Revolutionary War Soldiers
and
Patriots
with Ties to
Ripley County
Indiana

Compiled and Edited by
Marlene Jan McDerment

HERITAGE BOOKS
2017

HERITAGE BOOKS
AN IMPRINT OF HERITAGE BOOKS, INC.

Books, CDs, and more—Worldwide

For our listing of thousands of titles see our website
at
www.HeritageBooks.com

Published 2017 by
HERITAGE BOOKS, INC.
Publishing Division
5810 Ruatan Street
Berwyn Heights, Md. 20740

Copyright © 2017 Marlene Jan McDerment

Heritage Books by the author:

*Revolutionary Soldiers and the Wives of Soldiers
with Ties to Switzerland County, Indiana*

*Revolutionary War Soldiers and Patriots
with Ties to Ripley County, Indiana*

All rights reserved. No part of this book may be reproduced or transmitted in any form or by any means, electronic or mechanical, including photocopying, recording or by any information storage and retrieval system without written permission from the author, except for the inclusion of brief quotations in a review.

International Standard Book Number
Paperbound: 978-0-7884-5784-5

THIS BOOK IS DEDICATED TO THE MEN
WHO SERVED DURING THE REVOLUTIONARY WAR
AND THEN CONTRIBUTED TO THE SETTLEMENT OF
RIPLEY COUNTY

CONTENTS

ARNOLD, JAMES	1
BABBS, JOHN	6
BASSETT, WILLIAM	10
BEALL, NINIAN	18
BENEFIEL, GEORGE	27
BOLDEREY, JOHN	29
BUCHANNAH, GEORGE	33
BUMGARDNER, DANIEL	37
BURCHFIELD, JOHN	40
BURCHFIELD, ROBERT	45
BURROUGHS, JAMES	52
BUSKIRK (VAN BUSKIRK), JOHN	54
CAVENDAR, JOHN	60
CHAPMAN, LEMUEL	65
CHRISTY, JAMES	70
COLLINS, WILLIAM	76
CRANE, EDMUND	82
CRUZAN, BENJAMIN	85
DAVIS, PHILEMON	90
DELAP, JAMES	94
DOWERS, CONRAD	98
DOWERS, JACOB	105
FISK, ROBERT	109
FOX, ADAM	113
GIBSON, WILBOURNE	116
GOOKINS, SAMUEL	119
GRIMES, JAMES	128
HALL, BENJAMIN	134
HAMILTON, BENJAMIN	141
HENNEGIN, JOSEPH	144
HITE (HYATT), JACOB	149
HODGES, RICHARD	152
HOUSE, LEVI	158
HOWLETT, WILLIAM	162
HYATT, GIDEON	168
JOHNSON, JAMES	169
JOHNSON, PHILLIP	177
JOHNSON, ROSWELL	182
JOHNSTON, THOMAS	188

CONTENTS

LAMBERT, JAMES 194
LEVI, ISAAC 198
LIPPERD, WILLIAM 209
LIVINGSTON, GEORGE 216
LLOYD, INDIAN ROBIN ROBERT 218
MARQUEST, SAMUEL 222
MATHEWS, AMOS V 224
MAVITY, WILLIAM 228
MAXWELL, DAVID 232
McCULLOUGH, JOHN 235
McDONALD, JOSEPH 239
McMILLEN, DANIEL 243
MICHELLER, JACOB 249
MYERS, HENRY 253
NEWCOMER, PETER 258
O'NEAL, JOHN 263
OVERTURF, MARTIN 268
PARR, JOHN 272
PENDERGAST, EDWARD 277
PENMETENT, JOHN 282
PENNETENT, JOSEPH 286
PRATT, JONATHAN 287
PROTHERO, THOMAS 293
RESOR, PETER 295
ROBBINS, EPHRAIM 300
ROLFF, JAMES 304
RUTLEDGE, PETER 308
RYAN, GEORGE 313
STEPHENS, SAMUEL 318
STEWARD, CHARLES 322
THOMAS, HENRY 329
TUCKER, JOHN 333
VAN BIBBER, PETER 338
VAN BUSKIRK – SEE BUSKIRK 54

CONTENTS

WARD, JOHN 342
WAY, ISAAC 347
WELCH, DANIEL 350
WHETSTONE, DANIEL 355
WILSON, EPHRAIM 358
WILYARD, HENRY 363
WITTAKER, JOHN 368
WYCOFF, ISAAC 374
WYCOFF, JACOB 376
YOUNGER, KANARD 380
Appendix A 385
Appendix B 386
Appendix C 387

PREFACE

A few years ago, while researching my Revolutionary War ancestor, Griffith Dickinson, that research culminated in the publication of my book *Revolutionary Soldiers and the Wives of Soldiers with Ties to Switzerland County, Indiana*; Heritage Books, Inc., 2013. Some of the men who were presented in the Switzerland County book are included again in this publication. A few of them were living in the part of Switzerland County that later became Ripley County, and a few simply moved a little farther west.

After publication of that book I discovered that besides Griffith Dickinson, another man presented in the book, Gideon Tower, is also one of my ancestors. In addition, I knew that another ancestors, a John Whitacar (or Whitteker/Whittaker) served in the Revolutionary War and lived in either Switzerland or Ripley County, IN. As it turns out, there are two men by that name, one living in each county. As of this writing I still have not been able to determine which of these men I can claim as my ancestor.

As with the former book, in hopes of finding clues about my Whitacar/Whitteker/Whittaker ancestor, I identified all of the soldiers were who had ties to Ripley County who served in the Revolutionary War. This was done by searching through the county court ledgers, following leads from previous published lists and county histories. Then, pension records located at the National Archives, National Society Daughters of the American Revolution ancestor records, Revolutionary War muster and payroll records, and dozens of published records were consulted to prove service of the men I identified. The records compiled for all of these men are included in this volume.

Perhaps the greatest outcome of this Ripley County book, and the prior Switzerland County book is that new memorials have been erected in those courthouses to honor these men.

MARLENE JAN McDERMENT

ACKNOWLEDGMENT

I wish to express my gratitude to the many people who assisted in the compilation of this work by sharing their time, information, and encouragement.

First and foremost, I appreciate the courteous hospitality offered by Judy Kappes during my research trips to Ripley County. She has been generous with her time, knowledge, connections, and her enthusiasm for this project. Special thank you to Dan and Cheryl Welch, volunteers at the Ripley County Historical Society Archives for sharing the Violet Toph material.

Thanks to Cheryl Lane Welch, Janice Givan Wilson, and Judith "Judy" Bradford Kappes of the Ross' Run Chapter National Society Daughters of the American Revolution who joined me in forming a committee to see that a new memorial honoring these Revolutionary War patriots will be hung in the courthouse.

Additional thanks to the staff at the Ripley County Recorder's office; and to the researchers who kindly provided their family records.

INTRODUCTION

The purpose of this book is to bring into one volume the various records pertaining to the Revolutionary War soldiers who have ties to Ripley County, Indiana. Included are Ripley County inhabitants who have not previously been identified as having served in the Revolutionary War.

Earlier published works did not provide the source of the information presented about the patriots. This volume attempts to provide evidence placing them in Ripley County and to prove or, in some cases, disprove the soldier's Revolutionary service.

Several dozen sources were consulted to determine the service of these Revolutionary soldiers. Citation of each source is identified in these pages. If you find your subject herein, the listed sources provide direction to the original records.

When genealogical information was provided in the source material it is included. This work is not intended as a genealogical work. However, the family genealogist may find some useful clues within these pages. The compiler takes no responsibility for errors in these previously compiled records.

Every attempt has been made to present complete and accurate information. In a few cases the several records shown may be for another man with the same name. Even though the various spellings of surnames were used in searching records, as with any publication of this kind, some errors and omissions are unavoidable.

It is my sincere hope that this book serves as a useful guide for readers interested in joining lineage societies such as DAR, SAR, CAR, First Families of Indiana, and others, as well as supplementing family records.

The compiler, Marlene Jan McDerment, is interested in any additional information the reader can provide. Please send your information in an email to mjmcderment@aol.com.

ARNOLD, JAMES

Patriot: James Arnold
Birth: 1755 or 1756
Married Spouse 1: Lucy
Service state(s): VA
Rank: Private
Proof of Service: Pension application
Pension application No.: S30830
Residences: Culpeper Co., VA; Woodford & Franklin Co., KY; Ripley Co., IN
Died: Semi-annual pension payments ended 4 Mar 1838
Buried: Luther Hazelrigg Farm, Napoleon, Jackson Twp., Ripley Co., IN
DAR Ancestor No.: None as of 7 Jun 2017.

Pension Application Abstracted from National Archives microfilm Series M804, Roll 78, File S30830
Pension abstract for – James Arnold
Service state(s): VA
Date: 9 Aug 1832
County of: Woodford   State of: KY
Declaration made before a Judge or Court: County Court
Act of: 7 Jun 1832
Age: Between 76 & 77
Residence when he entered service: Culpeper Co., VA
Residence(s) since the war: not stated
Residence now: Woodford Co., KY
Volunteer, Drafted, or Substitute: Enlisted in Culpeper Co., VA. His brother Lewis Arnold enlisted at the same time, but Lewis never returned from service.
Rank(s): Private
Statement of service-

Period	Duration	Names of General and Field Officers
15 Jan 1777	3 yrs	10 VA Regt. - Lt. Thomas Barby (Barbee); Capt. John Gillison

Battles: Monmouth; Siege of Ft Mifflin on Mud Island
Discharge received: I was detached from my company & got no discharge.
Statement is supported by –
Living witness, name(s): Elizabeth Arnold (relationship not stated, she was wife of John Arnold), age 72-79, on 9 Aug 1832, gave testimony James Arnold enlisted in 1777, returned in 1781, his brother Lewis enlisted at the same time.
Evidence: Traditionary
Additional data in file: Letter of Katherine F. Goodwin, a descendant, states -The wife's name was evidently Lucy as the Woodford County court records give the following: "James Arnold and Lucy his wife deed to Jechonian Singleton, 79 acres on Greer's Creek, Sept. 1, 1827."

Revolutionary War Service Records; National Archives Publication number M881, Compiled service records of soldiers who served in the American Army during the Revolutionary War, 1775-1783.
https://www.fold3.com/image/23244201?terms=Arnold,%20James
Arnold, James – 10 Virginia Regiment   Private – Corporal
Gwathmey, John H.; *Historical Register of Virginians in the Revolution, Soldiers, Sailors, Marines, 1775-1783;* The Dietz Press, Richmond, VA, 1938, p. 22.
Arnold, James, Corp., 10 CL [10th Continental Line], also 6CL.

Revolutionary War Land Office Military Certificates; Records of the Executive Branch, Land Office (Record Group 4), microfilm reels 1-38; Library of Virginia, Richmond, VA.
In order to receive bounty lands for Revolutionary War service, a soldier or sailor must have served continuously for at least three years in a Virginia or Continental unit. Service in the militia did not count. The certificates were numbered 1-9926 and cover the period July 14, 1782-August 5, 1876. The warrant specified the amount of lands to be received and directed the surveyor of lands to set aside that quantity of land in the Virginia Military District in Kentucky and Ohio.
Arnold, James   Rank: Private   Military Certificate number: LO 1976

Bockstruck, Lloyd DeWitt; *Revolutionary War Bounty Land Grants Awarded by State Governments;* Genealogical Publishing Co., IN, Baltimore, MD, 1996. p.14.
Arnold, James. Va. Private. 26 Nov. 1783. 100 acres.

Wardell, Patrick G., comp.; *Virginia/West Virginia Genealogical Data From Revolutionary War Pension and Bounty Land Warrant Records, Vol. 1 ---Aaron through Cyrus;* Heritage Books, Inc., Bowie, MD, 1988, p. 26.
Arnold, James, esf 1777 Culpeper Co, VA; PN 1832 aec 77 Woodford Co, KY; bro Lewis never returned from RW svc; QLF states sol md to Lucy. R78.

Clift, G. Glens, Assistant Secretary, Kentucky Historical Society, Comp.; *"Second Census" of Kentucky – 1800, A Privately Compiled and Published Enumeration of Tax Payers Appearing in the 79 Manuscript Volumes Extant of Tax Lists of the 42 Counties of Kentucky in Existence in 1800;* Genealogical Publishing Co., Baltimore, MD, 1966, p. 8.

Name	County	Tax List Date
Arnold, John	Woodford	1800

[Note: Franklin Co. was formed from Woodford Co., KY in 1794]

Register of the Kentucky Historical Society; Early Kentucky Tax Records; Clearfield Publishing, Baltimore, Md., 1999; p. 47.
Department of State Archives – Franklin County Tax Lists, 1795.

A List of Taxable Property Within the District of Thomas Lillard, Commissioner for the County of Franklin for 1795.

Persons Named Chargable With the Tax	White Males Over 21	Total Blacks	Horses, Mares Colts & Mules	Cattle	Acres
Arnold, Jno.	1	2	9	34	1,500

Quisenberry, Anderson Chenault; <u>Revolutionary Soldiers in Kentucky</u>, containing a roll of the officers of Virginia line who received land bounties, a roll of the Revolutionary pensioners in Kentucky, a list of the Illinois regiment who served under George Rogers Clark in the Northwest campaign, also a roster of the Virginia Navy; Reproduction of the original which appeared in Sons of the American Revolution Kentucky Society Year Book, Louisville, 1896, Southern Book Co., Baltimore, MD, 1959. p. 241.

Woodford County
Pensioners under the Act of March 18, 1818.
Arnold, James, Private   Virginia line
    October 20, 1832; $80.   Age 79.

<u>Ripley County, Indiana Deed Records Vol. A, 11 Aug 1818-29 Jan 1827</u>
Page(s): 228-229.
Abstract of Deed/Patent for: James Arnold of Scott Co., KY
Purchaser (Grantee) or Seller (Grantor)?: Purchaser
Purchased from: Lewis C. Suggett & Fanny, his wife of Scott Co., KY
State & county where recorded: Ripley Co., Indiana
State & county where agreement was made: Scott Co., KY
Date entered: 27 Oct 1825
Description: County of Ripley, State of Indiana; NW qtr. of Sec. 9, Township 9,
    North of Range 11 E; containing 160 acres of the land directed to be
    sold at Jeffersonville by act of Congress providing for sale of lands in
    the Territory northwest of the Ohio and above the mouth of the
    Kentucky River.
Amount paid: $500.00 lawful money of Kentucky

Toph, Violet E.; <u>Peoples History of Ripley County, Indiana</u>; self-published, c. 1940, p. 120.
Revolutionary Soldiers Who Came to Ripley County
James Arnold was born in 1755 or 1756. He enlisted in Virginia, Jan. 15, 1777 and served to Jan. 15, 1781. He was a private under Capt. John Gillison and applied for a pension Aug. 9, 1832 from Woodford Co., Ky. He then moved to Indiana and died at Napoleon, Ind. where he is buried on the present James Hazelrigg farm. Edgar Arnold of Napoleon is his grandson.

O'Byrne, Mrs. Roscoe C., comp. & ed.; <u>Roster Soldiers and Patriots of the American Revolution Buried in Indiana</u>; Published by Indiana Daughters of the American Revolution, 1938, Reprinted Genealogical Publishing Co., Baltimore MD, 1968, p. 43-44.

ARNOLD, JAMES   Ripley County
Born – 1755 or 1756
Service – Enlisted as a pri. In Capt. Gillison's CO. of the 10th, subsequently The 6th Vir. Regt. Commanded by Col. Edward Stevens, Maj. Samuel Hawes, Col. John Green and Col. William Russell.
On the roll for 1779, he is reported as a corporal.
Proof – War Department Records. He applied for a pension while living in Woodford Co., Ky, in 1832.
Grave – In Old Cemetery near Napoleon, Ripley Co., Ind. Many descendants are living in Ripley Co.
Collected by Mrs. A. B. Wycoff, Batesville, Indiana.

<u>United States Headstone Applications for U.S. Military Veterans, 1925-1941</u>, database with images; (https://familysearch.org/ark:/61903/1:1:VHZW-93Q : 17 May 2016); Affiliate Publication Number: M1916; Affiliate Publication Title: Affiliate Film Number: 3; GS Film Number: 1878152; Digital Folder Number: 004831972; Image Number: 01912.
Application for Headstone; War Department O.Q.M.G. Form No. 623
Name: Arnold, James
Event Date: June 21, 1938
Name of Cemetery: Private on the Luther Hazelrigg farm
Located in or near: Napoleon, Ind.
Death Date: 1840
Enlistment Dates: Jan 15, 1777
Discharge Dates   Jan 15, 1781
Rank: Private
Company: Under Capt. John Gillison; VA Troops
To be shipped to: Ripley Co. Historical Society, Osgood, Ind., Ripley Co.
Whose post-office address is: Versailles, Ind.
This application is for the UNMARKED grave of a veteran. It is understood the stone will be furnished and delivered at the railroad station or steamboat landing above indicated, at Government expense, freight prepaid. I hereby agree to promptly accept the headstone at destination, remove it and properly place same at decedent's grave at my expense. Ripley Co. Historical Society, Applicant.
No fee should be paid in connection with this application.
Applicant: Ripley County Historical Society, Versailles, Ind.

Gibbs, A.; <u>Ripley County Historical Society Data on Revolutionary Soldiers</u>, 1973 review.
Exact location of marker: Rt. 421 north, about 1/4 mile north of 229intersection, about on Napoleon town limit, on east side, about 9-10 ft. down berm of road; stone chipped by mowing equipment (1973).
Burial nearby on old Hazelrigg Cem., Jackson Tw. Ripley Co. Ind.

Type of marker: Gov't
Date placed: noted in minutes of R.C.H.S. Nov. 14, 1938.
Placed by: Ripley County Historical Society
Additional comments: not on Court House list.
    Probate A. p. 73, Ripley Co. Ind.
    dec'd by Oct 20, 1828 Court. #S 30830.
Wording on marker:
James Arnold
Corp.
Gillison's Co.
Va. Troops
Rev. War
1840

Additional notation on this record: Is the tombstone date in error?

BABBS, JOHN

Patriot: John Babbs
Birth: 11 Aug 1756, Anne Arundel Co., MD
Married Spouse: Rebecca Lane (1770-1834)
Service state(s): MD
Rank: Orderly Sergeant
Proof of Service: Pension application
Pension application No.: S45241
Residences: MD, VA, Hamilton Co., OH, Ripley Co., IN
Died: 13 Feb 1844, Ripley Co., IN
Buried: Booher Farm Cemetery, Napoleon, Jackson Twp., Ripley Co., IN
DAR Ancestor No.: A133764

Pension Application Abstracted from National Archives microfilm Series M804, Roll 100, File S45241.
Pension abstract for – John Babbs
Service state(s): MD
Date: 30 Apr 1818
County of: Hamilton   State of: OH
Declaration made before a Judge or Court: Southern Circuit Court, State of Ohio
Act of: Not stated
Age: Not stated
Residence when he entered service: Not stated
Residence(s) since the war: Not stated
Residence now: Not stated
Volunteer, Drafted, or Substitute: Enlisted
Rank(s): Private, Duty Sergeant
Statement of service-

Period	Duration	Names of General and Field Officers
Summer 1776		Col. Smallwood's Regt. Maryland Line. Regt. broken up because of severe losses at Long Island; induced to join Capt. Scott, at White Plains.

Battles: Long Island, NY, White Plains, NY; leg badly broken by rock fragment knocked off by a cannon ball, hospitalized at Morristown, NJ, afterwards to Bethlehem and Cross Keys, PA. Acted as Duty Sergeant while hospitalized.
Discharge received: Yes, Mustered out and discharged at Annapolis
Signed by: Lt. Burgess & Major Price
What became of it?: Several years after his deployment he received Certificate of Right to Land when living in VA or MD. His Discharge and Certificate were in the hands of Francis Keys, Esquire (attorney) in Hampshire Co., VA to have land title perfected. Keys died on the way to Richmond. Discharge and Certificate have never been recovered.
&
Date: 28 Aug 1820
County of: Hamilton   State of: OH
Declaration made before a Judge or Court: Court of Common Pleas

Act of: 1 May 1820
Age: 68 years old
Residence now: Now resides with a son in Hamilton Co., OH
Statement of service-

Period	Duration	Names of General and Field Officers
1776	3 years	Regt. commanded by Capt. Scotts, Col. Smallwood; and 3rd Maryland Regt., Capt. Ford's company, Col. Ramey.

Battles: Long Island, White Plains
Wife: Not named
Names and ages of children: States he has children of age, not named.

Archives of Maryland; Muster Rolls and other records of service of Maryland Troops in the American Revolution; Reprinted with permission by Genealogical Publishing Co., Inc., Baltimore, 1972, p. 15.

Seventh Company

Commd. Jan 3d, '76		John Day Scott, Capt.	Present	
"	"	Thos. Harwood, 1 Lt.	"	
"	"	Thos. Goldsmith, 2 "	absent	on furlough
"	"	James Pale, Ensign.	present	

Rank	Date of Enlistment	Names		Remarks
Cadet		James Disney	absent	on furlough
Serjeant	Jan 20	Saml. Barber		disch. 23 May
"	"	Wilm. Sands	"	on furlough recruit'g
"	Mch 9	John Smith Selby	present	
"	Feb 15	Thos. Gordon	"	
Corporal	26	Wilm. Noyes	"	
"	15	Joshua Lamb	"	
"	"	Andw. Ferguson	"	
"	25	John Smith	absent	on furlough
Drummer	Jan 20	John Meek	present	
Fifer	Feb 3	Edward George	"	
Privates	Jan 20	John Babb	present	

p. 81.

MUSTERS OF MARYLAND TROOPS, VOL. 1
First Regiment

Names	Rank	Enlisted	Discharged	Remarks
Babbs, John	pt	10 Dec 76	20 Mar 77	discharged

p. 344.

A List of Men from Frederick. Return of Men sent to Annapolis By Capt. William Beatty. Delivered by Col. Baker Johnson 28th Aug. 1780.

Date of Enlistment	Men's Names
Aug 5	John Babbs, (followed the 1st Troops) } Marched

Newman, Harry Wright; Maryland Revolutionary Records; Tuttle Publishing, Rutland, VT, 1928. p. 8.

Maryland Revolutionary Pensioners				Misc. facts and
Name of Veteran	Birth	Rank	Establishment	other State services
Babbs, John	-	Pvt.	Maryland Line	Wounded

Senate Documents, Vol.9, No. 988, 63rd Congress, 3d Session, Washington, 1915; "Register of Certificates Issued by John Pierce, Esquire, Paymaster General and Commissioner of Army Accounts for the United States, to Officers and Soldiers of the Continental Army Under Act of July 4, 1783"; Seventeenth report of the National Society of the Daughters of the American Revolution; Genealogical Publishing Co., Inc., Baltimore, MD, 1984. p. 24.

Men listed in this volume with the same name.

No. of Certificate	To whom issued	Amount
18594	Babb, John	23.26
89507	Babb, John	20.00

O'Byrne, Mrs. Roscoe C., comp. & ed.; Roster Soldiers and Patriots of the American Revolution Buried in Indiana; Published by Indiana Daughters of the American Revolution, 1938, Reprinted Genealogical Publishing Co., Baltimore MD, 1968, p.47.

BABBS, JOHN   Ripley County
Service – Enlisted in Annapolis, Md., in 1776; pri. in Capt. Scott's CO., Col. Smallwood's Md. Regt. In the battle of Long Island and White Plains. Wounded in latter battle. While recovering in the hospital, he served as orderly sergeant. Later served in Capt. Ford's CO. of 3rd Md. Regt.
Proof – Pension claim S. 45241.
Died – About 1842. Buried in Booher Graveyard near Napoleon, Ind.
Daughter – Hannah, m. John Glass.
Collected by John Babbs Glass, Toulume Co., California.

O'Byrne, comp. Mrs. Roscoe C., comp.; Roster of Soldiers and Patriots of the American Revolution Buried in Indiana, Vol. III; Indiana Daughters of the American Revolution, 1966, p. 56.

Additional data and/or corrections received since 1966 to the records of the soldiers and patriots listed in Rosters I and II.
BABBS, JOHN   Roster I, p. 47   Ripley County
Died – Feb. 13, 1844.
Married – Rebecca Lane b. Aug. 28, 1820 d. Feb. 11, 1873. *[Family records indicate Rebecca was b. 17 Jan 1770, d. 1 Nov 1834 at Ohio Co., IN.]*
Children – John b, 1790; Mary b. 1792; Elizabeth b. 1793; Noah b. 1794; Hannah b. 1799 m. John Glass; William L. m. Rhoda Dixon b. 1801 and has 13 ch.
By Mrs. A. G. Charlton, 10 Sunnyside Avenue, Aurora, Indiana 47001.

Gibbs, A.; Ripley County Historical Society Data on Revolutionary Soldiers, 1973 review.
Exact location of marker: No information further on grave
Additional comments: Not on Court House tablet

Burial Notes: Rebecca (Lane) Babbs is buried in the Clark Hill Cemetery, Rising Sun, Ohio Co., IN. Tombstone inscription shows "Consort of John Babbs". John Babbs in buried in the Booher Cemetery, Napoleon, Ripley Co., IN. There is no tombstone.

Dailey, Mrs. Orville D., comp.; <u>The Official Roster of the Soldiers of the American Revolution Who Lived in the State of Ohio</u>; Greenfield Printing & Publishing Co., Greenfield, OH, 1938; p.45.
Enl 1776 in Col Smallwood's Regt. of the Md Line; b abt 1752 aged 68 yrs in 1820 (appl); resides with "son" (appl); pensd 9-25-1818 Hamilton co Ref Md S 45241.   Rept. By State D A R.

BASSETT, WILLIAM

Patriot: William Bassett, Sr.
Birth: 18 Apr 1755, Surry Co., England
Married Spouse 1: 27 Nov 1786, Mercer Co., KY
  Margaret "Peggy" McQuiddy/McGurdy (1768-1845)
Service state(s): VA Continental Line
Rank: Private
Proof of Service: Widow's pension application
Pension application No.: W9739
Residences: Botetourt Co., VA, Franklin Co., KY in abt 1818, Ripley Co., IN.
Died: 6 Feb 1840, Cross Plains, Brown Twp., Ripley Co., IN
Buried: Bassett Cemetery, Shields/Linkmeyer/Wm. Schuerman Farm,
  Cross Plains, Brown Twp., Ripley Co., IN
DAR Ancestor No.: A007276

Pension Application Abstracted from National Archives microfilm Series M804, Roll 171, File W9739.
Pension abstract for – William Bassett
Service state(s): VA Continental Line
Date: 29 Dec 1833
County of: Ripley   State of: IN
Declaration made before a Judge or Court: a Judge of the Circuit Court
Act of: 7 Jun 1832
Age: 79   Record of age: in my Bible
Where and year born: 18 Apr 1755 County of Surry, old England
Residence when he entered service: Botetourt Co., VA
Residence(s) since the war: Botetourt Co., VA, Kentucky in abt 1818,
  Ripley Co., IN.
Residence now: Ripley County, IN
Rank(s): Private in the Calvary [1st Regiment Continental Light Dragoons]
Statement of service-

Period	Duration	Names of General and Field Officers
Aug 1776- May 1779	2 yrs., 9 mos.	Gen. Paulaski, Col. George Bailor, Maj. Clough, Capt. John Stith, Lt. Custis.

Battles: White Plains, Morristown, Trenton, Princeton, Monmouth Courthouse, Massacre at Taupon (Tappan) where he was taken prisoner. In his escape he was bayonetted in the back.
Discharge received: Yes, in May 1779.
Signed by: Capt. John Stith by command of Col. Bailor.
What became of it?: It was consumed by fire at Craigs Station in KY which was
  burned by the Indians.
Wife: Not stated
Names and ages of children: Not stated
&
Pension abstract for – Peggy Bassett   Service state(s):
Date: 10 Mar 1840
County of: Ripley   State of: IN

Declaration made before a Judge or Court: Circuit Court
Act of: 7 Jul 1838
Age: 70 yrs.
Residence: Ripley Co., IN
Death of soldier: 6 Feb 1840
Marriage date and place: 27 Nov 1786
Proof of marriage: Family record from her Bible
Names and ages of children: Nancy b. 27 Aug 1787; Thomas b. 14 Apr 1791; James b. 18 Nov, 1793; Sally b. 13 Jan 1796; Elizabeth b. 2 Feb 1798; Polly b. 14 Aug 1801; Rebekah b. 13 Sep 1803; Melinda b. 8 Feb 1805; William b. 8 Oct 1806, m. Nancy 18 Jun 1829; Harriet b. 14 Jul 1811.
&
Pension abstract for – Peggy Bassett, widow of William Bassett
Date: 24 Jul 1843
County of: Ripley   State of: IN
Declaration made before a Judge or Court:
Act of: 3 Mar 1843
Age: 75
Residence: Ripley Co., IN

Abstract of Final Payment Voucher; General Services Administration, Washington, DC
NAME   BASSETT, WILLIAM
AGENCY OF PAYMENT   INDIANA
DATE OF ACT   1832
DATE OF PAYMENT   in 1840
DATE OF DEATH   Feb. 6, 1840
GENERAL ACCOUNTING OFFICE
National Archives and Records Service   NA-286
GSA DC 54-4891   November 1953

Abstract of Final Payment Voucher; General Services Administration, Washington, DC
NAME   Bassett, Peggy widow of William
AGENCY OF PAYMENT   Madison, Ind.
DATE OF ACT   1838, 1843 & 1844
DATE OF PAYMENT   2d Qr. 1845
DATE OF DEATH   Sept. 26, 1845
FINAL PAYMENT VOUCHER RECEIVED FROM
THE GENERAL ACCOUNTING OFFICE   Form
General Services Administration   GSA DC 70-7035   GSA Dec 69 7068

Gwathmey, John H.; *Historical Register of Virginians in the Revolution, Soldiers, Sailors, Marines, 1775-1783;* The Dietz Press, Richmond, VA, 1938, p. 46.
Bassett, William, 12 CL [12th Continental Line]

Senate Documents, Vol.9, No. 988, 63rd Congress, 3d Session, Washington, 1915; "Register of Certificates Issued by John Pierce, Esquire, Paymaster General and

Commissioner of Army Accounts for the United States, to Officers and Soldiers of the Continental Army Under Act of July 4, 1783"; <u>Seventeenth report of the National Society of the Daughters of the American Revolution</u>; Genealogical Publishing Co., Inc., Baltimore, MD, 1984. p.37.
Men listed in this volume with the same name.

No. of Certificate	To whom issued	Amount
2532	Bassett, William	21.42
3404	Bassett, William	97.53
3800	Bassett, William	79.18
4170	Bassett, William	80.00

Clift, G. Glens, Assistant Secretary, Kentucky Historical Society, Comp.; "Second Census" of Kentucky – 1800, A Privately Compiled and Published Enumeration of Tax Payers Appearing in the 79 Manuscript Volumes Extant of Tax Lists of the 42 Counties of Kentucky in Existence in 1800; Genealogical Publishing Co., Baltimore, MD, 1966, p. 17.

Name	County	Tax List Date
Bassett, William	Franklin	8/7/1801

Cowen, Janet C., comp; <u>Jeffersonville Land Entries 1808-1818</u>; McDowell Publications,
Utica, NY, 1984, p. 167.
Receipt #
13493   Bassitt   William   KY Franklin   NW S20 T06 N12E 160   1817 09 01

<u>Ripley County Indiana, Recorder's Office, Tract Book 1</u>, p. 34.
Bassett, William   28 Jan 1817   R12E, T6, S20   160 acres

<u>*U.S. Department of Interior, Bureau of Land Management, General Land Office Records; Land Patent Search*</u>
Name: BASSETT, WILLIAM
Accession Nr. IN2870-.297; Document Type – State Volume Patent; State - Indiana; Issue Date – 5/10/1848; Cancelled – No; Land Office – Jeffersonville; Authority – April 24, 1820: Sale-Cash Entry (3 Stat. 566); General Remarks – Incorrect Township Direction on Document Verified From Tract Book; Document Nr. 19844; Total Acres – 40.00; Land Descriptions: State – IN; Meridian – 2nd PM; Twp-Rng – 006N-012E; Aliquots – NW ¼ SW ¼; Section – 26; County - Ripley
Certificate No. 19844 To all to whom these Presents shall come, Greeting: Whereas William Henry Bafsett, of Ripley County Indiana…..

<u>*Ripley County, Indiana Deed Records Vol. A, 11 Aug 1818-29 Jan 1827*</u>
Page(s): 270-271.
Abstract of Deed/Patent for: John O'Neal & William Bassett, Deacons of the regular Baptist church known by the name Middle Fork Church.
Purchaser (Grantee) or Seller (Grantor)?: Purchaser

Purchased from: James Benham and Mary (dower) his wife of Ripley Co., IN.
State & county where recorded: Ripley Co., Indiana
Date entered: 6 May 1826
Recorded: 10 May 1826
Description: Part of the southeast quarter of Section 12, Township 6, Range 11 East, of the lands offered for sale at Jeffersonville, containing nearly one acre
Amount paid: Sixteen dollars ($16.00)
Name(s) of Witnesses: Jesse Marklin & Joseph McIntosh

Ripley County, Indiana Deed Records Vol. B., 29 Jan 1827-21 Sep 1832, Page(s) 387-389.
Abstract of Deed/Patent for: William Bassett and Peggy (dower) his wife
Purchaser (Grantee) or Seller (Grantor)?: Seller
Sold to: George Nicholson
State & county where recorded: Ripley Co., Indiana
Date entered: 19 Apr 1830
Recorded: 2 Aug 1830
Description: Part of the northwest quarter of Section 20, of Township 6, North of Range 12 East in the Jeffersonville district.
Amount paid: Fifty-six dollars and ninety-two cents ($56.92).
Name(s) of Witnesses: Thos. D. Bailey & John Cook.

Ripley County, Indiana Deed Records Vol. D., 7 Feb 1834 - 9 Feb 1836, Page 340-341
Abstract of Deed/Patent for: William Bassett, Sr. & Margaret (dower) his wife
Purchaser (Grantee) or Seller (Grantor)?: Seller
Sold to: William Bassett, Jr.
State & county where recorded: Ripley Co., Indiana
Date entered: 10 Feb 1835
Recorded: 8 Sep 1835
Description: Lot or parcel of land being part of the North West quarter of Section 20, Township 6 North of Range 12 East; of land directed to be sold at Jeffersonville, IN; containing 128 acres.
Amount paid: Six hundred dollars ($600.00)
Name(s) of Witnesses: John Steele & Preston Pribble

1820 U. S. Census, Ripley Co., IN, NARA Roll M33_15; EN 7 Aug 1820, p. 75, line 24.
William Bassett
Males 10-15=1, Males 16-25=1, Males 45>=1, Females 10-15=1, Females 16-25=2, Females 45>=1.

The Pension Roll of 1835 Volume IV, The Mid-Western States, Indexed Edition, *In Four Volumes; Genealogical Publishing Co., Inc., Baltimore, MD, Reprint 1968, p. 87.* Statement, &c. of Ripley county, Indiana.

INDIANA Names	Rank		Annual allowance.	Sums received	Description of service
William Bassett	Pri of Cav	100.00	300 00		Penn. State troops
When placed on pension roll	Commencement of pension		Ages		Laws under which they were formerly placed on the pension roll; and remarks.
Feb 4, 1834	Mar 4, 1831		81	-	

Judge Lewis Collins; <u>Franklin County, KY Revolutionary Soldiers</u>, Compiled from Kentucky Pension Roll of 1835 & History of Kentucky; http://www.rootsweb.ancestry.com/~kyfrankl/revwar.htm.

The following is a listing of soldiers that once lived in Franklin County, Kentucky. This list does not suggest the soldiers applied for a pension or died in Franklin County, only that they once resided in this county. Name, rank, birth and or death dates, place of service, pension and or Bounty Land file numbers are included.

WILLIAM BASSETT, SR., Private, b. 1755 England,
Continental Light Dragoons, New Jersey
    [Note: This is incorrect - he was in the VA Continental Line;
    he was in battles in NJ.]

<u>Ripley County, Indiana Complete Probate Book Vol. A.</u>, *12 May 1834-10 May 1842; p. 419-423. Also see* <u>Complete Probate Record Book Vol. C.</u>, *Feb. 1846-Nov. 1846; p. 212.*

Probate Court Term 8 Nov 1841

I, William Bassett, Sr. of Brown Township in the County of Ripley and State of Indiana do make and publish this my last Will and Testament thereby revoking and making void all former Wills by me at any time heretofore made. I direct that my body be decently interred and that my funeral be conducted in a manner corresponding with my estate and situation in life and as to such Worldly Estate as it has pleased God to entrust me with I dispose of the same in the following manner to wit: I direct first that all my just debts and funeral expenses paid as soon after my death as possible out of the first money that shall come to the hands of my Executors from any portion of my Estate Real or personal. I also direct that a fair valuation be made by three judicious neighbors of all my said estate including my house and furniture and after being signed with their names that a copy of the same be given by them to each of my Executors. I also direct that the whole of my household furniture shall be and remain the absolute property of my beloved wife is she shall be living at the time of my death but if she shall not survive me then that the same shall be equally divided amongst my children share and share alike and to be apportioned by three impartial neighbors mutually chosen by said heirs for that purpose. I also direct that my flock of sheep and cow and mare and colt and one note of hand on Robert Clark for one hundred dollars with ten per centum interest which shall be and remain the absolute property of my beloved wife and at mine and her death the above named property and money if any shall be equally divided amongst my beloved children share and share alike. I also will and bequeath to each of my children one dollar in cash out of my Estate and I hereby make and order my esteemed friends Thomas Bassett and William Bassett, Jr. Executors of this my last will and testament. In witness whereof I William Bassett Senior, the Testator have hereunto set my hand and seal this fourth day of October in the year of Our Lord One thousand Eight Hundred and thirty eight. William Bassett (his mark) Signed sealed published and declared by the above named William Bassett, Sen. as his last Will and Testament in the presence of us who have here unto subscribed our names as witnesses thereto in the presence of the said Testator and in their presence of each other Oct. 4th 1838 . G.W. Hunter, Harvey Lathrop

      Peggy Bassett (her mark) received goods and chattels and credits in accordance with the will of her said husband.

Wardell, Patrick G., comp.; Virginia/West Virginia Genealogical Data From Revolutionary War Pension and Bounty Land Warrant Records, Vol. 1 ---Aaron through Cyrus; Heritage Books, Inc., Bowie, MD, 1988, p. 55.
Bassett, William, esf 1776 Botetourt Co, VA; b 4/18/1755 Surry Co, England; mvd to KY, thence to Ripley Co, IN, where PN 1833; dd 2/6/1840; md 11/27/1786 Peggy ---, who PN ae 70 Ripley Co, IN, 1840; ch births: Nancy 8/27/1787; Thomas 4/14/91, James 11/18/93, Sally 1/13/96, Elizabeth 2/2/1798, Polly 8/14/1801, Rebecah 9/13/03, Melinda 2/8/05, William 10/8/08, & Harriet 7/14/1811; s William md 6/18/29 Nancy ---; QLF states sol dd near Cross Plains, IN, & buried there on the old family homestead; QLF 1924 from desc Mrs F E Battin, Pierre, SD, states sol wid dd 9/26/1844. R171.

Toph, Violet E.; Peoples History of Ripley County, Indiana; self-published, c. 1940, p. 130.
Revolutionary Soldiers Who Came to Ripley County
William Bassett entered the service from Virginia in 1776 under Colonel George Bailor and served two years and. nine months. He was born in 1754 and died February 6, 1840. He married his wife Peggy in 1780. He was pensioned from Ripley County. The Ripley County Historical Society placed a Government marker at his grave on the John Linkmeyer farm about one-half mile west of the Cross Plains School house, July 13, 1936.

O'Byrne, Mrs. Roscoe C., comp. & ed.; Roster Soldiers and Patriots of the American Revolution Buried in Indiana; Published by Indiana Daughters of the American Revolution, 1938, Reprinted Genealogical Publishing Co., Baltimore MD, 1968, p. 53.
BASSETT, WLLIAM   Ripley County
Born – 1754.
Service – Entered service from Virginia in 1776 under Col. George Bailor. Served 2 yrs. 9 mos.
Proof – Pension claim W.9739.
Died – Feb. 6, 1840. Buried on farm in Brown Twp. Government marker and name on bronze tablet in Versailles Court House.
Married – 1780, Margaret. Many descendants still living in Ripley Co.
Collected by Mrs. A. B. Wycoff, Batesville, Indiana

Gibbs, A.; *Ripley County Historical Society Data on Revolutionary Soldiers, 1973 review.*
Exact location of marker: on Wm. Schuerman farm)1973) on 800S, about four-tenths mile west off 129; cemetery not visible from road, but back 1/4 mi. sw of house in light wooded area. West of Cross Plains, Brown Tw. Ripley Co. Ind.
Burial: a family cemetery probably
Type of marker: Gov't; also family marker for him and wife: Peggy, consort of Wm. Bassett Sr. d. 26 Sept. 1844 age 76.
Date placed: 13 July 1936 (Toph notes)
Placed by: Ripley County Historical Society
Additional comments: family stone adds that Wm. Bassett was age 85 in 1840.
Pa Archives Series III, listed as Pennsylvanian residing in Ripley Co. Ind. age 81 (Feb. 1834).
On Court House tablet; Will- Probate Book B, Ripley Co. Ind.
Wording on marker:
William Bassett
Pvt. Smith' Co.
Baylor's Rgt.
Rev. War
Feb 6, 1840

United States Headstone Applications for U.S. Military Veterans, 1925-1949, database with images; (https://familysearch.org/ark:/61903/1:1:VHZW-HL7 : 17 May 2016); Affiliate Publication Number: M1916; Affiliate Publication Title: Applications for Headstones for U.S. Military Veterans, 1925-1941; Affiliate Film Number: 6; GS Film Number: 1878155; Digital Folder Number: 004832173; Image Number: 01576.
Application for Headstone; War Department O.Q.M.G. Form No. 623
Name: Bassett, William
Event Date: May 31, 1934
Name of Cemetery: Shields Private
Located in or near: Cross Plains, Ind.
Death Date: Feb. 6, 1840
Enlistment Dates: 1776
Discharge Dates: Served 2 years 9 mos
Rank: Private
Company: Under Col. George Baylor, Virginia Line
To be shipped to: Ripley Co. Historical Society, Osgood, Ind., Ripley Co.
Whose post-office address is: Versailles, Ind.
This application is for the UNMARKED grave of a veteran. It is understood the stone will be furnished and delivered at the railroad station or steamboat landing above indicated, at Government expense, freight prepaid. I hereby agree to promptly accept the headstone at destination, remove it and properly place same at decedent's grave at my expense. Ripley Co. Historical Society, Applicant.
No fee should be paid in connection with this application.
Applicant: Ripley Co. Historical Society, Versailles, Ind.

Tombstone location:	Bassett Cemetery located on the William Schuerman Farm, aka Shields Cemetery, Cross Plains, Brown Twp., Ripley Co., IN
Tombstone Inscription:	WILLIAM BASSETT PVT. STITH'S CO. BAYLOR'S REGT. REV WAR FEBRUARY 6, 1840
Tombstone Inscription:	IN Memory of WILLIAM BASSETT Who died Feb. 6, 1840 Aged 85 years

BEALL, NINION
Aka BELL, NINIAN, NING

Patriot:	Ninian Beall
Birth:	1761 MD
Married Spouse 1:	7 March 1780 Frederick Co., MD
	Ann Marie Stricker (- bef 1790) [a]
Married Spouse 2:	25 Jul 1790 Frederick Co., MD
	Christina Stull (1773-1855)
Service state(s):	MD Continental Line; VA
Rank:	Private
Proof of Service:	Widow's pension application
Pension application No.:	W9722

Residences: Frederick Co., MD; Butler Co., OH; Dearborn Co., IN; Ripley Co., IN
Died: 13 Jun 1836, Washington Twp., Ripley Co., IN
Buried: Old Washington Church Cemetery, Washington Twp., Ripley Co., IN
DAR Ancestor No.: A007888

[a] Anna Marie Striker's father, George Striker, served in the Revolutionary War.
DAR Ancestor No.: A111334.

Pension Application Abstracted from National Archives microfilm Series M804, Roll 187, File W9722.

Pension abstract for – Ning Beall
Service state(s): MD Continental Line
Date: 5 May 1818
County of: Frederick   State of: MD
Declaration made before a Judge or Court: Court
Act of: 18 Mar 1818
Age: 57 years
Volunteer, Drafted, or Substitute: Enlisted
Rank(s): Not stated
Statement of service-

Period	Duration	Names of General and Field Officers
1 Apr 1779 – 18 Sep 1782		Capt. Jones of the 3rd Regiment Light Dragoons in the Continental service.

Battles: Bacon's Bridge; Monks [Moncks] Corner; Santee River; Cowpens; Petersburg; and other skirmishes.
Discharge received: in the state of South Carolina
&
Pension abstract for – Ning Bell
Service state(s): MD Continental Line
Date: 5 Sep 1820
County of: Butler   State of: OH
Declaration made before a Judge or Court: Court of Common Pleas
Act of: 18 Mar 1818
Age: 59 years

Residence when he entered service: Enlisted at Frederick Town, MD
Residence now: St. Clair Twp., Butler Co., OH
Statement of service-

Period	Duration	Names of General and Field Officers
Apr 1778	3 yrs.	Col. William Washington, Capt. Jones in 3rd Regiment of Light Dragoons in the Virginia Line. [should be Maryland - transcription error by the clerk]

Discharge received: near Charles Town, SC
Signed by: S/Ambrose Gordon, Lt. & Pay Master 3rd Regt. Light Dragoons
What became of it?: Presented to the Court (copy in pension file)
Wife: Not named   Wife's age: 47 years
Names and ages of children: John age 15; Joseph age 12; Margaret age 10; James age 8; Sarah age 5.
&
Date: 14 Feb 1821, Butler Co., OH, he applied for transfer of his pension benefits to the Ohio agency, stating he intends to remain in Ohio and wishes his pension to be payable there.
&
Date: 7 Dec 1835, Dearborn Co., IN, he applied for transfer of his pension benefit to the Indiana agency, stating he moved to Indiana because he owned no land in Ohio and could purchase land cheaper in Indiana.
&
Pension abstract for – Christina Beall, widow of Ning Beall
Date: 11 Nov 1839
County of: Ripley   State of: IN
Declaration made before a Judge or Court: Probate Court
Act of: 4 Jul 1836 & 3 Mar 1837
Age: 66
Affidavit supporting widow's statement: Zephaniah Beall & Ninian Beall
Death of soldier: 13 Jun 1836
Marriage date and place: Aug 1790, Frederick County, MD
Proof of marriage: The marriage was published, no record was kept of the same.
&
Abstract for – Ninian Beall, Jr, in support of his mother's application
Alternate spelling(s): His father, Ninian or Ning Beall
Date: 8 Oct 1842
County of: Ripley   State of: IN
Declaration made before a Judge or Court: before James Early, J.P.
Act of: 7 Jun 1838
Age: 50 yrs on the 27th of the present month
Record of age: abt. 22 yrs ago the family Bible was consumed by fire in the house of Zephaniah Bell, a brother of mine and next oldest to myself. Abt. one yr. bef. the burning he had taken a copy of his own birth which he encloses. He remembers his brother William's age was set there & he was b. 1 Oct 1790.
Where and year born: Frederick Co., MD, 27 Oct 1792
Persons who certify character: James Early, J.P.
Death of soldier: 13 Jun 1836

Marriage date and place: His parents Ninian & Christina were married in 1790, and his brother William was first born after said marriage.

&

Abstract for – Zepeniah Beall, in support of his mother's application
Alternate spelling(s): His father, Ninian or Ning Beall
Date: 8 Oct 1842
County of: Ripley   State of: IN
Declaration made before a Judge or Court: before James Early, J.P.
Act of: 7 Jun 1838
Age: 48 yrs on 10 Apr next (1843)
Record of age: abt. 22 yrs ago the family Bible was consumed by fire in his own house. He inspected the copy of the entry in the Bible & is positive it is the same.
Where and year born: Place not stated, 1 Oct 1790
Persons who certify character: James Early, J.P.
Marriage date and place: He has understood his parents were married 1790 in Frederick Co., MD.
Note: Affidavit given by Daniel Zacharias, pastor German Evangelical Church, Frederick, Frederick Co., MD states marriage of Ninian Beall to Christina Stoll (or Stull) took place 25 Jul 1790, by Rev. William Runkle.

Letter in the Pension application for Adam Fox
Versailles Indiana September the 19th 1839

Dear Sir Thomas Johnson who was a soldier of the Revolutionary war and who resided at the time of his death in the County of Dearborn and State of Indiana and who drew a pension for many years before his death also Ning Bell and William Lippard and Henry Wilyard all of whom was soldiers of the Revolutionary War and resided in the county of Ripley and State of Indiana and was in the receipt of pensions at the time of their death. They have all left surviving widows to wit Sarah Johnson, Agnes Willyard, Christina Beall, and Mary Lippard all of whom wish to apply for pensions under and by Authority of the Act of Congress of the 4th of July 1836, and the 3rd of March 1837. The said Thomas Johnson, Ning Beall, William Lipperd and Henry Wilyard at the time of their deaths left a draw of pensions due and in order to obtain the same, sayeth widows, was requested to surrender the pension Certificates of their deceased husbands which said Certificated I suppose has been returned to the proper office. In order to enable the widows of deceased pensioner to identify themselves as the widows of the deceased it is necessary for them to set out the original pension certificate of their deceased husbands and as they must be on file in the office over which you preside please transfer to me at Versailles Indiana the original certificated of the said Johnson, Beall, Lipperd, and Wilyard if it is in accordance with the custom of your office. If not, please send me a Certified Copy of the same

I herewith send the papers of Mr. Adam Fox who claims a pension. If the papers are different please point out the deficiency to me.

Let me hear from you as soon as convenient.   Yours respectfully
                                                                                Joseph Robinson

Abstract of Final Payment Voucher; General Services Administration, Washington, DC
NAME   BELL, NING (KING)?
AGENCY OF PAYMENT   INDIANA
DATE OF ACT   1818
DATE OF PAYMENT   3rd Qr. 1836
DATE OF DEATH   June 13, 1836
GENERAL SERVICES ADMINISTRATION
National Archives and Records Service   NA-286
GSA DC 54-4891   November 1953

Brumbaugh, Gaius Marcus & Hodges, Margaret Roberts, comp.; *Revolutionary Records of Maryland;* Clearfield Company, Inc., Baltimore, MD, 1999, p. 22.
Frederick County, Maryland, 1778
"A List of the names of Sundry Persons who made their appearance in Open Court, and who after giving reasons which the Court deemed satisfactory, why they did not take the Oath of Fidelity and Support to the State of Maryland, agreeable in the last Act of Assembly, by permission of the said Court did severally and respectively take and repeat agreeable to the provision in the same Act contained".
[Included in the list] Beall, Ninian

Brumbaugh, Gaius Marc M.S., M.D., comp.; *Maryland Records – Colonial, Revolutionary, County and Church from Original Sources, Vol. I;* Genealogical Publishing Co., Inc., Baltimore, MD, 1985, p. 284.
Official Poll of Presidential Election in Frederick County, Md., November 9 to 12, 1796; 1917 Voters.
"Poll taken at the Court House in Frederick Town in and for Frederick County. Begun on the Second Wednesday of November 1796, from day to Day until the Twelfth day of the same Month inclusive for Electing an Elector of the President and Vice-President of the United States of America to wit:"
Candidates: John Tyler (Federalist voters marked F), and Geo. Murdock (Democratic-Republican voters marked D-R.)
Voter's Names:
[Included in list] Ninian Beall (F)

Brumbaugh, Gaius Marc M.S., M.D.,Litt.D., Washington, D.C., comp.; *Maryland Records – Colonial, Revolutionary, County and Church from Original Sources, Vol. II;* Lancaster Press, Inc., Lancaster, PA, 1928, p. 502
Frederick County - Marriages
Beall, Ninian and Christina Stoll, July 25, 1790.

Clements, S. Eugene and Wright, F Edward; *The Maryland Militia in the Revolutionary War;* Family Line Publications, Westminster, MD 21157, 1987, p. 198.
Muster Rolls and Other Lists - Montgomery County, Lower Battalion
Officers and Privates for the 29th (Lower) Battalion – Col. John Murdock; Lieut. Wm. Dakins; Maj. George Beall - 2 Co.: Nin: Edmn. Beall

p. 206.
Muster Rolls and Other Lists - Montgomery County
Sixth Company
Class No. 8: Ninn E. Beall

Newman, Harry Wright; *Maryland Revolutionary Records*; Tuttle Publishing, Rutland, VT, 1928. p. 9, 110, 130.
p. 9.

Maryland Revolutionary Pensioners				Misc. facts and
Name of Veteran	Birth	Rank	Establishment	other State services
Beall, Ninian*	1761	Pvt.	---	Va. Service

* Indicates that the widow applied for pension

p. 110
Marriage Records
Ninian Beall Christina Stull July 25, 1790 Fred. Co., Md.

p. 130.
Miscellaneous Lists Other States
Beall, Ninian Virginia

Barnes, Robert, Comp.; *Maryland Marriages 1778-1800*; Genealogical Publishing Co., Inc., 1979; p. 14.

Beall, Ninian,   7 March 1780,   Ann Marie Stricker   4 FR*
Beall, Ninian,   25 July 1790,   Christina Stoll   2 FR-1108**

*4 FR – Frederick County – Frederick County Marriage Licenses, 1778-1800, copied from the originals at the court house, and published in the DAR Magazine, Vol. 85.
**2 FR – Frederick County - First German Evangelical Reformed Church, Frederick, copy made in 1903, at MHS.

Myers, Margaret E., comp.; *Marriage Licenses of Frederick County 1778-1810*, Second Edition; Family Line Publications, Westminster, MD, 1994, p. 8.
Mar 7   1780   Beall, Ninian   to   Stricker, Ann Maria

Clark, Murtie June; *The Pension List of 1820 [U.S. War Department]* Reprinted with an Index; Genealogical Publishing Co., Inc., Baltimore, 1991. Originally published 1820 as Letter from the Secretary of War, p. 540.
MARYLAND
Names of the Revolutionary Pensioners which have been placed on the Roll of Maryland, under the Law of the 18th of March, 1818, from the passage thereof, to this day, inclusive of the Rank they held, and the Lines in which they served, viz: -

Names	Rank	Line
Included in the list –		
Ning Bell	private	Maryland

Ripley County Indiana, Recorder's Office, Tract Book 2, p.53.
Beall, Ninian   22 Jun 1829   R12, T7, S11   160 acres

Ripley County, Indiana Deed Records Vol. C., 21 Sep 1832 - 4 Feb 1834, Page 492.
Abstract of Deed/Patent for: Ninian Beall and Margaret (dower) his wife.
Purchaser (Grantee) or Seller (Grantor)?: Seller
Sold to: Richard Blair
State & county where recorded: Ripley Co., Indiana
Date entered: 25 Jun 1831
Recorded: 9 Dec 1833
Description: The lot in Presley Gray's donation to the county of Ripley known and designated on the plat thereof by number seven.
Amount paid: Twelve dollars ($12.00)

Ripley County, Indiana Deed Records Vol. D., 7 Feb 1834 - 9 Feb 1836, Page 116.
Abstract of Deed/Patent for: Ninian Beale, Sr.
Purchaser (Grantee) or Seller (Grantor)?: Purchaser
Purchased from: David Aspy and Maria (dower) his wife
State & county where recorded: Ripley Co., Indiana
Date entered: 23 May 1834
Recorded: 6 Sep 1834
Description: Tract of parcel of land in the South East quarter of Section 13, Township 7 North in Range 12 East; in the district of lands subject to sale at Jeffersonville, IN; containing 80 acres.
Amount paid: One hundred twenty five dollars ($125.00)
Name(s) of Witnesses: Daniel Gano, Clerk of Common Pleas Court, Hamilton Co., OH

The Pension Roll of 1835 Volume IV, The Mid-Western States, Indexed Edition, In Four Volumes; Genealogical Publishing Co., Inc., Baltimore, MD, Reprint 1968, p. 51.
A Statement, &c. of Ripley county, Indiana.

INDIANA Names	Rank	Annual allowance.	Sums received	Description of service
Ning Bell	Private	96.00	1519 99	Maryland line

When placed on pension roll	Commencement of pension	Ages	Laws under which they were formerly placed on the pension roll; and remarks.
June 30, 1818	May 5, 1818	73	-

Rejected or Suspended Applications for Revolutionary War Pensions; Reprinted for Clearfield Company Inc. by Genealogical Publishing Co., Inc., Baltimore, MD, 1998. p. 416.
A list of persons residing in Indiana who have applied for pensions under the act of July 4, 1836, whose claims have been suspended; prepared in conformity with the resolution of the Senate of the United States, September 16, 1850.

Names	Residence	Reason for suspension
Beall, Christina, widow of King	Versailles, Ripley	For proof of marriage

Pierce, Alycon Trubey DG, abstracted by; *Selected Final Payment Vouchers 1818-1864, Baltimore, Maryland;* Willow Bend Books, Lovettsville, VA, 1997, p. 15.

Bell, Ning   Maryland   1818
Butler Co., Ohio, 7 Jul 1821, Ning Bell (signature) (former dragoon in army of Rev.) resident of this county for two and a half years and previous thereto of Maryland, appoints Alexander Fridge attorney to collect pension due from 5May 1818 to 4 Mar 1820; sworn before M(atthew) Hueston J.P. (signature), Hartley Malone (signature), and Thomas Lloud (signature).
   Baltimore, 23 Jul 1821, Alexr. Fridge (signature) collected $176.00.

Ripley County, Indiana Complete Probate Book Vol. A., 12 May 1834-10 May 1842; p. 271-279.

His will is also recorded in -
Ripley Co., IN Probate Order Book, Vol.1 Wills, Sep 1821-Apr 1839, p. 31.
Abstract of will and administration for: Ninian Beall
      (also referred to as Ninian Bell)
State & county where will was made: Indiana, Ripley County
Date will made: 21 May 1836
Witnesses to will: William Brown & John L. Craig
Date entered in probate: 4 Jul 1836
Name(s) of administrator(s): Ninian Bell & John Bell
Bonded by and amount of bond: Ninian & John Beall; $3,000.00.
Names of heirs and others mentioned in will: my beloved wife Christina Beall;
   son Joseph Beall; son Ninian Beall, Jr.; son John Beall.
Date of division & disbursement, or final return: 12 Aug 1839

Toph, Violet E.; *Peoples History of Ripley County, Indiana;* self-published, c. 1940, p. 126, 128, 129-130.
Revolutionary Soldiers Who Came to Ripley County
Ninian (Ning) Beall was a soldier of Maryland Cavalry during the Revolutionary War. His name appears on a record under the following heading "A list of soldier of the Virginia Line on Continental Establishment who have received certificated of the balance of their full pay agreeable to the Act of Assembly passed November Session, 1781 which record shows that he received his recompense July 13, 1836. The Ripley County Historical Society placed a Government Marker to his grave in the Old Washington Cemetery.

p. 128.
In July, 1936, the Ripley County Historical Society, aided by subscriptions from descendants of the five Revolutionary soldiers buried in Old Washington cemetery, Edward Pendergast, Ninian Beall, James Grimes, Joseph McDonald and William Lipperd enclosed the cemetery with a durable wove wire fence and placed Government markers for each of the five soldiers, thus making a notable Revolutionary Shrine for Washington Township.

p. 129-130.
Ninian Beall entered the service from Maryland in April, 1778 under Col. William Washington. He was pensioned from Maryland, later moving to Cincinnati, O. then to Dearborn Co. Ind. and later to Washington Township, Ripley County, Ind. where he died June 13, 1836. He was born in 1761 and married Christine Stull.

Daughters of the American Revolution of the State of Ohio, comp. Official Roster III, Soldiers of the American Revolution Who Lived in the State of Ohio; Painesville Publishing, Painesville, OH, 1959, p. 33.
BELL, NING - -   ? Co.
D 6-13-1836. Pvt. in Cavalry; drew pens on Cert No 1800 on June 30, 1818; was transferred from O to Ind. on Mar 16, 1836. Widow, Christina, on Cert No 2649, dated Dec 28, 1848. Ref: DAR Magazines, July 1949, p. 609; Nov. 1949, p. 928.

O'Byrne, Mrs. Roscoe C., comp. & ed.; Roster Soldiers and Patriots of the American Revolution Buried in Indiana; Published by Indiana Daughters of the American Revolution, 1938, Reprinted Genealogical Publishing Co., Baltimore MD, 1968, p. 54.
BEALL (BELL), NINIAN (NING)   Ripley County
Born – 1761, Maryland.
Service – Enlisted from Maryland in April, 1778, under Col. Wm. Washington.
Proof – Pension claim W. 9722.
Died – June 13, 1836. Buried Washington Cemetery, near Versailles, Ind. Stone. Government marker and name on bronze tablet in Versailles Court House.
Married – Christine Stull. Many descendants living in Ripley Co., Ind.
Collected by Mrs. A. B. Wycoff, Batesville, Indiana.

Gibbs, A.; Ripley County Historical Society Data on Revolutionary Soldiers, 1973 review.
Exact location of marker: east out of Elrod on 525 to 50N, right; to Thurmon Boyd farm (1973); mile ne of house going down across creek and up a hill; no road. Old Washington Cemetery north-east of Elrod, Washington Tw. Ripley Co. Ind.
Type of marker: Gov't
Date placed: Oct. 1936 (minutes of R.C.H.S.)
Placed by: Ripley County Historical Society
Additional comments: on Court House tablet
Wording on marker: Ninian Beall - Pvt. Jones Co. –
              3 Continental Dragoons - Rev. War - June 13, 1836

<u>United States Headstone Applications for U.S. Military Veterans, 1925-1949, database with images</u>; *(https://familysearch.org/ark:/61903/1:1:VHZW-C11 : 17 May 2016); Affiliate Publication Number: M1916; Affiliate Publication Title: Applications for Headstones for U.S. Military Veterans, 1925-1941; Affiliate Film Number: 7; GS Film Number: 1878156; Digital Folder Number: 004832174; Image Number: 00056.*
Application for Headstone; War Department O.Q.M.G. Form No. 623
Name: Beall, Ninian
Event Date: May 31, 1934
Name of Cemetery: Old Washington
Located in or near: Milan, Ind.
Death Date: June 13, 1836
Enlistment Dates: Previous to 1781
Discharge Dates: -
Rank: Private
Company: Capt. Jones Co., Col. Wm. Washington's 3rd Regt. of Virginia Cavalry
To be shipped to: Ripley Co. Historical Society, Osgood, Ind., Ripley Co.
Whose post-office address is: Versailles, Ind.
This application is for the UNMARKED grave of a veteran. It is understood the stone will be furnished and delivered at the railroad station or steamboat landing above indicated, at Government expense, freight prepaid. I hereby agree to promptly accept the headstone at destination, remove it and properly place same at decedent's grave at my expense. Ripley Co. Historical Society, Applicant. No fee should be paid in connection with this application.
Applicant: Ripley Co. Historical Society, Versailles, Ind.

Tombstone Location: Old Washington Church Cemetery, Elrod, Washington Twp., Ripley Co., IN

Tombstone Inscription:
NINIAN
BEALL
PVT. JONES' CO,
CONTINENTAL
DRAGOONS
REV WAR
JUNE 13, 1836

Tombstone Inscription:
IN
memory of
Ninian Beall
who departed this life
June 13, 1836
Aged 75 years
& 10 days

BENEFIEL, GEORGE

George Benefiel's name appears on the original "Bronze Tablet" at the Ripley County Courthouse. There is no evidence that he ever resided, or had any court appearances in Ripley County. Information about this soldier is included here for those who are researching this man.

Patriot: George Benefiel
Birth: 25 Dec 1759, York Co., PA
Married Spouse 1: 1782 PA, Mary Buchanan (1764-1857) [a]
Service state(s): PA
Rank: Private
Proof of Service: PA Archives, Series 3, Vol. 23, p. 704.
Pension application No.: None
Residences: York Co., PA; Jefferson Co., IN
Died: 1 Apr 1832, Jefferson Co., IN
Buried: Jefferson Church Cemetery, Shelby Twp., Jefferson Co., IN
DAR Ancestor No.:A009069

(a) Mary Buchanan's father, George Buchanan, served in the Revolutionary War. See his record in this book. DAR Ancestor No.: A016392.

Pennsylvania Archives, Series 3, Vol. 23, p. 704.
Muster Rolls of Cumberland County Militia for the year 1780
Class Roll of the Seventh Company of the Fourth Battalion of Cumberland County Militia, Commanded by Colonel Samuel Culbertson, August 19, 1780.
Captain James Patton; Ensign John Dickey; Sergeant Mich'l McElhatton, Andrew Campbell, Andrew Dickey, John Haws
Fourth Class
[Included in list] George Benefield

U.S. Department of Interior, Bureau of Land Management, General Land Office Records; Land Patent Search
Name: BENEFIEL, GEORGE
Accession Nr. CV-0077-274; Document Type – Credit Volume Patent; State – Indiana; Issue Date – 12/9/1872; Cancelled – No; Names on Document - : Land Office – Jeffersonville; Authority – April 24, 1820: Sale-Cash Entry (3 Stat. 566); Document Nr. 395; Total Acres – 80.00; Land Descriptions: State – IN; Meridian – 2nd PM; Twp-Rng – 05N-011E; Aliquots – E 1/2SE 1/4; Section – 4; County - Jefferson

Toph, Violet E.; Toph Papers; collected during her lifetime 1878-1956, p. 1807-1808.
Excerpt – Told by George Buchanan in 1911. I was born in 1828, where the old fort, or what was commonly known as Buchanan's Station was built. My grandfather, George Buchanan, (a soldier of the Revolution) moving from Paris, Kentucky, and building the fort in the autumn of 1819. The fort of station was a log building with a projecting story having rifle ports set in the ground and

sharpened at the top. My father, Willson Buchanan, built his cabin on the tract of land he had entered just south of the post or station. West of him was Uncle George McLaughlin's home. These were all in Jefferson County, but are now in Ripley County, adjoining the Jefferson County line. What is now in Ripley County was then a part of Jefferson County. South of them, in what is still Jefferson County, was the cabin home of my uncle, George Benefiel, (also a Revolutionary soldier).

O'Byrne, Mrs. Roscoe C., comp. & ed.; <u>Roster Soldiers and Patriots of the American Revolution Buried in</u> Indiana; Published by Indiana Daughters of the American Revolution, 1938, Reprinted Genealogical Publishing Co., Baltimore MD, 1968, p. 57.

BENEFIEL, GEORGE   Jefferson County
Born – Dec. 25, 1759, York Co., Penn.
Service - Pri. in Capt. James Patton's Company, 4th Battalion, Cumberland Co. Penn. Militia, Col. Samuel Culbertson's Regt. Aug. 19, 1780.
Proof – Penn. Archives 3rd Series, Vol. 23, p. 704.
Died – April 1, 1832. Buried Jefferson Church Cemetery. Government marker placed by John Paul Chapter D.A.R.
Married – 1787, Mary Buchanan (1754-1857). Ch. Robert b. 1787, m. Ann Stewart; Martha b. 1789, m. John West; William b. 1791, m. Phebe Conner; Esther b. 1793, m. Robert McClelland; George b. 1795, m. first to Ann Ryker, second to Marjorie Van Cleave; Mary b. 1797, m. first to James McCarty, second to Isaiah Stewart; Jane b. 1798; Jesse b. 1800, m. Sarah ----; Wilson b. 1802, m. Eliza Buchanan; James b. 1806, m. Eliza Taylor; Samuel b. 1806, m. Elizabeth Stewart; Eliza b. 1808, m. ----- Russell.
Collected by John Paul Chapter D.A.R.

Gibbs, A.; <u>Ripley County Historical Society Data on Revolutionary Soldiers</u>, *1973 review.*
Additional comments: On Court House tablet
    Claimed by Jefferson Co. Ind. where he died.

Tombstone Location: Jefferson Church Cemetery, Shelby Twp., Jefferson Co., IN

Tombstone Inscription (nearly illegible):
GEO. BENEFIEL
[Illegible]
REV. WAR

Tombstone Inscription: TO THE
Memory of
GEORGE BENEFIEL
Departed this Life
April 1, 1832
72 Years 3 mo & 7 days

BOLDREY (BOLDEREY), JOHN

Patriot: John Bolderey
Birth: 1756 America
Married Spouse 1: Deborah (abt 1758-aft 1820)
Service state(s): MA Continental Line; MA Sea Service
Rank: Private & Marine
Proof of Service: Pension application
Pension application No.: S35785
Residences: Bristol Co., MA; Ontario Co., NY; Dearborn Co., IN
Died: 12 Jun 1821, Ripley Co., IN *[Incorrect date – was on 1840 census list]*
Buried: Franklin Church Cemetery, Franklin Twp. Ripley Co., IN
DAR Ancestor No.: None as of 6 Nov 2015

Pension Application Abstracted from National Archives microfilm Series M804, Roll 281, File S35785
Pension abstract for – John Bolderey
Service state(s): Continental MA, MA Sea Service
Alternate spelling(s): Boldrey
Date: 15 Apr 1818
County of: Ontario   State of: NY
Declaration made before a Judge or Court: Circuit Court
Act of: 18 Mar 1818
Age: 61 yrs.
Where and year born: Native of America
Residence when he entered service: Not stated
Residence(s) since the war: Bristol Co., MA; Ontario Co., NY; Dearborn Co., IN
Residence now: Ontario Co., NY
Volunteer, Drafted, or Substitute: Enlisted
Rank(s): Pvt. (1775-1776) & Marine (1777)
Statement of service-

Period	Duration	Names of General and Field Officers
Apr 1775	8 mos.	MA Line, Capt. Silas Cobb, Col. Walker's Regt.
1776	1 yr.	Capt. Oliver Soper, Col. Reed's Regt.
20 Feb 1777		Served on the frigate Boston
1779 – end of War		Served on the Caesar

Battles: Caesar captured, held prisoner in Port Royal, Jamaica
Discharge received: Left service each time with permission of his officers
&
Date: 23 Sep 1820
County of: Dearborn   State of: IN
Declaration made before a Judge or Court: Circuit Court
Age: 64   Record of age:
Statement of service-
Period   Names of General and Field Officers
Regt. commanded by Col. Reed, company commanded by Capt. Oliver Soper
Wife: Deborah   Wife's age: 62

Clark, Murtie June; *The Pension List of 1820 [U.S. War Department]Reprinted with an Index; Genealogical Publishing Co., Inc., Baltimore, 1991. Originally published 1820 as Letter from the Secretary of War, p. 352.*
NEW YORK
Names of the Revolutionary Pensioners which have been placed on the Roll of New York, under the Law of the 18th of March, 1818, from the passage thereof, to this day, inclusive of the Rank they held, and the Lines in which they served, viz: -

Names	Rank	Line
Included in the list –		
John Boldery	private	Massachusetts

Ripley County Indiana, Recorder's Office, Tract Book 3, p. 88.

Boldery, John	13 Jun 1827	R13, R9, S32	80 acres

The Pension Roll of 1835 Volume IV, The Mid-Western States, Indexed Edition, In Four Volumes; Genealogical Publishing Co., Inc., Baltimore, MD, Reprint 1968, p. 51.
Statement, &c. of Ripley county, Indiana.

INDIANA Names	Rank	Annual allowance.	Sums received	Description of service
John Boldery	Private	96.00	1525 29	Massachusetts line

When placed on pension roll	Commencement of pension	Ages	Laws under which they were formerly placed on the pension roll; and remarks.
Mar 24, 1819	Ap'l 15, 1818	78	Transferred from Ontario county, New York

A Census of Pensioners for Revolutionary or Military Services with their Names, Ages, and Places of Residence Under the Act for Taking the Sixth Census in 1840; Genealogical Publishing Co., Inc., Baltimore, Maryland, 1965. p. 184.

Names of pensioners for revolutionary or military services.	Ages	Names of heads of families with whom pensioners resided June 1, 1840.
RIPLEY COUNTY		
JOHNSON		
John Boldry	84	Samuel Boldry

Toph, Violet E.; *Peoples History of Ripley County, Indiana;* self-published, c. 1940, p. 130.
Revolutionary Soldiers Who Came to Ripley County
John Boldery entered the service from Massachusetts in April, 1775 under Col. Walker. He was born in 1756 and died June 12, 1821. He moved to Ripley County, Ind. in 1820. He is buried in the Franklin cemetery about three miles north of Milan and about three miles south of Sunman, Ind.

O'Byrne, Mrs. Roscoe C., comp. & ed.; Roster Soldiers and Patriots of the American Revolution Buried in Indiana; Published by Indiana Daughters of the American Revolution, 1938, Reprinted Genealogical Publishing Co., Baltimore MD, 1968, p. 64.

BOLDREY, JOHN   Ripley County
Born – 1756.
Service – Entered service from Mass. In April, 1775, under Col Walker.
Proof – Pension claim S.35785.
Died – June 12, 1821. Probably buried in Franklin Cemetery, Ripley Co. Name on bronze tablet in Versailles Court House.
Collected by Mrs. A. B. Wycoff, Batesville, Indiana.

Hatcher, Patricia Law, Comp.; Abstract of Graves of Revolutionary Patriots (4 volumes); Pioneer Heritage Press, Dallas, TX, 1987, Vol. I, p. 94.
Boldrey   John   Pilgrim's Home Ch, Old Regular Bapt Cem, Ripley Co IN 74
[Pilgrims Home Church is also known as Franklin Church Cemetery]

Gibbs, A.; Ripley County Historical Society Data on Revolutionary Soldiers, 1973 review.
Exact location of marker: Grave not located (1973); Gov't marker at Old Franklin Church (Regular Baptist) or Franklin Free Will Baptist Church, now (1974) called Pilgrims Home Church of Old Regular Baptist; cemetery adjoins. On State rd. 101 from Old Milan to Sunman on local 700N one mile east from 700E; Franklin Tw. Ripley Co. Ind., Sec. 5 T8 R13E; near what used to be called Clinton that was laid out by John and Samuel Boldrey – no longer on map.
Type of marker: Gov't
Date placed: Nov. 1938. R. C. H. S. minutes indicate that a marker (Gov't) was placed at the same time as those of James Arnold and Daniel McMillen's.
Placed by: Ripley County Historical Society
Additional comments: On Court House tablet.
> It must be noted that this man's name appears on the Pension list of 1840 census as age 84, so that it [is] very probable that the death date on the marker is incorrect.

Wording on marker:

John Boldrey
Pvt
Rev. War
Walker's Mass. Regt.
June 12, 1821

United States Headstone Applications for U.S. Military Veterans, 1925-1949, database with images; (https://familysearch.org/ark:/61903/1:1:VHZW-K9V : 17 May 2016); Affiliate Publication Number: M1916; Affiliate Publication Title: Applications for Headstones for U.S. Military Veterans, 1925-194; Affiliate Film Number: 10; GS Film Number: 1878159; Digital Folder Number: 00483217; Image Number: 01260.

Application for Headstone; War Department O.Q.M.G. Form No. 623
Name: Bolderey, John
Event Date: June 21, 1939
Name of Cemetery: Franklin
Located in or near: Milan, Ind.
Death Date: June 12, 1821
Enlistment Dates: April 1775
Discharge Dates: -
Rank: Private
Company: Cobbs Co., under Col. Walker's Massachusetts Regt.
To be shipped to: Ripley Co. Historical Society, Osgood, Ind., Ripley Co.
Whose post-office address is: Versailles, Ind.
This application is for the UNMARKED grave of a veteran. It is understood the stone will be furnished and delivered at the railroad station or steamboat landing above indicated, at Government expense, freight prepaid. I hereby agree to promptly accept the headstone at destination, remove it and properly place same at decedent's grave at my expense. Ripley Co. Historical Society, Applicant. No fee should be paid in connection with this application.
Applicant: Ripley County Historical Society, Versailles, Indiana

Location of tombstone: Franklin Church Cemetery, Stumpke Corner,
                             Franklin Twp., Ripley Co., IN

Tombstone Inscription:

JOHN
BOLDEREY
PVT
WALKER'S MASSACHUSETTS
REV. WAR
JUNE 12, 1821

BUCHANAN, GEORGE

Patriot: George Buchanan
Birth: 1721, Pennsylvania or County Donegal, Ireland
Married Spouse 1: Esther Campbell
Service state(s): PA
Rank: Pvt.
Proof of Service: 4th PA Regiment; Patriotic Service
Pension application No.: None
Residences: Fannett Township, Cumberland Co., PA; Paris, KY; Ripley Co., IN; Jefferson Co., IN
Died: 1818, Jefferson Co., IN
Buried: McLaughlin Cemetery, Brown Twp., Ripley Co, IN
– moved to Buchanan Cemetery, Brown Twp., Ripley Co., IN
DAR Ancestor No.: A016392
Children: His daughter, Mary Buchanan, married George Benefiel. See his record in this book. DAR Ancestor No.: A009069.

Revolutionary War Service Records; National Archives Publication number M881, Compiled service records of soldiers who served in the American Army during the Revolutionary War, 1775-1783.
https://www.fold3.com/image/21189617?terms=Buchanan,%20George
Buchanan, George - 4th Pennsylvania Regiment
Card Numbers 39146026, 6279.

Pennsylvania Archives, Series 3, Vol. 20, p. 159.
County of Cumberland – 1779
Fannett Township
Supply Rates [tax]

	Acres.	Horses.	Cattle.	Negroes.
Buchanan, George	100	2	3	..

Stemmons, John D and E. Diane (comp);Pennsylvania in 1780, A Statewide Index of Circa 1780 Pennsylvania Tax Lists, Self-published, 1978, p. 27.
BUCHANAN
    George   CUMB: FN [Fannett Twp.]

[Although not mentioned in family records and other records, he may have been in Kentucky prior to moving to Indiana. The following record, although not a Revolutionary War record, is of interest, and might be for him. – mjm]
Clark, Murtie June, Comp.; *American Militia in the Frontier Wars, 1790-1796;* Genealogical Publishing Co., Inc., 1990, p. 55.

Kentucky Militia

Pay Roll of a Company of Mounted Volunteers Commanded by Captain Anthony Bartlett, Major William Prince's Battalion, called into the service by the President of the United States in 1794.

Nr	Rank	Name	Remarks
76	Private	Buchanan, George	-

Toph, Violet E.; Toph Papers; collected during her lifetime 1878-1956, p. 1807-1808.

Excerpt – Told by George Buchanan in 1911. I was born in 1828, where the old fort, or what was commonly known as Buchanan's Station was built. My grandfather, George Buchanan, (a soldier of the Revolution) moving from Paris, Kentucky, and building the fort in the autumn of 1819. The fort of station was a log building with a projecting story having rifle ports set in the ground and sharpened at the top. My father, Willson Buchanan, built his cabin on the tract of land he had entered just south of the post or station. West of him was Uncle George McLaughlin's home. These were all in Jefferson County, but are now in Ripley County, adjoining the Jefferson County line. What is now in Ripley County was then a part of Jefferson County. South of them, in what is still Jefferson County, was the cabin home of my uncle, George Benefiel, (also a Revolutionary soldier).

O'Byrne, Mrs. Roscoe C., comp. & ed.; Roster Soldiers and Patriots of the American Revolution Buried in Indiana; Published by Indiana Daughters of the American Revolution, 1938, Reprinted Genealogical Publishing Co., Baltimore MD, 1968, p. 75.

BUCHANAN, GEORGE   Ripley County
Born – 1721, Pennsylvania.
Service – In 4th Penn. Cont'l Line as Pri. 1777-1781, 4 years. *[This is a different man named George Buchannan who died abt. 1786 – mjm]*
Proof – A. L. Buchanan, Larned, Kansas; Penn. Archives.
Died – 1818. There is a question as to his exact grave. A government marker placed by Ripley Co. Hist. Society in McLaughlin Cemetery in 1935. John Paul Chapter D. W. R placed one in Jefferson Church Cemetery in 1924.
Married – Esther Campbell. Ch Mary b. 1764, m. George Benefiel (Rev. S.); Harriet b. 1768, m. ---- McLaughlin; Margaret b. 1770, m. John Cowan; William b. 1771; David b. 1774; Wilson b. 1775; John b. 1778.
Collected by Mrs. A. B. Wycoff, Batesville, Indiana, and John Paul Chapter D.A.R.

O'Byrne, comp. Mrs. Roscoe C., comp.; Roster of Soldiers and Patriots of the American Revolution Buried in Indiana, Vol. III; Indiana Daughters of the American Revolution, 1966, p. 58.

Additional data and/or corrections received since 1966 to the records of the soldiers and patriots listed in Rosters I and II.
BUCHANAN, GEORGE   Roster I, p. 75   Ripley County
Children – (Additional) William b. 1771 m. (1) Catherine Yount or Young, (2) Edna Hawkins; David b. 1774 m. Nov. 1814 Nancy Jane Buchanan; Wilson b. 1775 m. (1) 1817 Zella Forester (2) Hannah Ricketts *[DAR has determined that Wilson is not the son of George Buchannan]*; John b. 1778 m. Rachel Short.
By Mrs. A. G. Charlton, 310 Sunnyside Avenue, Aurora, Indiana 47001.

Gibbs, A.; Ripley County Historical Society Data on Revolutionary Soldiers, 1973 review.

Exact location of marker: on County Line between Ripley and Jefferson Co. Ind., rd. 1100S, on knoll in an enclosed cemetery across from the Buchanan Fort Marker. Buchanan Cemetery, Brown Tw. Ripley Co. Ind.

Type of marker: Gov't (in 1973, it is sinking)
Date placed: (guess?) 1936
Placed by: Ripley County Historical Society
Additional comments: On Court House tablet
Wording on marker:	George Buchanan
		4 Pa Rgt.
		Rev. War
		1815

United States Headstone Applications for U.S. Military Veterans, 1925-1949, database with images; (https://familysearch.org/ark:/61903/1:1:VHZW-1Y8 : 17 May 2016) Affiliate Publication Number: M1916; Affiliate Publication Title: Applications for Headstones for U.S. Military Veterans, 1925-1941; Affiliate Film Number: 15; GS Film Number: 1878164; Digital Folder Number: 004832182; Image Number: 00082.

Application for Headstone; War Department O.Q.M.G. Form No. 623
Name: Buchanan, George
Event Date: 7 Oct 1937
Name of Cemetery: Family
Located in or near: Ripley County, Indiana
Death Date: 1815
Enlistment Dates: 1777
Discharge Dates: 1781
Rank: Pvt.
Company: 4th Regiment, Pennsylvania Continental Line
To be shipped to: George T. Buchanan at Madison, Indiana
Whose post-office address is: Buchanan Station Farm, R.F.D.
This application is for the UNMARKED grave of a veteran. It is understood the stone will be furnished and delivered at the railroad station or steamboat landing above indicated, at Government expense, freight prepaid. I hereby agree to promptly accept the headstone at destination, remove it and properly place same at decedent's grave at my expense. Ripley Co. Historical Society, Applicant. No fee should be paid in connection with this application.
Applicant: Mrs. Minnie E. Wycoff, 219 Maplewood Ave., Batesville, Indiana

Tombstone Location:	McLaughlin Cemetery, on Barbersville Rd., Brown Twp., Ripley Co., IN

Tombstone Inscription:

                  GEORGE
                 BUCHANAN
                4 PA. REGT.
                 REV. WAR
                    1815

[Note: this tombstone shows his death occurred in 1815; National Society Daughters of the American Revolution and family records show his death was in 1818.]

BAUMGARDNER (BUMGARDNER), DANIEL

Patriot: Daniel Bumgardner
Birth: 1761, Berks Co., PA
Married Spouse 1: 1 Jan1780/1781 Rowan Co., NC   Elizabeth
Service state(s):   NC
Rank: Private
Proof of Service: Pension application
Pension application No.: S32150
Residences: Berks Co., PA; Rowan Co., NC; KY; OH; St. Joseph Co., IN
Died: 25 Oct 1834, St. Joseph Co., IN
Buried: Byrkit Cemetery, Penn Twp., Mishawaka, St. Joseph Co., IN
DAR Ancestor No.: None as of 6 Nov 2015

Pension Application Abstracted from National Archives microfilm Series M804, Roll 404, File S32150
Pension abstract for – Daniel Baumgardner
Service state(s): NC State Troops
Date: 11 Dec 1833
County of: St. Joseph   State of: IN
Declaration made before a Judge or Court: Circuit Court
Act of: 7 Jun 1832
Age: 72 yrs.
Record of age: father's family Bible, I took a copy now in my possession
Where and year born: Berks Co., PA   1761
Residence when he entered service: Rowan Co., NC
Residence(s) since the war: NC, KY, OH, IN
Residence now: Indiana
Volunteer, Drafted, or Substitute: Volunteered 1st tour; drafted 2nd tour; drafted 3rd tour
Rank(s): Private
Statement of service-

Period	Duration	Names of General and Field Officers
Mar 1779	3 mos.	Capt. Armstrong; transferred to Capt. Garrison's company of light infantry, Major Lewis
Abt Jul 1779	3 mos.	Gen. Readerforth [Rutherford], under Col. Lock [Locke], Capt. Lps [Lopps] Company
Abt late 1779	3 mos.	Capt. Lop's light-horse company; Capt. Bodenhammer [Boldenheimer] after Lop was taken prisoner.

Battles: Stono, NC;
1st tour Discharge received: Discharged abt. 6 mi. from Stono, SC
What became of it?: Lost
2nd tour Discharge received: Discharged at Anson Courthouse
What became of it?: Lost
3rd tour Discharge received: Discharged in Randolph Co., NC

What became of it?: Lost
Statement is supported by –
Documentary proof: Knows of no documentary evidence
Person now living who can testify to service: No one
Persons in neighborhood who certify character: Solomon Michael and
                               Edmund Byrket
&

Pension abstract for – Elizabeth Bumgardner, widow of Daniel Bumgardner
Date: 7 Apr 1835
County of: St. Joseph   State of: Indiana
Declaration made before a Judge or Court: Circuit Court
Age: 73 years, 4 months, 3 days   Record of age:
Declaration: Widow's claim – they marred 1 Jan 1780 or 1781, Rowan Co., NC and she lived with him until 25 Oct 1834 (his death). Daniel Bumgardner, private, to receive $30.00 annually beginning 4 Mar 1831. Widow says no part of pension was received.
Residence now: St. Joseph Co., IN
Witness testimony: Jacob Byrket made declaration he was acquainted with
           Daniel Bumgardner and says he is the same as in the certificate and that
           Elizabeth & Daniel have lived in Indiana for 40 years and the couple
           raised children
Witness testimony: Solomon Michael attests that he knew the couple for 5 years
           and their children.
Names and ages of children: Not shown

Abstract of Final Payment Voucher; General Services Administration, Washington, DC
NAME   BUMGARDNER, DANIEL
AGENCY OF PAYMENT   INDIANA
DATE OF ACT   1832
DATE OF PAYMENT   3rd Qt. 1835
DATE OF DEATH   Oct 24, 1834
GENERAL ACCOUNTING OFFICE
National Archives and Records Service   NA-286
GSA DC 54-4891   November 1953

The Pension Roll of 1835 Volume IV, The Mid-Western States, Indexed Edition, In Four Volumes; Genealogical Publishing Co., Inc., Baltimore, MD, Reprint 1968, p. 87.
Statement, &c. of Ripley county, Indiana.

INDIANA Names	Rank	Annual allow-ance.	Sums re-ceived	Description of service
Daniel Bumgardiner	Pvt	30.00	-	N.C. State troops
When placed on pension roll	Commencement of pension	Ages		Laws under which they were formerly placed on the pension roll; and remarks.
Jan 18, 1834	March 4, 1831	81		-

Toph, Violet E.; Peoples History of Ripley County, Indiana; self-published, c. 1940, p. 125.
Revolutionary Soldiers Who Came to Ripley County
Daniel Bumgardner enlisted from North Carolina in March 1779 and was pensioned while living in St Joseph County, Ind. He died in 1835.

Mrs. Roscoe C. O'Byrne, comp. & ed.; Roster Soldiers and Patriots of the O'Byrne, Mrs. Roscoe C., comp. & ed.; Roster Soldiers and Patriots of the American Revolution Buried in Indiana; Published by Indiana Daughters of the American Revolution, 1938, Reprinted Genealogical Publishing Co., Baltimore MD, 1968, p. 54.
BAUMGARDNER, DANIEL   Ripley County
Service – Enlisted from N.C. in March, 1779.
Proof – Pension claim S. 32150.
Died – 1835. Name on bronze tablet in Versailles, Court House.
Collected by Mrs. A. B. Wycoff, Batesville, Indiana.

Gibbs, A.; Ripley County Historical Society Data on Revolutionary Soldiers, 1973 review.
Exact location of marker: No information further on grave
Additional comments: On Court House tablet
> Toph notes: was pensioned while living in St. Joseph Co. Ind. No probate record in St. Joseph Co. said clerk.

Princess Mishawaka Society Children of the American Revolution, Revolutionary War Soldiers Final Rest, St. Joseph Co., Indiana; Mishawaka, IN, 2011; http://www.rootsweb.ancestry.com/~insccdar/princess/st-jo-veterans.html.
Daniel Bumgardner
B. 1761, Berks County, Pa - D. October 25, 1834
Buried: Byrkit Cemetery
Enlisted: Rowan County, North Carolina, March 1779
Private, North Carolina Militia
Note: Edmund Byrkit and Solomon Michael, witnesses

Burial: The Schuyler Colfax Chapter National Society Daughters of the American Revolution, South Bend, IN Re-dedicated the grave of Daniel Bumgardner, and dedicated a marker for his wife, Elizabeth in 2008. Per Chapter member, Carol Nichols in 2016, there is a "military tombstone" for Daniel, and Elizabeth has a "rock". *[I have not been able to locate transcriptions for these – mjm.]*

BURCHFIELD, JOHN

Patriot: John Burchfield
Birth: 6 Jun 1765, Guilford Co., NC
Married Spouse 1: 22 Dec 1815, Bourbon Co., KY
                                  Mary "Polly" Patterson (abt 1797 - 1862)
Service state(s): NC
Rank: Private
Proof of Service: Pension application
Pension application No.: W8175
Residences: NC; Abbeville District, SC; Warren Co., KY; Franklin Co., IN
Died: 28 Dec 1849   Jefferson Co., IN
Buried: possibly Whitham Cemetery, Rexville, Shelby Twp., Ripley Co., IN
DAR Ancestor No.: None as of 7 Jun 2017.

Pension Application Abstracted from National Archives microfilm Series M804, Roll 409, File W8175
Pension abstract for – John Burchfield
Service state(s): NC
Date: 14 Feb 1833
County of: Franklin   State of: IN
Declaration made before a Judge or Court: Probate Court
Act of: 7 Jun 1832
Age: 67 yrs.   Record of age:
Where and year born: Guilford Co., NC   6 Jun 1765
Residence when he entered service: Cathy's Station on Catawba River, NC
                      [Cathey's Station]; volunteered in Burke Co., NC
Residence(s) since the war: Abbeville District, SC (13 yrs), Warren Co., KY (abt
                      21 yrs), Indiana in 1822 [date illegible, might be 1812]
Residence now: Franklin Co., IN
Volunteer, Drafted, or Substitute: 1st tour Volunteered; 2nd tour volunteered
Rank(s): 1st tour as Private; 2nd tour as a spy
Statement of service-

Period	Duration	Names of General and Field Officers
7 Apr 1780 – 1 Feb 1781	10 mos.	Capt. Joseph McDowell, Lt. Joseph McKiney [McKinney], Ensign Harry Highland
May, 1781	6 mos.	Capt. Gilliam Johnson at Turkey Cove, NC spying against the Cherokee Indians.

Battles: Cowpens – wounded in the forehead by a sword
1st tour Discharge received: Received no discharge, he was dismissed at Quaker Meadows until called again; not called again.
2nd tour Discharge received: at Warford's Station, Turkey Coves, NC
Signed by: Capt. Johnson
What became of it?: Lost
Documentary proof: Has no documentary evidence
Clergyman: Daniel St. John

Persons in neighborhood who certify character: Joseph Evans, Esq.; Charles Test, Judge Rush Co., IN; William Gillen
&

Pension abstract for – Mary Burchfield, widow of John Burchfield
Date: 4 Nov 1851
County of: Dearborn   State of: IN
Declaration made before a Judge or Court: Notary Public
Act of: 28 Sep 1850 [War of 1812]
Age: 51
Residence now: Hamilton Co., OH
Rank(s): She states he was a private then a sergeant [War of 1812]
Widow's Statement of soldier's service-

Period	Names of General and Field Officers
War of 1812	Company commanded by Capt. Henry C. Guess (or Guest), in the 28th Regiment of Regulars commanded by Col. Thomas [Illegible].

Statement is supported by –
7 Nov 1851, Fayette Co., IN, Rebeckar Ward gave an affidavit supporting the application of Mary Burchfield described as a resident of Hamilton Co., OH; that she is the sister of Mary Burchfield; that their father's name was James Patterson who lived in Bourbon County Kentucky. In the latter part of the year 1815, she recalls the marriage of John Burchfield to her sister Mary Patterson; they removed to Bracken Co., KY shortly after their marriage; in 1823 they removed to Fayette Co., IN, then to Rush and then to Franklin Co., IN
&

Pension abstract for – Mary Burchfield, widow of John Burchfield
Date: 7 Nov 1856
County of: Marion   State of: IN
Declaration made before a Judge or Court:
Age: 59, nearly 60
Residence now: Soldier lived in Franklin Co., IN; went to Hamilton Co., Oh for abt. 2 yrs.; then to Ripley Co., IN; then to Jefferson Co., IN where he died.
Death of soldier: 28 Dec 1849, Jefferson Co., IN – recorded in clerk's office in Madison, IN.
Widow's name before marriage: Mary Patterson
Marriage date and place: 22 Dec 1815   Bourbon Co., KY
Proof of marriage: No proof, she stated they were married by Stephen Riddle, Baptist preacher.
The original one [record] of the birth of our children has been destroyed; have a copy which dates the birth of our first child – not named.
Names and ages of children: 1st child b. 24 Sep 1817
Statement is supported by –
Living witness, name(s): Eliza Ann Brisbin, daughter age 35, resident of Ripley Co., IN, gave affidavit supporting her mother's testimony
&

Proof of Marriage: An Extract from the Marriage Returns of Records in the Clerk's Office of Bourbon Co., KY –

Date	Parties Names	By Whom Married
1815 Dec 22nd	John Burchfield and Polly Patterson	Rev'd Steven Riddle

Certified by R. J. Bromwell, 11 Nov 1856

Abstract of Final Payment Voucher; General Services Administration, Washington, DC
NAME   Burchfield, John
AGENCY OF PAYMENT   INDIANA
DATE OF ACT   1832
DATE OF PAYMENT   1st Qr. 1850
DATE OF DEATH   Dec. 28 1849
GENERAL SERVICES ADMINISTRATION
National Archives and Records Service   NA-286
GSA DC 54-4891   November 1953

Abstract of Final Payment Voucher; General Services Administration, Washington, DC
NAME   BURCHFIELD, MARY WIDEO OF JOHN
AGENCY OF PAYMENT   INDIANA
DATE OF ACT   1853 2d Sect
DATE OF PAYMENT   March 1862
DATE OF DEATH   -
last ~~FINAL~~ PAYMENT VOUCHER RECEIVED FROM
        THE GENERAL ACCOUNTING OFFICE   Form
General Services Administration   GSA DC 70-7035   GSA DEC 69 7068

Kentucky, County Marriages, 1797-1954; Bourbon, Kentucky, United States, Madison County Courthouse, Richmond, p. 55; accessed 11 April 2016) from https://familysearch.org/ark:/61903/1:1:V5Z4-BS6
Name: John Burchfield
Event Date: 22 Dec 1815
Event Place: Bourbon, Kentucky, United States
Spouse's Name: Polly Patterson
GS Film number: 000183145
Digital Folder Number: 004542764; Image Number: 00084
FHL microfilm 183,145.

Ripley County Indiana, Recorder's Office, Tract Book 3, p. 40.
Burchfield, John   18 Nov 1816   R12E, T6, S17   160 acres

U.S. Department of Interior, Bureau of Land Management, General Land Office Records; Land Patent Search
Name: Burchfield, John

Accession Nr. CV-0076-374; Document Type – Credit Volume Patent; Issue Date – 5/17/1821; Cancelled – No
Land Office – Jeffersonville; authority – April 24, 1820:Sale-Cash Entry (3 Stat. 566); Document Nr. 3971; Total Acres – 160.00
Land Descriptions: State – IN; Meridian – 2nd; Twp-Rng – 006N-012E; Aliquots – SE1/4; Section – 17; County - Ripley

Cowen, Janet C., comp; *Jeffersonville Land Entries 1808-1818;* McDowell Publications, Utica, NY, 1984, p. 130.
Receipt #
11088   Burchfield John IN Jefferson SE S17 T06 N12E 160 1816 11 18
The Pension Roll of 1835 Volume IV, The Mid-Western States, Indexed Edition, In Four Volumes; Genealogical Publishing Co., Inc., Baltimore, MD, Reprint 1968, p. 71.
Statement, &c. of Franklin county, Indiana.

INDIANA Names	Rank	Annual allow-ance.	Sums received	Description of service
John Burchfield	Private	22.33	56 32	Virginia militia

When placed on pension roll	Commencement of pension	Ages	Laws under which they were formerly placed on the pension roll; and remarks.
May 13, 1833	March 4, 1831	74	-

A Census of Pensioners for Revolutionary or Military Services with their Names, Ages, and Places of Residence Under the Act for Taking the Sixth Census in 1840; Genealogical Publishing Co., Inc., Baltimore, Maryland, 1965. p. 184.

Names of pensioners for revolutionary or military services.	Ages	Names of heads of families with whom pensioners re-Sided June 1, 1840.
RIPLEY COUNTY		DELAWARE
John Burchfield	74	John Burchfield

1840 U. S. Census, Delaware Twp., Ripley County, IN; Roll 92; p. 100, line 6.
John Burchfield
Males 10-14=1, Males 15-19=1, Males 60-69=1, Females <5=1, Females 5-9=1, Females 10-14=1, Females 40-49=1.

Toph, Violet E.; *Peoples History of Ripley County, Indiana;* self-published, c. 1940, p. 129.
Revolutionary Soldiers Who Came to Ripley County
John Burchfield entered the service from North Carolina in 1779 and served fifteen months and 24 days. He was born in Guildford [Guilford] Co. North Carolina June 6, 1765, lived in Warren Co., Ky. and afterwards moved to Rush and Franklin Co. He moved to Hamilton, Ohio and then to Ripley Co., Ind and later to Jefferson county, Ind. where he died Dec. 28, 1849. He was pensioned in Franklin.

O'Byrne, Mrs. Roscoe C., comp. & ed.; <u>Roster Soldiers and Patriots of the American Revolution Buried in Indiana</u>; Published by Indiana Daughters of the American Revolution, 1938, Reprinted Genealogical Publishing Co., Baltimore MD, 1968, p. 77.

BURCHFIELD, JOHN   Ripley County
Born – June 6, 1765, Guilford Co., North Carolina.
Service – Entered service from N.C. in 1779. Served 15 mos. and 24 days.
Proof – Pension claim W. 8175.
Died – Dec. 28, 1849, in Ripley Co. Name on bronze tablet in Versailles Court House.
Married – 1815, Polly Patterson.
Collected by Mrs. A. B. Wycoff, Batesville, Indiana.

Gibbs, A.; <u>Ripley County Historical Society Data on Revolutionary Soldiers</u>, 1973 review.

Exact location of marker: No further information on grave site.
    Penciled on Toph's notes is "buried in Jefferson Co. Ind."
Additional comments: On Court House tablet.
        1840 census Ripley Co. Ind., p. 198, John Burchfield age 72.

BURCHFIELD, ROBERT

Patriot: Robert Burchfield
Birth: 18 Dec 1759, Baltimore, Baltimore Co., MD
Married Spouse 1: March 1787 Burke Co., NC, Elizabeth Hill (1768-1845)
Service state(s): NC
Rank: Private
Proof of Service: Pension application
Pension application No.: R1444
Residences: Rowan Co., NC; abt. 1787 to [Franklin Co.] KY; Ripley Co., IN
Died: 29 Oct 1844, Ripley Co., IN
Buried: Whitham Cemetery, Shelby Twp., Ripley Co., IN
DAR Ancestor No.: A017098

Pension Application Abstracted from National Archives microfilm Series M804, Roll 409, File R1444
Pension abstract for – Robert Burchfield
Service state(s): NC
Date: 13 Nov 1832
County of: Ripley   State of: IN
Declaration made before a Judge or Court: Probate Court
Act of: 7 Jun 1832
Age: 73 yrs.
Where and year born: Baltimore, on Pipe Creek, MD   18 Dec 1759
Residence when he entered service: Rowan Co., NC
Residence(s) since the war: Rowan Co., NC; abt. 1787 to KY; Ripley Co., IN
Residence now: Ripley Co., IN
Volunteer, Drafted, or Substitute: Volunteer
Rank(s): Private - Ranger & Guard
Statement of service-

Period	Duration	Names of General and Field Officers
Mar/Apr 1775-Jun 1775	3 mos.	Capt. George Cathie's company, Col. Mathew Locke's regiment. Served as ranger & guard on the frontier against the Cherokee Indians.
Jun 1775-Sep 1775	3 mos.	Capt. Samuel Davis' company, Col. Locke's regiment. Against the Cherokee Indians.
Nov 1778-Apr 1779	5 mos.	Capt. Robert Alexander's company, Col. Locke's regiment & Captain Richardson's company, Col. Lytle's regiment.
Nov 1781-Dec 1781	1 mo.	Capt. William Trimble's company, Col. John Sevier's regiment. In engagement with Cherokees on Boyd Creek.
May 1782-Aug 1782	3 mos.	Capt. James Davis' company, Col. Joseph McDowell's regiment. His brother, Meshac Burchfield was Ensign.
Mar 1783-Jun 1783	3-4 mos.	Capt. George Cathie's company, Col. Joseph McDowell's regiment. Against the Cherokees. His father (not named) was killed by the Cherokees about this time.

Battles: Gen. Ashe's defeat at Briar Creek; Boyd's Creek, NC (now TN); Battle of Cherokee Towns.
Discharge received: Yes – received two written
Signed by: 3rd term – Col. Locke; 4th term – Capt. Davis.
What became of it?: Not stated
Person now living who can testify to service: Eugene [?], Col. John Hunter, Doct. Cornett, Col. Robinson or Versailles.
Clergyman: Elias Robinson
Persons in neighborhood who certify character: John Hunter
Death of soldier: 29 Oct 1844   Ripley Co., IN
Wife: Elizabeth Hill
Marriage date and place: Mar 1787
&
Pension abstract for – Elizabeth Burchfield widow of Robert
Date: 26 Feb 1845
County of: Ripley   State of: IN
Declaration made before a Judge or Court: Circuit Court
Act of: 3 Mar 1843
Widow's Age: 77 yrs.
Persons in neighborhood who certify character: John Burchfield, ag 77, (no relation indicated), became acquainted with the applicant.
Death of soldier: 29 Oct 1844   Ripley Co., IN
Marriage date and place: Mar 1787   Burke Co., NC
Names and ages of children: Mary Burchfield Roberts; Sally Kelly; Betsey O'Neal; John Burchfield of Ripley Co., IN; Nancy Whitam; Kitty Smith; Robert Burchfield Jr. (in 1854 resident of Delaware Twp., Ripley Co., IN).

Abstract of Final Payment Voucher; General Services Administration, Washington, DC

~~FINAL~~ LAST PAYMENT VOUCHER RECEIVED FROM THE GENERAL ACCOUNTING OFFICE

NAME	BURCHFIELD, ROBERT
AGENCY OF PAYMENT	INDIANA
DATE OF ACT	1832
DATE OF PAYMENT	Sept. 3, 1844
DATE OF DEATH	-
GENERAL SERVICES ADMINISTRATION	
National Archives and Records Service	NA-286
GSA-WASH DC 54-4891	November 1953

Register of the Kentucky Historical Society; Early Kentucky Tax Records; *Clearfield Publishing, Baltimore, Md., 1999; p. 50.*
List of Taxable Property Within the District of Isaac E. Gano, Commissioner in the County of Franklin for the Year 1795.

Persons Named Chargeable with the Tax	White Males Above 21	Horses, mares, colts & mules	Cattle
Burchfield, Robert	1	1	10

Ripley County Indiana, Recorder's Office, Tract Book 1, p. 34.
Burchfield, Robert   02 Apr 1818   R11E, T6, 24   160 acres
U.S. Department of Interior, Bureau of Land Management, General Land Office Records; Land Patent Search
Name: Burchfield, Robert
Accession Nr. IN0250_.283; Document Type – State Volume Patent; Issue Date – 7/16/1832; Cancelled – No
Land Office – Jeffersonville; authority – April 24, 1820: Sale-Cash Entry (3 Stat. 566); Document Nr. 2798; Total Acres – 53.32
Land Descriptions: State – IN; Meridian – 2ndPM; Twp-Rng – 008N-012E; Aliquots – E1/2SW1/4; Section – 7; County - Ripley
&
Name: Burchfield, Robert
Accession Nr. IN0250_.399; Document Type – State Volume Patent; Issue Date – 6/8/1833; Cancelled – No
Land Office – Jeffersonville; authority – April 24,: Sale-Cash Entry (3 Stat. 566); Document Nr. 2913; Total Acres –   40.00
Land Descriptions: State – IN; Meridian –2ndPM; Twp-Rng –008N-12E; Aliquots –NE1/4NW1/4; Section –   17; County - Ripley
&
Name: Burchfield, Robert
Accession Nr. IN0280_.138; Document Type – State Volume Patent; Issue Date – 10/8/1834; Cancelled – No
Land Office – Jeffersonville; authority – April 24, 1820:Sale-Cash Entry (3 Stat. 566); Document Nr. 4147; Total Acres – 40.00
Land Descriptions: State – IN; Meridian – 2ndPM; Twp-Rng – 008N-012E; Aliquots – SE1/4SW1/4; Section – 8; County - Ripley
&
Name: Burchfield, Robert
Accession Nr. IN2630_.400; Document Type – State Volume Patent; Issue Date – 8/10/1837; Cancelled – No
Land Office – Jeffersonville; Authority – April 24, 1820: Sale-Cash Entry (3 Stat. 566); Document Nr. 7929; Total Acres – 80.00
Land Descriptions: State – IN; Meridian – 2ndPM; Twp-Rng – 008N-01E; Aliquots – W1/2NE1/4; Section –   7; County - Ripley
&
Name: Lacock, William & Burchfield, Robert
Accession Nr. CV-005-220; Document Type – Credit Volume Patent; Issue Date – 8/20/1827; Cancelled – No
Land Office – Jeffersonville; Authority – April 24, 1820: Sale-Cash Entry (3 Stat. 566); Document Nr. 2108; Total Acres – 80.00
Land Descriptions: State – IN; Meridian – 2ndPM; Twp-Rng – 006N – 012E; Aliquots – W1/2NW1/4; Section – 15; County - Ripley
&
Name: Whitham, James & Burchfield, Robert
Accession Nr. CV-0052-171; Document Type – Credit Volume Patent; Issue Date – 6/23/1820; Cancelled – No

Land Office – Jeffersonville; Authority – April 24, 1820: Sale-Cash Entry (3 Stat. 566); Document Nr. 0; Total Acres – 160.00
Land Descriptions: State – IN; Meridian – 2ndPM; Twp-Rng – 006N – 011E; Aliquots – NE1/4; Section – 24; County - Ripley

Cowen, Janet C., comp; Jeffersonville Land Entries 1808-1818; McDowell Publications, Utica, NY, 1984, p. 102.
Receipt # 09396
Burchfield ?? Robert IN Jefferson NE S24 T06 N11E 160 1816 04 18
Burchfield ?? Robert IN Jefferson NE S24 T06 N11E 160 1816 04 18

1820 U. S. Census, Ripley Co., IN, NARA Roll M33_15; EN 7 Aug 1820, p. 75, line 28.
Robert Burchfield
Males 10-15=1, Males 16-25=2, Males 45>=1, Females 10-15=1, Females 45>=1.

Ripley County, Indiana Deed Records Vol. B., 29 Jan 1827-21 Sep 1832,
Page(s) 205-206.
Abstract of Deed/Patent for: Robert Burchfield, Junior
Purchaser (Grantee) or Seller (Grantor)?: Purchaser
Purchased from: Brazella Leonard
State & county where recorded: Ripley Co., Indiana
Date entered: 9 Mar 1829
Recorded: 9 Mar 1829
Description: North half of the southwest quarter of Section 24, of Township 8, North of Range 11 East
Amount paid: One hundred dollars ($100.00).
Name(s) of Witnesses: Jno. Hunter & Conrad Overturf

Ripley County, Indiana Deed Records Vol. D., 7 Feb 1834 - 9 Feb 1836, Page 114-115.
Abstract of Deed/Patent for: Robert Burchfield and Elizabeth (dower) his wife
Purchaser (Grantee) or Seller (Grantor)?:
Sold to: Jeremiah Burchfield
State & county where recorded: Ripley Co., Indiana
State & county where agreement was made:
Date entered: 5 Aug 1834
Recorded: 2 Sep 1834
Description: Lot or parcel of land being in the North East 1/4 of the South West 1/4 of Section 24, Township 8 North of Range 11 East; of the lands sold at Jeffersonville, IN; containing 40 acres.
Amount paid: Fifty dollars ($50.00)
Name(s) of Witnesses: William Markland & Henry Hess

The Pension Roll of 1835 Volume IV, The Mid-Western States, Indexed Edition, In Four Volumes; Genealogical Publishing Co., Inc., Baltimore, MD, Reprint 1968, p. 87.
Statement, &c. of Ripley county, Indiana.

INDIANA Names	Rank	Annual allowance.	Sums received	Description of service
Robert Burchfield	Private	60.00	1830 00	N. Carolina militia
When placed on pension roll	Commencement of pension		Ages	Laws under which they were formerly placed on the pension roll; and remarks.
April 9, 1833	March 4, 1831		81	-

A Census of Pensioners for Revolutionary or Military Services with their Names, Ages, and Places of Residence Under the Act for Taking the Sixth Census in 1840; Genealogical Publishing Co., Inc., Baltimore, Maryland, 1965. p. 184.

Names of pensioners for revolutionary or military services.	Ages	Names of heads of families with whom pensioners resided June 1, 1840.
RIPLEY COUNTY DELAWARE		
Robert Burchfield	81	Robert Burchfield

Toph, Violet E.; *Peoples History of Ripley County, Indiana;* self-published, c. 1940, p. 125.
Revolutionary Soldiers Who Came to Ripley County
Robert Burchfield enlisted from North Carolina in April 1775 and served at different times to 1783 in March. Total service eighteen months. He was born in 1759 and died Oct. 29, 1844 and was pensioned from Ripley County, Ind. The Ripley County Historical Society placed a Government Marker a short distance west of his grave on the Clyde Whitham farm near Benham, Ind. July 13, 1936.

O'Byrne, Mrs. Roscoe C., comp. & ed.; *Roster Soldiers and Patriots of the American Revolution Buried in Indiana;* Published by Indiana Daughters of the American Revolution, 1938, Reprinted Genealogical Publishing Co., Baltimore MD, 1968, p. 78.
BURCHFIELD, ROBERT   Ripley County
Born – 1759.

Service – Enlisted from N. C. in April, 1775. Served at different times to March, 1783. Total service, 18 mos.
Proof – Pension claim R. 1444.
Died – Oct. 29, 1844. Buried Whitham cemetery, Brum Twp. Name on bronze tablet in Versailles Court House.
Child – A daughter, m. Daniel Kelly. Descendants still living in Ripley Co.
Collected by Mrs. A. B. Wycoff, Batesville, Indiana.

Hatcher, Patricia Law, Comp.; *Abstract of Graves of Revolutionary Patriots (4 volumes)*; Pioneer Heritage Press, Dallas, TX, 1987, Vol. I, p. 133.
Burchfield, Robert Whitham Cem, Brum Twp, Wabash Co IN 72
[Note: Wabash Co. is shown in error. Whitham Cemetery is in Ripley Co. - mjm]

United States Headstone Applications for U.S. Military Veterans, 1925-1949, database with images; (https://familysearch.org/ark:/61903/1:1:VHZ4-9G3 : 17 May 2016); *Affiliate Publication Number: M1916; Affiliate Publication Title: Applications for Headstones for U.S. Military Veterans, 1925-1941; Affiliate Film Number: 15; GS Film Number: 1878164; Digital Folder Number: 004832182; Image Number: 01381.*
Application for Headstone; War Department O.Q.M.G. Form No. 623
Name: Burchfield, Robert
Event Date: May 31, 1934
Name of Cemetery: Whitham Private
Located in or near: Benham, Ind.
Death Date: Oct. 29, 1844
Enlistment Dates: April 1775
Discharge Dates: March 1783
Rank: Private
Company: Capt. Geo Cathies Co., Col. Matthew Locke's Regt., Capt. Samuel Davis Co., North Carolina Line
To be shipped to: Ripley Co. Historical Society, Osgood, Ind., Ripley Co.
Whose post-office address is: Versailles, Ind.
This application is for the UNMARKED grave of a veteran. It is understood the stone will be furnished and delivered at the railroad station or steamboat landing above indicated, at Government expense, freight prepaid. I hereby agree to promptly accept the headstone at destination, remove it and properly place same at decedent's grave at my expense. Ripley Co. Historical Society, Applicant.
No fee should be paid in connection with this application.
Applicant: Ripley Co. Historical Society, Versailles, Ind.

Gibbs, A.; *Ripley County Historical Society Data on Revolutionary Soldiers*, 1973 review.
Exact location of marker: west on 800S out of Cross Plains, turn left on 50E; about 1/2 mile; on left, in hedgerow or fence line; overgrown, partially buried. The Whitham Cemetery, about 1/4 mile back from the Concord Church, is abandoned and all stones except that of a child, are gone. This used to be the

Whitham farm where Burchfield was buried. West out of Cross Plains, Brown Tw. Ripley Co. Ind.
Type of marker: Gov't
Date placed: about 1936?
Placed by: Ripley County Historical Society
Additional comments: on Court House tablet.
    1840 census Ripley Co. Ind. Pension list, p. 198. Robert Burchfield 81. Probate A., p. 133 Ripley Co. Ind. appl. for pension Nov. 1832

Wording on marker:
    Robert Burchfield
    Pvt. Davis' Co.
    Locke's Rgt.
    Rev. War
    Oct. 1844

BURROUGHS, JAMES

The patriot, James Burroughs, died in New Jersey. His son, Jeremiah, resided in Ripley Co., IN where he married Jemima Scudder.

Patriot: James Burroughs
Birth: 1735   NJ
Married Spouse 1:   Mary Jones
Service state(s):   NJ, 3rd Regiment
Rank: Musician
Proof of Service: Revolutionary War Service Records
Pension application No.: None
Residences: NJ
Died: 1784   Trenton, Hunterdon Co., NJ
DAR Ancestor No.: A019098

Revolutionary War Service Records; National Archives Publication number M881, Compiled service records of soldiers who served in the American Army during the Revolutionary War, 1775-1783.
Muster Roll of Maj. Hollingshead's Company, 3d New Jersey Regiment in the Service of the United States of America Commanded by Colo. Elias Dayton for the month of July, Aug, and September 1779.
Drums and Fifes
James Burroughs

Gibbs, A.; Ripley County Historical Society Data on Revolutionary Soldiers, 1973 review.
    The following is from a miscellaneous scrap of paper from among the papers of Violet Toph. She penciled at the top 'copied', but no data on John [James] Burroughs has come up in her known papers as of Oct. 1973.
    History notes given by Mr. George Stevens of Elrod, Ind. – James Burroughs was a Revolutionary soldier who lived about one and one-half miles from the Ripley and Dearborn Co., line over in Ripley Co. The story was told of him that he was too young to go to war, but that one day he made an elder fife and was laying it when a body of Continental soldiers came along. After listening to him for a while, they asked his father to let him go with them, but the father refused. But soon after, young James ran away and became a fifer in the American Army.

[The following record was used to prove the Revolutionary War service of James Burrough for acceptance by the National Society Daughters of the American Revolution – mjm]
New Jersey Adjutant General; *Revolutionary War Records*
Name: James Burroughs
File – BU
Ref -   MSS NO 3774   page2
        Casualty Book
Rank -   Musician

Term of Enlistment – War
Mustered – Oct 1777
Elizabeth B. Satterthwaite, Notary Public who made this statement: I, Elizabeth B. Satterthwaite, Notary Public have compared the above copy of service with the official record on file at the office of N.J. ADJ. GEN's and it correct as pr said records.　　　Signed and sealed 9 mo. 28, 1921.
{Seal}　　Elizabeth B. Satterthwaite, Notary Public

BUSKIRK (Van BUSKIRK), JOHN

Patriot: John Buskirk (formerly VanBuskirk)
　　　　　Recorded erroneously by War Department as Aaron Buskirk
Birth: 26 Sep 1757, Frederick Co., MD
Married Spouse 1: 1780/1782 PA, Mary Little (Littell) (1762-1822)
Service state(s): VA & PA
Rank: Private, Ensign, Lieutenant
Proof of Service: Pension application
Pension application No.: S32148
Residences: Frederick Co., MD; Dunmore Co., VA; Hampshire Co., VA; Fayette Co., PA; Shelby Co., KY, since 1822 in IN (Greene Co.).
Died: 1 Dec 1840, Greene Co., IN
Buried: McIntosh Cemetery, Greene Co., IN
DAR Ancestor No.: A117274

Pension Application Abstracted from National Archives microfilm Series M804, Roll 434, File S32148
Pension abstract for – John Buskirk
Service state(s): VA
Alternate spelling(s): John VanBuskirk
Date: 10 Oct 1832
County of: Monroe　　　　　　　　　State of: IN
Declaration made before a Judge or Court: Circuit Court
Act of: 7 Jun 1832
Age: 75
Where and year born: Frederick Co., MD, in 1757
Record of age: None except one made for himself
Residence when he entered service: Dunmore Co., VA (now Shenandoah Co.)
Residence(s) since the war: Hampshire Co., VA; Fayette Co., PA; KY; since 1822 in IN.
Residence now: Green Co., IN – being no attorney in that county he was advised to apply in Monroe Co., IN
Volunteer, Drafted, or Substitute: 1st service – prob. enlisted
2nd service - Substitute – man's name he does not remember
3rd service – drafted (called up)
4th service – not stated
Rank(s): 1st service – not stated; 2nd service – private; 3rd service – entered as ensign, elected lieutenant; 4th service – not stated.
Statement of service-

Period	Duration	Names of General and Field Officers
1775	1 week	Capt. Jonathan Clark
Aug 1775	3 mos.	Col. Netherton; Lt. Abraham Byrd; Josiah Allen, orderly sergeant. Placed with 8th Regt. VA Line called the German Regiment.
1780	3 mos.	Gen. George R. Clarke, Capt. Parminas Briscoe, Maj. Bulge or Bulzer, Adjutant Sandford Edwards.
1781	3 weeks	Capt. Virgin & Capt. Pigmon.

Battles: Not stated
Discharge received: 1st service – no discharge in writing
2nd service – in writing
3rd service – dismissed at mouth of Licking by Col. Clarke, no written discharge.
4th service – not stated
Signed by: 2nd service - Brigadier General Scott
What became of it?: Wore out carrying it in his pocket, has not seen it for 40 yrs.
Statement is supported by –
Living witness, name(s): Isaac VanBuskirk, his brother, states the original name was VanBuskirk, that his brothers dropped the "Van". States he knew of the performance of the first service; he did not live with his brother during the remains of his service.
&
Pension abstract for – John Buskirk
Service state(s): VA & PA
Alternate spelling(s): John VanBuskirk
Date: 7 Jun 1834 – amendment to application of 10 Oct 1832
County of: Monroe   State of: IN
Declaration made before a Judge or Court: Justice of the Peace
Age: 77 on the 26th day of Sep next.
Record of age: record copied from my father's old Dutch Bible now in my possession.
Where and year born: Frederick Co., MD
Residence when he entered service: Dunmore Co., VA (now Shenandoah);
Residence(s) since the war: Kentucky Co., VA, organized into Jefferson Co. (he thinks); Fayette Co. (claimed by both VA & PA); then KY abt. 4 yrs; then IN abt. 12 yrs.
Residence now: Greene Co., IN
Volunteer, Drafted, or Substitute:
    1st service – volunteer
    2nd service - Substitute – man's name he does not remember
    3rd service – drafted (called up)
    4th service – volunteer
    5th service – volunteer
    6th – service - volunteer
Rank(s): 1st service – private; 2nd service - private; 3rd service – ensign then lieutenant; 4th service – private; 5th service – private; 6th service - private.
Statement of service-

Period	Duration	Names of General and Field Officers
1st	1 week	Militia State of VA, company commanded by Capt. Jonathan Clark, Regt. commanded by Col. Mulenburgh; change of command to German Regt. No. 8.
2nd	3 mos.	Militia State of VA, placed in 8th VA Regt., commanded by Col. Bowman.
3rd	2 mos. 1 wk.	Militia State of VA, Capt. Parmenas Briscoe, under Col. George Rodgers Clark.

4th	3 weeks	Militia State of VA, part of time under Capt. Virgin, part under Capt. Pigman.
5th	1 week	Militia of Pennsylvania (territory disputed with VA where I lived), Regt. commanded by Col. Hays.
6th	2 weeks	Militia of VA, small detachments of organized troops, officers names forgotten.

I was drafted another time but my brother Isaac took my place.
Discharge received: only one
Signed by: Gen. Scott
What became of it?: worn out and lost
Statement is supported by –
Person now living who can testify to service: my brother Isaac V Buskirk
Clergyman: None convenient who was well acquainted with him.
Persons in neighborhood who certify character: David Durn & Henry Jackson,
    Esq'rs; Thomas Harvey; John Johnston Esq'r; Luke Vaughn. Also
    known to Jonathan Legg; George H. Johnston Esq'r; & others in
    Monroe Co.
Wife: Not named
Names and ages of children: Not named
    He has no family of his own. His land lies in Greene Co.
    He spends his time principally with his son in Greene Co.
Notes: A letter in the file dated 6 Nov 1834 states that John Buskirk's first pension certificate was erroneously issued under the name "Aaron Buskirk." This pension certificate remains in the National Archives and Records Administration in a separate folder for the nonexistent Aaron Buskirk with the file number Certificate 26833.
A letter dated 11 Dec 1844 states that John Buskirk had died.

Abstract of Final Payment Voucher; General Services Administration, Washington, DC

NAME	BUSKIRK, JOHN
AGENCY OF PAYMENT	INDIANA
DATE OF ACT	1832
DATE OF PAYMENT	4th QUARTER 1840
DATE OF DEATH	

    FINAL PAYMENT VOUCHER RECEIVED FROM
    THE GENERAL ACCOUNTING OFFICE   Form
General Services Administration GSA DC 70-7035   GSA DEC 69 7068

Register of the Kentucky Historical Society; <u>Early Kentucky Tax Records</u>; *Clearfield Publishing, Baltimore, Md., 1999; p. 229.*
Department of State Archives – Shelby County Tax Lists, 1795.
A List of Taxable Property Taken and Returned by Thomas Shannon, Esquire, Commissioner of the Tax for Shelby County for the Year 1795.

Persons Named Charged With Taxes	Horses	Cattle	County	Water Course	Acres of Land
Buskirk, John	4	9	Shelby	Bearshears Creek	318
Buskirk, John			Shelby	Bearshears Creek	200

Gwathmey, John H.; *Historical Register of Virginians in the Revolution, Soldiers, Sailors, Marines, 1775-1783;* The Dietz Press, Richmond, VA, 1938, p. 116.
Buskirk, John, Ripley Co., Ind. mpl [Militia Pension List compiled by Secretary of War 1835]

Virginia Military Records from the Virginia Magazine of History and Biography, the William and Mary College Quarterly, and Tyler's Quarterly; Genealogical Publishing Co., Baltimore, MD, 1983, p. 144.
The First Independent Company of Dunmore, from VMHB, Vol. XLIV (1936), 102-104.
The following is a list of the men comprising the First Independent Company of Dunmore and their resolutions:
In the list - #   57.   John Vanbuskerk

McAllister, J.T.; *Virginia Militia in the Revolutionary War;* McAllister Publishing Co., Hot Springs, VA, 1913, Part V.
Alphabetical List of Pensioners Residing Outside of Virginia in 1835, whose Pensions were Granted for Services as Virginia Militiamen.
This list was compiled from a repot made by the Secretary of War in 1835. The ages are those given in that report, and are believed to be the ages of the pensioners in 1835. The names of the pensioners in what is now West Virginia are embraced under Part IV.
Buskirk, Jno.   69   Ripley   IN

Clift, G. Glens, Assistant Secretary, Kentucky Historical Society, Comp.; *"Second Census" of Kentucky – 1800, A Privately Compiled and Published Enumeration of Tax Payers Appearing in the 79 Manuscript Volumes Extant of Tax Lists of the 42 Counties of Kentucky in Existence in 1800;* Genealogical Publishing Co., Baltimore, MD, 1966, p. 42.

Name	County	Tax List Date
Buskirk, John	Shelby	8/25/1800

Clark, Murtie June, Comp.; *Index to U.S. Invalid Pension Records 1801-1815;* Genealogical Publishing Co., Inc., 1991, p. 101.

Indiana Territory

Name	Rank	Page	Remarks
Buskirk, John V.	Private	140	began Oct 19, 1813

Message from The President of the United States, transmitting a Report of The Secretary of War in Compliance with a Resolution of the Senate, March 28, 1818,

Revolutionary Pensioners of 1818; Reprinted for Clearfield Company, Inc. by Genealogical Publishing Co., Inc., Baltimore, MD, 1992, p. 178.
List of Invalid Pensioners U. States, belonging to the state of Indiana, and payable at Vernon, Indiana, with the annual allowance to each annexed, viz:
John V. Buskirk   Private   At 96 per annum

The Pension Roll of 1835 Volume IV, The Mid-Western States, Indexed Edition, In Four Volumes; Genealogical Publishing Co., Inc., Baltimore, MD, Reprint 1968, p. 87.
Statement, &c. of Ripley county, Indiana.

INDIANA Names	Rank	Annual allowance	Sums received	Description of service
John Buskirk	Private	23.33	-	Virginia militia

When placed on pension roll	Commencement of pension	Ages	Laws under which they were formerly placed on the pension roll; and remarks.
July 16, 1834	March 4, 1831	69	-

A Census of Pensioners for Revolutionary or Military Services with their Names, Ages, and Places of Residence Under the Act for Taking the Sixth Census in 1840; Genealogical Publishing Co., Inc., Baltimore, Maryland, 1965. p. 182.

Names of pensioners for revolutionary or military services.	Ages	Names of heads of families with whom pensioners re-Sided June 1, 1840.
INDIANA, GREENE COUNTY		
John Buskirk	83	Joseph Buskirk

Scott, Craig R.; *The "Lost" Pensions, Settled Accounts of the Act of 6 April 1838;* Willow Bend Books, Lovettsville, VA, 1996, p. 49.
An Act directing the transfer of money remaining unclaimed [for the term of eight months] by certain pensioners, and authorizing payment of the same at the Treasury of the United States.
Buskirk, John; Pension Office – Madison, INd.; Box - 44; Account - #4370.
Buskirk, John; Pension Office – a/o, INd.; Box 92; Account #19709.
Buskirk, John V.; Pension Office – INd.; Box 57; Account #7612.

Toph, Violet E.; *Peoples History of Ripley County, Indiana;* self-published, c. 1940, p. 124.
Revolutionary Soldiers Who Came to Ripley County
John Buskirk enlisted from Virginia in 1775. He served one week, later re-enlisted 1777 and served as substitute in place of a man whose name he did not remember. He served about three months, re-enlisted 1780, served three months and then he again re-enlisted in 1781 and served three weeks. He was born in 1757.

O'Byrne, Mrs. Roscoe C., comp. & ed.; Roster Soldiers and Patriots of the American Revolution Buried in Indiana; Published by Indiana Daughters of the American Revolution, 1938, Reprinted Genealogical Publishing Co., Baltimore MD, 1968, p. 80.

BUSKIRK, JOHN   Ripley County
Born - 1757, Frederick Co., Maryland
Service – Enlisted from Virginia in 1775, served one wk. Re-enlisted in 1777, as a substitute for 3 mos. In 1780, for 3 mos. Again in 1781. For 3 wks.
Proof – Pension claim S. 32148. Soldier's brother, Isaac Van Buskirk, testified that soldier had dropped the Van from his name.
Died – In Ripley Co. Name on bronze tablet in Versailles Court House.
Married - ------- Little. Ch. George Abram, b. 1783, m. Anna Boswell.
Collected by Mrs. A. B. Wycoff, Batesville, Indiana.

O'Byrne, comp. Mrs. Roscoe C., comp.; Roster of Soldiers and Patriots of the American Revolution Buried in Indiana, Vol. III; Indiana Daughters of the American Revolution, 1966, p. 48.

VAN BUSKIRK, JOHN   Greene County
Born – Sept. 26, 1757 Frederick Co., Md.
Service – Lt. under Capt. Jonathan Clark and Col. Muhlenberg in Va. Militia against Lord Dunsmore when he robbed Magazine in Williamsburg; served under Lt. Abram Bird and Col. Netherton in Va. Militia.
Proof – Dept. of Int. Rev. & 1812 War Depts.; Pension #S32145; DAR #588726; Patriot Index, p. 689.
Died – Dec. 1, 1840 Greene Co., Ind.
Married – 1782 Mary Little d. Apr. 16, 1792.
Children – George Abram b. 1783 m. Nov. 2, 1808 Mary A. Boswell; John Little m. Elizabeth Young; Hester (Esther) b. 1787 m. John Martin; Hannah b. Apr. 16, 1796 m. 1822 John Cochran; Joseph; Alfred m. Jan 13, 1822 Lithia Dayhoff; Isaac m. Jan. 1817 Patience Stillwell; Mary m. Elliott Veech; Michael. From A Roster of Revolutionary Ancestors of the Indiana Daughters of the American Revolution, Vol. II, p. 324.

Gibbs, A.; Ripley County Historical Society Data on Revolutionary Soldiers, 1973 review.
Exact location of marker: no further information of grave site.
Additional comments: Toph note: pensioned from Monroe Co. Ind.
        On Court House tablet.

Tombstone Location: McIntosh Cemetery (aka Buskirk & Light Cemetery, Highland Twp., Greene Co., IN

Tombstone Inscription:

SACRED
to the memory of
JOHN BUSKIRK
born Sept. 26, 1757
died Dec. 1, 1840

CAVENDER, JOHN

John Cavender has no ties to Ripley County, Indiana. His wife Margaret came to Ripley County after his death where she applied for widow's pension.

Patriot: John Cavender
Birth: 1760 New Castle Co., DE
Married Spouse 1: Aug 1784/5, Newark, New Castle Co., DE Margaret X
Service state(s): DE Continental, MD, NC
Rank: Private
Proof of Service: Pension application
Pension application No.: W9776
Residences: New Castle Co., DE; Cecil Co., MD; PA; Hamilton Co., OH
Died: 12 Sep 1837 Hamilton Co., OH
Buried: Crosby Twp, Hamilton Co., OH
DAR Ancestor No.: A023485

Pension Application Abstracted from National Archives microfilm Series M804, Roll 501, File W9776.
Pension abstract for – John Cavender
Service state(s): DE Continental, MD, NC
Date: 5 Sep 1832
County of: Hamilton State of: OH
Declaration made before a Judge or Court: Common Pleas Court
Act of: 7 Jun 1832
Age: 72 yrs. Record of age: None
Where and year born: New Castle Co., DE
Residence when he entered service: Red Lyon hundred, New Castle Co., DE
Residences during the war: Red Lion Hundred, New Castle Co., DE; Cecil County, MD in spring 1778.
Residence(s) since the war: DE, MD, PA, Hamilton Co., OH
Residence now: Hamilton Co., OH
Volunteer, Drafted, or Substitute: 1st tour -Drafted with his team of horses; 2nd tour – Drafted; 3rd tour – Drafted.
Rank(s): 1st tour - Teamster; 2nd & 3rd tour – Private.
Statement of service-

Period	Duration	Names of General and Field Officers
Aug-Dec 1777	3+ mos.	Continental Service, Gen. Wade; taken to Wilmington under Cheesebury of NC, under Gen. Nash.
Jan 1778	3 mos.	DE Militia, Capt. William Rankins
May 1778	3 mos.	MD Militia, Capt. John Crow, 1st Sgt. Alexander Brown

Battles: 1st tour – with my team, and lost one wagon horse, very severe, in guarding the shores of the Delaware River, often laying on our arms all night, without fire, escaping barely with my life, when

most of our companions were buried – and many of them by my own hands.
Discharge received: None other than verbal from one of my officers
Person now living who can testify to service: William Wakefield, Henry Wile
Persons in neighborhood who certify character: Judge Othniel Looker; Esq. Hoppin; Esq. Henry Linkhorn; Adam Ritenhouse, Joseph Sater; John McMahan.
&
Pension abstract for – Margaret Cavender widow of John Cavender
Date: 21 Aug 1843
County of: Franklin   State of: IN
Declaration made before a Judge or Court:
Act of: 7 Jul 1835
Age of widow: 85 yrs.
Residence now: town of Brookville, Franklin Co., IN
Death of soldier: 12 Sep 1837
Marriage date and place: Aug 1784 Newark, New Castle Co., DE,
    by Parson Edwards, a "settled" minister. She cannot positively state
    whether it was 1784 or 1785 that she married.
Proof of marriage: Family record [included in pension file]
&
Pension abstract for – Margaret Cavender
Date: 1 Sep 1843
County of: Ripley   State of: IN
Declaration made before a Judge or Court: Justice of the Peace
Act of: 7 Jul 1838
Declaration: She provides a Family record as evidence of marriage and children.
Witness: John Cavender (grandson)
Names and ages of children: Easter, died in infancy; John, died in infancy;
    Alexander, b. 1 Jan 1791, d. 1843; Robert, b. 22 Apr 1793; Polly, b. 18
    Sep 1795; Eliza, b. 30 Jan 1805, d. 1839 (her son was living in Ripley
    Co., IN in 1843).
&
Pension abstract for – Margaret Cavender
Date: 27 Mar 1844
County of: Franklin   State of: IN
Declaration made before a Judge or Court: Justice of the Peace
Act of: 3 Mar 1843
Age: 80 yrs.
Residence: Brookville, Franklin Co., IN
Declaration: She is the widow of John Cavender, who was a Private in the army of the Revolution; she is still a widow.

Abstract of Final Payment Voucher; General Services Administration, Washington, DC
NAME   Cavender, John
AGENCY OF PAYMENT   Cincinnati, Ohio
DATE OF ACT   1832
DATE OF PAYMENT   3rd qr 1837

DATE OF DEATH -
    last FINAL PAYMENT VOUCHER RECEIVED FROM
    THE GENERAL ACCOUNTING OFFICE   Form
General Services Administration   FSA DC 70-7035   GSA DEC 69 7068

Abstract of Final Payment Voucher; General Services Administration, Washington, DC
NAME   CAVENDER, MARGARET
AGENCY OF PAYMENT   INDIANA
DATE OF ACT   1844
DATE OF PAYMENT   3rd QUARTER 1847
DATE OF DEATH
    LAST ~~FINAL~~ PAYMENT VOUCHER RECEIVED FROM
    THE GENERAL ACCOUNTING OFFICE   Form
General Services Administration   GSA DC 70-7035   GSA DEC 69 7068

The National Archives Publication Number M881, National Archives Catalog ID 570910, Record Group 93
Compiled service records of soldiers who served in the American Army during the Revolutionary War, 1775-1783.
Delaware - Individual Record
Surname: Cavender,   Given Name: John

The National Archives Publication Number M881, National Archives Catalog ID 570910, Record Group 93
Compiled service records of soldiers who served in the American Army during the Revolutionary War, 1775-1783.
Continental Troops - Patton's Regiment - Individual Record
Surname: Cavender   Given Name: John

U.S. Department of Interior, Bureau of Land Management, General Land Office Records; Land Patent Search
Name: Cavender, John
Accession Nr. IN0250_.383; Document Type – State Volume Patent; Issue Date – 6/8/1833; Cancelled – No
Land Office – Jeffersonville; Authority – April 24, 1820: Sale-Cash Entry (3 Stat. 566); Document Nr. 2897; Total Acres – 80.00
Land Descriptions: State – IN; Meridian – 2nsPM; Twp-Rng – 007N – 012E; Aliquots – E1/2SE1/4; Section – 23; County - Ripley

Ripley County Indiana, Recorder's Office, Tract Book 3, p. 61.
Cavender, John   24 May 1832   R12, T7, S23   80 acres

The Pension Roll of 1835 Volume IV, The Mid-Western States, Indexed Edition, In Four Volumes; Genealogical Publishing Co., Inc., Baltimore, MD, Reprint 1968, p. 253.
Statement, &c. of Hamilton county, Ohio.

OHIO Names	Rank	Annual allowance	Sums received	Description of service
John Cavender	Private	20.00	60	Del. State troops
When placed on pension roll	Commencement of pension		Ages	Laws under which they were formerly placed on the pension roll; and remarks.
Nov 30, 1832	March 4, 1831		74	-

Henderson, Frank D., the adjutant-general, comp.; <u>The Official Roster of the Soldiers of the American Revolution Buried in the State of Ohio</u>; Daughters of the American Revolution, Ohio; The F. J. Heer Printing Co., Columbus, OH, 1929-1959. p. 73.
CAVENDER, JOHN, (Hamilton Co.)
Br. Delaware. D 1837. Ref: S.A.R. Fur infor Cincinnati Chap.

Daughters of the American Revolution of the State of Ohio, comp. <u>Official Roster III, Soldiers of the American Revolution Who Lived in the State of Ohio</u>; Painesville Publishing, Painesville, OH, 1959, p. 69.
CAVENDER, JOHN – Hamilton Co
by Mrs. W. Earle Johnson, Batavia, O
Roster I, p. 73
Widow, Margaret, drew pens in Franklin Co, Ind. Ref: Ind. State Library, Indianapolis, Ind.

Michael B. Gunn, Ohio Society Graves Committee Chairman, & Michael Blum, Vice Chairman, (Editors) 2015; <u>Revolutionary War Patriots Buried in Ohio</u>; http://ohssar.org/wp-content/uploads/2015/09/Revolutionary-War-Soldiers-Buried-in-Ohio.pdf.
CAVENDER, JOHN, (Hamilton Co.) Crosby Township [39.275 -84.721]
Br New Castle, Delaware, enlisted 1775. In May 1778 moved to Cecil Co., Maryland and enlisted there as well. Mar Margaret ? in August 1784-5 in Newark, New Castle Co., Delaware. Lived in PA before going to Hamilton Co., OH. D September 12, 1837. May be Bur in Crosby Twp., Ham., Co., OH or in Franklin Co. Ind. Ref : S. A. R. Fur infor Cincinnati Chap.

Historic Sites Committee, Cincinnati Chapter Daughters of the American Revolution; <u>Revolutionary Soldiers Buried in Hamilton County, Ohio</u>; Little Miami Publishing Co., Milford, OH, 2010; p. 84.
CROSBY TOWNSHIP – Cemetery Unknown
CAVENDER, JOHN 1760-1837 - He was born in New Castle, Delaware, in 1760 and was living there when he enlisted. In May 1778 he moved to Cecil County, Maryland, and enlisted there as well. He served on the Delaware, Maryland, and North Carolina Lines. He married Margaret (- ? -) in August 1784-85 in Newark, New Castle County, Delaware, and lived in Pennsylvania before going to Hamilton County, Ohio. He applied for a pension September 12, 1837. His widow, Margaret, drew a pension in Franklin County, Indiana.

Margaret R. Waters; Revolutionary Soldiers Buried in Indiana (1949) With Supplement (1954) Two Volumes in One; Genealogical Publishing Company, Baltimore, MD, 1970. p. 132.

The following 121 soldiers did not die in Indiana. Their widows later moved to Indiana. Of the 121 widows, there are pension files for 120. Since these are not Revolutionary soldiers who died in Indiana, I jotted down only the sketchiest of data which may, however, help some reader. When known, Indiana residence is given for widow.

CAVENDAR, JOHN & MARGARET   Franklin & Ripley
He d. 1837, Hamilton Co., O. (See "Ohio Rev. Sold.", v.1, & Natl. Gen. So. Quart., Dec. 1944, p. 106). She liv. Ripley Co., Ind., first. Pens. W9776.

Ohio Deaths and Burials, 1854-1997, Database; FamilySearch,
(https://familysearch.org/ark:/61903/1:1:F68Q-RPF : 12 December 2014), John Cavender, 1837; citing , reference ; FHL microfilm 182,715, Indexing Project (Batch) Number: I00001-3, System Origin: Ohio-EASy; accessed 14 June 2016. Index based upon data collected by the Genealogical Society of Utah, Salt Lake.
Name: John Cavender
Death Date: 1837

CHAPMAN, LEMUEL

Patriot: Lemuel Chapman
Birth: 1 Sep 1757, Middletown, CT
Married Spouse 1: XX
Married Spouse 2: Anne Brayman (1765-1818)
Service state(s): NY & CT
Rank: Private
Proof of Service: Pension application (1818 application was originally in a file for Samuel Chapman. Error was corrected in 1819).
Pension application No.: S35831
Residences: CT; Rutland Co., VT; Ripley Co., IN
Died: 17 Sep 1847, Versailles, Johnson Twp., Ripley Co., IN
Buried: Unknown, Ripley Co., IN
DAR Ancestor No.: A020931

Pension Application Abstracted from National Archives microfilm Series M804, Roll 521, File S35831.
Pension abstract for – Lemuel Chapman
Service state(s): NY & CT
Date: 7 Apr 1818
County of: Rutland   State of: VT
Declaration made before a Judge or Court: Judge of Rutland Co. Court
Act of: 18 Mar 1818
Age: 59 yrs.
Where and year born: Connecticut
Residence when he entered service: Not stated
Residence(s) since the war: 14 yrs. Clarendon, Rutland Co, VT;
            then 1 yr. Middletown, Rutland Co., VT.
Residence now: Middletown, Rutland Co., VT
Volunteer, Drafted, or Substitute: 1st tour – Enlisted; 2nd tour – enlisted.
Rank(s): Private
Statement of service-

Period	Duration	Names of General and Field Officer
1st tour -		
Jan 1777	2 yrs.	Capt. Philip DuBois Bovier's company, Col. DuBois' NY Regt.
Jan 1779	1 yr.	Capt. Johnson's company, Col. DuBois NY Regt.
2nd tour -		
Spring 1782	1 yr.	Capt. D. Strong's company, Col. [Heman] Swift's CT Regt. [7th Co, 2d Regt.]

Battles: None stated
Discharge received: at Morristown, NJ
What became of it?: Kept until abt. 8 yrs. ago since which time I have not seen.
&
Pension abstract for – Lemuel Chapman
Date: 28 Jun 1820

County of: Rutland State of: VT
Declaration made before a Judge or Court: County Court
Age: 61 yrs.
Residence now: Rutland Co., VT
Names and ages of children: daughter named Alvina, aged 14 yrs.
&
Pension abstract for – Lemuel Chapman – Request for Transfer
Date: 31 Jan 1837
County of: Ripley State of: IN
Declaration made before a Judge or Court: Justice of the Peace
Reason: for removing from VT to IN – he has no family & removed here for the purpose of spending the remainder of his life with one of his children.
&
Letter in file:
Cambridge, Vermont
March 18th 1935
Veterans Administration Lemuel Chapman
Washington S. 35831
DC 3A-J/MLB
Dear Sirs:

 Since I wrote you last Act, asking for Rev. war record of Lemuel Chapman I have spent much time in searching records and writing different towns for help in establishing my lineage but cannot find anything more or different than I already have.

 In your reply you state that "after the war Lemuel Chapman resided in Clarendon, Rutland Co, Vermont for fourteen years, then moved to Middletown same county." I have an old deed dated 1817, deeding land in Middletown to Lemuel Chapman stating that he was formerly from Clarendon.

 Lemuel Chapman, Rev. soldier moved after this to Fletcher with his son Lemuel, when his grand-daughter Amelia Chapman (my grandmother) was six months old, and lived with them until he was seventy seven years old when he went west to live with his youngest daughter in Vevay, Ind.

 Mrs. E.M. Perry of Ft. Akinson, Wis. Joined the D.A.R. from his war service and her father HM. Lucuis B. Caswell was a 1st. cousin of my grandmother and used to visit us from his home in Washington and Mrs. Perry writes me that- "he was the one that introduced the bill while he was in congress. I have a letter written by him to my grandmother.

 I also have a six page written account of "her grandfathers war service" written by my grandmother Amelia Chapman Ellsworth.

 In lieu of the fact that I have all this evidence would you please advise me how to proceed to get my D.A.R. membership.
Yours very truly,
Kittie E. Lang
Mrs. Chas. J.
[From the material in this file we are able to determine that Lemuel Chapman had at least three children whose names are: Lemuel, Alvina, & Amelia.]

Abstract of Final Payment Voucher; General Services Administration, Washington, DC
        FINAL PAYMENT VOUCHER RECEIVED FROM
        THE GENERAL ACCOUNTING OFFICE
NAME   Chapman, Samuel [Samuel on voucher]
AGENCY OF PAYMENT   INDIANA
DATE OF ACT   1818
DATE OF PAYMENT   per Act 6 April (Jan. '55)
DATE OF DEATH   Sept. 17, 1847
GENERAL SERVICES ADMINISTRATION
National Archives and Records Service   NA-286
GSA-WASH DC 54-4891   November 1953

Revolutionary War Service Records; National Archives Publication number M881, Compiled service records of soldiers who served in the American Army during the Revolutionary War, 1775-1783.
https://www.fold3.com/image/20750210?terms=Chapman,%20Lemuel
New York 5th Regiment, D. B. Vier's Co., Copied form Rolls
Lemuel Chapman, Private - Enlisted for 3 yrs.; Discharged 6 January 1780.
&
Connecticut 2s Formation, 1781. 7th Co., in the 2d Reg't, commanded by Col. Heman Swift.
Lemuel Chapman, Private – Appears on Company Muster Roll for Apr 1782- May 23, 82; May 82-Jun 16, 82; Jun 82-Jul 26, 82; Jul, 1782-Aug 6, 82; Aug 82- Sep 10, 82; Sep 82-Oct 15, 82; Oct 82-Nov 13, 82; Nov 82-Dec 82; Dec 82 & Jan 83-Jun 28, 83; Feb 83-Mar 15, 83; Mar 83-Apr 28, 83.

Adjutants-General, by the Authority of the General Assembly, comp.; Record of Service of Connecticut Men in the I. War of the Revolution; The Case, Lockwood & Brainard Company Printers and Binders, Hartford, CT, 1889, p. 329.
Regiments, "Connecticut Line", 17811783.
"Names of Men engaged for 8 months, a year, or shorter term, joined 2d Connecticut Regt. 1783."

Names	Time Enlisted	Term	Residence
Lemuel Chapman	Apr. 1, '82	1 year	Sharon

Senate Documents, Vol.9, No. 988, 63rd Congress, 3d Session, Washington, 1915; "Register of Certificates Issued by John Pierce, Esquire, Paymaster General and Commissioner of Army Accounts for the United States, to Officers and Soldiers of the Continental Army Under Act of July 4, 1783"; *Seventeenth report of the National Society of the Daughters of the American Revolution;* Genealogical Publishing Co., Inc., Baltimore, MD, 1984. p. 96.
Men listed in this volume with the same name.

No. of Certificate	To whom issued	Amount
43614	Chapman, Lemuel	16.37
44227	Chapman, Lemuel	80.00
45064	Chapman, Lemuel	37.10
51929	Chapman, Lemuel	60.00

Clark, Murtie June; *The Pension List of 1820 [U.S. War Department]Reprinted with an Index;* Genealogical Publishing Co., Inc., Baltimore, 1991. Originally published 1820 as Letter from the Secretary of War, p. 298.

VERMONT

Names of the Revolutionary Pensioners which have been placed on the Roll of Vermont, under the Law of the 18th of March, 1818, from the passage thereof, to this day, inclusive of the Rank they held, and the Lines in which they served, viz:

Names	Rank	Line
Included in the list –		
Lemuel Chapman	private	New York

The Pension Roll of 1835 Volume I, New England States, Indexed Edition, In Four Volumes; Genealogical Publishing Co., Inc., Baltimore, MD, Reprint 1968, p. 897.

A statement showing the names, rank, &c., or persons residing in Rutland county, in the State of Vermont, who have been inscribed on the pension list under the act of Congress passed March 18, 1818.

Names	Rank	Annual allowance.	Sums received	Description of service
Lemuel Chapman	Private	96.00	1,527 43	N. York cont'l line

When placed on pension roll	Commencement of pension	Ages	Laws under which they were formerly placed on the pension roll; and remarks.
Sept 22, 1818	Apr 7, 1818	75	-

A Census of Pensioners for Revolutionary or Military Services with their Names, Ages, and Places of Residence Under the Act for Taking the Sixth Census in 1840; Genealogical Publishing Co., Inc., Baltimore, Maryland, 1965. p. 184.

Names of pensioners for revolutionary or military services.	Ages	Names of heads of families with whom pensioners resided June 1, 1840.
RIPLEY COUNTY		
JOHNSON		
Lemuel Chapman	82	

Toph, Violet E.; <u>Peoples History of Ripley County, Indiana</u>; self-published, c. 1940, p. 129.
Revolutionary Soldiers Who Came to Ripley County
Lemuel Chapman entered the service from New York in 1777 under Colonel Swift and Captain Strong and served five months. He was born in 1759, pensioned in Vermont and moved to Ripley County, Ind. in 1837.

O'Byrne, Mrs. Roscoe C., comp. & ed.; <u>Roster Soldiers and Patriots of the American Revolution Buried in</u> Indiana; Published by Indiana Daughters of the American Revolution, 1938, Reprinted Genealogical Publishing Co., Baltimore MD, 1968, p. 94.
CHAPMAN, LEMUEL   Ripley County
Born – 1759, Conn.
Service – Entered service from N.Y. in 1777, under Col. Swift and Capt. Strong. Served 5 mos.
Proof – Pension claim S. 35831. Pensioned first in Vermont. Moved to Ripley Co., Ind., in 1837.
Died – Sept. 17, 1847. Thought to be buried near Versailles, Ind. Name on bronze tablet in Versailles Court House.
Had a daughter, Alvina, aged 14, in 1820.
Collected by Mrs. A. B. Wycoff, Batesville, Indiana.

Gibbs, A.; <u>Ripley County Historical Society Data on Revolutionary Soldiers</u>, 1973 review.
Exact location of marker: no further information on grave site.
Additional comments: may have been living with D.C. Ingols.
    On Court House
        1840 Ripley Co. Ind. pension list, p. 208, Samuel Chapman age 82.

CHRISTY, JAMES

James Christy has no ties to Ripley County. His wife, Sarah, died in Ripley. His record is included for the purpose of verification.

Patriot: James Christy
Birth: 16 Aug 1758 Lancaster Co., PA
Married Spouse 1: 20 Mar 1781, Orange Co., VA Sarah Lemen (1782- 1844)
Service state(s): VA
Rank: Private
Proof of Service: Pension application
Pension application No.: W9782
Residences: Pittsylvania Co., VA; NC; Franklin Co., VA;
                  Lincoln Co., KY; Shelby Co., KY.
Died: 8 Mar 1837 Shelby Co., KY
Buried: prob. Shelby Co., KY
DAR Ancestor No.: A021784

Pension Application Abstracted from National Archives microfilm Series M804, Roll 540, File W9782.
Pension abstract for – James Christie
Service state(s): VA
Date: 18 Sep 1832
County of: Shelby   State of: KY
Declaration made before a Judge or Court: County Court
Act of: 7 Jun 1832
Age: 74 yrs.   Record of age: copy from the record of my age
Where and year born: Lancaster Co., PA, on 16 Aug 1758
Residence when he entered service: Pittsylvania Co., VA
Residence(s) since the war: Pittsylvania Co., VA; NC; Franklin Co., VA;
                  Lincoln Co., KY; Shelby Co., KY.
Residence now: Shelby Co., KY
Volunteer, Drafted, or Substitute: 1st tour – Volunteered; 2nd tour – Drafted; 3rd tour – Substitute; 4th tour – Volunteered.
Rank(s): Private
Statement of service-

Period	Duration	Names of General and Field Officers
May 1777	3 mos.	VA State Line, under Capt. Donaldson
Feb-Jul 1779	6 mos.	VA Militia, under Capt. William Witcher
Mar/Apr 1780	5 mos.	VA, Capt. Clement, Col. Faulkner
Abt. Sep 1780	5 mos.	VA, Capt. Clement, Col. Faulkner

Battles: Battle of Camden
Discharge received: 1st tour – Capt. Donaldson; 2nd tour -
What became of it?: 1st tour – not stated; 2nd tour – presented to court; 3rd & 4th tour – a portion presented to court.
Statement is supported by –
Living witness, name(s): name illegible
Clergyman: Abraham Cook

&

Pension abstract for – Sarah Christie widow of James Christie
Date: 10 Sep 1838
County of: Shelby   State of: KY
Declaration made before a Judge or Court: Justice of the Peace
Act of: 7 Jul 1838
Age: 76 yrs.
Residence now: Shelby Co., KY
Death of soldier: 8 Mar 1837, Shelby Co., KY
Widow's birth: 19 Apr 1762
Widow's death: 27 Mar 1844, Ripley Co., IN
Marriage date and place: 20 Mar 1781 or 1782, Orange Co., VA
Proof of marriage: The original record of marriage, and birth of her children, was burned accidentally some years since; Affidavits, signed by Oswald C. Herring & Sarah Ford, states he/she was acquainted with James Christie & that he left a widow Sarah; Affidavit of son, Israel, affirms statements by his mother.
Names and ages of children: 6th child, Israel, 45 yrs. in 1838; James of Ripley Co., IN; William of Hendricks Co.; John; of Switzerland Co., IN; 3 daughters – not named.
[Note: correspondence in file indicates that Sarah's, aka, Sallie, maiden name is Lemen.

&

Pension abstract for – Sarah Christie
Date: 13 Jan 1844
County of: Jefferson   State of: IN
Declaration made before a Judge or Court: Justice of the Peace
Act of: 3 Mar 1843
Age: 82
Declaration: She is still a widow

Gwathmey, John H.; *Historical Register of Virginians in the Revolution, Soldiers, Sailors, Marines, 1775-1783*; The Dietz Press, Richmond, VA, 1938, p. 150, 151, 192.

p. 150
Christee, James (Christy)   Pvt. WD [War Department, emphasizing record is there]

p. 151
Christie, James (Christy) Drummer, 8 CL [8th Continental Line]
Christie, James, 85, Shelby Co., Ky., mpl [Militia Pension List 1835]
Christy, James, Drummer, 8 CL
Christy, James, Cav. [Name appeared on Army Register but had not received bounty land]. Rom. [A list of militia paid at Romney in 1775. It is probable that these were Colonial troops late in receiving their pay. It is noted that practically all of them immediately joined the army of the Revolution.
Christy, James M., E [.—"Index of the Revolutionary records in the

Virginia State Archives", compiled by Dr. H. J. Eckenrode in 1912 and 1914.]

p. 192
Cristy, James (Christy) Drummer, 8 CL

<u>Revolutionary War Land Office Military Certificates</u>; *Records of the Executive Branch, Land Office (Record Group 4), microfilm reels 1-38; Library of Virginia, Richmond, VA.*
In order to receive bounty lands for Revolutionary War service, a soldier or sailor must have served continuously for at least three years in a Virginia or Continental unit. Service in the militia did not count. The certificates were numbered 1-9926 and cover the period July 14, 1782-August 5, 1876. The warrant specified the amount of lands to be received and directed the surveyor of lands to set aside that quantity of land in the Virginia Military District in Kentucky and Ohio.
Christee, James   Rank: Private   Military Certificate number: LO 309

Senate Documents, Vol.9, No. 988, 63rd Congress, 3d Session, Washington, 1915; "Register of Certificates Issued by John Pierce, Esquire, Paymaster General and Commissioner of Army Accounts for the United States, to Officers and Soldiers of the Continental Army Under Act of July 4, 1783"; <u>Seventeenth report of the National Society of the Daughters of the American Revolution</u>; *Genealogical Publishing Co., Inc., Baltimore, MD, 1984. p. 99.*
Men listed in this volume with the same name.

No. of Certificate	To whom issued	Amount
8615	Christey, James	$ 102.60
56124	Christey, James	23.00
70833	Christie, James	111.69
70854	Christie, James	234.00
71157	Christie, James	436.19
71316	Christie, James	400.00
72979	Christie, James	24.00
73295	Christie, James	800.00
73296	Christie, James	800.00
73297	Christie, James	447.30
84434	Christie, James	300.00
9096	Christy, James	80.00
24624	Christy, James	44.66
25270	Christy, James	80.00
72260	Chrystie, James	36.60

Wilson, Samuel L., comp.; <u>Year Book of the Society, Sons of the American Revolution in the Commonwealth of Kentucky, 1894-1913, and Catalogue of</u>

Military Land Warrants Granted by the Commonwealth of Virginia; Lexington, KY, 1913, p. 202.

No. of Warrant	Name of Officer or Soldier	No. of Acres	Character of Service as Private or Officer, If Officer, what Grade	Department of Service: Continental or State Line or Navy
309	Christee, James	20	Private	Va. State Line

No. of Years of Service		Date of Warrant		
war		Apr. 9, 1783		

Wardell, Patrick G., comp.; Virginia/West Virginia Genealogical Data From Revolutionary War Pension and Bounty Land Warrant Records, Vol. 1 ---Aaron through Cyrus; Heritage Books, Inc., Bowie, MD, 1988, p. 200.
Christie, James, esf 1777 Pittsylvania Co, VA; b 8/16/1758 Lancaster Co, PA; mvd after RW to NC, thence Franklin Co, VA, thence Lincoln Co, KY, thence Shelby Co, KY, where PN 1832 & dd there 3/8/37; md 3/20/1781-2 Sarah, Orange Co, VA, who b 4/19/1762; wid PN 1838 Shelby Co, KY, & dd 3/27/44 Ripley Co, IN; heirs of sol & w 1853 (all Christie); James & Isaac (Ripley Co), William (Hendricks Co), John (Switzerland Co) & their 3 sis's; in 1838 sol 6th ch Israel ae 45, Shelby Co, IN; QLF 1900 from great gdd M Katherine Wise, Bloomfield, IA, states sol md Sarah/Sally Lemon, further family res Christiansburgh, Shelby co, IN; QLF 1939 from desc Dora Lewis Sanders, Donna, TX, states sol md Sarah Lemon; QLF states sol s/o William who also RW sol, further sol md Sarah Lemon of Franklin Co, VA; QLF 1913 from Simeon Bush Christy, Murfreesboro, IN. R540.

Quisenberry, Anderson Chenault; Revolutionary Soldiers in Kentucky, containing a roll of the officers of Virginia line who received land bounties, a roll of the Revolutionary pensioners in Kentucky, a list of the Illinois regiment who served under George Rogers Clark in the Northwest campaign, also a roster of the Virginia Navy; Reproduction of the original which appeared in Sons of the American Revolution Kentucky Society Year Book, Louisville, 1896, Southern Book Co., Baltimore, MD, 1959. p. 225.
Shelby County - Pensioners Under the Act of March 18, 1818

Christie, James, private February 11, 1833; $56. Age 76	Virginia militia [Note: Rangers on the Frontier were Virginia militiamen.]

McAllister, J.T.; Virginia Militia in the Revolutionary War; McAllister Publishing Co., Hot Springs, VA, 1913, Part V.
Alphabetical List of Pensioners Residing Outside of Virginia in 1835, whose Pensions were Granted for Services as Virginia Militiamen.
This list was compiled from a repot made by the Secretary of War in 1835. The ages are those given in that report, and are believed to be the ages of the pensioners in 1835. The names of the pensioners in what is now West Virginia are embraced under Part IV.

Christie, James	85	Shelby	KY

Cowen, Janet C., comp; *Jeffersonville Land Entries 1808-1818;* McDowell Publications, Utica, NY, 1984, p. 171.
Receipt #
13782 Christie James IN Jefferson NE S17 T05 N11E 160 1817 09 22

Ripley County, Indiana Deed Records Vol. B., 29 Jan 1827-21 Sep 1832,
Page(s) 192-193.
Abstract of Deed/Patent for: Deed of Gift by James Christie *[son of the patriot]*
Purchaser (Grantee) or Seller (Grantor)?: Seller
Gifted to: Baptist Church at the west fork of Indian Kentucky [Creek]. Granted to David Shepherd, John Robinson and David Perkins, Trustees of said church and their successors.
State & county where recorded: Ripley Co., Indiana
Date entered: 6 Feb 1829
Recorded: 6 Feb 1829
Description: A certain lot or parcel of ground lying in the northwest quarter of Section 31, in Township 6, North of Range 11 East in the Jeffersonville district, containing one acre more or less.
Amount paid: Consideration of the love, goodwill and affection which I have and do bear towards the Baptist church at the west fork of Indian Kentucky.
Name(s) of Witnesses: C. Overturf & Jesse Miles

Ripley County, Indiana Deed Records Vol. D., 7 Feb 1834 - 9 Feb 1836,
Page 435-436.
Abstract of Deed/Patent for: James Christie *[son of patriot]*
Purchaser (Grantee) or Seller (Grantor)?: Purchaser
Purchased from: Isaac Christie & Susannah (dower) his wife
State & county where recorded: Ripley Co., Indiana
Date entered: 2 Apr 1835
Recorded: 4 Jan 1836
Description: Parcel or tract of land being part of the South West quarter of Section 31, Township 6 North of Range 11 East; in the Jeffersonville district; containing 10 acres and twenty two hundredths
Amount paid: Thirty six dollars ($36.00)
Name(s) of Witnesses: Preston Christie & Maryann Mavity

Margaret R. Waters; Revolutionary Soldiers Buried in Indiana (1949) With Supplement (1954) Two Volumes in One; Genealogical Publishing Company, Baltimore, MD, 1970. p. 132, 140, 141.
p. 132.
The following 121 soldiers did not die in Indiana. Their widows later moved to Indiana. Of the 121 widows, there are pension files for 120. Since these are not Revolutionary soldiers who died in Indiana, I jotted down only the sketchiest of data which may, however, help some reader. When known, Indiana residence is given for widow.
CHRISTIE, JAMES & SARAH   Ripley
He d. 3-8-1837, Shelby Co., Ky. Pens. 9782 Va.

p. 140.
In list of spouses buried in Indiana for Ripley Co., - Christie, Sarah-w. James.
p. 141.
In list of "Soldiers Who Died in Other States" (husbands of widows on list of spouses) – Kentucky – Christie, James.

Notes:
James Christie's burial is believed to be at Indian Fork Baptist Church in Shelby Co. KY. This has not been verified.
In 2015, descendants placed a Memorial Stone for Sarah Lemmon Christie in West Fork Cemetery, Rexville, Ripley Co., IN.]

COLLINS, WILLIAM

Patriot: William Collins
Birth: 6 May 1764, Orange Co., VA
Married Spouse 1: 1818   Orange Co. VA   Frances Williams
Service state(s): VA & PA
Rank: Private
Proof of Service: Pension application
Pension application No.: S31613
Residences: Orange Co., VA; Garrard Co., KY; Ripley Co., IN
Died: 1838
Buried: Unknown
DAR Ancestor No.:None as of 7 Jun 2017.

Pension Application Abstracted from National Archives microfilm Series M804, Roll 615, File S31613
Pension abstract for – William Collins
Service state(s): VA & PA
Date: 10 Feb 1834
County of: Ripley   State of: IN
Declaration made before a Judge or Court: Probate Court
Act of: 7 Jun 1832
Age: 6? [illegible]   Record of age: it is now in Jessamine Co., KY
Where and year born: Orange Co., VA 6 May 1764
Residence when he entered service: Orange Co., VA
Residence(s) since the war: Not stated
Residence now: Ripley Co., IN
Volunteer, Drafted, or Substitute: Tour 1 - Substitute for his father John Collins who was drafted; tour 2 – Substitute for Benjamin Stevens; tour 3 – Substitute for James Porter; tour 4 – Volunteer.
Rank(s): Private
Statement of service-

Period	Duration	Names of General and Field Officers
1 Nov 1780 - 2 May 1781	2 mos.	VA Militia, Gen. Weeden, Col. MacWilliams, Lt. Co. Murray, Maj. James Thompson, Capt. James Legg, etc.
5/6 May 1781 - [abt Jul 1781]	2 mos.	Gen. Nelson, Col. Thomas Bar???, Lt. Col. John Williams, Maj. Moore, etc..
[Abt Jul 1781 - 3 Sep 1781	2 mos.	Gen. Stevens, Col. James Mathews, Lt/ Col. John Riggs, Maj. Jones, etc..
3 Sep 1781 - 8 Nov 1781	2 mos. 5 days	PA Continental Line, Gen. Anthony Wayne, Col. James Edmonds, Lt. Col. Bridges, Maj. Wise, Adj. Bridges, Capt. James Jamison, Lt. Jones, etc.

Additional statement: Tour 4 – he volunteered in Capt. May Bentons Co. of VA Militia and there was 8 men more than his command called for and he with some others were transfer[ed] to the company of Regulars commanded by Capt. James Jameson who had not his full command at

that time. (Applicant deems it necessary to state these particulars to the Department, that it may readily explain how he came to serve under Capt. Jamison……).
Battles: Yorktown – was present at the surrender of Lord Cornwallis.
Statement is supported by –
Living witness, name(s): Knows of no person
Clergyman: Mishack Hyatt
&
Date: 16 May 1834
County of: Ripley   State of: IN
Declaration: Amendment to the Declaration he made on 10 Feb 1834
..in said declaration he was greatly mistaken in regard to his age as there set down that he was not born as stated in his answer to the 1st of the 7 questions presented by the War Department on the 6 day of May 1767 but in 1764 which makes the error three years. Deponent is of opinion that the mistake did not originate with him self, but with his Attorney Mr Harding as he well remembers that he was 16 years of age the May prior to his entering the Army the 1st time which was on the 1st day of November 1780. Deponent recollects of seeing the Record of his age in Jessamine County Ky. …….

Gwathmey, John H.; Historical Register of Virginians in the Revolution, Soldiers, Sailors, Marines, 1775-1783; The Dietz Press, Richmond, VA, 1938, p. 169.
Collins, William, Ky. Mil. ["Collins History of Kentucky"-accredited work.]

[Note: Garrard County was created 17 December 1796 from Lincoln, Madison and Mercer Counties.]

Register of the Kentucky Historical Society; Early Kentucky Tax Records; Clearfield Publishing, Baltimore, Md., 1999; p. 132.
A List of Taxable Property in the District of Reuben Ewing, Commissioner in the County of Logan for the Year 1795.

Persons Names Chargeable with Tax	Males Over 16	Horses	Cattle	Males Over 21
Collins, William	1	1	15	1

Revolutionary War Land Office Military Certificates; Records of the Executive Branch, Land Office (Record Group 4), microfilm reels 1-38; Library of Virginia, Richmond, VA.
In order to receive bounty lands for Revolutionary War service, a soldier or sailor must have served continuously for at least three years in a Virginia or Continental unit. Service in the militia did not count. The certificates were numbered 1-9926 and cover the period July 14, 1782-August 5, 1876. The warrant specified the amount of lands to be received and directed the surveyor of lands to set aside that quantity of land in the Virginia Military District in Kentucky and Ohio.
Collins, William   Rank: Private   Military Certificate number: LO 6150

Bockstruck, Lloyd DeWitt; <u>Revolutionary War Bounty Land Grants Awarded by State Governments</u>; Genealogical Publishing Co., IN, Baltimore, MD, 1996, p. 111.
Collins, William. Pa. [rank not shown]. 19 Feb. 1787. 200 acres to
                                              Ralph Philips, assignee.
Collins, William. Va. Private. 23 Mar. 1814. 200 acres.

Senate Documents, Vol.9, No. 988, 63rd Congress, 3d Session, Washington, 1915; "Register of Certificates Issued by John Pierce, Esquire, Paymaster General and Commissioner of Army Accounts for the United States, to Officers and Soldiers of the Continental Army Under Act of July 4, 1783"; <u>Seventeenth report of the National Society of the Daughters of the American Revolution</u>; Genealogical Publishing Co., Inc., Baltimore, MD, 1984. p. 112.
Men listed in this volume with the same name.

No. of Certificate	To whom issued	Amount
13938	Collins, William	34.60
14372	Collins, William	12.14
15198	Collins, William	120.00
25976	Collins, William	80.00
26648	Collins, William	25.00
28067	Collins, William	89.07
28520	Collins, William	108.00
30418	Collins, William	54.81
29200	Collins, William	80.00
29490	Collins, William	20.01
47090	Collins, William	11.28
69837	Collins, William	47.10
71619	Collins, William	40.60
71913	Collins, William	80.00
80396	Collins, William	58.30

Wardell, Patrick G., comp.; <u>Virginia/West Virginia Genealogical Data From Revolutionary War Pension and Bounty Land Warrant Records, Vol. 1 ---Aaron through Cyrus</u>; Heritage Books, Inc., Bowie, MD, 1988, p. 226.
Collins, William, est 1780 as sub for f John, Orange Co, VA, where b 5/17/1767; mvd to KY after RW, thence 1816 to Ripley Co, IN, where PN 1834. R615

[He did not state where he lived in KY in his Pension Application. He may have participated in the Frontier Wars which would not be mentioned in application because they occurred after the close of the Revolutionary War. The following record might be for him (I have not definitive proof.) – mjm]

Clark, Murtie June, Comp.; <u>American Militia in the Frontier Wars, 1790-1796</u>; Genealogical Publishing Co., Inc., 1990, p. 116.
Muster Roll of a Company of Infantry Commanded by Captain Morgan Murray in the Regiment of Washington County Militia, Southwest Territory, in the

Service of the United States Commanded by Gilbert Christian, Esquire, from Aug 31 to Dec 3, 1793.

Nr	Rank	Name	Remarks
44	Private	Collins, William	-

[He did not state where he lived in KY in his Pension Application. The following record lists all men named William Collins who were in KY in 1799 – mjm]
Clift, G. Glens, Assistant Secretary, Kentucky Historical Society, Comp.; <u>"Second Census" of Kentucky – 1800, A Privately Compiled and Published Enumeration of Tax Payers Appearing in the 79 Manuscript Volumes Extant of Tax Lists of the 42 Counties of Kentucky in Existence in 1800</u>; Genealogical Publishing Co., Baltimore, MD, 1966, p. 59.

Name	County	Tax List Date
Collins, William	Green	1800
Collins, William	Mason	1800
Collins, William	Shelby	8/25/ 1800
Collins, William	Warren	1800/1801
Collins, William E.	Shelby	8/29 1800

<u>Virginia, Orange County Marriage Records, 1757-1938</u>, database with images, FamilySearch (<u>https://familysearch.org/ark:/61903/1:1:VP1P-SD8</u> : 5 December 2014), Wm W Collins and Frances Williams, 07 Apr 1818; citing , , County Courthouse, Orange; FHL microfilm 33,031.

Name: Wm W Collins
Event Type: Marriage
Event Date: 07 Apr 1818
Event Place: Orange Co., VA
Spouse's Name: Frances Williams
Spouse's Titles and Terms:
Spouse's Father's Name: Jacob Williams
Spouse's Mother's Titles and Terms:
GS Film number: 33031
Digital Folder Number: 4810100
Image Number: 00233

<u>Ripley County Indiana, Recorder's Office, Tract Book 1, p. 10.</u>
Collins, William   Jun 1816   R10, T7, S35   160 acres

<u>U.S. Department of Interior, Bureau of Land Management, General Land Office Records; Land Patent Search</u>
Name: Collins, William
Accession Nr. CV-0077-314; Document Type – Credit Volume Patent; Issue Date – 12/16/1822; Cancelled – No
Land Office – Jeffersonville; Authority – April 24, 1820: Sale-Cash Entry (3 Stat. 566); Document Nr. 438; Total Acres – 160.00
Land Descriptions: State – IN; Meridian – 2ndPM; Twp-Rng – 07N – 010E; Aliquots – SW1/4; Section – 35; County - Ripley

Cowen, Janet C., comp; Jeffersonville Land Entries 1808-1818; McDowell Publications, Utica, NY, 1984, p. 107.
Receipt # 09709 Collins William KY Garrard SW S35 T07 N10E 160
Date: 1816 08 10

Ripley County, Indiana Deed Records Vol. B., 29 Jan 1827-21 Sep 1832,
Page(s) 389-390.
Abstract of Deed/Patent for: William Collins and Frances (dower) his wife of
Purchaser (Grantee) or Seller (Grantor)?: Seller
Sold to: Thomas Collins
State & county where recorded: Ripley Co., Indiana
Date entered: 14 Apr 1830
Recorded: 2 Aug 1830
Description: Southwest quarter of Section 35, in Township 7, North of Range 10
    East, containing one hundred sixty acres.
Amount paid: Fifty dollars ($50.00).
Name(s) of Witnesses: James Wobley & Anna Collins

Message from The President of the United States, transmitting a Report of The Secretary of War in Compliance with a Resolution of the Senate, March 28, 1818, Revolutionary Pensioners of 1818; Reprinted for Clearfield Company, Inc. by Genealogical Publishing Co., Inc., Baltimore, MD, 1992, p. 178.
List of Invalid Pensioners U. States, belonging to the state of Indiana, and payable at Vernon, Indiana, with the annual allowance to each annexed, viz:
William Collins   Private   At 48 per annum

1820 U. S. Census, Ripley Co., IN, NARA Roll M33_15; EN 7 Aug 1820, p. 74, line 15.
Males 10-15=1, Males 16-25=2, Males 45>=1, Females 10-15=1, Females 16-25=1, Females 45>=1.

The Pension Roll of 1835 Volume IV, The Mid-Western States, Indexed Edition, In Four Volumes; Genealogical Publishing Co., Inc., Baltimore, MD, Reprint 1968, p. 87.
Statement, &c. of Ripley county, Indiana.

INDIANA Names	Rank	Annual allowance.	Sums received	Description of service
William Collins	Private	20.22	-	Penn. militia

When placed on pension roll	Commencement of pension	Ages	Laws under which they were formerly placed on the pension roll; and remarks.
July 12, 1834	March 4, 1831	82	-

Scott, Craig R.; The "Lost" Pensions, Settled Accounts of the Act of 6 April 1838; Willow Bend Books, Lovettsville, VA, 1996, p. 70.
An Act directing the transfer of money remaining unclaimed [for the term of eight months] by certain pensioners, and authorizing payment of the same at the Treasury of the United States.
Name – Collins, William; Pension Office – INd.; Box – 44; Account - #4313.

Toph, Violet E.; Peoples History of Ripley County, Indiana; self-published, c. 1940, p. 122.
Revolutionary Soldiers Who Came to Ripley County
William Collins enlisted Nov. 1, 1780. He entered and left the service four times coming out of the service Nov. 8, 1781. He served eight months and three days altogether. He was born in 1763 and died in 1838. He was pensioned from Madison, Ind.

O'Byrne, Mrs. Roscoe C., comp. & ed.; Roster Soldiers and Patriots of the American Revolution Buried in Indiana; Published by Indiana Daughters of the American Revolution, 1938, Reprinted Genealogical Publishing Co., Baltimore MD, 1968, p. 101.
COLLINS, WILLIAM   Ripley County
Born – 1763.
Service – Enlisted Nov. 1, 1780. Entered and left service four times. Final discharge was Nov. 8, 1781. Entire time, 8 mos. 3 days.
Proof – Pension claim S. 31613.
Died – 1838. Name is on bronze tablet in Versailles Court House.
Collected by Mrs. A. B. Wycoff, Batesville, Indiana.

Gibbs, A.; Ripley County Historical Society Data on Revolutionary Soldiers, 1973 review.
Exact location of marker: no further information on grave site
Additional comments: On Court House tablet.
       Toph: pensioned from Madison, Ind.
          Pa. Archives Series III Pennsylvanians residing in Ripley Co. Ind.
            pr P.M. 12 July 1834 age 82.

Analysis of determination of wife:
Marriage record of 7 Apr 1818, Orange Co., VA –
    Frances Williams m. William w. Collins.
Francis relinquished dower rights on deed dated 14 Apr 1830, Ripley Co., IN

CRANE, EDMUND

Patriot: Edmund Crane
Birth: 15 Oct 1760
Married Spouse 1: Unidentified
Service state(s): NJ
Rank: Private & Corporal
Proof of Service: Pension application
Pension application No.: R2448
Residences: Morris Co., NJ; NY; IN; Vermillion Co., IL; Washbourne, Prairie, MO; Benton Co., AR.
Died: prob. Benton Co., AR
Buried: Unknown
DAR Ancestor No.: None as of 7 Jun 2017.

Pension Application Abstracted from National Archives microfilm Series M804, Roll 682, File R2443.
Pension abstract for – Edmond Crane
Service state(s): NJ
Date: 29 Oct 1832
County of: Vermillion   State of: IL
Declaration made before a Judge or Court: County Commissioner's Court
Act of: 7 Jun 1832
Age: 71 yrs.
Residence when he entered service: Morris County NJ
Residence now: Vermillion Co., IL
Volunteer, Drafted, or Substitute:
Rank(s): Private, Corporal
Statement of service-

Period	Duration	Names of General and Field Officers
1776	3 mos.	NJ Militia, Capt. Jonas Ward
1776/1777 3 Jun 1780	3 yrs. 6 mos.	Capt. Daniel Balding, Maj. Witherspoon, Col. Mathias Ogden.

Battles: Ash Swamp, Tappen Battle, Brandywine, German Town, Monmouth, Scotch Plains, Short Hills, Springfield, Elizabeth Town, Mud Island.
Statement is supported by –
Evidence: Traditionary
&
Pension abstract for – Edmond Crane
Date: 15 Oct 1842
County of: Benton   State of: AR
Declaration made before a Judge or Court: Justice of the Peace
Act of: 7 Jun 1832
Age: 82 yrs, now confined to his bed by disease. Record of age: Have none
Where and year born: 1760
Residence when he entered service: abt. 7 miles from Morristown, NJ
Residence(s) since the war: NJ; NY; IN; IL; Washbourne, Prairie, MO; Benton Co., Arkansas.

Residence now: Benton Co., AR
Volunteer, Drafted, or Substitute: 1st tour – Volunteered; 2nd tour – Volunteered; 3rd tour – Enlisted, sent home on furlough; 4th tour – Enlisted;
Rank(s): Private, Colonel (4th tour)
Statement of service-

Period	Duration	Names of General and Field Officers
1)Fall 1776	not less than 2 wks.	NJ Militia, Capt. Jonas Ward
2)Fall 1776	not less than 2 wks.	Same
3)1776	not less than 2 mos. 20 days	Same
4)1777	3 yrs. plus 5 mos. over term	NJ Continental Line 1st NJ Regt, under Capt. Daniel Balding, Col. Mathias Ogden, Gen Maxwell.

Battles: [see previous application]
Discharge received: 1st tour – Discharged; 4th tour – I was entitled to my discharge. But my Captain Balding, being wounded at Germantown in the leg and thrown into the hospital I was prevented from getting discharged.
Persons in neighborhood who certify character & belief of your service: Samuel Burk, David J. Long, Even Morgan.
Remarks: The claim was rejected on the ground that he deserted from the service and it does not appear that he ever rejoined the Army.

1820 U S Census; Ripley Co., IN; *NARA Roll*: *M33_15*; *Image: 49*; *EN 7 Aug 1820, p. 72, 2nd line from bottom of page.*
Edmund Crane
Males 10-15=1, Males 26-44=1, Males 45 & over= 5 (Edmund is one of these), Females under 10=3, Females 10-15=1, Females 26-44=1.

[There is a marriage record in Ripley County, IN for Edmond Crane to Nancy Burk, dated 5 May 1820 (there is no return). This record might be a second marriage for this man. In 1842, Samuel Burk lived in the Benton Co., AR neighborhood and testified for Crane's character and belief of service (see above pension application). – mjm]

Rejected or Suspended Applications for Revolutionary War Pensions; Reprinted for the Clearfield Publishing Co., Inc. by Genealogical Publishing Co., Inc., Baltimore, MD, 1991, p. 424.
A list of persons residing in Illinois who have applied for pensions under the act of June 7, 1832, whose claims have been rejected; prepared in conformity with the resolution of the Senate of the United States, September 16, 1850.

Name	Residence	Reason for rejection
Crane, Edmond	Danville, Vermillion	Desertion

Margaret R. Waters; Revolutionary Soldiers Buried in Indiana (1949) With Supplement (1954) Two Volumes in One; Genealogical Publishing Company, Baltimore, MD, 1970. p. 116.
CRANE, EDMUND   Ripley

(Uncertain). Name obtained after this Suppl was started. An Edmund Crane of Indiana is on the 1831 list of rejected pens., reason: "deserted the service". He is prob. Pens. R.2443 N.J. on Natl. Gen Soc. Quart. pens. Index. There is an Edmund Crane in 1820 Cens. of Ripley Co., Ind., v. 6, p.72. REF: "Rej. Appl. for Pens." (1831) p. 48.
[There is an Edmond Crane listed in Danville, Vermillion Co., Illinois list of rejected pensions. He is not listed in the Indiana rejected pensions. See citation above. – mjm]

CRUZAN (CRUIDSON, CRUIDSON, KRUZEN), BENJAMIN

Patriot: Benjamin Cruzan
Birth: 1751-1753, VA
Married Spouse 1: c. 1785   Jane DeVault (1754- 1840)
Service state(s):   VA Continental Line
Rank: Private
Proof of Service: Pension application
Pension application No.: S35869
Residences: NC; Adams Co., OH; KY(?); Rush Co., IN; Ripley Co., IN
Died: 5 Jun 1848, Brown Twp., Ripley Co., IN
Buried: Cross Plains Methodist Church Cemetery, Cross Plains,
   Brown Twp., Ripley Co., IN
DAR Ancestor No.: A028388

Pension Application Abstracted from National Archives microfilm Series M804, Roll 706, File S35869.
Pension abstract for – Benjamin Cruzan
Service state(s): VA Continental Line
Alternate spelling(s): Cruidson & Kruzan
Date: 18 Apr 1825
County of: Adams   State of: OH
Declaration made before a Judge or Court: Common Pleas Court
Act of: 18 Mar 1818
Age: 67
Residence when he entered service: Not stated
Where he entered the service: Hillsborough, NC
Residence(s) since the war: Not stated
Residence now: Adams Co., OH
Volunteer, Drafted, or Substitute: Enlisted
Rank(s): Private
Statement of service-

Period	Duration	Names of General and Field Officers
Fall 1780 - end of war 1783		VA Continental Line, 1st Regt. Horse – Capt. Fauntleroy, Regt. commanded by Col. Anthony Walton White

Battles: Not stated
Discharge received: in South Carolina
&
Pension abstract for – Benjamin Cruzan
Declaration: Application for Transfer
Alternate spelling(s): alias Cruidson
Date: 22 Mar 1838
County of: Ripley   State of: IN
Declaration made before a Judge or Court: Justice of the Peace
Statement of service-

Period	Duration	Names of General and Field Officers
		Capt. James Quin [?], Col. Anthony

Walton White.
Reason for Removing from: Ohio - moved to Ripley County "his children having moved to the state of Indiana he wished to follow them".

Abstract of Final Payment Voucher; General Services Administration, Washington, DC
    FINAL PAYMET VOUCHER RECEIVED FROM
    THE GENERAL ACCOUNTING OFFICE
NAME   Cruzan, Benjamin
AGENCY OF PAYMENT   INDIANA
DATE OF ACT   1818
DATE OF PAYMENT   4th Qr. 1848
DATE OF DEATH   June 5, 1848
GENERAL SERVICES ADMINISTRATION
National Archives and Records Service   NA-286
GSA DC 54-4891   November 1953

Virginia Military Records from the Virginia Magazine of History and Biography, the William and Mary College Quarterly, and Tyler's Quarterly; Genealogical Publishing Co., Baltimore, MD, 1983, p. 424.
Va. Officers and Men in the Continental Line, from VMHB, Vol.II (1895), 241-258, 357-370; III (1895), 92.
Doc. No. 34, House of Delegates, 1833-34
A List of some Officers and Soldiers (of Virginia) of the Revolutionary Army. Included in list of Privates – Benjamin Crewson

Revolutionary War Land Office Military Certificates; Records of the Executive Branch, Land Office (Record Group 4), microfilm reels 1-38; Library of Virginia, Richmond, VA.
In order to receive bounty lands for Revolutionary War service, a soldier or sailor must have served continuously for at least three years in a Virginia or Continental unit. Service in the militia did not count. The certificates were numbered 1-9926 and cover the period July 14, 1782-August 5, 1876. The warrant specified the amount of lands to be received and directed the surveyor of lands to set aside that quantity of land in the Virginia Military District in Kentucky and Ohio.
Cruidson, Benjamin   Rank: Private   Military Certificate number: LO 4042

Gwathmey, John H.; Historical Register of Virginians in the Revolution, Soldiers, Sailors, Marines, 1775-1783; The Dietz Press, Richmond, VA, 1938, p. 196.
Cruidson, Benjamin (Crewson)   1 Light Dragoons.

Wilson, Samuel L., comp.; Year Book of the Society, Sons of the American Revolution in the Commonwealth of Kentucky, 1894-1913, and Catalogue of

Military Land Warrants Granted by the Commonwealth of Virginia; Lexington, KY, 1913, p. 208.

No. of Warrant	Name of Officer or Soldier	No. of Acres	Character of Service as Private or Officer, If Officer, what Grade	Department of Service: Continental or State Line or Navy
4042	Cruidson, Benjamin	200	Private	Cont. Line

	No. of Years of Service	Date of Warrant		
	war	Dec. 15, '85		

Wardell, Patrick G., comp.; *Virginia/West Virginia Genealogical Data From Revolutionary War Pension and Bounty Land Warrant Records, Vol. 1 ---Aaron through Cyrus*; Heritage Books, Inc., Bowie, MD, 1988, p. 272.
Cruzan, Benjamin, esf 1780 NC for svc with VA regiment; PN ae 67 Adams Co, IN, 1825; PN transferred 1838 to Ripley Co, IN where sol address P O Lawrenceburgh District; PN last paid 12/1846. R706

[Note: In his pension application he did not state that he had lived in KY. There was a man by the name Benjamin Cruzan in Scott Co., KY in 1799. The name is not common so there is a possibility the following are records for him. – mjm]

Clift, G. Glens, Assistant Secretary, Kentucky Historical Society, Comp.; *"Second Census" of Kentucky – 1800, A Privately Compiled and Published Enumeration of Tax Payers Appearing in the 79 Manuscript Volumes Extant of Tax Lists of the 42 Counties of Kentucky in Existence in 1800*; Genealogical Publishing Co., Baltimore, MD, 1966, p. 69.

Name	County	Tax List Date
Cruzan, Benjamin	Scott	1800

Register of the Kentucky Historical Society; Early Kentucky Tax Records; Clearfield Publishing, Baltimore, Md., 1999; p. 44.
A List of Taxable Property in 1790, Taken in the Third District of the County of Mason (Afterwards Floyd County).

Persons Chargeable with the Tax	Horses
Crusan, Benjamin	1

The Pension Roll of 1835 Volume IV, The Mid-Western States, Indexed Edition, In Four Volumes; Genealogical Publishing Co., Inc., Baltimore, MD, Reprint 1968, p. 52.
Statement, &c. of Rush county, Indiana.

INDIANA Names	Rank	Annual allowance.	Sums received	Description of service
Benjamin Cruzan,				

alias Cruidson	Private	96.00	851 96	Virginia line

When placed on pension roll	Commencement of pension	Ages	Laws under which they were formerly placed on the pension roll; and remarks.
May 12, 1825	Ap'l 18, 1825	76	-

Ripley County Indiana Complete Probate Record Book Vol. E., Dec. 1848- Sept. 1850; p. 188-194.
Abstract of administration for: John Crusan
Names of executors/administrator: John Crusan
Date of death: (if specifically mentioned): More than 15 days prior to the first day of the present term of this court [which was 18 June 1848].
Place of death: Ripley Co., IN
Date recorded: 21 Jun 1848
Bonded by and amount of bond: James Miller $600.00
Names of heirs and others mentioned in will and relationship if shown: Son, John
    Crusan; Isaac Crusan; Thomas Crusan; Benjamin Crusan; Isrial Crusan; Garret Crusan; Lemuel Crusan; Rosemary Crusan; Polly Glaize wife of William Glaize; Elizabeth Butts wife of Providence Butts; Jane Mathena.
Date of division & disbursement, or final return: 18 Jun 1849

Daughters of the American Revolution of the State of Ohio, comp. Official Roster III, Soldiers of the American Revolution Who Lived in the State of Ohio; Painesville Publishing, Painesville, OH, 1959, p. 89.
CRUZAN, BENJAMIN - - ? Co
Pvt, drew pens in Ind on Cert No 19436, May 12, 1825. From Apr. 13, 1838.
Ref: DAR Magazine, July 1949, p. 610.

O'Byrne, Mrs. Roscoe C., comp. & ed.; Roster Soldiers and Patriots of the American Revolution Buried in Indiana; Published by Indiana Daughters of the American Revolution, 1938, Reprinted Genealogical Publishing Co., Baltimore MD, 1968, p. 110.
CRUZAN (CRUIDSON), BENJAMIN   Ripley County
Born – About 1758.
Service – Pri. in company commanded by Capt. Fauntleroy, Regt. Of Col. A.W. White, Vir. Line, 1780-1783. Discharged in S.C.
Proof – Pension claim S. 35868. [s/b S.35869 – mjm]
Died – June 5, 1848, in Ripley Co., Ind. Had children living in Ripley County.

Gibbs, A.; Ripley County Historical Society Data on Revolutionary Soldiers, 1973 review.
Exact location of marker: M.E. Cemetery adjoining the M.E. Church, east side of Rt. 129 Cross Plains, Brown Tw. Ripley Co. Ind.
Type of marker: Gov't
Additional comments: to Ripley Co. Ind. in 1828 from Ohio.
    Book D. Ripley Co. Ind. Probate (Sept. 19, 1848). Now at this time it is

proven to the satisfaction of the Court by the Oath of Jonathan Shrieve that Benjamin Crusan was a pensioner of the United States at the rate of Eight dollars per month was a resident of the County of Ripley and State of Indiana, and died in Brown Township of said County in the year 1848 on the 5th day of June, that he left eleven children whose names are as follows viz: Isaac Crusan, Thomas Crusan, Benjamin Crusan, John Crusan, Israel Crusan, Polly Glaze, Elizabeth Butt, Garret Crusan, Lemuel Crusan, Jane Mathna and Rosman Crusan, all of which is ordered to be certified.

Book E. Ripley Records p. 188. John Cruzan appointed administrator; his father, Benj. Cruzan, had "died more than 15 days prior to the present term of court". Court date, entry: 21 June 1848.

His son Isaac lived in Brown Tw. Ripley Co. Ind. 1850 census

Wording on marker:

Benjamin Cruzan
Pvt.
Rev. War
Va. Troops
1753-1848

<u>United States Headstone Applications for U.S. Military Veterans, 1925-1949</u>
Application for Headstone or Marker; War Department O.Q.M.G. Form No. 646
Name: Cruzan, Benjamin
Event Date: 19 Nov 1953
Name of Cemetery: Methodist Church Cemetery, Cross Plains, Indiana
Located in or near: Cross Plains, IN
Death Date: 5 Jun 1848
Enlistment Dates: 1780
Discharge Dates: 1783
Rank: Private
Company: Commanded by Capt. Fauntleroy, Regt. of Col. A.W. White, VA Line
To be shipped to: Mrs. Jeannette G. Farley, 416 E. Main St., Madison, IN
Applicant: Mrs. Jeannette G. Farley, 416 E. Main St., Madison, IN
I certify this application is submitted for a stone or marker for the unmarked grave of a deceased member or former member of the Armed Forces of the United States (Revolutionary War noted at top of application). I hereby agree to accept responsibility for properly placing the stone or marker as the grave at no expense to the Government.

Tombstone Location: Cross Plains Methodist Church Cemetery, Cross Plains, Brown Twp., Ripley Co., IN

Tombstone Inscription:

BENJAMIN
CRUZAN
PVT
VA TROOPS
REV WAR

DAVIS, PHILEMON (PHILAMON)

Patriot: Philemon Davis
Birth: Mar 1758, Chesapeake Bay, MD
Married Spouse 1: Unidentified
Service state(s): MD
Rank: Private & Sergeant
Proof of Service: Pension application
Pension application No.: S31640
Residences: Chesapeake Bay, MD; Nicholas Co., KY; OH; Ripley Co., IN
Died: 5 Jun 1841   Ripley Co., IN
Buried: Unknown
DAR Ancestor No.: None as of 7 Jun 2017.
Child: Son John mentioned in Pension Application

Pension Application Abstracted from National Archives microfilm Series 804, Roll 762, File S31640.
Pension abstract for – Davis, Philamon
Service state(s): MD
Alternate spelling(s): Davis, Philemon
Date: 11 Feb 1834
County of: Ripley   State of: IN
Declaration made before: Probate Court
Age: 75 years old   Record of age: None
Where and year born: March 1758   Chesapeake Bay, MD
Residence when he entered service: Chesapeake Bay, MD
Residence(s) since the war: Chesapeake Bay, MD until end of War; KY; Ripley Co., IN.
Residence now: Ripley County, IN
Volunteer or Drafted or Substitute: Volunteered
Rank(s): Private
Statement of service-

Period	Duration	Names of General and Field Officers
Aug 1775-Feb 1776	6 mos.	Gen. Gates, Gen. Schuyler, Col. William Clark, Maj. Charles White, Capt. Fountleroy, Ensign Charles Taylor
Feb 1776 -Jul 1776	6 mos.	Same officers
Jul 1776-Jul 1777	11 mos.	Same officers

Battles: Three Rivers in Canada
Discharge received: Yes
Statement is supported by –
Living witness, name(s): None
Documentary proof: None
Person now living who can testify to service: None
Clergyman: Rev. Mischack Hyatt
Persons in neighborhood who certify character: Illegible
Wife: None mentioned

Additional: In Jefferson Co., IN, on 7 Nov 1838, he requested a copy of his Pension Certificate. He names commanding officers Taylor & Hardin. He states his name was on the pension roll of Indiana, which was taken at the City of Louisville by John Davis, who delivered it to Nancy Jackson who put it in a box, and taken from the same by her little boy and torn up. His son, John Davis, testifies to the same.

In Vevay, Switzerland Co., IN, on 30 Jan 1838, William C. Keen makes request for a copy of the certificate.

In Madison, on 9 Nov 1839, application for copy was submitted.

A document from the Treasury Department shows payment has been made from 4 Sept. 1834 to 4 March 1838.

In Madison, on 24 Nov 1841, his heirs make request for balance of pension due him at the time of his decease. The certificate was surrendered and in the possession of (illegible) the writer.

Elijah Martin, well acquainted with pensioner, that he resided in IN and prev. resided in OH.

Abstract of Final Payment Voucher; General Services Administration, Washington, DC

FINAL PAYMENT VOUCHER RECEIVED FROM
THE GENERAL ACCOUNTING OFFICE

NAME	DAVIS, PHILOMEN
AGENCY OF PAYMENT	INDIANA
DATE OF ACT	1832
DATE OF PAYMENT	4th Qt. 1841
DATE OF DEATH	June 5, 1841

GENERAL SERVICES ADMINISTRATION
National Archives and Records Service   NA-286
GSA DC 54-4891   November 1953

Clements, S. Eugene and Wright, F Edward; The Maryland Militia in the Revolutionary War; Family Line Publications, Westminster, MD 21157, 1987, p. 154.

From the Sharf Collection, held by the State Archives -
CAROLINE COUNTY – A return of the 28th Battalion, returned 13 Aug. 1777, by William Whitely Lieutenant and Commander in Chief of the aforesaid County.

1777 Aug 13/John Fountleroy, Capt; Young Keen, 2 Lieut; Richard Keen, Ensign.

[Included in list]   Phillimon Davis

Archives of Maryland; Muster Rolls and other records of service of Maryland Troops in the American Revolution; Reprinted with permission by Genealogical Publishing Co., Inc., Baltimore, 1972, p. 199, 278, 645, 651.

p. 199.
MUSTERS OF MARYLAND TROOPS, VOL. ll.
Fifth Regiment

| | | Time of Service | | |
Names	Rank	Enlisted	Discharged	Remarks
Davis, Philemon'	pt	26 Apr 78	16 May 80	

To Hawkins', I mustr. April 78
p. 278.

MUSTERS OF MARYLAND TROOPS, VOL. lll.
Fifth Regiment
Non Commissioned Officers and Soldiers of the Fifth Maryland
Regiment left out of the Rolls February, 1778.

Davis, Philemon	27 July 77	wounded and gone home

p. 645.

From the records of the Council of Safety, see MD. Archives, see Md. Archives, Vol. XI.
A list of the Minute Company that march'd from Queen Anns County, Maryland the 3d Feby., 1776.

James Kent, Capt.   John Dames, Ensign
Thomas Tilltson, 1st Lieut.   James Browne, Surgeon
John Charris 2nd Lieut.
    Sergts.   Corporals
George Findley   John Jackson
Ephraim Wyn Story   Thomas Meridith Bryon
Philemon Davis   Thomas Freshwater, DRumr.
Samuel Cooper   John Findley, Fifer.
p. 651.

Roll of Capt. Robert Wright Company of Militia, in the Service of the United States by a Resolution of Congress, under the command of Col. Wm. Richardson. Aug. and Sept., 1777.

Rank	Appointed	Names	Remarks
Privates	July 3d	Philn. Davis	Enlisted in another Company Sept.

Newman, Harry Wright; *Maryland Revolutionary Records*; Tuttle Publishing, Rutland, VT, 1928. p. 17.

| Maryland Revolutionary Pensioners | | | | Misc. facts and |
Name of Veteran	Birth	Rank	Establishment	other State services
Davis, Philemon	1759	Pvt.	Continental Line	

Clift, G. Glens, Assistant Secretary, Kentucky Historical Society, Comp.; *"Second Census" of Kentucky – 1800, A Privately Compiled and Published Enumeration of Tax Payers Appearing in the 79 Manuscript Volumes Extant of Tax Lists of the 42 Counties of Kentucky in Existence in 1800*; Genealogical Publishing Co., Baltimore, MD, 1966, p. 75.

Name	County	Tax List Date
Davis, Philimon	Nicholas	1800

The Pension Roll of 1835 Volume IV, The Mid-Western States, Indexed Edition, In Four Volumes; Genealogical Publishing Co., Inc., Baltimore, MD, Reprint 1968, p. 87.

Statement, &c. of Ripley county, Indiana.

INDIANA Names	Rank	Annual allowance.	Sums received	Description of service
Philamore Davis	Private	63.33	199 99	Md. State troops

When placed on pension roll	Commencement of pension	Ages	Laws under which they were formerly placed on the pension roll; and remarks.
March 6, 1834	March 4, 1831	77	

Scott, Craig R.; *The "Lost" Pensions, Settled Accounts of the Act of 6 April 1838;* Willow Bend Books, Lovettsville, VA, 1996, p. 87.

An Act directing the transfer of money remaining unclaimed [for the term of eight months] by certain pensioners, and authorizing payment of the same at the Treasury of the United States.

Name – Davis, Philomon; Pension Office – INd.; Box – 47; Account - #5027

Toph, Violet E.; *Peoples History of Ripley County, Indiana;* self-published, c. 1940, p. 124.

Revolutionary Soldiers Who Came to Ripley County

Philamon (or Philemon) Davis entered the service from Maryland in August 1775 and served one year and seven months. He was born in 1750 and died in 1841 while a resident of Ripley County.

O'Byrne, Mrs. Roscoe C., comp. & ed.; *Roster Soldiers and Patriots of the American Revolution Buried in Indiana;* Published by Indiana Daughters of the American Revolution, 1938, Reprinted Genealogical Publishing Co., Baltimore MD, 1968, p. 115-116.

DAVIS, PHILEMON   Ripley County
Born – 1750.
Service – Enlisted in Maryland in Aug., 1775. Served 1 year and 7 mos.
Proof – Pension claim S. 31640.
Died – 1841, Ripley Co., Ind. Name on bronze tablet in Versailles Court House.
Collected by Mrs. A. B. Wycoff, 219 Maplewood Ave., Batesville, Indiana.

Gibbs, A.; *Ripley County Historical Society Data on Revolutionary Soldiers,* 1973 review.

Exact location of marker: no further information on grave site
Additional comments: on Court House tablet.
                Was a resident of Ripley County in 1832 (Toph note).

DELAP, JAMES

Patriot: James Delap
Birth: 15 Sep 1755, Burlington, NJ
Married Spouse 1: abt 1793, X Sidney (1763-abt 1840)
Service state(s): NJ
Rank: Private, Minute Man
Proof of Service: Pension application
Pension application No.: S32215
Residences: NJ; OH abt. 14 yrs.; Ripley Co., IN
Died: 10 Jul 1840, Ripley Co., IN
Buried: Green Cemetery, Washington Twp., Ripley Co., IN
DAR Ancestor No.: A031500

Pension Application Abstracted from National Archives microfilm Series M804, Roll 790, File S32215.
Pension abstract for – James Delap
Service state(s): NJ
Date: 13 Nov 1832
County of: Ripley   State of: IN
Declaration made before a Judge or Court: Probate Court
Act of: 7 Jun 1832
Age: 77
Where and year born: Burlington Co., NJ   15 Sep 1755
Residence when he entered service: Galloway, Gloucester Co., NJ
Residence(s) since the war: NJ; OH abt. 14 yrs.; Ripley Co., IN
Residence now: Ripley Co., IN
Volunteer, Drafted, or Substitute: Volunteered all tours
Rank(s): Private; last tour as Minute Man
Statement of service-

Period	Duration	Names of General and Field Officers
Dec 1777- end Apr/early Mar 1777	little over 2 mos.	NJ Militia under Col. Robert Taylor, Capt. Hillman.
May 1781- Jun 1781	1 mo.	Capt. Thomas Doughty, Lt. Col. Enoch Leeds, Maj. John Steelman, Capt. Richard Higbee.
July 1781	6 mos.	Capt. Davis & Capt. Cooper's companies, Lt. James Bell, Adj. Sgt. William Brown.

Battles: He was wounded in the thigh by a musket ball in a skirmish at Thomson's Point on the Delaware River. He was in the affair at Clam Town on the shore at Little Egg Harbor, and many other skirmishes.
Discharge received: 1st tour – at Sandtown, NJ; 2nd & 3rd – verbal discharge.
What became of it?: Long since been lost
Statement is supported by –
Documentary proof: Has none
Evidence: Traditionary
Person now living who can testify to service: James Leeds, cousin of deponent

and resident of Dearborn Co., makes affidavit he knew James Delap in Gloucester Co., NJ, knows most positively that he served ... [service described]
Clergyman: Elias Robinson
Persons in neighborhood who certify character: Edward Pendergast
Death of soldier: 10 Jul 1840
Wife: Not named
Names and ages of children: A son was referred to, but his name not stated [probably James]. On 10 Jul 1840, Nathaniel Delap heir of James Dunlap deceased leaving no widow his wife having died before him, appoints an attorney; Elizabeth G. Delap witness.
Notes: Correspondence in file refers to brothers William and Samuel Delap.

Abstract of Final Payment Voucher; General Services Administration, Washington, DC

LAST FINAL PAYMENT VOUCHER RECEIVED FROM THE GENERAL ACCOUNTING OFFICE
NAME   DELAP, JAMES
AGENCY OF PAYMENT   INDIANA
DATE OF ACT   1832
DATE OF PAYMENT   March 1, 1840
DATE OF DEATH   -
GENERAL SERVICES ADMINISTRATION
National Archives and Records Service   NA-286
GSA-WASH DC 54-4891   November 1953

Possible reference –
William S. Stryker, Adjutant General, Compiled Under Orders of His Excellency Theodore F. Randolph, Governor; Official Register of the Officers and Men of New Jersey in the Revolutionary War; by Printed by the Authority of the Legislature; Wm. T. Nicholson & Co., Printers, Trenton, NJ, 1872, Facsimile Reprint by Heritage Books, Inc., Bowie, MD, 1993; p. 570.
Delop, James.   Essex.

The Pension Roll of 1835 Volume IV, The Mid-Western States, Indexed Edition, In Four Volumes; Genealogical Publishing Co., Inc., Baltimore, MD, Reprint 1968, p. 87.
Statement, &c. of Ripley county, Indiana.

INDIANA Names	Rank	Annual allowance.	Sums received	Description of service
James Delap	Private	30.00	90 00	N. Jersey cont'l line
When placed on pension roll	Commencement of pension	Ages		Laws under which they were formerly placed on the pension roll; and remarks.
Nov 29, 1833	March 4, 1831	80		-

A Census of Pensioners for Revolutionary or Military Services with their Names, Ages, and Places of Residence Under the Act for Taking the Sixth Census in 1840; Genealogical Publishing Co., Inc., Baltimore, Maryland, 1965, p. 184.

Names of pensioners for revolutionary or military services.	Ages	Names of heads of families with whom pensioners resided June 1, 1840.
RIPLEY COUNTY		
JACKSON		
James Delapp	85	Nathaniel Delapp

Toph, Violet E.; *Peoples History of Ripley County, Indiana*; self-published, c. 1940, p. 130.
Revolutionary Soldiers Who Came to Ripley County
James Delap entered the service from New Jersey in 1777 under Col. Robert Taylor and served nine months. He was born in 1755 and died July 10, 1840 and is buried in the Green graveyard near Elrod, Ind. He was pensioned from Ripley County. The Ripley County Historical Society placed a Government marker at his grave July 13, 1936. His heir was Nathaniel Delap of Elrod, Ind.

O'Byrne, Mrs. Roscoe C., comp. & ed.; *Roster Soldiers and Patriots of the American Revolution Buried in Indiana*; Published by Indiana Daughters of the American Revolution, 1938, Reprinted Genealogical Publishing Co., Baltimore MD, 1968, p. 119.
DELAP, JAMES   Ripley County
Born – 1755, Burlington, N.J.
Service – Entered service from N.J., under Col. Robert Taylor in 1777. Served 9 mos.
Proof – Pension claim S. 32215.
Died – July 10, 1840. Buried near Versailles, Ind. Stone and government marker and name on bronze tablet in Versailles Court House.
Married - ------- Sidney, b. 1763. Son, Nathaniel, 1793-1841, m. Mary Kindle.
Collected by Mrs. A. B. Wycoff, Batesville, Indiana.

Gibbs, A.; *Ripley County Historical Society Data on Revolutionary Soldiers*, 1973 review.
Exact location of marker: off Rt. 50 east from Versailles, turn s. on 400E, then left on 300S 4/10ths mi.; in left. Green Cemetery, south of Elrod and Versailles area, Washington Tw. Ripley Co. Ind.
Type of marker: Gov't and somewhat worn family marker
Date placed: family marker probably at time of death;
        Gov't one, July 13, 1936 (Toph notes).
Placed by: Ripley County Historical Society
Additional comments: on Court House tablet
        Family marker reads: 84yr 10mo 5da.
        1840 census Ripley Co. Ind. census list p. 164, James Delap 85.

Probate Book A, Ripley Co., p. 133, appl. for pension Nov. 1832
Wording on marker:
James Delap
Pvt. Rev. War N.J.
Hillman's Co.
Taylor's
d. July 10, 1840

United States Headstone Applications for U.S. Military Veterans, 1925-1949, database with images; (https://familysearch.org/ark:/61903/1:1:VHZH-WF8 : 17 May 2016); Affiliate Publication Number: M1916; Affiliate Publication Title: Applications for Headstones for U.S. Military Veterans, 1925-1941; Affiliate Film Number: 29; GS Film Number: 1878178; Digital Folder Number: 004832196; Image Number: 01150.
Application for Headstone; War Department O.Q.M.G. Form No. 623
Name: James Delap
Event Date: May 31, 1934
Name of Cemetery: Green
Located in or near: Versailles, Ind.
Death Date: July 10, 1840
Enlistment Dates: 1777
Discharge Dates: Served 9 mos.
Rank: Private
Company: Col. Robert Taylor, NJ Troops, New Jersey Line
To be shipped to: Ripley Co. Historical Society, Osgood, Ind., Ripley Co.
Whose post-office address is: Versailles, Ind.
This application is for the UNMARKED grave of a veteran. It is understood the stone will be furnished and delivered at the railroad station or steamboat landing above indicated, at Government expense, freight prepaid. I hereby agree to promptly accept the headstone at destination, remove it and properly place same at decedent's grave at my expense. Ripley Co. Historical Society, Applicant. No fee should be paid in connection with this application.
Applicant: Ripley Co. Historical Society, Versailles, Ind.

Tombstone Location: Green Cemetery, Washington Twp., Ripley Co., IN

Tombstone Inscription: JAMES
DELAP
PVT. HILLMAN'S CO.
TAYLOR'S N J TROOP
REV. WAR
JULY 10, 1840

DOWERS (TOWERS, TOWERHOUSE), CONRAD

Patriot: Conrad Dowers
Birth: Aug 1764 near Philadelphia, Philadelphia Co., PA
Married Spouse 1: 2 Jun 1788, Philadelphia, PA Mary Shields (1764-1853)
Service state(s): PA
Rank: Private
Proof of Service: Widow's pension
Pension application No.: W9839
Residences: Lancaster, PA; York Co., PA; OH until 1824; Ripley Co., IN
Died: 27 Feb 1844   Ripley Co., IN
Buried: Pleasant Hill Cemetery (aka Weakman), near Cross Plains,
        Brown Twp., Ripley Co., IN
DAR Ancestor No.:A034067

Pension Application Abstracted from National Archives microfilm Series M804, Roll 844, File W9839.
Pension abstract for – Conrad Dowers
Service state(s): PA Continental
Date: 11 Feb 1833
County of: Ripley   State of: IN
Declaration made before a Judge or Court: Probate Court
Act of: 7 Jun 1832
Age: 68   Record of age: No record, only what my parents told me.
Where and year born: seven miles from Philadelphia, PA   1764
Residence when he entered service: Lancaster, Lancaster Co., PA
Residence(s) since the war: Lancaster, PA; OH until 1824; Ripley Co., IN
Residence now: Ripley Co., IN
Volunteer, Drafted, or Substitute: Volunteer
Rank(s): Private
Statement of service-

Period	Duration	Names of General and Field Officers
Mar 1778 - Nov 1778	9 mos.	PA Line - Gen. Mulenburg, Capt. Weltner's German Regt., Maj. Burchant.

Battles: Battle of Monmouth
Discharge received: Verbal discharge from Maj. Burchant
Statement is supported by –
Documentary proof: Has none
Person now living who can testify to service: Know no one
Clergyman: Meshack Hyatt
Persons in neighborhood who certify character: Edward Pendergast
Persons who believe service & character: Col. John Hunter, Col. Thomas Smith, Maj. Johnson, John J. Craig Esq.
&
Pension abstract for – Mary Dowers
Alternate name(s): Mary Towerhouse or Tauhauer which is the German
        for Towers or Dowers.
Date: 13 May 1844

County of: Ripley State of: IN
Declaration made before a Judge or Court: Probate Court
Act of: 7 Jul 1838
Age: 79 yrs.
Where and year born: Aug 1764
Residence when he entered service:
Residence now: Ripley Co., IN
Death of soldier: 27 Feb 1844 Ripley Co., IN
Widow's former name: Mary Sheilds
Marriage date and place: 2 Jun 1788 Philadelphia, PA
Proof of marriage: Pastor's Certificate & Corporate Seal of the German Lutheran Congregation, Second Street, Philadelphia, PA.
Names and ages of children:
    Sarah Towerhouse, which is the German for Dowers, b. 6 Aug 1789.
        Baptismal certificate for Mary is in file – German Lutheran Congregation, Second Street, Philadelphia, PA.
        Correspondence in file shows she marr. John Likes.
    Catherine (Catherine Prentice) was living in Ripley Co., IN in 1854.
Death of Widow: 7 Feb 1853

Abstract of Final Payment Voucher; General Services Administration, Washington, DC
    FINAL PAYMENT VOUCHER RECEIVED FROM
    THE GENERAL ACCOUNTING OFFICE
NAME
AGENCY OF PAYMENT INDIANA
DATE OF ACT 1832
DATE OF PAYMENT 2d Qr. 1844
DATE OF DEATH Feb. 27, 1844
GENERAL SERVICES ADMINISTRATION
National Archives and Records Service NA-286
GSA-WASH DC 54-4891 November 1953

Abstract of Final Payment Voucher; General Services Administration, Washington, DC
NAME Dowers, Mary widow of Conrad
AGENCY OF PAYMENT Madison, Ind.
DATE OF ACT 1848
DATE OF PAYMENT 3rd Qr. 1853
DATE OF DEATH Feb. 8, 1853
    FINAL PAYMENT VOUCHER RECEIVED FROM
    THE GENERAL ACCOUNTING OFFICE Form
General Services Administration GSA DC 70-7035 GSA DEC 69 7068

Ripley County Indiana, Recorder's Office, Tract Book 3, p. 61.
Dowers, Conrad 21 Aug 1832 R12, T7, S23 40 acres

U.S. Department of Interior, Bureau of Land Management, General Land Office Records; Land Patent Search
Name: Dowers, Cunrod
Accession Nr. IN0260_.260; Document Type – State Volume Patent; Issue Date – 8/1/1833; Cancelled – No
Land Office – Jeffersonville; Authority – April 24, 1820: Sale-Cash Entry (3 Stat. 566); Document Nr. 3269; Total Acres – 40.00
Land Descriptions: State – IN; Meridian – 2ndPM; Twp-Rng – 007N – 012E; Aliquots – SE1/4SW1/4; Section – 23; County - Ripley

Ripley County, Indiana Deed Records Vol. C., 21 Sep 1832 - 4 Feb 1834,
Page(s) 3-4.
Abstract of Deed/Patent for: Conrad Dowers
Purchaser (Grantee) or Seller (Grantor)?: Purchaser
Purchased from: James Leeds and Evey (dower) Leeds his wife
State & county where recorded: Ripley Co., Indiana
Date entered: 19 Feb 1830
Recorded: 6 Oct 1832
Description: A certain tract of land lying in part of the southeast quarter of Section 27, Township 7, Range 12, containing one hundred ten acres.
Amount paid: Two hundred dollars ($200.00).
Name(s) of Witnesses: Thomas Hubbell & Benjamin Rogers

Ripley County, Indiana Deed Records Vol. C., 21 Sep 1832 - 4 Feb 1834,
Page(s) 267.
Abstract of Deed/Patent for: Conrad Dowers and Mary Dowers (dower) his wife.
Purchaser (Grantee) or Seller (Grantor)?: Seller
Sold to: George Warren
State & county where recorded: Ripley Co., Indiana
Date entered: 6 Oct 1830
Recorded: 17 Aug 1832
Description: Part of the southeast quarter of Section 27, Township 7, Range 12.
Amount paid: One hundred dollars ($100.00).
Name(s) of Witnesses: James Wilson & Richard Welden

The Pension Roll of 1835 Volume IV, The Mid-Western States, Indexed Edition, In Four Volumes; Genealogical Publishing Co., Inc., Baltimore, MD, Reprint 1968, p. 87.
Statement, &c. of Ripley county, Indiana.

INDIANA Names	Rank	Annual allow- ance.	Sums re- ceived	Description of service
Conrad Dowers	Private	30.00	90 00	Penn. militia

When placed on pension roll	Commencement of pension	Ages	Laws under which they were formerly placed on the pension roll; and remarks.
July 15, 1833	March 4, 1831	70	-

A Census of Pensioners for Revolutionary or Military Services with their Names, Ages, and Places of Residence Under the Act for Taking the Sixth Census in 1840; Genealogical Publishing Co., Inc., Baltimore, Maryland, 1965, p. 184.

Names of pensioners for revolutionary or military services.	Ages	Names of heads of families with whom pensioners resided June 1, 1840.
RIPLEY COUNTY		
JACKSON		
Conrad Dowers	76	Conrad Dowers

Rejected or Suspended Applications for Revolutionary War Pensions; Reprinted for Clearfield Company Inc. by Genealogical Publishing Co., Inc., Baltimore, MD, 1998. p. 418.

A list of persons residing in Indiana who have applied for pensions under the act of July 7, 1838, whose claims have been suspended; prepared in conformity with the resolution of the Senate of the United States, September 16, 1850.

Names	Residence	Reason for suspension
Dowers, Mary, widow of Conrad	Versailles, Ripley	Barred by the act of April 30, 1814 reinstated under acts March 8, 1843, and July 1, 1848.

Ripley County, Indiana Deed Records Vol. C., 21 Sep 1832 - 4 Feb 1834, Page 3.
Abstract of Deed/Patent for: Conrad Dowers
Purchaser (Grantee) or Seller (Grantor)?: Purchaser
Purchased from: James Leeds & his wife Evey.
State & county where recorded: Ripley Co., Indiana
Date entered: 19 Feb 1830
Recorded: 6 Oct 1830
Description: Tract of land lying in the County of Ripley, State of Indiana, and known as a part of the South east quarter of Section twenty-seven, in Township Seven, Range twelve.
Amount paid: Two hundred dollars ($200.00)
Name(s) of Witnesses: Thomas Hubbell & Benjamin Rogers

Ripley County, Indiana Deed Records Vol. C., 21 Sep 1832 - 4 Feb 1834, Page 267.
Abstract of Deed/Patent for: Conrad Dowers
Purchaser (Grantee) or Seller (Grantor)?: Seller
Sold to: George Warren
State & county where recorded: Ripley Co., Indiana
Date entered: 6 Oct 1830
Recorded: 17 Aug 1832

Description: Part of the South east quarter of Section twenty-seven, in Township Seven, Range twelve.
Amount paid: One hundred dollars ($100.00)
Name(s) of Witnesses: James Wilson & Richard Welden

Ripley County Indiana Probate Order Book C., Nov. 1843-Feb. 1846; p. 28, 35, 85, 95, 121, 140, 142, 176, 178. & Complete Probate Record Book Vol. C., Feb. 1846- Nov. 1846; p. 332-352.
Abstract of administration for: Conrad Dowers
Name of Administrator: Mary Dowers for the estate of her late husband relinquished 14 Mar 1844 to George Likes;
Place of death: Ripley Co., IN
Date recorded: 15 Jul 1844
Bonded by and amount of bond: Joseph Beall $300.00
Names of heirs and others mentioned and relationship if shown: Catherine Dowers (no relation stated) brought claim against estate, jury found in favor of her, assessed damages at $190.00; heirs of Nancy (Dowers) Terrill; Ann Jane Terrill; Nancy Terrill; Benjamin Terrill; Lauretta Terrill; Jackson Terrill; Joshua Terrill; John Likes; Sarah Likes William Miller; Mary Miller; Sarah Rubecamp, her husband's given name not known.

Toph, Violet E.; Peoples History of Ripley County, Indiana; self-published, c. 1940, p. 127.
Revolutionary Soldiers Who Came to Ripley County
Conrad Dowers enlisted from Pennsylvania in March 1778. He was discharged in November 1778. He died Feb. 27, 1844.
The Ripley County Historical Society placed Government markers for the Dowers brothers in the Weakman cemetery one mile south of Olean, Indiana July 13, 1936

O'Byrne, Mrs. Roscoe C., comp. & ed.; Roster Soldiers and Patriots of the American Revolution Buried in Indiana; Published by Indiana Daughters of the American Revolution, 1938, Reprinted Genealogical Publishing Co., Baltimore MD, 1968, p. 127.
DOWERS, CONRAD   Ripley County
Born – 1764, Philadelphia, Pennsylvania.
Service – Enlisted from Penn., in March, 1778, and served as pri. in Capt. Bonner's CO., Col. Weltner's German Regt. For 9 mos. In battle of Monmouth. Discharged Nov. 1778.
Proof – Pension claim W. 9839.
Died – Feb. 27, 1844, Ripley Co. Name on bronze tablet in Versailles Court House.
Married – Mary Shields, 1788, d. 1853. Ch. Sarah; Catherine.
Collected by Mrs. A. B. Wycoff, Batesville, Indiana.

Gibbs, A.; Ripley County Historical Society Data on Revolutionary Soldiers, 1973 review.
Exact location of marker: 129 south of Versailles, about 1 mi. s. of Olean on Rt;

(or 1-7/10 mi. n. from Cross Plains on left. Weakman or Pleasant Hill Cemetery, Brown Tw. Ripley Co. Ind. The 2 Dowers stones are together *[one on each side of main path]* at the front edge of the cemetery, somewhat visible from road.
Type of marker: Gov't
Date placed: about 1936?
Placed by: Ripley County Historical Society
Additional comments: on Court House tablet
    1840 census Ripley Co. Ind., p. 162, Conrad Dowers age 75.
    Applied for pension: Ripley Co. Probate Book A, p. 135, Feb. 1833
Wording on marker:

                    Conrad Dowers
                    Pvt. Bruner's Co.
                    Weltner's
                    German Rgt.
                    Rev. War
                    Feb. 27, 1844

United States Headstone Applications for U.S. Military Veterans, 1925-1949, database with images; (https://familysearch.org/ark:/61903/1:1:VHZH-DD4 : 17 May 2016); *Affiliate Publication Number: M1916; Affiliate Publication Title: Applications for Headstones for U.S. Military Veterans, 1925-1941; Affiliate Film Number: 31; GS Film Number: 1878180; Digital Folder Number: 004832198; Image Number: 02132.*
Application for Headstone; War Department O.Q.M.G. Form No. 623
Name: Dowers, Conrad
Event Date: May 31, 1934
Name of Cemetery: Pleasant Grove
Located in or near: Cross Plains, Ind.
Death Date: Feb. 27, 1844
Enlistment Dates: March 1778
Discharge Dates: Nov. 1778
Rank: Private
Company: Capt. Bruntiss(?) Co., Col. Weltner's German Regt.,
                    Pennsylvania Line
To be shipped to: Ripley Co. Historical Society, Osgood, Ind., Ripley Co.
Whose post-office address is: Versailles, Ind.
This application is for the UNMARKED grave of a veteran. It is understood the stone will be furnished and delivered at the railroad station or steamboat landing above indicated, at Government expense, freight prepaid. I hereby agree to promptly accept the headstone at destination, remove it and properly place same at decedent's grave at my expense. Ripley Co. Historical Society, Applicant.
No fee should be paid in connection with this application.
Applicant: Ripley Co. Historical Society, Versailles, Ind.

Tombstone Location: Pleasant Hill (Grove) Cemetery
(aka Weakman Cemetery),
Brown Twp., Ripley Co., IN

Tombstone Inscription:

CONRAD
DOWERS
PVT. BRUNNER'S CO
WELTNER'S
GERMAN REGT.
REV. WAR
FEBRUARY 27, 1844

DOWERS (TOWERS, TOWERHOUSE), JACOB

Patriot: Jacob Dowers
Birth: Aug 1760 near Philadelphia, Philadelphia Co., PA
Married Spouse 1: abt 1790 XX (abt 1770-1840/44/47)
Service state(s): PA
Rank: Private
Proof of Service: Pension application
Pension application No.: S16371
Residences: Lancaster Co., PA; York Co., PA; MD; VA;
           Adams Co., OH; Ripley Co., IN
Died: 2 Jun 1840 per tombstone; Pension file 2nd qtr. 1847 (final payment 3rd qtr.); Will written in 1846, Recorded 25 Jan 1847   Ripley Co., IN
Buried: Pleasant Hill Cemetery (aka Weakman Cemetery), near Cross Plains, Brown Twp., Ripley Co., IN
DAR Ancestor No.: A034069

Pension Application Abstracted from National Archives microfilm Series M804, Roll 844, File S16371.
Pension abstract for – Jacob Dowers
Service state(s): PA
Date: 23 Aug 1832
County of: Ripley   State of: IN
Declaration made before a Judge or Court: Aug - Circuit Court
Act of: 7 Jun 1832
Age: 72 yrs.
Where and year born: Philadelphia, PA 1760
Residence when he entered service: Lancaster, Lancaster Co., PA
Residence(s) since the war: PA, MD, VA, IN
Residence now: Ripley Co., IN
Volunteer, Drafted, or Substitute: Enlisted
Rank(s): Private
Statement of service-

Period	Duration	Names of General and Field Officers
Aug 1780- Feb 1781	6 mos.	Capt. Bartley's Co., Col. Johnston's 5th Penn. Regt.

Battles: None stated
Discharge received: yes
Signed by: Col. Menges
What became of it?: Conrad Dowers stated his mother, if living, has it in York Co., PA
Statement is supported by –
Living witness, name(s): I knew Gen. Wayne, Col. Johnson, Col. Menges, Maj. Tailor, Adj. Bartley
Person now living who can testify to service: Conrad Dowers
Persons in neighborhood who certify character: Conrad Dowers, Azariah Dowers
Death of soldier: 2 Jun 1840 [from correspondence in file]

Abstract of Final Payment Voucher; General Services Administration, Washington, DC
FINAL PAYMENT VOUCHER RECEIVED FROM
THE GENERAL ACCOUNTING OFFICE
NAME   DOWERS, JACOB
AGENCY OF PAYMENT   INDIANA
DATE OF ACT   1832
DATE OF PAYMENT   3rd Qr. 1847
DATE OF DEATH   Jan. 9, 1847
GENERAL SERVICES ADMINISTRATION
National Archives and Records Service   NA-286
GSA-WASH DC 54-4891   November 1953

Cowen, Janet C., comp; Jeffersonville Land Entries 1808-1818; McDowell Publications, Utica, NY, 1984, p. 95.
Receipt # 08025 Dowers Jacob OH Adams SW S03 T06 N12E 160
Date - 1816 01 29

U.S. Department of Interior, Bureau of Land Management, General Land Office Records; Land Patent Search
Name: Dowers, Cunrod
Accession Nr. IN0260_.260; Document Type – State Volume Patent; Issue Date – 8/1/1833; Cancelled – No
Land Office – Jeffersonville; Authority – April 24, 1820: Sale-Cash Entry (3 Stat. 566); Document Nr. 3269; Total Acres – 40.00
Land Descriptions: State – IN; Meridian – 2ndPM; Twp-Rng – 007N – 012E; Aliquots – SE1/4SW1/4; Section – 23; County - Ripley

1830 U. S. Census, Ripley County, IN; Series M19, Roll 32; p. 14, line 23.
Jacob Dowers
Males <5=1, Males 70-79=1, Females 5-9=1, Females 20-29=1, Females 60-69=1.

A Census of Pensioners for Revolutionary or Military Services with their Names, Ages, and Places of Residence Under the Act for Taking the Sixth Census in 1840; Genealogical Publishing Co., Inc., Baltimore, Maryland, 1965, p. 184.

Names of pensioners for revolutionary or military services.	Ages	Names of heads of families with whom pensioners re-sided June 1, 1840.
RIPLEY COUNTY		
JACKSON		
Jacob Dowers	79	Jacob Dowers

Ripley County, Indiana Will Records Vol. B, June 1839-May 1862; p. 68-69
Abstract of will and administration for: Jacob Dowers
Date and place will was made: 16 Sep 1846 in Ripley Co., Indiana
Witnesses to will: Berryman Spiller, John D. White, Hosea Weatherbee
Names of executors: son Azariah Dowers

Place of death: Ripley Co., IN
Date recorded: 25 Jan 1847
Names of heirs and others mentioned in will and relationship if shown: Daughter, Sarah Jolly; son, Isaac Dowers; daughter Perlina Sames; heirs of son George Dowers; heirs of Elizabeth Weldon; daughter Nancy; sons Azriah and Henry.

Toph, Violet E.; Peoples History of Ripley County, Indiana; self-published, c. 1940, p. 127.
Revolutionary Soldiers Who Came to Ripley County
Jacob Dowers enlisted from Pennsylvania in August 1780 and was discharged in February, 1781. The Ripley County Historical Society placed Government markers for the Dowers brothers in the Weakman cemetery one mile south of Olean, Indiana July 13, 1936

O'Byrne, Mrs. Roscoe C., comp. & ed.; Roster Soldiers and Patriots of the American Revolution Buried in Indiana; Published by Indiana Daughters of the American Revolution, 1938, Reprinted Genealogical Publishing Co., Baltimore MD, 1968, p. 128.
DOWERS, JACOB   Ripley County
Born – 1760, Philadelphia, Pennsylvania.
Service – While a resident of Lancaster Co., Penn., enlisted in Aug. 1780, served in Capt. Bartley's CO., Col. Johnston's Fifth Penn. Regt., and was discharged by Col. Mentges after 6 mos. service.
Proof – Pension claim S. 16371.
Died – Jan. 9, 1847, Ripley Co., Ind. Name on bronze tablet in Versailles Court House.
Children – Azariah; Henry; Isaac; Sally; Jolly; Purlina Sams; Nancy Johnson.
Collected by Mrs. A. B. Wycoff, Batesville, Indiana.

Gibbs, A.; Ripley County Historical Society Data on Revolutionary Soldiers, 1973 review.
Exact location of marker: 129 south of Versailles, about 1 mi. s. of Olean on Rt; (or 1-7/10 mi. n. from Cross Plains on left. Weakman or Pleasant Hill Cemetery, Brown Tw. Ripley Co. Ind. The 2 Dowers stones are together *[one on each side of main path]* at the front edge of the cemetery, somewhat visible from road.
Type of marker: Gov't   Date placed: about 1936?
Placed by: Ripley County Historical Society
Additional comments: on Court House tablet.
    1840 census Ripley Co. Ind., p. 160, Jacob Dowers 79.
    Book B Wills Ripley Co., 16 Sep 1846; probated 25 Jan '47. *[Same man? Too many years between death & entered into probate – mjm]*
Wording on marker:
Jacob Dowers
Pvt.
Johnson's Pa. Rgt.
Rev. War
June 2, 1840

<u>United States Headstone Applications for U.S. Military Veterans, 1925-1949, database with images</u>(https://familysearch.org/ark:/61903/1:1:VHZH-DDH : 17 May 2016; *Affiliate Publication Number: M1916; Affiliate Publication Title: Applications for Headstones for U.S. Military Veterans, 1925-1941; Affiliate Film Number: 31; GS Film Number: 1878180; Digital Folder Number: 004832198; Image Number: 02133.*
Application for Headstone; War Department O.Q.M.G. Form No. 623
Name: Dowers, Jacob
Event Date: Illegible, 1939
Name of Cemetery: Pleasant Grove
Located in or near: Cross Plains, Ind.
Death Date: June 2, 1840
Enlistment Dates: Aug 1780
Discharge Dates: Feb 1781
Rank: Private
Company: Capt. Bailey's C0., Col. Johnston's Regt. Pennsylvania Line
To be shipped to: Ripley Co. Historical Society, Osgood, Ind., Ripley Co.
Whose post-office address is: Versailles, Ind.
This application is for the UNMARKED grave of a veteran. It is understood the stone will be furnished and delivered at the railroad station or steamboat landing above indicated, at Government expense, freight prepaid. I hereby agree to promptly accept the headstone at destination, remove it and properly place same at decedent's grave at my expense. Ripley Co. Historical Society, Applicant. No fee should be paid in connection with this application.
Applicant: Ripley Co. Historical Society, Versailles, Ind.

Tombstone Location: Pleasant Hill (Grove) Cemetery
                                     (aka Weakman Cemetery),
                                     Brown Twp., Ripley Co., IN

Tombstone Inscription:
                                     JACOB DOWERS
                                     PENNSYLVANIA
                                     PVT.
                                   JOHNSTON'S 5 PA REGT.
                                     REV. WAR
                                     JUNE 2, 1840

FISK, ROBERT

Patriot: Robert Fisk
Birth: 1758　　Lexington, MA
Married Spouse 1: 3 Aug 1782, Hackensack, NY　　Elizabeth Jones (1760-1843)
Service state(s): MA Continental Line
Rank: Sergeant
Proof of Service: Pension application
Pension application No.: W9438
Residences: Lexington, MA; Dutchess Co., NY; Pope Co., IL
Died: 19 Apr 1824　　Golconda, Pope Co., IL
Buried: Unknown
DAR Ancestor No.: A039834 [Note: Only the member applications for his son Abraham J. Fisk is correct.]
Child: Son, Abraham J. Fisk

Pension Application Abstracted from National Archives microfilm Series M804, Roll 982 File W9438; BLWt 2332-100.
Pension abstract for – Robert Fisk
Service state(s): MA Continental Line
Date: 8 Jun 1819
County of: Pope　　　　　　　　　　　　State of: IL
Declaration made before a Judge or Court: Circuit Court
Act of: 18 Mar 1818
Age: Not stated
Residence when he entered service: Not stated
Residence(s) since the war: Not stated
Residence now: Pope Co., IL
Volunteer, Drafted, or Substitute: Enlisted
Rank(s): Sergeant
Statement of service-

Period	Duration	Names of General and Field Officers
8 May 1775 - 8 Jun 1783	8 yrs. 1 mo.	3rd Regt. MA Continental Line, Capt. North, Col. Greaton

Battles: Not stated
Discharge received: Yes, dated 8 Jun 1783
What became of it?: Accompanies this document
&
Pension abstract for – Robert Fisk
Declaration: Schedule of Property
Service state(s): MA Continental Line
Date: 13 Apr 1824 – Clerk of Court certified on 19 Apr 1824
　　　　　　　　[same date as reported death date]
County of: Pope　　　　　　　　　　　　State of: IL
Declaration made before a Judge or Court: Circuit Court
Act of: 1 Mar 1823
Age: 66 yrs.

Residence now: Pope Co., IL
Statement of service-
Period   Duration   Names of General and Field Officers
         He served eight years and one month
                                              He last belonged to the 3rd Regiment of
                                              Infantry Massachusetts Line
Discharge received: yes
What became of it?: Has been sent to the Secretary of War's office – No. 15,257.
Wife: Elizabeth Fisk   Wife's age: 58 yrs.
Names and ages of children: [family consists of] "and a little girl, Eliza Fisk, 11 years of age, and incapable of supporting herself".
&
Pension abstract for – Elizabeth Fisk widow of Robert Fisk
Date: 27 Jul 1841
County of: Ripley   State of: IN
Declaration made before a Judge or Court: Circuit Court
Act of: 4 Jul 1836
Widow's age: 75 yrs.
Soldier's where and year born: Lexington, MA
Soldier's Residence when he entered service: Lexington, MA
Widow's Residence now: Ripley Co., IN
Volunteer, Drafted, or Substitute: Enlisted
Rank(s): Orderly Sergeant
Statement of service: His name appears on the pension list of Illinois agency. She
                         noted that a few days before his death he made
                         application to the Pension agent…
Battles: Battle of Lexington
Persons in neighborhood who certify character: her grandson Robert W. Fisk
Death of soldier: 19 Apr 1824   Golconda, Pope Co., IL
Marriage date and place: she stated abt. middle of Aug 1782
&
Bounty Land application for: Elizabeth Fisk widow of Robert Fisk
Date: 24 Jul 1843
County of: Jefferson   State of: IN
Declaration made before a Judge or Court:
Act of: 4 Jul 1836
Statement is supported by –
Documentary proof: Robert Fisk's name can be found on the Pension Roll of the
                                Illinois Agency
Death of soldier: 19 Apr 1824 in IL
Widow's former name: Elizabeth Jones   Widow's age:
Marriage date and place: 3 Aug 1782   "Both parties were of Rumbolts precinct
               which comprised that part of Fishkill in which they lived"
Proof of marriage: Certification – Reformed Dutch Church of Hackensack,
                               Dutchess Co., NY
Names and ages of children: Only son Abraham J. Fisk

Abstract of Final Payment Voucher; General Services Administration, Washington, DC
    FINAL PAYMENT VOUCHER RECEIVED FROM
    THE GENERAL ACCOUNTING OFFICE
NAME   FISK, ELIZABETH   WIDOW OF ROBERT
AGENCY OF PAYMENT   INDIANA
DATE OF ACT   1836
DATE OF PAYMENT   1st Qr. 1844
DATE OF DEATH   August 10, 1843
GENERAL SERVICES ADMINISTRATION
National Archives and Records Service   NA-286
GSA-WASH DC 54-4891   November 1953

Bockstruck, Lloyd DeWitt; *Revolutionary War Pensions Awarded by State Governments 1775-1874, the General and Federal Governments Prior to 1814, and by Private Acts of Congress to 1905;* Genealogical Publishing Co., Baltimore, MD, 2011, p. 265.
Fisk, Robert.   Mass. -   He was in the 3rd Regiment and was paid $20.00.

Senate Documents, Vol.9, No. 988, 63rd Congress, 3d Session, Washington, 1915; "Register of Certificates Issued by John Pierce, Esquire, Paymaster General and Commissioner of Army Accounts for the United States, to Officers and Soldiers of the Continental Army Under Act of July 4, 1783"; *Seventeenth report of the National Society of the Daughters of the American Revolution;* Genealogical Publishing Co., Inc., Baltimore, MD, 1984. p. 177.

No. of Certificate	To whom issued	Amount
13715	Fisk, Robert	85.77
14165	Fisk, Robert	11.18
15045	Fisk, Robert	120.00
60783	Fisk, Robert	79.54
61545	Fisk, Robert	80.00

New York Marriages, 1686-1980, accessed 11 April 2016 from https://familysearch.org/ark:/61903/1:1:F64L-G4Q
Name: Robert Fisk
Spouse's Name: Elizabeth Jones
Event Date: 03 Aug 1782
Event Place: Reformed Dutch Church, New Hackensack, Dutchess, New York
Indexing Project (Batch) Number: M50617-1
System Origin: New_York-ODM; GS Film number: 1206459
FHL microfilm 1,206,459.

Clark, Murtie June; *The Pension List of 1820 [U.S. War Department]*Reprinted with an Index; Genealogical Publishing Co., Inc., Baltimore, 1991. Originally published 1820 as Letter from the Secretary of War, p. 661.
ILLINOIS
Names of the Revolutionary Pensioners which have been placed on the Roll of

Illinois, under the Law of the 18th of March, 1818, from the passage thereof, to this day, inclusive of the Rank they held, and the Lines in which they served, viz:

Names	Rank	Line
Included in the list –		
Robert Fisk	sergeant	Massachusetts

The Pension Roll of 1835 Volume IV, The Mid-Western States, Indexed Edition, In Four Volumes; *Genealogical Publishing Co., Inc., Baltimore, MD, Reprint 1968, p. 10.*Statement, &c. of Sangamon county, Illinois.

ILINOIS Names	Rank	Annual allow- ance.	Sums re- ceived	Description of service
Robert Fisk	Sergeant	96.00	70 92	Mass. continental

When placed on pension roll	Commencement of pension	Ages	Laws under which they were formerly placed on the pension roll; and remarks.
Oct 12, 1819	June 8, 1819	-	Suspended act May 1, 1820

Pensioners of the Revolutionary War Struck Off the Roll with an Added Index to States; Reprinted by Genealogical Publishing Co., Baltimore, MD for Clearfield Company, Inc., 1989. p. 102.

Pensioners in the State of Illinois who have been dropped from the pension roll under the act of the 1st of May, 1820; prepared in conformity with the resolution of the House of Representatives of the 17th of December, 1835.

Names	Acts under which restored	Remarks
Include in list –		
Robert Fisk	March 1, 1823	-

Margaret R. Waters; *Revolutionary Soldiers Buried in Indiana (1949) With Supplement (1954) Two Volumes in One;* Genealogical Publishing Company, Baltimore, MD, 1970, p.133.

The following 121 soldiers did not die in Indiana. Their widows later moved to Indiana. Of the 121 widows, there are pension files for 120. Since these are not Revolutionary soldiers who died in Indiana, I jotted down only the sketchiest of data which may, however, help some reader. When known, Indiana residence is given for widow.

FISK, ROBERT & ELIZABETH   Ripley
He d. 4-19-1824, Ill. Pens. W.9438 Mass.

[Note: There is a Sgt. Robert Fisk of MA Continental, d. 12 Oct 1819, Sangamon Co., IL; listed in 1835 Invalid Pension (copy in his folder) and on plaque in courthouse. Not the same man as this. – mjm]

FOX, ADAM

Patriot: Adam Fox
Birth: 16 Jul 1764 Frederick Co., MD
Married Spouse 1: 2 Nov 1798 Frederick Co., MD Ann Gaver
Service state(s): MD, possibly VA
Rank: Private
Proof of Service: Rejected pension application
Pension application No.: R3721
Residences: Frederick Co., MD; Augusta Co., VA; Knox Co., OH; Hamilton Co., OH; Ripley Co., IN
Died: Unknown
Buried: Unknown
DAR Ancestor No.: None as of 7 Jun 2017.
Child: Son, Jacob Fox of Cincinnati, OH, letter in pension file.
Jacob says papers were destroyed by the Ohio River Flood of 1883.

Pension Application Abstracted from National Archives microfilm Series M804, Roll 1012, File R3721.

Pension abstract for – Adam Fox   Service state(s): MD and VA
Date: 13 Aug 1839
County of: Ripley   State of: IN
Declaration made before: Probate Court
Act of: Jun 1832
Age: Record of age: Recorded in father's family Bible when I left VA 30 yrs. ago
Where and year born: 16 Jul 1764   (Illegible) Co., MD
Residence when he entered service: Frederick Co., MD; from there to Augusta Co., VA
Residence(s) since the war: 27 yrs. Augusta Co., VA; abt. 4 yrs. Knox Co., OH; Hamilton Co., OH; Ripley Co., IN.
Residence now: Ripley Co., IN
Volunteer, Drafted, or Substitute: Substitute for Henry Reed; I was 15-16 y/o.
Rank(s): not stated
Statement of service-

Period	Duration	Names of General and Field Officers
Oct 1779	2 mos.	MD Capt. Valentine Creager; Lieutenant Levy

Battles: None
Discharge received: Yes
Signed by: Capt. Valentine Creeger
What became of it?: I have lost my discharge.
Statement is supported by –
Living witness, name(s): John Stockwell, John Craven, & Joseph Stockwell
Clergyman: Meshack Hyatt
Names and ages of children: Son, Jacob Fox, wrote letter inquiring about status of claim. The claim was rejected because his father only rendered two months of service.

&

Letter in the above Pension application R3721 for Adam Fox
Versailles Indiana September the 19th 1839
    Dear Sir Thomas Johnson who was a soldier of the Revolutionary war and who resided at the time of his death in the County of Dearborn and State of Indiana and who drew a pension for many years before his death also Ning Bell and William Lippard and Henry Wilyard all of whom was soldiers of the Revolutionary War and resided in the county of Ripley and State of Indiana and was in the receipt of pensions at the time of their death. They have all left surviving widows to wit Sarah Johnson, Agnes Willyard, Christina Beall, and Mary Lippard all of whom wish to apply for pensions under and by Authority of the Act of Congress of the 4th of July 1836, and the 3rd of March 1837. The said Thomas Johnson, Ning Beall, William Lipperd and Henry Wilyard at the time of their deaths left a draw of pensions due and in order to obtain the same, sayeth widows, was requested to surrender the pension Certificates of their deceased husbands which said Certificated I suppose has been returned to the proper office. In order to enable the widows of deceased pensioner to identify themselves as the widows of the deceased it is necessary for them to set out the original pension certificate of their deceased husbands and as they must be on file in the office over which you preside please transfer to me at Versailles Indiana the original certificated of the said Johnson, Beall, Lipperd, and Wilyard if it is in accordance with the custom of your office. If not, please send me a Certified Copy of the same
I herewith send the papers of Mr. <u>Adam Fox</u> who claims a pension. If the papers are different please point out the deficiency to me.
Let me hear from you as soon as convenient.
                                          Yours respectfully
                                          Joseph Robinson

Newman, Harry Wright; *Maryland Revolutionary Records*; Tuttle Publishing, Rutland, VT, 1928. p. 22.

Maryland Revolutionary Pensioners				Misc. facts and
Name of Veteran	Birth	Rank	Establishment	other State services
Fox, Adam	1764	Pvt.	Militia	-

Possible record –
Gwathmey, John H.; *Historical Register of Virginians in the Revolution, Soldiers, Sailors, Marines, 1775-1783*; The Dietz Press, Richmond, VA, 1938, p. 285.
Fox, Adam, 11 and 15 CL, 15 CL. [Continental Line]

Revolutionary War Land Office Military Certificates; Records of the Executive Branch, Land Office (Record Group 4), microfilm reels 1-38; Library of Virginia, Richmond, VA.
In order to receive bounty lands for Revolutionary War service, a soldier or sailor must have served continuously for at least three years in a Virginia or Continental unit. Service in the militia did not count. The certificates were numbered 1-9926 and cover the period July 14, 1782-August 5, 1876. The warrant specified the amount of lands to be received and directed the surveyor of lands to set aside that quantity of land in the Virginia Military District in Kentucky and Ohio.
Fox, Adam   Rank: Private   Military Certificate number: LO 8311-12

Rejected or Suspended Applications for Revolutionary War Pensions; Reprinted for Clearfield Company Inc. by Genealogical Publishing Co., Inc., Baltimore, MD, 1998. p.407.
A list of persons residing in Indiana who have applied for pensions under the act of July 7, 1832, whose claims have been suspended; prepared in conformity with the resolution of the Senate of the United States, September 16, 1850.

Names	Residence	Reason for suspension
Fox, Adam	Versailles, Ripley	Service short of six months.

Bockstruck, Lloyd DeWitt; *Revolutionary War Bounty Land Grants Awarded by State Governments;* Genealogical Publishing Co., IN, Baltimore, MD, 1996, p. 186.
Fox, Adam. Va. Private. 24 Jul. 1835. 100 acres.

Margaret R. Waters; *Revolutionary Soldiers Buried in Indiana (1949) With Supplement (1954) Two Volumes in One;* Genealogical Publishing Company, Baltimore, MD, 1970, p. 37.
FOX, ADAM   Ripley
b. 7-16-1764, Frederick Co., Md.; mar.; chn. (at least): Jacob. Pens Appl. 8-12-1837, ae. 75, Ripley Co., Ind. After War liv. Frederick Co., Md; Augusta Co., Va., ca 27 yr.; Knox Co., O., ca. 4 yr.; Ripley Co., Ind. Affid. of Ninian Beall ("Roster" p. 54). Letter 4-30-1887 from son, Jacob Fox, Cincinnati, O.; mother dead. Service: enl. ae 15-16 yr., while liv. with Col. Joseph Wood in Frederick Co., Md., as subst. for Henry Reede (sp?), Oct. 1779, Capt. Valentine Cregger (Cregor?). REF: Pens. R.3721 Md.; Rej. Pens. List, p. 407—did not serve 6 mos.

O'Byrne, Mrs. Roscoe C., comp.; *Roster of Soldiers and Patriots of the American Revolution Buried in Indiana, Vol. II;* Indiana Daughters of the American Revolution, 1980, p. 40-41.
FOX, ADAM   Ripley County
Born – July 16, 1764, Frederick Co., Md.
Service – Enl., age 15 or 16 yrs., while living with Col. Joseph Wood in Frederick Co., Md, as a substitute for Henry Reede (?), Oct. 1779. Capt. Valentine Creeger (Cregor).
Proof – Pens. R. 3721, Md. Did not serve 6 mos. Appl. for pension Aug. 12, 1837, age 75, Ripley Co., Ind.
Married – Had son Jacob.
From Water's Sup., p. 37.

Gibbs, A.; *Ripley County Historical Society Data on Revolutionary Soldiers,* 1973 review.
Exact location of marker: no further information on grave site

GIBSON, WILBOURNE

Patriot: Wilbourne Gibson
Birth: 1763 NC
Married Spouse 1: 1783, NC   Rebecca (- 3 Mar 1839)
Service state(s): NC
Rank: Private
Proof of Service: Pension application
Pension application No.: R4000
Residences: Randolph Co., NC; OH; IN; now Ripley Co., IN
Died: 4 Apr 1843   Ripley Co., IN
Buried: Unknown
DAR Ancestor No.: None as of 7 Jun 2017.
Child: Daughter, Mary Ann Lewis, assigned Power of Attorney (Pension file).

Pension Application Abstracted from National Archives microfilm Series M804, Roll 1067, File R4000.
Pension abstract for – Wilbourne Gibson
Service state(s): NC
Date: 10 May 1838
County of: Ripley   State of: IN
Declaration made before a Judge or Court: Probate Court
Act of: 7 Jun 1832
Age: 75 yrs. last Jan   Record of age: It was recorded in my father's Bible which is long ago worn out and destroyed
Where and year born: Guilford Co., NC   1763
Residence when he entered service: Randolph Co., NC
Residence(s) since the war: Randolph Co., NC; OH; IN; now Ripley Co., IN
Residence now: Ripley Co., IN
Volunteer, Drafted, or Substitute: Drafted
Rank(s): Private
Statement of service-

Period	Duration	Names of General and Field Officers
Spring 1781	3 mos.	Capt. John Knight, Col. Dugan,

Battles: "Menden Hall's mill [Battle of Lindley's Mill]
Discharge received: Yes
Signed by: Capt. John Knight
What became of it?: "considering it of no value or importance whatever and being totally unlearned It has long ago been lost and destroyed"
Person now living who can testify to service: knows of no person living by whom he can prove his service – that he has for years past been endeavoring to procure such testimony but cannot succeed – his officers were old men mostly and those of his acquaintance who were known to him are all dead or gone where he is unable to hear from them.
Clergyman: John Ruby
Persons in neighborhood who certify character and reputation as soldier:
      Mr. Ruby, Mr. Griggs, Mr. Dadly, Mr. Davis.
[Note: Claim was Rejected because he did not serve six months.]

&
Power of Attorney assigned to obtain a pension
Assigners: Mary Ann Lewis, daughter of solider;
& George Lewis, son-in-law
Date: 19 Oct 1852
Declaration made before a Judge or Court: Probate Court
Statement: They are the Heirs of Wilburn Gilbson who was a Revolutionary Soldier in the State of North Carolina and that he died on the 4th day of April 1843and that Mary Ann Lewis' mother, named Rebecca Gibson died on the 3rd March 1839 and they were married on the – day of – in the year 1783 and they were residents of the State of North Carolina and that they resided there -------- years, and that they affiants reside in Ripley County Ind. and that furthermore By These Presents, constitute, appoint, and fully empower, and authorize, irrevocably and with powers of substitution, F. E. Hassler, of Washington city, D.C., as our true and lawful Attorney for us an in our name and stead, to examine into, to prosecute, to demand, and to receive from the U. S. Government and State officers our rights in all and any manner of claim for increase or arrears of Pension or Land that may be due us as Heirs of Wilburn Gibson who died leaving the same undrawn, as in right of law he may be entitled.
[Note: response is not in the file.]

Rejected or Suspended Applications for Revolutionary War Pensions; Reprinted for Clearfield Company Inc. by Genealogical Publishing Co., Inc., Baltimore, MD, 1998. p.407.
A list of persons residing in Indiana who have applied for pensions under the act of July 7, 1832, whose claims have been suspended; prepared in conformity with the resolution of the Senate of the United States, September 16, 1850.

Names	Residence	Reason for suspension
Gibson, Wilbourne	Versailles, Ripley	He did not serve six months.

Toph, Violet E.; Peoples History of Ripley County, Indiana; self-published, c. 1940, p. 131.
Revolutionary Soldiers Who Came to Ripley County
Wilbourne Gibson entered the service from North Caroline in 1781 and served three months. He was born in 1763 and died April 4, 1843. He applied for a pension from Ripley County, Ind. in 1838.

O'Byrne, Mrs. Roscoe C., comp. & ed.; Roster Soldiers and Patriots of the American Revolution Buried in Indiana; Published by Indiana Daughters of the American Revolution, 1938, Reprinted Genealogical Publishing Co., Baltimore MD, 1968, p. 155.
GIBSON, WILBOURNE (WELLBORN)   Ripley County
Born – 1763.
Service – Entered service from N.C. in 1781, served 3 mos.
Proof – Pension claim R. 4000.
Died – April 4, 1843, Ripley Co., Ind.
Collected by Mrs. A. B. Wycoff, Batesville, Indiana.

Gibbs, A.; Ripley County Historical Society Data on Revolutionary Soldiers, 1973 review.
Exact location of marker: no further information on grave site
Additional comments: on Court House tablet.

GOOKINS, SAMUEL

Patriot: Samuel Gookins
Birth: 19 Sep 1762 CT
Married Spouse 1: 13 Mar 1786 Pawlet, VT Polly/Mary Andrus
(b. 4 Mar 1764 Norwich, CT - d. 13 Jun 1848 Delaware Twp., Ripley Co., IN)
Service state(s): CT
Rank: Private
Proof of Service: Pension application W10064
Pension application No.: W10064
Residences: Danbury, Fairfield Co., CT; Rutland Co., VT; Ontario Co., NY; Ripley Co., IN
Died: 11 Dec 1842 Delaware Twp., Ripley Co., IN
Buried: Gookins Family cemetery, Delaware Twp., Ripley Co., IN
DAR Ancestor No.: A045930

Pension Application Abstracted from National Archives microfilm Series 805, Roll 365, File W10064.
Pension abstract for – Samuel Gookins Service state(s): Connecticut
Date: 19 Aug 1820
County of: Ontario State of: New York
Declaration made before a Court of the Common Pleas
Age: 58
Residence(s) since the war: Sussex, Hartford Co., CT, now Ontario Co., NY
Residence now: Freeport, Ontario Co., NY
Volunteer or Drafted or Substitute: Not stated
Rank(s): Private
Statement of service-

Period	Duration	Names of General and Field Officers
Spring 1777	until June 1783	Capt. Samuel Granger, Col. Clarke Well's [3rd] regt. of Connecticut line. Transferred to Col. Samuel B. Well's regt. CT line.

Battles: Stony Point
Discharge received: Regularly discharged
&
Widow's application for pension –
Date: 19 May 1843
County of: Ripley State of: Indiana
Declaration made before a Judge. Due to bodily infirmity she is unable to appear in court.
Soldier died: 4 Dec 1842, in Delaware Twp., Ripley Co., IN.
Widow's name: Polly Gookins Age: 79
Marriage date and place: 1 March 1886 in Pollet, Rutland Co., VT
Proof of marriage: On 1 Sep 1843, Asa Gookins, resident of Ripley Co., IN, makes oath that he is the fourth child of Samuel & Polly Gookins, they had seven children all living. He provides a copy of Family Record from a Bible now in his hands. Record lists these children – Naomi Gookins, b. Oct. 11, 1785; Lydia

Gookins, b. Aug'st. 19, 1788; Anna Gookins, b. March 10, 1791; Asa Gookins, b. August 26, 1795; Samuel Gookins, b. January 25, 1797; Polley Gookins, b. May 21st, 1801; Olive Gookins b. March 22th, 1803.

Abstract of Final Payment Voucher; General Services Administration, Washington, DC
FINAL PAYMENT VOUCHER RECEIVED FROM
THE GENERAL ACCOUNTING OFFICE
NAME   Gookins, Samuel
AGENCY OF PAYMENT   Indiana
DATE OF ACT   1818
DATE OF PAYMENT   3rd Qr. 1843
DATE OF DEATH   Dec. 11, 1842
GENERAL SERVICES ADMINISTRATION
National Archives and Records Service   NA-286
GSA-WASH DC 54-4891   November 1953

Revolutionary War Service Records; National Archives Publication number M881, *Compiled service records of soldiers who served in the American Army during the Revolutionary War, 1775-1783.*
https://www.fold3.com/image/14700467?terms=Gookins,%20Samuel%20CT
3 Connecticut Regiment, Light Infantry, commanded by Col. Samuel B. Webb.
Gookins, Samuel – Private; Feb, 1783-Mar 13, 83; Mar 83-Apr 28, 83; Apr 1, 83- May 26, 83.

Adjutants-General, by the Authority of the General Assembly, comp.; Record of Service of Connecticut Men in the I. War of the Revolution; The Case, Lockwood & Brainard Company Printers and Binders, Hartford, CT, 1889, p. 162, 353, 642.
p. 162.
Regiments, "Connecticut Line," 1777-1781.

Names	Company	Date of Enlistment	Term	Remarks
Privates				
Gookins, Samuel	Granger	Apr. 26, "77	War	-

p. 353.
Regiments, "Connecticut Line," 1777-1781.
Captain Welles' Company
("Pay abstract of the Officers and Privates who were at the Southward, under Command of the Marquis de la Fayette in Capt. Roger Welle's Company drafted from the 3d Connecticut Regt., and were charged with one month's pay of new Continental Emission in stateing their accounts for the year 1781, which charge was ordered by the Gen' Assembly in Jan. 1783, to be deducted and to be so part of their three month's pay."
Captain   Roger Welles   Wethersfield   Slightly wounded at assault or redoubt
Lieutenant   William Lynn   Killingsworth
Ensign   Jacob Kinsbury Norwich
Privates

Names and Rank
Samuel Gookins
p. 642.
Connecticut Pensioners, Act of 1818, Residing in New York

Name	Rank, etc.
Samuel Gookins	Priv.

Connecticut Historical Society; <u>Collections of the Connecticut Historical Society, Vol. III</u>; facsimile reprint, Heritage Books, Inc., Bowie, MD, 1995, p. 53, 121.
p. 53.
Connecticut Line, 1777-1781; Second Regiment – Col. Butler; Return 1779.
Return of Lieut Coloney Halts Company in the 2nd Connecticut Regiment of Foot Commanded by Zebulon Butler Esq. Col. of the Non Commis. Officrs and Soldiers who are engaged for the war Dec. 12th 79.
[Included in list]   Sam Gookins   Suffield
p. 121.
Connecticut Line, 1781-1783; Light Infantry, 1781.
Pay abstract of the Infantry who Marched to the Southard under the Command of Marq. De la Fayette and were Omitted in the Abstract for February 1781.
Infantry Co.

Names	Rank	Fro	To
[Included in list]			
Samuel Gookins	Priv.	Feb. 1	Mar. 1

Connecticut Historical Society; <u>Lists and Returns of Connecticut Men in the Revolution, 1775-1783, Vol. XII</u>; Connecticut Historical Society, 1909; facsimile reprint Heritage Books, 2008, p. 306, 328, 352.
p. 306.
Connecticut Line, 1781-1783;
p. 306.
Light Infantry Company – Capt. Welles.
(The muster rolls of this company for February, May, June, July, September and October 1782 as preserved. Only the earlies of these is here copied, with such changes noted as appear on any of the later rolls.)
Muster Roll of Capt. Roger Welles's Company of Light Infantry in the 3d Connecticut Regiment in the Service of the United States Commanded by Col. B. Webb, For the Month of Feb'r 1782.

Inlisted	Term		Notes
Included in list –			
Dec. 22 - 1780	D.W. [Duration War]	Sam'l Gookins	-

p. 328.
Connecticut Line, 1783; Third Regiment – Col. Webb.
Light Infantry Company – Capt. Welles.

Roll and Muster of the Light Infantry Company in the 3rd Regiment of Connecticut Troops Commanded by Col. Sam. B. Webb.

Ranks	Names	Term of Enlistment	
Privates	Samuel Gookins	DW	[Duration of War]

p. 352.
Connecticut Line, 1781-1783; Connecticut Line – Hartford County Returns.
A List of Names of Men taken from the Returns from the Continental Army & those Claim'd by & allow'd to the Several Towns by the Committee for Hartford County.
Those below not Return'd from the Army
    Suffield
[Included in list]
Sam'l Gookins

Senate Documents, Vol.9, No. 988, 63rd Congress, 3d Session, Washington, 1915; "Register of Certificates Issued by John Pierce, Esquire, Paymaster General and Commissioner of Army Accounts for the United States, to Officers and Soldiers of the Continental Army Under Act of July 4, 1783"; *Seventeenth report of the National Society of the Daughters of the American Revolution;* Genealogical Publishing Co., Inc., Baltimore, MD, 1984. p. 207.
Men listed in this volume with the same name.

No. of Certificate	To whom issued	Amount
4092	Gookin, Samuel	49.26
4461	Gookins, Samuel	80.00
2421	Gookins, Samuel	4.52

Vermont Vital Records, 1760-1954; State Capitol Building, Montpelier; accessed 11 April 2016 from https://familysearch.org/ark:/61903/1:1:XFFG-Z36
Name: Samuel Gookins
Event Type: Marriage
Event Date: 13 Mar 1786
Event Place: Rupert, Vermont, United States
Gender: Male
Spouse's Name: Polly Andrus
Spouse's Gender: Female
GS Film Number: 27461
Digital Folder Number: 004542939; Image Number: 00389
FHL microfilm 27,461.

U.S. Department of Interior, Bureau of Land Management, General Land Office Records; Land Patent Search – accessed 27 June 2012.
GOOKINS, SAMUEL
Accession Nr. CV-0087-396; Document Type – Credit Volume Patent; Issue Date – 9/6/1831; Cancelled – No
Names on Document: Crowley, Ellis; Gookins, Samuel; Craig, George
Land Office – Jeffersonville; authority – April 24, 1820 Sale-Cash Entry (3 Stat. 566); Document Nr. 2644; Total Acres – 160.00

Land Descriptions: State – IN; Meridian – 2nd PM; Twp-Rng – 009N-012E; Aliquots – SW1/4; Section – 28; County - Ripley
&
Accession Nr. IN2750_.005; Document Type – State Volume Patent; State – Indiana; Issue Date – 8/1/1839; Cancelled – No
Names on Document: Gookins, Samuel
Land Office – Jeffersonville; Authority – April 24, 1820 Sale-Cash Entry (3 Stat. 566); Document Nr. 1346; BLM Serial Nr. – In No S/N; Total Acres – 80.00
Land Descriptions:

State	Meridian	Twp-Rng	Aliquots	Section	County
IN	2nd PM	009N-012E	SW1/4NW1/4		32
	Ripley				
IN	2nd PM	009N-012E	NW1/4SW1/4		32
	Ripley				

Ripley County Indiana, Recorder's Office, Tract Book 3, p. 75.
Gookins, Samuel   15 Apr 1837   R12, T9, S32   40 acres

Ripley County, Indiana Deed Records Vol. C., 21 Sep 1832 - 4 Feb 1834,
Page 287-288.
Abstract of Deed/Patent for: Samuel Gookins of Ripley County
Purchaser (Grantee) or Seller (Grantor)?: Seller
Sold to: George Craig of Switzerland County
State & county where recorded: Ripley Co., Indiana
Date entered: 4 Aug 1832
Recorded: 13 Oct 1832
Description: Said lot is the west part of the southwest quarter of Section 29, in
        Township 9, North of Range 12 East of the lands directed to be sold at
Jeffersonville, containing one hundred ten acres.
Amount paid: Two hundred dollars ($200.00).
Name(s) of Witnesses: Samuel Gookins Jr., Elias Jenison, Asa Gookins

Ripley County, Indiana Deed Records Vol. C., 21 Sep 1832 - 4 Feb 1834,
Page 360-361.
Abstract of Deed/Patent for: Samuel Gookins
Purchaser (Grantee) or Seller (Grantor)?: Purchaser
Purchased from: George Craig & Jane B. Craig (dower) his wife
State & county where recorded: Ripley Co., Indiana
Date entered: 3 Aug 1832
Recorded: 4 Aug 1832
Description: All that tract or parcel of land; said lot in the East part of the south west quarter of Section 20, in Township 9 North of Range 12 East, of the lands directed to be sold at the Jeffersonville Land Office; containing 110 acres.
Amount paid: Three hundred dollars ($300.00)
Name(s) of Witnesses: James Eaton & Uzal Cory

Ripley County, Indiana Deed Records Vol. D., 7 Feb 1834 - 9 Feb 1836,
Page 386-387.

Abstract of Deed/Patent for: Samuel Gookins, the wife being departed
Purchaser (Grantee) or Seller (Grantor)?: Seller
Sold to: Ellis Crowley
State & county where recorded: Ripley Co., Indiana
Date entered: 10 Nov 1834
Recorded: 16 Nov 1835
Description: Tract or parcel of land in the South West half of the South West quarter of Section 28, Township 9 North of Range 12 East; sold at Jeffersonville; containing 80 acres.
Amount paid: One hundred dollars ($100.00)
Name(s) of Witnesses: H. Fisher & Asa Gookins

1830 U. S. Census, Ripley County, IN; Series M19, Roll 32; p. 5, line 14.
Samuel Gookins
Males 30-39=1, Males 60-69=1, Females 20-49=1.

The Pension Roll of 1835 Volume IV, The Mid-Western States, Indexed Edition, *In Four Vo13 Oct 1832lumes; Genealogical Publishing Co., Inc., Baltimore, MD, Reprint 1968, p. 51.*
Statement, &c. of Ripley county, Indiana.

INDIANA Names	Rank	Annual allow- ance.	Sums re- ceived	Description of service
Samuel Gookins	Private	96.00	1,525 29	Connecticut line

When placed on pension roll	Commencement of pension	Ages	Laws under which they were formerly placed on the pension roll; and remarks.
Mar 23, 1819	Ap'l 15, 1818	72	Transferred from Ontario county, New York

A Census of Pensioners for Revolutionary or Military Services with their Names, Ages, and Places of Residence Under the Act for Taking the Sixth Census in 1840; Genealogical Publishing Co., Inc., Baltimore, Maryland, 1965, p.184.
INDIANA, RIPLEY COUNTY, DELAWARE

Names of Pensioners for Revolutionary or Military services	Ages	Names of heads of families with whom pensioner resided June 1, 1840
Samuel Gookins	78	Asa Gookins

Ripley Co., IN Probate Order Book, Vol. B. 8 May 1837-17 Aug 1843, p. 471.
Be it remembered that on this 2d day of September A.D. 1843 comes George Osborn of the Subscribing witnesses to the last Will and Testament of Samuel Gookins late of the County of Ripley & State of Indiana, and files his affidavit in proof the Same and the same is entered & Recorded in the Will Book of the Ripley Probate Court by me.   Conrad Overturf, Clerk

Ripley County, Indiana Will Records vol. B, June 1839-May 1862; p. 40.
&
Ripley County Indiana Probate Order Book B, 8 May 1837-17 Aug 1843; p. 471.
Abstract of will and administration for: Samuel Gookins
Date and place will was made: 18 Feb 1833, Delaware Twp., Ripley Co., IN
Witnesses to will: George Osborn
Place of death: Delaware Twp., Ripley Co., IN
Date recorded: 2 Sep 1843
Names of heirs and others mentioned in will and relationship: Son, Asa Gookins
    I give and bequeath unto my son Asa Gookins the tract or parcel of land on which I know live it being the West part of the South West quarter of Section twenty nine Township nine range twelve East of the lands offered for sale at Jeffersonville; containing one hundred and ten acres.

O'Byrne, Mrs. Roscoe C., comp. & ed.; Roster Soldiers and Patriots of the American Revolution Buried in Indiana; Published by Indiana Daughters of the American Revolution, 1938, Reprinted Genealogical Publishing Co., Baltimore MD, 1968, p. 160.
GOOKINS, SAMUEL   Switzerland County
Born – Sept. 19, 1762, Suffolk, Connecticut
Service – Enlisted April 26, 1777, for the term of the war in Capt. Samuel Granger's CO., 2nd Regt. Conn. Line, Col. Chas. Webb. Was later in Cpt. Roger Well's CO., 3rd Conn. Line, Col. Samuel B. Webb.
Proof – Family records furnished by Mrs. Clara Gookins Scherer.
Died – Dec. 4, 1842. Buried in family cemetery, Delaware Twp., Ripley Co. Stone. Name on bronze tablet in Versailles Court House.
Grandchildren of Soldier – Samuel; Lydia; William.
Collected by Mrs. A. B. Wycoff, Batesville, Indiana.

Patricia Law Hatcher; Abstract of Graves of Revolutionary Patriots (4 volumes); Pioneer Heritage Press, Dallas, TX, 1987, Vol. 2, p. 83.
This is an abstract and an index to information reported to the Daughters of the American Revolution and published in their annual reports to the Smithsonian Institution, printed as Senate Documents (1900-1974) and published annually in the DAR magazine (1978-1987).
Published 1977.
GOOKINS, Samuel Fam cem, Rt 48, Delaware Twp., Ripley Co IN

Toph, Violet E.; Peoples History of Ripley County, Indiana; self-published, c. 1940, p. 121-122, 132.
Revolutionary Soldiers Who Came to Ripley County
p. 121-122.
Mrs. Clara E. Gookins, a relative of Samuel Gookins, also a Revolutionary soldier, and of Joseph Hennegin, said this of these soldiers: " How very young both of these soldiers were at the time they enlisted. Samuel Gookins was less than fifteen years old. Joseph Hennegan was only eighteen years old. The boys of these days are not husky like they were in olden times. They did not have the diet they live on now and grew stronger".

The following Revolutionary Claim Document is in the War Memorial Museum a Versailles, Ind.

"I certify that in conformity with the law of the United States of the 18th of March 1818, Samuel Gookins late private in the army of the Revolution is inscribed on the pension role of the New York Agency, at the rate of eight dollars per month to commence on the fifteenth day of April one thousand eight hundred and eighteen.

Given at the War office of the United States this twenty-third day of March one thousand eight hundred and nineteen.   J. C. Calhoun, Secretary of State

Know all men by these presents that I, Samuel Gookins of Ripley County and State of Indiana, a Revolutionary pensioner of the United States of America, do hereby constitute and appoint James Ranstead my true and lawful attorney for and in my name to receive for me the agent of the United States for paying the pension of invalids in the State of Indiana my pension from the 14th day of March 1825 to the 4th day of September, 1825. Witness my hand and seal this – day of September, 1825.   Sealed and delivered in the presence of -

State of Indiana, Ripley County, SS.

Be it known that before me Adolpaus Huggins, Justice of the Peace, in the county aforesaid personally appeared Samuel Gookins above named and acknowledged the foregoing power of attorney to be his act and deed; in testimony whereof I have hereunto set my hand and seal the day and year last above mentioned.

Be it known that before me Adolphus Huggins Esq, Justice of the Peace in the county aforesaid, personally appeared Samuel Gookins named in the original certificate in his possesson of which the above is a copy that he is entitled to a pension of eight dollars per month for services rendered in the United States during the Revolutionary War, that he now resides in Ripley County and State of Indiana and has resided there for the last two years, previous thereto he resided in the State of New York.

James Ranstead, the attorney, named in the within mentioned power of attorney appeared and made oath that the same was not given to him by request of any Sale, transfer or mortgage of the pension or arrears of pension herein authorized to be received by him.   Sworn to and subscribed the day and year last above mentioned.   JP

p. 132.

Samuel Gookins was born Sept. 19, 1762. He enlisted April 26, 1777 for the term of the War in Captain Samuel Grainger's Company of the 2nd Regiment Connecticut Line Commanded by Charles Webb. Later due to consolidation of certain Connecticut lines regiments he seems to have been in Captain Roger Wells' company of the 3rd Connecticut Line under col. Samuel B. Webb and was in Gimats' Battalion of that regiment at the Battle of Yorktown which led in the assault upon the works of the British. He lived at Suffolk, Conn at the time of the War but later lived at Rupert, Vermont. Before coming to Indiana he lived in New York State. He died in Ripley County, Ind. Dec. 4, 1842 and is buried on the old Gookins farm still owned by his descendant Miss Lydia Gookins near Lookout, Ind.   Mrs. Clara E. Gookins Scherer, Batesville, R.1, Ind.

Brakebill, Clovis H. (comp. & ed.), <u>National Society of the Sons of the American Revolution - Revolutionary War Graves Register</u>; db Publications, Dallas, TX, 1993, p. 246.
Gookins Samuel; ?-?; Old Gookins Family Cem, W fr Lookout, [Ripley Co.], IN

Gibbs, A.; <u>Ripley County Historical Society Data on Revolutionary Soldiers</u>, 1973 review.
Exact location of marker: 8/10 th mi. west of Lookout, Ind. on Rt. 48, in back of Drockelman place, about 1/8 mi. from road. Old Gookins family cemetery. Delaware Tw. Ripley Co. Ind.
Type of marker: Gov't (upright); & family marker
Date placed: 7 Nov 1976(Gov't); time of death (family)
Placed by: Ross' Run Chapter Daughters of the American Revolution;
    by Hill Monument Co.
Additional comments: on Court House tablet
   Toph noted: less than 15yr old at time of enlistment
   His will: Ripley Co. Wills Book B, p. 40
   1840 census Ripley Co., p. 200, Samuel Gookins age 78

Wording on DAR marker:
        Samuel Gookins
        Conn Line
        Rev. War
        Sept 14, 1762
        Dec 4, 1842
Wording on family marker:
        Samuel Gookins
       Soldier of the Revolution
        d. Dec. 4, 1842
       age 80yr 2mo 15da
      A Patriot's Dust Lies Here

GRIMES, JAMES

Patriot: James Grimes
Birth: 1764 County Down, North Ireland
Married Spouse 1: Isabella X (- prob 1833)
Service state(s): VA Militia & VA Continental Line
Rank: Private, Orderly Sergeant
Proof of Service: Pension application
Pension application No.: S17455
Residences: Augusta Co., VA; Rockingham Co., VA; KY;
　　　　　　 Ripley Co., IN
Died: 11 Nov 1833　　Ripley Co., IN
Buried: Old Washington Church Cemetery, Washington Twp.,
　　　　 Ripley Co., IN
DAR Ancestor No.: A201803

Pension Application Abstracted from National Archives microfilm Series M804, Roll 1135, File S17455.
Pension abstract for – James Grimes
Service state(s): VA
Date: 23 Aug 1832
County of: Ripley　　　　　　　　　　State of: IN
Declaration made before a Judge or Court: Circuit Court
Act of: 7 Jun 1832　　　　　　　　　　Age: 78 yrs.
Record of age: No record, can only speak from what my parents told me.
Where and year born: County of Down in North Ireland　　1754
Residence when he entered service: Augusta Co., VA
Residence(s) since the war: Rockingham Co., VA; KY; last 12 yrs. in
　　　　　　　　　　　　　　Ripley Co., IN
Residence now: Ripley Co. IN
Volunteer, Drafted, or Substitute: Drafted
Rank(s): Private, Orderly Sergeant
Statement of service-

Period	Duration	Names of General and Field Officers
1777-1781	18 mos. as Pvt. & 6 mos. as Ord. Sgt	VA Militia under Gen, Mulenburgh, Col. [VA Continental, 13 Regt. of Foot, aka West Augusta Volunteers] Benjamin Harrison, Capt. George Houston, Lt. Shanklin

Battles: Battle of Burnt Chimnis, Williamsburgh
Discharge received: Never received a discharge
Statement is supported by –
Documentary proof: None
Names of Regular Officers: I was acquainted with Gen. Anthony Wayne &
　　　　　　　　　　　　　Gen. Morgan
Persons in neighborhood who certify character: Joseph Richard, Esq. Lippard,
　　　　　　　　　　　　　　　　　　　　　　John Bell & many others
Death of soldier: 11 Nov 1833

Abstract of Final Payment Voucher; General Services Administration, Washington, DC
FINAL PAYMENT VOUCHER RECEIVED FROM
THE GENERAL ACCOUNTING OFFICE
NAME   GRIMES, JAMES
AGENCY OF PAYMENT   INDIANA
DATE OF ACT   1832
DATE OF PAYMENT   2d Qt. 1834
DATE OF DEATH   Nov. 12, 1833
GENERAL SERVICES ADMINISTRATION
National Archives and Records Service   NA-286
GSA-WASH DC 54-4891   November 1953

Gwathmey, John H.; Historical Register of Virginians in the Revolution, Soldiers, Sailors, Marines, 1775-1783; The Dietz Press, Richmond, VA, 1938, p. 329, 332.
p. 329.
Grimes, James, 80, Ripley Co., Ind., mpl. [Militia Pension List. Compiled from a report of the Secretary of War in 1835, "Pensions", Volume II, of men receiving pensions for services as Virginia Militiamen.]
Grimes, James, 1 VA. State Reg., 3 CL, 3 and 4 CL, 3 and 7 CL. Rom. [A list of militia paid at Romney in 1775. It is probable that these were Colonial troops late in receiving their pay. It is noted that practically all of them immediately joined the army of the Revolution.]
p. 332.
Grymes, James (Grimes) 1 Va. State Reg.

McAllister, J.T.; Virginia Militia in the Revolutionary War; McAllister Publishing Co., Hot Springs, VA, 1913, Part V.
Alphabetical List of Pensioners Residing Outside of Virginia in 1835, whose Pensions were Granted for Services as Virginia Militiamen.
This list was compiled from a repot made by the Secretary of War in 1835. The ages are those given in that report, and are believed to be the ages of the pensioners in 1835. The names of the pensioners in what is now West Virginia are embraced under Part IV.
Grimes, James   80   Ripley   IN

Virginia Military Records from the Virginia Magazine of History and Biography, the William and Mary College Quarterly, and Tyler's Quarterly; Genealogical Publishing Co., Baltimore, MD, 1983, p. 785.
List of Officers, Sailors and Marines of the Va. Navy in the American Revolution, from VMHB, Vol. I (1893), 64-75.
Non-Commissioned Officers, Seamen and Marines of the State Navy.
In list is –   Grymes, James,   Ord'y   Seaman

[In his pension application he indicated he lived in KY, but did not say what county. He was likely one of the men on the following list. – mjm]

Clift, G. Glens, Assistant Secretary, Kentucky Historical Society, Comp.; "Second Census" of Kentucky – 1800, A Privately Compiled and Published Enumeration of Tax Payers Appearing in the 79 Manuscript Volumes Extant of Tax Lists of the 42 Counties of Kentucky in Existence in 1800; Genealogical Publishing Co., Baltimore, MD, 1966, p. 117.

Name	County	Tax List Date	
Grimes, James	Fayette		1800
Grimes, James	Fleming	8/11/	1800
Grimes, James	Fleming	8/11/	1800
Grimes, James	Garrard		1800
Grimes, James	Washington		1800
Grimes, James, Jr.	Fleming	8/11	1800
Grimes, James, Jr.	Logan	8/26	1800
Grimes, James Sr.	Logan	8/26/	1800
Grymes, James	Montgomery	8/22/	1800

1830 U. S. Census, Ripley County, IN; Series M19, Roll 32; p. 12, line 2.
James Grimes
Males 15-19=1, Males 70-79=1, Females 70-79=1.

Ripley County, Indiana Deed Records Vol. D., 7 Feb 1834 - 9 Feb 1836, Page 74-75.
Abstract of Deed/Patent for: James Grimes
Purchaser (Grantee) or Seller (Grantor)?: Purchaser
Purchased from: Joacum Williamson & Elizabeth (dower) his wife
State & county where recorded: Ripley Co., Indiana
Date entered: 7 Dec 1833
Recorded: 16 Jun 1834
Description: Tract or parcel of land lying in the North East corner of the South West quarter of Section 24, Township 7 North of Range 12 East; containing 60 acres.
Amount paid: Eighty dollars ($80.00)
Name(s) of Witnesses: Edward Pendergast & John Cavender

The Pension Roll of 1835 Volume IV, The Mid-Western States, Indexed Edition, In Four Volumes; Genealogical Publishing Co., Inc., Baltimore, MD, Reprint 1968, p. 87.
Statement, &c. of Ripley county, Indiana.

INDIANA Names	Rank	Annual allow- ance.	Sums re- ceived	Description of service
James Grimes	Private	80.00	-	Virginia militia

When placed on pension roll	Commencement of pension	Ages	Laws under which they were formerly placed on the pension roll; and remarks.
Mar. 25, 1833	March 4, 1831	80	Died November 11, 1833.

Ripley Co., IN, Probate Order Book, Vol. A, 19 Nov 1818-Feb. 1837, p. 147.
February Term, 1834
Isabella Grimes now appeared in open Court & proved to the satisfaction of the Court that she is the widow of James Grimes Deceased & that he died on the 12th day of November 1833. This she proves in order to obtain the Balance of Pension due her 3d Husband.

Toph, Violet E.; Peoples History of Ripley County, Indiana; self-published, c. 1940, p. 122-123, 128.
Revolutionary Soldiers Who Came to Ripley County
James Grimes entered the service in 1777 from Virginia and served two years. He last resided near Versailles, Indiana. James Grimes came with his family to Indiana in 1816 and settled in Ripley County. He lived until 1841, died and was buried in the old Washington Cemetery in Washington Township in Ripley County.
His son John Grimes was born in Virginia about 1790. He came with his father to Kentucky then to Indiana. John Grimes was a soldier in the War of 1812 and the Harrison Indian War and was present at Tippecanoe in 1811.
John Grimes married Mary McDonald, daughter of Joseph McDonald who served in Colonel Thomas Clark's company in the First North Carolina Regiment. He enlisted July 1, 1777 for three years and his name is last borne on a return dated March 12, 1779. He is buried in the Old Washington cemetery near James Grimes.
To John and Mary McDonald were born Thomas, James, Henry, Joseph, John W. and Samuel Grimes, six sons, all but Thomas born in Indiana. Also three daughters Rachel, Elizabeth, and Mary, who died unmarried at the age of sixteen. Rachel married Jacob Green and Elizabeth married Thornton Rogers. All but Mary lived to a ripe old age and had large families.
The Grimes family is of North Ireland stock and probably migrated from the Clan Graham in early history as the member of the Grhams (Grames or Grimes).
The Pension Records will show that James Grimes and Joseph McDonald received pensions up to about 1840 from Ripley County, Ind. The McDonalds came from Fredericktown, Maryland and Joseph was a Scotchman by birth and came down to Maysville, Ky. in Indian times and from Kentucky to Indiana.
The forebearer of James Grimes was probably born in Virginia of Irish parentage. The writer has no record of the size of James Grimes Sr's family except that James, a second brother of John Sr. moved to Missouri in early days. Except that one daughter Betsy married Jack McKittrick of Ripley County. This sketch of the Grimes was given by Rev. Walter B. Grimes, 4906 Manlove Ave. Indianapolis, Ind., son of John W. Grimes, and Pastor of Bellaire M.E Church. Walter B. Grimes was formerly of Ripley County.
p. 128.
In July, 1936, the Ripley County Historical Society, aided by subscriptions from descendants of the five Revolutionary soldiers buried in Old Washington cemetery, Edward Pendergast, Ninian Beall, James Grimes, Joseph McDonald and William Lipperd enclosed the cemetery with a durable wove wire fence and placed Government markers for each of the five soldiers, thus making a notable Revolutionary Shrine for Washington Township.

O'Byrne, Mrs. Roscoe C., comp. & ed.; Roster Soldiers and Patriots of the American Revolution Buried in Indiana; Published by Indiana Daughters of the American Revolution, 1938, Reprinted Genealogical Publishing Co., Baltimore MD, 1968, p. 165.

GRIMES, JAMES   Ripley County
Service – Enlisted in Virginia in 1777, 2 years.
Died – Nov. 11, 1833. Buried Old Washington Cemetery near Versailles, Ind. Government marker placed by Ripley Co. Hist. Society.
Married – Mary McDonald. Ch. John; Thomas; Henry; and probably others.
Collected by Mrs. A. B. Wycoff, Batesville, Indiana.

Gibbs, A.; Ripley County Historical Society Data on Revolutionary Soldiers, 1973 review.

Exact location of marker: east out of Elrod on 525 to 50N, right, to Thermon Boyd farm (1973); mile n.e. of house, going down across creek and up a hill; no road. Old Washington Cemetery north-east of Elrod, Washington Tw. Ripley Co. Ind.
Type of marker: Gov't
Date placed: Oct 1936 (minutes of R.C.H.S.)
Placed by: Ripley County Historical Society
Additional comments: on Court House tablet
Rev. Walter B. Grimes of Indianapolis, Ind. speaker at dedication of tablet in Court House, Versailles, Ind. on May 30, 1928, was a descendant of James Grimes.
Toph noted: lived in Versailles, Ind.
Probate A, p. 147, Feb 1834, widow appl. for pension (this negates the 1840 date on the tombstone). His wife Isabella says he died Nov. 12, 1833.
Wording on marker:

James Grimes
Pvt. Houston's Co.
Harrison's Va. Rgt.
Rev. War
1840

United States Headstone Applications for U.S. Military Veterans, 1925-1949, database with images; (https://familysearch.org/ark:/61903/1:1:VHZC-VCV : 17 May 2016); Affiliate Publication Number: M1916; Affiliate Publication Title: Applications for Headstones for U.S. Military Veterans, 1925-1941; Affiliate Film Number: 45; GS Film Number: 1878194; Digital Folder Number: 004832212; Image Number: 02103.

Application for Headstone; War Department O.Q.M.G. Form No. 623
Name: Grimes, James
Event Date: May 31, 1934
Name of Cemetery: Old Washington
Located in or near: Milan, Ind.
Death Date: not provided
Enlistment Dates: 1777

Discharge Dates: Served 2 years
Rank: Private
Company: Capt. George Houston's Co., Col. Benj. Harrison's VA Regt,
Virginia Line
To be shipped to: Ripley Co. Historical Society, Osgood, Ind., Ripley Co.
Whose post-office address is: Versailles, Ind.
This application is for the UNMARKED grave of a veteran. It is understood the stone will be furnished and delivered at the railroad station or steamboat landing above indicated, at Government expense, freight prepaid. I hereby agree to promptly accept the headstone at destination, remove it and properly place same at decedent's grave at my expense. Ripley Co. Historical Society, Applicant. No fee should be paid in connection with this application.
Applicant: Ripley Co. Historical Society, Versailles, Ind.

Tombstone Location: Old Washington Church Cemetery, Washington Twp., Ripley Co., IN

Tombstone Inscription:

JAMES
GRIMES
GEO. HOUSTON'S CO.
HARRISON'S VA REGT.
REV. WAR
[ILLEGIBLE]

HALL, BENJAMIN

Patriot: Benjamin Hall
Birth: Jun 1753   Hopkinton, Providence Co. [later Washington Co.], RI
Married Spouse 1: 1780-1790   Phebe (1753 – aft 10 Aug. 1833)
Service state(s): RI State Regiment & RI Continental
Rank: Private, Sergeant
Proof of Service: Pension application S32295
Pension application No.: R5362-1/2 & S32295
Residences: Hopkinton, Providence Co. (current Washington Co.), RI; NY;
    Switzerland Co., IN; Ripley Co., IN, Jefferson Co., IN
Died: Jan 1850 Jefferson Co., IN
Buried: Unknown
DAR Ancestor No.: A049461

Revolutionary War Service Records; National Archives Publication number M881, Compiled service records of soldiers who served in the American Army during the Revolutionary War, 1775-1783.
https://www.fold3.com/image/21649201?terms=Hall,%20BEnjamin%20RI
Topham's Regiment, New Jersey State Troops
Hall, Benjamin – Private –Appears in the Company Muster Roll of Capt. Benjn, West's Company, Col. John Topham's Regiment, now engaged in the service of the United States for twelve months from the 16th day of March, 1778. The organization taken to Tiverton.
Hall, Benjamin, Enlisted March 14, 1778; May 16, 1778; Jul 11, 78; Sep 13, 78-Oct 17, 78; Nov 10 ,78; Dec 6, 78; Jan 17, 79 on furlough; Feb 20, 79 on command.
&
1 and 2 Rhode Island Regiments Consolidated.
Hall, Benjamin – Private – 7th Company Rhode Island Reg't of Foot, Company Muster Roll; May, 1782-Jun 16, 82; Jun, 82-Jul 29, 82; Aug, 82-Sep 7, 82; Sep, 82- Oct 15, 82; Oct, Nov, Dec 82.

Note: There are two pension applications for Benjamin Hall that are entertwined.
It **appeared** that there are two men by the same name (see my book *Revolutionary Soldiers and Wives of Soldiers With Ties to Switzerland County Indiana*). After hours of analysis I am convinced the applications are for the **same man**. I base that conclusion on the fact that in both Pension Applications (R5362-1/2 and S32295) service is shown under Col. Angle/Angel & Capt. Elijah Lewis. Also, the probability that two men of the same name served in Rhode Island, and moved to the same area is unlikely.   mjm

Confusion regarding this man has continued for many years (see citations following). This statement, dated 23 Aug 1832, addressed to the Secretary of War, written by William C. Keen, of Printers Retreat, IN adds to the confusion:

Printers Retreat, Ind					Aug. 23, 1832
"Enclosed I send you the application of Benjamin Hall, (who now resides in Ripley County) for a pension made out in 1820. I am informed, also, that he made an application through O. H. Smith some 4 or 5 years since = you can compare those enclosed with those filed by Smith. He called on me a few days since to make out an application under the Act of Congress of June 7, 1832. His statement differs so widely that I declined sending it on. He may make application from Ripley, Dearborn, or Jefferson = if so, you will be enable to judge of his claims. I will copy his last statement, made to me, and forward it by next mail.		Yours, William C, Keen

Pension Application Abstracted from National Archives Microfilm Series 804, Roll 1158, File R5362-1/2.
Pension abstract for – Benjamin Hall
Alternative spelling: Hale
Service state(s):	RI
Date: 16 Oct 1819
County of: Switzerland				State of: IN
Declaration made before a Judge or Court: Circuit Court
		Act of: 18 Mar 1818
Age:	abt, 70 yrs.
Residence when he entered service: Not stated
Residence now: Switzerland Co., IN
Volunteer, Drafted, or Substitute:	1) Enlisted at Washington Co., RI;
					2) Enlisted in Eastern PA
Rank(s): Private
Statement of service-

Period	Duration	Names of General and Field Officers
Apr or May 1776 - 1779	3 yrs.	CT Line, Capt. Elijah Lewis, Col. John Angle.
Sep 1780 - end of war		In Eastern PA, Artillery under Maj. Ebenezer Adams. [Maj. RI troops]

Discharge received: 1) At White Plains by Col. John Angle
			2) In NY by Maj. Adams
&
Date: 28 Feb 1820
County of: Switzerland				State of: IN
Age:	70 yrs.
Residence now: Switzerland Co., IN
Volunteer, Drafted, or Substitute: 1) Enlisted in Rhode Island (crossed out),
					Massachusetts written above.
Rank(s): Private
Statement of service-

Period	Duration	Names of General and Field Officers
1) 9 /10 Dec 1776 - 1779	3 yrs.	RI Line, Capt. Elijah Lewis, Regt. commanded by Col. John Angle.

2) Sep 1780 –   In Eastern PA, artillery under Maj.
    End of war   Ebenezer Adams [Maj. RI troops],
commanded
                                                by (illegible).
Battles: 1) Stillwater, Trenton
Discharge received: 1) At King's Ferry, NY
                                2) City of New York
Note: Ralph Cotton, Judge, certified the first application was dated 16 Oct 1819.

Pension Application Abstracted from National Archives Microfilm Series 804, Roll 1158, File S32295.
Date: 18 Sep 1832
County of: Switzerland   State of: Indiana
Declaration made before: Circuit Court
Age: 80 years   Record of age: None
Where and year born: estimate 1752/1753
Residence when he entered service: Hopkinton, Little Neck Co., [Providence Co.] RI
Residence(s) since the war: none stated
Residence now: Ripley Co., IN
Volunteer or Drafted or Substitute: Volunteered (4th term as a substitute)
Rank: Private (poss. Sergeant)
Statement of service-

Period	Duration	Names of General and Field Officers
1st May or June 1775	8 mos	Gen. Greene, Capt. Samuel Ward, 1st Regt Rhode Island Line
2nd April 1776	9 mos	Gen Correll, Capt. Wm. Parker, Col. Pritchard
3rd 12 May 1777	1 year	Col. Geo. Tappan [Topham], 1st Regt. Rhode Island Line
4th 1778	3 years	Capt. Elijah Lewis, Col. Angel [Angle]

Battles: Battle of Rhode Island known as Sullivan's Expedition, Bunker Hill, White Plains, Saratoga, Monmouth, Battle of Red Banks on the Delaware.
He was wounded in the shoulder in 1776 in Sullivan's Expedition.
Discharge received & signed by: 1st 8 Dec 1775; 2nd Jan 1777 by Col. Hitchcock; 3rd by Col. Tappan [Topham]; 4th in 17881 by Col. Angel.
Statement is supported by –
Living witness, name(s): Phebe Hall – gave deposition in Ripley Co., IN on 10 Aug 1833. She was born in Nov. (26 day), 1753, in Little Rest (?), RI; since the 10th year of age she has known and been well acquainted with Benjamin Hall who appeared 18 Sep 1832, before the Switzerland Co. Circuit Court; she well remembers the time said Hall entered the service as an enlisted soldier, also as a substitute; to the best of her recollection he served as in his declaration; she cannot state from her personal knowledge the regiments, companies, or who commanded him.
No family information is given.
&
Additional notations in file:

Certificate of pension issued 18 Oct 1833
Benjamin Hall of Ripley Co. in the State of Indiana who was a private in the company of Capt.
> Ward of the regiment commanded by Col. Tappen (Topham) in the RI line for 2 years.

Letter of Steven Harding, attorney, Versailles, IN, dated 12 Aug 1833, request that pension be allowed.

Letter of Marshall Walker, attorney, dated 6 Sep 1850: Benjamin Hall died in January last [Jan 1850]; having been a sergeant in the RI troops during nearly the whole of the Rev. War; his pension has been suspended and his son claims he is entitled to eleven years back pay; letter requests a copy of certificate of pension, information concerning this matter.

Abstract of Final Payment Voucher; General Services Administration, Washington, DC   Page 1 of 2
LAST   FINAL PAYMENT VOUCHER RECEIVED FROM THE GENERAL ACCOUNTING OFFICE
NAME   ~~HALE~~ HALL, BENJAMIN
AGENCY OF PAYMENT   INDIANA
DATE OF ACT   1832
DATE OF PAYMENT   Sept. 3, 1838
DATE OF DEATH
GENERAL SERVICES ADMINISTRATION
National Archives and Records Service   NA-286
GSA-WASH DC 54-4891   November 1953

Abstract of Final Payment Voucher; General Services Administration, Washington, DC   Page 2 of 2
LAST   FINAL PAYMENT VOUCHER RECEIVED FROM THE GENERAL ACCOUNTING OFFICE
NAME   HALL, BENJAMIN
AGENCY OF PAYMENT   INDIANA
DATE OF ACT   1832
DATE OF PAYMENT   1st Qr. 1850
DATE OF DEATH   Jan. 10, 1850
GENERAL SERVICES ADMINISTRATION
National Archives and Records Service   NA-286
GSA-WASH DC 54-4891   November 1953

National Archives Microfilm Publication M246, 138 rolls; Revolutionary War Rolls, 1775-1783; War Department Collection of Revolutionary War Records, Record Group 93; National Archives, Washington. D.C.
Rhode Island   Topham's Regiment and Battalion   11 July 1778
A Muster Role of Capt. Benjamin Wests Company, Col. John Tophams Regt. Now In the Service of the United States Engaged For Twelve Months from the Sixteenth of March 1778

Commissioned officers	{Benjamin West, Capt. {Barber Ledham {Charles Hunt		March 6th March 6th March 6th	
	Sergeants		Corporals	
No.	Name	When enlisted	No.	Name When enlisted
1	Caleb Lewis Feby 5	March 9th 1778	1	William Barber
2	Azariah Brigs Feby 3d	Feby 2	2	James ?hebins
3	Job Wait Jo	Feby 2	3	Bowen Greene ?
4	Jonathan Foster March 10t	? 9	4	George Congdon
	Privates			
27	Benjamin Hall	March 14th		

National Archives Microfilm Publication M246, 138 rolls; <u>Revolutionary War Rolls, 1775-1783</u>; War Department Collection of Revolutionary War Records, Record Group 93; National Archives, Washington. D.C.

Rhode Island   Topham's Regiment and Battalion   20 Feb 1779
A Muster Role of Capt. Benjamin Wests Company, Col. John Tophams Regt. of Rhode Island State Troops Now Engaged In the Service of the United States for one year from 16th of March 1778 taken to 20th Feb'ry 1779.

Commissioned officers	{Benjamin West {Barber Ledham {Charles Hunt	Capt. 1t Lieut. 2d Lieut.	on command	} } }
	Sergeants		Corporals	
No.	Name	Remarks	No.	Name
1	Caleb Lewis		1	George Congdon
2	Jonathan Foster	on Duty	2	George Hyram
3	James Rhobins		3	Caleb Whitman
4	John Congdon		4	George ???nale
	Privates			
19	Benjamin Hall	on command		

<u>Register of Certificates Issued by John Pierce, Esquire, Paymaster General and Commissioner of Army Accounts for the United States, to Officers and Soldiers of the Continental Army Under Act of July 4, 1783</u>; Originally Published as Senate Documents, Vol.9, No. 988, 63rd Congress, 3d Session, Washington, 1915; Seventeenth report of the National Society of the Daughters of the American Revolution; Genealogical Publishing Co., Inc, Baltimore, MD, 1984. p. 222.
Men listed in this volume with the same name.

No. of Certificate	To whom issued	Amount
45069	Hall, Benjamin	64.80
83743	Hall, Benjamin	56.58

Senate Documents, Vol.9, No. 988, 63rd Congress, 3d Session, Washington, 1915; "Register of Certificates Issued by John Pierce, Esquire, Paymaster General and

Commissioner of Army Accounts for the United States, to Officers and Soldiers of the Continental Army Under Act of July 4, 1783"; Seventeenth report of the National Society of the Daughters of the American Revolution; Genealogical Publishing Co., Inc., Baltimore, MD, 1984. p. 222.

Men listed in this volume with the same name.

No. of Certificate	To whom issued	Amount
45069	Hall, Benjamin	64.80
83743	Hall, Benjamin	56.58

The Pension Roll of 1835 Volume IV, The Mid-Western States, Indexed Edition, In Four Volumes; Genealogical Publishing Co., Inc., Baltimore, MD, Reprint 1968, p. 87.

Statement, &c. of Ripley county, Indiana.

INDIANA Names	Rank	Annual allowance.	Sums received	Description of service
Benjamin Hall	Private	80.00	-	R.I. State troops

When placed on pension roll	Commencement of pension	Ages	Laws under which they were formerly placed on the pension roll; and remarks.
Oct 18, 1833	March 4, 1831	69	-

Rejected or Suspended Applications for Revolutionary War Pensions; Reprinted for Clearfield Company Inc. by Genealogical Publishing Co., Inc., Baltimore, MD, 1998. p. 407.

A list of the names of persons residing in Indiana who have applied for pensions under the act of June 7, 1832, whose claims have been rejected; prepared in conformity with the resolution of the Senate of the United States of September 16, 1850.

Names	Residence	Reasons for rejection
HALL, BENJAMIN	Vevay, Switzerland	Caveat to this claim from Wm. C. Keen, Printer's Retreat, August 23, 1832.

Toph, Violet E.; *Peoples History of Ripley County, Indiana;* self-published, c. 1940, p. 125. Revolutionary Soldiers Who Came to Ripley County
Benjamin Hall enlisted from Rhode Island in May or June 1775 and was discharged on December 8, 1775 and again enlisted in April, 1776 and was discharged in January, 1777 and re-enlisted May 12, 1777 and served for twelve months. His total service was two years and five months. He was pensioned from Switzerland county, moved to Ripley County from three he evidently moved to Madison, Ind. He died in January 1850.

O'Byrne, Mrs. Roscoe C., comp. & ed.; *Roster Soldiers and Patriots of the American Revolution Buried in Indiana;* Published by Indiana Daughters of the

American Revolution, 1938, Reprinted Genealogical Publishing Co., Baltimore MD, 1968, p. 170.
HALL, BENJAMIN   Ripley County
Service – Enlisted from Rhode Island in May or June, 1775. Discharged on Dec. 8, 1775. Re-enlisted April, 1776. Discharged Jan., 1777. Re-enlisted May 12, 1777. Served 1 yr., total service 2 yrs. 5 mos. *[Switzerland Co. man]*
Proof – Pension claim S 32295.
Died – Jan., 1850. Name on bronze tablet in Versailles Court House.
Collected by Mrs. A. b. Wycoff, Batesville, Indiana.

Waters, Margaret E.; <u>Revolutionary Soldiers Buried in Indiana A Supplement</u>; 485 Names Not Listed in the Roster of Soldiers and Patriots of the American Revolution Buried in Indiana (1938) nor in Revolutionary Soldiers Buried in Indiana (1949); Indianapolis, 1954. p.44.
HALL, BENJAMIN   Ripley (?)
(Note: this man is not the one of Ripley Co., Ind, "Roster" p. 1170, Pens. S.32295. However, this man's res. is uncertain; see below). b. 1749. Pens. appl. 10-16-1819, ae. ca. 70, Switzerland Co., Ind.; again 2-28-1820, ae. 70. Letter 8-23-1838 from William C. Keen, Printer's Retreat, Switzerland Co., Ind., says that sold. may make another appl. from Ripley, Dearborn, or Jefferson Co., Ind. Service: enl. Apr.-May 1776 for 3 yr., Lexington, Conn., Capt. Elijah Lewis, Col. John Angle, Conn. Line; disch. At White Plains, N.Y.; again enl. Sept. 1780, Easton, Pa., Maj. Ebenezer Adams, Artillery, & serv. till end of War. REF: Pens. R.5362-1/2 R.I.; Rej. Pens. List, p. 407—Caveat to this claim from William C. Keen, Printer's Retreat, 8-28-19832.
[As concluded above, this is the same man as the one of Ripley Co., Inc. – mjm]

Gibbs, A.; <u>Ripley County Historical Society Data on Revolutionary Soldiers</u>, 1973 review.
Exact location of marker: No further information on grave site.
Additional comments: on Court House tablet
        Probate A, p. 138, Aug. 1833 Ripley Co. Ind. appl. for pension.
        On 1850 Mortality Schedule of Jefferson Co. Ind.
        Claimed by Jefferson Co. Ind.

HAMILTON, BENJAMIN

Patriot: Benjamin Hamilton
Birth: Oct 1760   Bucks Co., PA
Married Spouse 1: XX
Service state(s):   PA
Rank: Private
Proof of Service: Pension application
Pension application No.: S16400
Residences: Bucks Co., PA; KY; Ripley Co., IN
Died: Final Pension Payment 3 Sep 1840, Indiana
Buried: Unknown
DAR Ancestor No.:None as of 7 Jun 2017.

Pension Application Abstracted from National Archives microfilm Series M804, Roll 1170, File S16400.
Pension abstract for – Benjamin Hamilton
Service state(s): PA
Alternate spelling(s):
Date: 11 Feb 1833
County of: Ripley   State of: IN
Declaration made before a Judge or Court: Probate Court
Act of: 7 Jun 1832
Age: 73 yrs.   Record of age: No
Where and year born: Bucks Co., PA   16 Oct 1760
Residence when he entered service: Bucks Co., PA
Residence(s) since the war: Not stated
Residence now: Ripley Co., IN
Volunteer, Drafted, or Substitute: 1st tour – Volunteer; 2nd tour – Drafted; 3rd tour – Substitute for his brother John Hamilton; 4th tour – Volunteered.
Rank(s): Private
Statement of service-

Period	Duration	Names of General and Field Officers
Nov 1776-Jan 1777		PA Line under Capt. Andrew Long
Apr 1777 -May 1777		Capt. George McGrandy
Jan 1778	8 mos.	Flying Camp under Maj. John Beaty, Capt. William Baxter, Lt. John Crawford, Ensign Miller
Fall 1778	2 wks.	Gen. Lacy

          Total 10 mos. 2 dys.
Battles: Fort Washington; under Gen. Washington on Christmas Eve 1777 on the Delaware near Philadelphia.
Discharge received: 3rd tour – Capt. Baxter
Clergyman: Meshack Hyatt

Abstract of Final Payment Voucher; General Services Administration, Washington, DC
LAST FINAL PAYMENT VOUCHER RECEIVED FROM
           THE GENERAL ACCOUNTING OFFICE
NAME   HAMILTON, BENJAMIN
AGENCY OF PAYMENT   INDIANA
DATE OF ACT   1832
DATE OF PAYMENT   Sept. 3, 1840
DATE OF DEATH   -
GENERAL SERVICES ADMINISTRATION
National Archives and Records Service   NA-286
GSA-WASH DC 54-4891   November 1953

1820 U. S. Census, Ripley Co., IN, NARA Roll M33_15; EN 7 Aug 1820, p. 77, line 16.
Benjamin Hamilton
Males 16-25=1, Males 45>=1, Females 16-25=1, Females 45>=1.

The Pension Roll of 1835 Volume IV, The Mid-Western States, Indexed Edition, In Four Volumes; Genealogical Publishing Co., Inc., Baltimore, MD, Reprint 1968, p. 87.
Statement, &c. of Ripley county, Indiana.

INDIANA Names	Rank	Annual allow-ance.	Sums re-ceived	Description of service
Benjamin Hamilton	Pvt	36.00	108 00	Penn. militia

When placed on pension roll	Commencement of pension	Ages	Laws under which they were formerly placed on the pension roll; and remarks.
June 29, 1833	March 4, 1831	75	-

Toph, Violet E.; Peoples History of Ripley County, Indiana; self-published, c. 1940, p. 122.
Revolutionary Soldiers Who Came to Ripley County
Benjamin Hamilton entered the service in November, 1776 from Pennsylvania. He entered and left the service four times serving altogether ten months and twenty-four days. He was born in October 1760.

O'Byrne, Mrs. Roscoe C., comp. & ed.; Roster Soldiers and Patriots of the American Revolution Buried in Indiana; Published by Indiana Daughters of the American Revolution, 1938, Reprinted Genealogical Publishing Co., Baltimore MD, 1968, p. 172.
HAMILTON, BENJAMIN
Born – Oct., 1760.
Service – Entered in Penn., Nov., 1776. Four enlistments with total service 10 mos. and 24 days.

Proof – Pension claim S. 16400.
Collected by Mrs. A. B. Wycoff, Batesville, Indiana.

Revolutionary Soldiers Buried in Indiana (1949) With Supplement (1954) Two Volumes in One; Margaret R. Waters; Genealogical Publishing Company, Baltimore, MD, 1970. p. 44, 119.

p. 44.
HALL, BENJAMIN   Ripley (?)
(Note: this man is not the one of Ripley Co., Ind., "Roster" p. 170, Pens. S.32295. .However, this man's res. is uncertain; see below). b. 1749. Pens. appl. 10-16-1819, ae. Ca. 70, Switzerland Co., Ind.; again 2-28-1820, ae. 70. Letter 8-23-1832 from William C. Keen, Printer's Retreat, Switzerland Co., Ind., says that sold may make another appl. from Ripley, Dearborn, or Jefferson Co., Ind. Service: enl. Apr.-May 1776 for 3 yr., Lexington, Conn., Capt. Elijah Lewis, Col. John Angle, Conn. Line; disch. at White Plains, N.Y.; again enl. Sept. 1780, Easton, Pa., Maj. Ebenezer Adams, Artillery, & serv. till end of War. REF: Pens. R.5362-1/2 R.I.; Rej. Pens. List, p. 4077—Caveat to this claim from William C. Keen, Printer's Retreat, 8-28-1832. (See. p. 119 later).

p. 119.
Additional Notes to Soldiers in Section I
HALL, BENJAMIN – p. 44. Confusion between a Rev. sold., Benajah Hall, d. 11-4-1840, Cayuga Co., N.Y., who liv. after Rev. at Hartford, Conn., & Dutchess Co., N.Y.; had pens.; had son Benajah who is incorrectly given as Benjamin Hall, 61 Conn.; wife Margaret, 54, N.Y.; chn. Simon, 26, N.Y.; George W., 19, N.Y.; Margaret C., 16, N.Y.; Lewis, 12, Ohio, in 1850 Cens., Ripley Co., Ind., Washington Twp., p. 312-1/2, fam. 70. The Rhode Island man in "Roster", p. 170., should be Benjamin and not Benajah.

Gibbs, A.; *Ripley County Historical Society Data on Revolutionary Soldiers, 1973 review.*
Exact location of marker: no further information on grave site
Additional comments: on Court House tablet
    Probate A, p. 135, Ripley Co. Ind. appl. for pension Feb 1833.
    Pa. Archives Series 3; Pennsylvanians residing in Ripley Co. Ind. pr. P.M. 29 June 1833, age 75.

HENNEGIN, JOSEPH

Patriot: Joseph Hennegin
Birth: 6 Feb 1759 Holland
Married Spouse 1: 20 Mar 1785, Kingsbury, Washington Co., NY
Rhoda Harris (1763/1768 -) [a]
Service state(s): NY Continental Line
Rank: Private
Proof of Service: Pension application
Pension application No.: S10097
Residences: NY, Ripley Co., IN
Died: 6 Apr 1833 Ripley Co., IN
Buried: George Hennegin Family Cemetery, Delaware Twp., Ripley Co., IN
DAR Ancestor No.: A055062

[a] Rhoda's father, Moses Harris, served in the Revolutionary War.
DAR Ancestor No.: A051790.

Pension Application Abstracted from National Archives microfilm Series M804, Roll 1254, File W10097.
Pension abstract for – Joseph Hennegin
Service state(s): NY Continental Line
Alternate spelling(s): Hennegan, Hennagin
Date: 14 Apr 1818
County of: Onondaga   State of: NY
Declaration made before a Judge or Court: Common Pleas Court
Act of: 18 Mar 1818
Age: 57 yrs.
Where and year born: 6 Jan 1759   place not stated
Residence when he entered service: Not stated
Residence now: Onondaga Co., NY
Volunteer, Drafted, or Substitute: Enlisted
Rank(s): Private
Statement of service-

Period	Duration	Names of General and Field Officers
Apr 1776	1 yr.	NY Continental Line under Capt. Henry O'Hara, Col. Wynkoop' Regt.
1777-1 Jan 1781	3 yrs.	Same company under Col. Moses Hazen

Battles: None
Discharge received: at Fish Kill, NY
What became of it?: Lost
&
Date: 27 May 1820
County of: Onondaga   State of: NY
Declaration made before a Judge or Court: Common Pleas Court
Act of: 1 May 1820
Declaration: Same as 14 Apr 1818

Age: 61 yrs.
Residence now: Onondaga Co., NY
&

Pension abstract for – Rhoda Hannegan widow of Joseph Hannegan
Date: 12 Feb 1839
County of: Dearborn   State of: IN
Declaration made before a Judge or Court: Probate Court
Act of: 7 Jul 1838
Age: 76 yrs. as of yesterday 11 Feb 1839
Where and year born: 11 Feb 1763
Residence now: Sparta Twp., Dearborn Co., IN
Affidavits provided by: Son Peter; Daniel Welsh who since 1875, in Washington Co., NY, was acquainted with Joseph & Rhoda Hennegan.
Death of soldier: 6 Apr 1833 Ripley Co., IN
Marriage date and place: 20 Mar 1785 Kingsbury, NY
Proof of marriage: Family record in the family Bible which she produced
Names and ages of children: From the Family Record –

Peter born	8 Jun 1786		
Margaret	9 Jul 1788		
Dorothy	3- Jun 1790		
Prudence	23 Dec 1792	died	Aug 7 -
Barbara	7 Aug 1795	died	23 Apr 1796
Diadama	6 Oct 1796		
Poly	- Feb 1799		
Hennery	27 Jun ----		
Gorg	17 Oct ----		
Emily	10 May 1806		

&

Pension abstract for – Rhoda Hennegin widow of Joseph Hennegin
Date: 12 Oct 1848
County of: Ripley   State of: IN
Declaration made before a Judge or Court: Justice of the Peace
Act of: 2 Feb 1848
Age: 88 yrs.
Statement is supported by –
Documentary proof: She has no documents to show under whom he served and her memory is so impaired by age she cannot remember.

Abstract of Final Payment Voucher; General Services Administration, Washington, DC

LAST   FINAL PAYMENT VOUCHER RECEIVED FROM
         THE GENERAL ACCOUNTING OFFICE
NAME   HENEGIN, JOSEPH
AGENCY OF PAYMENT   INDIANA
DATE OF ACT   1818
DATE OF PAYMENT   March 1, 1833 (dead)
DATE OF DEATH

GENERAL SERVICES ADMINISTRATION
National Archives and Records Service   NA-286
GSA-WASH DC 54-4891   November 1953

1830 U. S. Census, Ripley County, IN; Series M19, Roll 32; p. 10, line 22.
Joseph Henigen
Males 60-69=1, Females 30-39=1, Females 60-69=1.

Ripley County Indiana, Recorder's Office, Tract Book 3, p. 74.
Hennigin, Joseph   02 Apr 1833   R12, T9, S28   40 acres

Ripley County, Indiana Deed Records Vol. D., 7 Feb 1834 - 9 Feb 1836,
Page 165-166.
Abstract of Deed/Patent for: Rhoda Hennegin, Widow of Joseph Hennegin
Purchaser (Grantee) or Seller (Grantor)?: Seller
Sold to: Dorothy Hennegin
State & county where recorded: Ripley Co., Indiana
Date entered: 3 May 1834
Recorded: 24 Dec 1834
Description: That certain tract or parcel of land lying in the South West quarter of the South East quarter of Section 28, Township 9 North of Range 12 East; containing 40 acres.
Amount paid: In consideration of love and affection
Name(s) of Witnesses: Thomas Harrison & Adonijah Gleason; and Rhody Henigin, Peter Henigin, John G. Jackson, Margaret Jackson, Joseph Churchill, Polly Churchill, George Henigin, Suan Hennigin, John Horton, Emily Horton, Henry Henigin, & Mary Henigin.

Toph, Violet E.; Peoples History of Ripley County, Indiana; self-published, c. 1940, p. 120-121.
Revolutionary Soldiers Who Came to Ripley County
Joseph Hennegin (Hennegan) was born in Holland Feb. 6, 1759. He came to New York City with his family two years before the Revolution and enlisted as a Private Feb. 16, 1777 in Captain Henry O'Hara's Company. Then was in Captain Richard Lynde also designated the 12th Company; then in Colonel Moses Hazen's Regiment Continental Troops. He was discharged Jan. 1781. He died in Ripley County, Indiana April 6, 1833 and was buried in the family burying ground 1/2 mile southeast of Lookout Indiana. Mr. Otto Fruchtnicht now owns the farm. His grave was marked when he died but the stone seems to have been of poor materials that it crumbled and was so obliterated that the inscription could not be read. The Ripley County Historical Society secured and placed a Government marker at this grave July 13, 1936.
Mrs. Clara E. Gookins, a relative of Samuel Gookins, also a Revolutionary soldier, and of Joseph Hennegin, said this of these soldiers: " How very young both of these soldiers were at the time they enlisted. Samuel Gookins was less than fifteen years old. Joseph Hennegan was only eighteen years old. The boys of these days are not husky like they were in olden times. They did not have the diet they live on now and grew stronger".

O'Byrne, Mrs. Roscoe C., comp. & ed.; *Roster Soldiers and Patriots of the American Revolution Buried in Indiana*; Published by Indiana Daughters of the American Revolution, 1938, Reprinted Genealogical Publishing Co., Baltimore MD, 1968, p. 185.
HENNEGIN, JOSEPH
Born – Feb. 6, 1759, Holland.
Service – Entered service from N.Y., 1776, under Capt. Henry O'Hara and served two yrs. In Capt. Richard Layden's CO. Later in Col. Moses Hazen's Regt. of Penn. Troops. Discharged Jan. 4, 1781.
Proof – Pension claim S. 10097.
Died – April 6, 1833. Buried in Delaware Twp. Stone. Government marker and name on bronze tablet in Versailles Court House.
Married – 1785, Rhoda Harris, b. 1763. Ch. Peter, b. 1786; Margaret, b. 1788; Dorothy, b. 1790; Prudence, b. 1792; Barbara, b. 1793; Diadema, b. 1796, m. John Shue; Polly, b. 1799, m. Joseph Churchill; Henry, b. 1800, m. Mary Chamberlain; Emily, b. 1806, m. John Horton; George, b. 1811, m. Susan Montgomery.
Collected by Mrs. A. B. Wycoff, Batesville, Indiana.

Gibbs, A.; *Ripley County Historical Society Data on Revolutionary Soldiers*, 1973 review.
Exact location of marker: turn south off Rt. 48 at Lookout, onto Delaware Rd; go 4/10th mile; turn 1. on unmarked rd., go ½ mi.; cemetery on left, not visible from road. Old Hennegin Cemetery; Delaware Tw. Near Fr. Tw. line Ripley Co. Ind.
Type of marker: Gov't; family marker too worn to read
Date placed: about 1936?
Placed by: Ripley County Historical Society
Additional comments: on Court House tablet
    Cemetery is on the old John G. Jackson farm now owned by Mrs. Oscar Grigsby.
    Marker for Rhoda Hennegin: d. May 16, 1857 age 89.
    Mrs. Leroy Shockley of Cincinnati – May 1928- who unveiled the tablet at the Court House at time old dedication was a descendant of Joseph Hennegin.
    Toph note: Joseph Hennigin age 18 at enlistment.
Wording on marker:
Joseph Hennegin
Pvt. O'Hara's Co.
Hazen's Continental Troops
Rev. War
April 6, 1833

United States Headstone Applications for U.S. Military Veterans, 1925-1949, database with images; (https://familysearch.org/ark:/61903/1:1:VHZZ-9JM : 17 May 2016); Affiliate Publication Number: M1916; Affiliate Publication Title: Applications for Headstones for U.S. Military Veterans, 1925-1941; Affiliate

Film Number: 52; GS Film Number: 1878201; Digital Folder Number: 004832219; Image Number: 00685.
Application for Headstone; War Department O.Q.M.G. Form No. 623
Name: Hanagin, Joseph
Event Date: May 31, 1934
Name of Cemetery: Hennegin Private
Located in or near: Delaware, Ind.
Death Date: April 6, 1833
Enlistment Dates: Feb. 16, 1777
Discharge Dates: Jan. 4, 1781
Rank: Private
Company: Henry O'Hara's Co., Moses Hansen's Regt., Continental Troops
To be shipped to: Ripley Co. Historical Society, Osgood, Ind., Ripley Co.
Whose post-office address is: Versailles, Ind.
This application is for the UNMARKED grave of a veteran. It is understood the stone will be furnished and delivered at the railroad station or steamboat landing above indicated, at Government expense, freight prepaid. I hereby agree to promptly accept the headstone at destination, remove it and properly place same at decedent's grave at my expense. Ripley Co. Historical Society, Applicant. No fee should be paid in connection with this application.
Applicant: Ripley Co. Historical Society, Versailles, Ind.

Tombstone Location: Jackson & Hennegin Family Cemetery, Delaware Twp., Ripley Co., IN

Tombstone Inscription: JOSEPH
HENNEGIN
PVT. O'HARA'S CO.
HAZEN'S CONTINENTAL
TROOPS
REV. WAR
APRIL 6, 1833

HITE (HYATT), JACOB

Toph's indicates he was in Ripley County, IN. However, no evidence has been located indicating he was in the county. He lived in, was pensioned in, and was buried in Rush Co., IN.

Patriot: Jacob Hyatt (Hite)
Birth: 14 Feb 1761 MD
Married Spouse 1: 4 Apr 1786, Frederick Co., VA
                                     Catherine Sheiner (1769 – 1844)
Service state(s): VA
Rank: Private
Proof of Service: Pension application
Pension application No.: S16414
Residences: MD; VA; Rush Co., IN
Died: 27 Oct 1839 Rush Co., IN
Buried: Richland Cemetery, Rush Co., IN
DAR Ancestor No.: A055686

Pension Application Abstracted from National Archives microfilm Series M804, Roll 1291, File S16414.
Pension abstract for – Jacob Hite, Sr.
Service state(s): VA
Date: 22 Sep 1832
County of: Rush   State of: IN
Declaration made before a Judge or Court: Circuit Court
Act of: 7 Jun 1832
Age: 72 years
Where and year born: Frederick Co., MD   14 Feb 1761
       His father, when deponent was abt. 1 y/o emigrated to Frederick Co., VA
Residence when he entered service: Frederick Co., VA
Residence(s) since the war: Not stated
Residence now: Richland Twp., Rush Co., IN
Volunteer, Drafted, or Substitute: Enlisted (in his words he was "detailed")
Rank(s): Private
Statement of service-

Period	Duration	Names of General and Field Officers
1778	abt. 2 mos.	Capt. Gillison [Capt. Samuel Gilkerson].
1 Oct 1781	6 mos.	Virginia Line, Capt. Armistead, Lt. Mann; aft. Yorktown Capt. Newell

Statement is supported by –
Documentary proof: None stated
Death of soldier: 27 Oct 1839
Wife: Not named   Wife's age: 64 years

Abstract of Final Payment Voucher; General Services Administration, Washington, DC
LAST   FINAL PAYMENT VOUCHER RECEIVED FROM
        THE GENERAL ACCOUNTING OFFICE
NAME   HITE, JACOB
AGENCY OF PAYMENT   INDIANA
DATE OF ACT   1832
DATE OF PAYMENT   Sept. 3, 1839
DATE OF DEATH   -
GENERAL SERVICES ADMINISTRATION
National Archives and Records Service   NA-286
GSA-WASH DC 54-4891   November 1953

Revolutionary War Service Records; National Archives Publication number M881, Compiled service records of soldiers who served in the American Army during the Revolutionary War, 1775-1783.
https://www.fold3.com/image/23349150?terms=Hite,%20Jacob%20VA
VA – Jacob Hite, Sol., Appears in a Book under the following heading: "A List of State Soldiers and Seaman who have received Certificated for the balance of their full pay. Agreeable to Act of Assembly passed November Session 1781". By whom drawn – Nath'l Ashby, Time – June 28, 1786, Sum £8, S7, P4.

Gwathmey, John H.; Historical Register of Virginians in the Revolution, Soldiers, Sailors, Marines, 1775-1783; The Dietz Press, Richmond, VA, 1938, p. 380.
Hite, Jacob   Inf.,   [Name appeared on Army Register but had
                           not received bounty land. An extensive compilation
                           in the War Department.]

Toph, Violet E.; Peoples History of Ripley County, Indiana; self-published, c. 1940, p. 131.
Revolutionary Soldiers Who Came to Ripley County
Jacob Hite (Hyatt) was born in Maryland and entered the service from Virginia in 1778 under Captain Armstrong and served eight months. He was born February 14, 1761 and died October 27, 1839. He **was** pensioned in Rush County, Ind.

O'Byrne, Mrs. Roscoe C., comp. & ed.; Roster Soldiers and Patriots of the American Revolution Buried in Indiana; Published by Indiana Daughters of the American Revolution, 1938, Reprinted Genealogical Publishing Co., Baltimore MD, 1968, p. 191.
HITE, JACOB, SR.   Rush County
Born – Feb. 14, 1761.   Frederick Co., Maryland
Service – Enlisted from Frederick Co., Vir., under Capt. Gilkison. Was in the company of General McIntosh, Armistead, and Newall. As a pri., served 2 mos. in 1778, from Oct. 1, 1781, served 6 mos. Present at Yorktown.
Proof – Pension claim S.16414.
Died – 1839. Buried Richland Cemetery. Name on bronze tablet in Rush Co. Court House.

Married – Catherine Shimer. Ch. John; George (War of 1812); William; Jacob, Jr.; Polly m. Archibald Crowdy; Alexander.
Collected by Mrs. Willard Amos, Rushville, Indiana.

HODGES, RICHARD

Patriot: Richard Hodges
Birth: 1756 Essex Co., VA
Married Spouse 1: abt 1781 Sarah Rosemond (abt 1760-1821)
Service state(s): SC
Rank: Private, Lieutenant
Proof of Service: SC Accounts Audited of Claims Growing Out of the Revolution
Pension application No.: None
Residences: VA; SC; TN; Boone Co., KY; Ripley Co., IN
Died: 7 Jan 1823 Ripley Co., IN
Buried: Blair Cemetery, Johnson Twp., Ripley Co., IN
DAR Ancestor No.: A056210

South Carolina Department of Archives and History; Columbia, SC; <u>Accounts Audited of Claims Growing Out of the Revolution, Richard Hodges 3650</u>; Reproduction of Microfilm Roll #AD400, AA3650, RW2756, copied 2016, pp. FRS:72-75.

[First image - from the account book]
 ??? No. 28 25th April 1785
Mr. Rich.d Hodges
his Acco.t of Duty in the Militia done alternately from <u>1779 to 1783</u> pay
Pay Script
on Horse } 106 Dy.s   £238:10
as lieut.t
on foot } 85 Dy.s   £148:151
as private
on foot } 21 Dy.s   10:10
                        ~~~~~~~~
             Curr.y = 397:151
             £sd   56:16:5
Fifty Six Pounds, Sixteen Shill.gs And five Pence
Sterling ~~~~~ £.97:14:11
19.5p
[Written vertically in account book to the right of the above accounting image]
Received April 25th 1785 the full amount of the [illegible] [illegible] in a
Treasury Indent No.503 Book C for Rich.d Hodges
by Virtue of an Order   James BosemonJ
[Second image in file]
State So Carolina   Dr to Rich.d Hodges
for Duty in the Militia for Pay Bills of Capt. Sam.l Rosamond comm.nd – 79
[illegible] for 188 days as Lieut
        on Horse 101 Dys 451 £238.10.
                  85 Dys 351 148.15._
        as Private 21 Dys 161 10.10._
                              ~~~~~~~
                Curry 397.151
                £sd   £ 56:16:5

[Third image in file]
Abbeville County 25th June 1785
Gentlemen
        Please to deliver my Indents to Mr. James Boseman the bearer hereof and oblige   Gentlemen

Edwd. Blake & Peter Boequet Esqr.	}your very humble Servant
Comm.rs of the Treasury	}Rich'd Hodges
The above order was Signed in	}
my presence 25th June 1785 - John Bowie J.P.	}

Moss, Bobby Gilmer; <u>Roster of South Carolina Patriots in the American Revolution</u>; Genealogical Publishing Co., IN., Baltimore, MD, 1983, p. 452.
Hodges, Richard
He served as a private and lieutenant in the militia from 1779 to 1783 alternately under Capt. Samuel Rosamond. A.A.3650; 0503.

<u>Ripley County Indiana, Recorder's Office, Tract Book 1</u>, p. 38.
Hodges, Richard   11 Aug 1814   R12, R7, S33   160 acres

<u>U.S. Department of Interior, Bureau of Land Management, General Land Office Records; Land Patent Search</u>
Name: Hodges, Richard
Accession Nr. CV-0030-226; Document Type – Credit Volume Patent; Issue Date – 8/2/1816; Cancelled – No
Land Office – Jeffersonville; Authority – April 24, 1820: Sale-Cash Entry (3 Stat. 566); Document Nr. 0; Total Acres – 0.00
Land Descriptions: State – IN; Meridian – 2ndPM; Twp-Rng – 007N – 012E; Aliquots – SE1/4; Section – 33; County - Ripley
&
Name: Hodges, Richard
Accession Nr. CV-0041-370; Document Type – Credit Volume Patent; Issue Date – 9/30/1818; Cancelled – No
Land Office – Jeffersonville; Authority – April 24, 1820: Sale-Cash Entry (3 Stat. 566); Document Nr. 0; Total Acres – 0.00
Land Descriptions: State – IN; Meridian – 2ndPM; Twp-Rng – 007N – 012E; Aliquots – NW1/4; Section –33; County - Ripley

Cowen, Janet C., comp; <u>Jeffersonville Land Entries 1808-1818</u>;McDowell Publications, Utica, NY, 1984, p. 58 & 108.
p. 58.
Receipt #
03680 Hodges Richard KY Boone SE S33 T07 N12E 160 1814 08 11
03681 Hodges Richard KY Boone NW S33 T07 N12E 160 1814 08 11
p. 108.
Receipt #
09735 Hodges Richard KY Boone SE S33 T07 N12E 160 1816 06 11
09736 Hodges Richard KY Boone NW S33 T07 N12E 160 1816 06 11

Ripley County, Indiana Deed Records Vol. A, 11 Aug 1818-29 Jan 1827
Page(s): 4-6.
Abstract of Deed/Patent for: Richard Hodges, Senr. and Sarah (dower) his wife of the county of Ripley, State of Indiana.
Purchaser (Grantee) or Seller (Grantor)?: Seller
Sold to: Richard Hodges, Junr.
State & county where recorded: Ripley Co., Indiana
Date entered: 21 Sep 1818
Description: All that part of the Southeast quarter of Section thirty-three, Township 7, North of the last line in Range twelve East of the second principal meridian of lands directed to be sold at Jeffersonville
Amount paid: Twenty-five cents (25¢)
Name(s) of Witnesses: Samuel Hodges & Hezekiah Norris.

Ripley County, Indiana Deed Records Vol. A, 11 Aug 1818-29 Jan 1827
Page(s): 54-56.
Abstract of Deed/Patent for: Richard Hodges and Sarah (dower) his wife of the County of Ripley, State of Indiana.
Purchaser (Grantee) or Seller (Grantor)?: Seller
Sold to: George Roberts
State & county where recorded: Ripley Co., Indiana
Date entered: 10 Jan 1822
Recorded: 9 Feb 1822
Description: Part of the northwest quarter of section numbered thirty-three of Township seven, North of Range 12 East of the lands directed to be sold at Jeffersonville, containing seventy acres and a half.
Amount paid: One dollar ($1.00).
Name(s) of Witnesses: Daniel Ross & Richard Burchfield.

Ripley Co., IN Probate Order Book, Vol.1 Wills, Sep 1821-Apr 1839, p. 17-19.
Will was written 22 Aug 1821, probated 26 Jan 1824.
Last will and testament of Richard Hodges of the County of Ripley and State of Indiana, I Richard Hodges, considering the uncertainty of this mortal life and being of sound mind and memory possessed, be almighty god for the same, do make and publish this my last will and testament, in manner and form following that is today.
1st I give and bequeath unto my beloved wife, Sarah Hodges, the use of the plantation whereon I now live, together with all m household goods and debts and moveable effects together with all my negroes in the state of South Carolina and Kentucky to be forever her own use during the time shall remain my widow and unmarried, but at her marriage, as decease, all movable effects to equally divided among the legates, which their names as follows = John B. Hodges, Samuel Hodges, Reuben B. Hodges, Elizabeth Weldon, Sarah H. Norris, Margaret Pate, Mary Boyse, Jane Ross, and after my wife Sarah Hodges, death as marriage, a I also give to and bequeath unto my said son younger son, Reuben Hodges, 100 acres of land, whereon I now live, to have and to hold his heirs and assigns forever, and I hereby give and bequeath unto my son, William Hodges,

100 acres of land, whereon he now lives and I hereby give and bequeath unto my daughter Sarah Harris, 23 acres of land, an I also give and bequeath unto my granddaughter, Elizabeth Welch, 1 cow and calf and a feather bed and bedding, and lastly as to all the rest residue and remainder of my personal estate good and chattels of what kind and nature soever I give and bequeath the same to my wife Sarah Hodges, and Samuel Hodges, and James Hodges, and James Wilson whom I hereby appoint sole executors of this my last will and testament, hereby revolking all former wills by me made.

In witness whereof i have hereunto set my hand and seal, the 22nd of august 1821.

Witnesses   Joshua Conn
George Swisher
Richard Blair

Toph, Violet E.; Peoples History of Ripley County, Indiana; self-published, c. 1940, p. 126-127.

Revolutionary Soldiers Who Came to Ripley County

The name Richard Hodges, Private, Captain Joshua Miles Company, in the 6th Maryland Regiment, commanded by Colonel Williams, appears on a roll dated Sept. 9, 1778, which shows that he enlisted for one year. That name also appears on an undated account of clothing delivered by Lieut. Colonel Smith of Fort Mifflin to the soldiers of the 6th Maryland Regiment. At the time Hodges is shown as a member of Chaplain's company. July 13, 1936 the Ripley County Historical Society placed a Government marker at his grave in the Blain Cemetery near Friendship, Ind.

p. 132.

Richard Hodges, private of Capt. Miles' Company in the 6th Maryland Regiment, commanded by Col. Williams appears on a roll dated Sept. 9, 1778 which shows that he enlisted for one year. That name also appears on an undated account for clothing delivered by Lieut. Colonel Smith of Fort Mifflin to the soldiers of the 6th Maryland Regiment. At that time Hodges is shown as a member of Chaplin's Company, Date of death as sent in Jan. 7, 1823. A marker was placed at his grave in the Blair cemetery in 1936.

[Note the service in both of these citations is not correct. There was another man by the same name who served in Maryland. Richard Hodges, who settled in Ripley Co., lived and served in SC.]

O'Byrne, Mrs. Roscoe C., comp. & ed.; Roster Soldiers and Patriots of the American Revolution Buried in Indiana; Published by Indiana Daughters of the American Revolution, 1938, Reprinted Genealogical Publishing Co., Baltimore MD, 1968, p. 192.

HODGES, RICHARD   Ripley County

Service – Pri. in Capt. Joshua Miles' Regt., the 6th Maryland under Col. Williams. Enlisted Sept. 9, 1778, for one year. Later was a member of Chaplain's CO. Discharged Jan., 1780.

Proof – Pension record.

Died – Buried in Blair Cemetery, Brown Twp. Stone crumbled. Name appears on bronze tablet in Versailles Court House.

Descendants are: Mrs. Nora Newman Crouch, Osgood, Ind.; Mrs. Madge Crouch Franke, Spades, Ind.; and J. L. Hodges, 1432 N. 17th St., Philadelphia, Penn. Collected by Mrs. A. B. Wycoff, Batesville, Indiana.

Gibbs, A.; Ripley County Historical Society Data on Revolutionary Soldiers, 1973 review.
Exact location of marker: Buried beside his daughter Mrs. Anna B. Roberts in the Blair Cemetery, Johnson Tw. Ripley Co. Ind.; on Cave Hill Rd near Little Turkey Branch, about 1/2 mi. from 425, on west side of road. Cemetery is visible from road, and is surrounded by old field-stone wall.
Type of marker: Gov't
Date placed: 1936
Placed by: Ripley County Historical Society
Additional comments: on Court House tablet
Ripley Co. Ind. Will Book, p. 4.
Wording on marker:

      Richard Hodges
       Maryland
     Pvt. 6 Md. Rgt.
       Rev. War
      Jan. 7, 1823

United States Headstone Applications for U.S. Military Veterans, 1925-1949, database with images; (https://familysearch.org/ark:/61903/1:1:VHZZ-H31 : 17 May 2016); Affiliate Publication Number: M1916; Affiliate Publication Title: Applications for Headstones for U.S. Military Veterans, 1925-1941; Affiliate Film Number: 54; GS Film Number: 1878203; Digital Folder Number: 004832221; Image Number: 00295.
Application for Headstone; War Department O.Q.M.G. Form No. 623
Name: Hodges, Richard
Event Date: Sept. 2, 1935
Name of Cemetery: Blair
Located in or near: Friendship, Ind.
Death Date: Jan. 7, 1823
Enlistment Dates: Sept. 9, 1778
Discharge Dates: One year later
Rank: Private
Company: Joshua Miles Co., 6th Maryland [determined later to be incorrect]
To be shipped to: Ripley Co. Historical Society, Osgood, Ind., Ripley Co.
Whose post-office address is: Versailles, Ind.
This application is for the UNMARKED grave of a veteran. It is understood the stone will be furnished and delivered at the railroad station or steamboat landing above indicated, at Government expense, freight prepaid. I hereby agree to promptly accept the headstone at destination, remove it and properly place same at decedent's grave at my expense. Ripley Co. Historical Society, Applicant.
No fee should be paid in connection with this application.

Applicant: Ripley Co. Historical Society, Versailles, Ind.

Tombstone Location: Blair Cemetery, Johnson Twp., Ripley Co., IN

Tombstone Inscription:
>RICHARD
>HODGES
>MARYLAND
>PVT. 6 MD REGT.
>REV. WAR
>JANUARY 7, 1823

HOUSE, LEVI

Patriot: Levi House
Birth: 1754 Bedford Co., VA (per DAR)
Married Spouse 1: abt 1782, Mercer Co., KY   Sarah Pressley (1765-1850)
Service state(s): PA and VA
Rank: Private, Patriotic Service
Proof of Service: Pension application
Pension application No.: R5265
Residences: Washington Co., VA (now PA); Mercer Co., KY; Jefferson Co., IN
Died: 8 Oct 1846   Napoleon, Jackson Twp., Ripley Co., IN
   Will administered in Franklin Co., KY
Buried: Culver Cemetery, Napoleon, Jackson Twp., Ripley Co., IN
DAR Ancestor No.: A057507

Pension Application Abstracted from National Archives microfilm Series M804, Roll 1336, File R5265.
Pension abstract for – Levi House
Service state(s): PA & VA
Date: 13 Feb 1835
County of: Jefferson   State of: IN
Declaration made before a Judge or Court:
Act of: 7 Jun 1832
Age: 80 yrs.
Where and year born: Not stated
Residence when he entered service: Washington Co., VA (now PA)
Residence(s) since the war: Not stated
Residence now: Jefferson Co., IN
Volunteer, Drafted, or Substitute: Enlisted
Rank(s): Private
Statement of service-
   He enlisted in the Army of the United States in May 1777 with Capt. James Hook's Calico Hunting Shirt Company of the Virginia Line, under the following named officers, Lieutenant Adam Row, Capt. I. Hook and Col. Broadhead. Left service in November 1778.
   In the month of February 1779 went to Jackson Fort, Penn. where he served 3 months under Capt. Wm. Harrod in scouting.
   Then performed same kind of service under Captain Archer, served six months
   Then was in Crawford's Defeat. Served under Col. Crawford as a volunteer. This was early 1782.
   Served as a spy for a period of nine months.
Battles: Crawford's Defeat
Discharge received: Yes
What became of it?: Lost
Statement is supported by –
Living witness, name(s): William Hall - stated he is well acquainted

with Levi House. Been acquainted with him since this applicant was 13 or 14 years old. That when he was about that age they lived in the same neighborhood not far apart. Says said House is a little older then him, how much he does not know. Knows that said House served under Capt. Hook in his Calico Shirt Company & saw him march in said Company…. Saw House march in the company when they started on said expedition and talked with him and good many of the company that went with him that he known when they were starting about their going, saw him when he come back and served in the same company in the frontier scouting. Saw him often times when in the service. Knows that he served until that company was discharged….Affiant knows also that he was in Crawford's defeat. Heard said House talk about soon afterwards & heard others say that House was in that defeat.

&

Pension abstract for – Elizabeth Hall daughter of Levi House
Date: - Apr 1851
County of: Franklin   State of: KY
Declaration made before a Judge or Court: Court
Declaration: She believes that he is entitled to a pension under the Act of Congress passed 7th day of June 1832. Since she most respectfully asks the Hon. Commissioner of Pensions to allow it to him, to commence on the 4th of March 1831 and terminate on the 8th day of October 1846 which was the day of his death.
Act of: 7 Jun 1832
Her Age: 67 on 14 Aug next
Death of soldier: 8 Oct 1846
Her Spouse: John Hall
Her Marriage date and place: 19 Feb 1803/4
Names and ages of children:

&

Letter in file – from Aaron Culver, husband of Cassandra House, to John and Elizabeth (House) Hall –
Napoleon, Ripley County, In
Oct 11, 1846

Dear Brother and Sister Hall I take my pen in hand to inform that Father House has departed this life on the eight of the month he was sensable of his near approach to Death for some days before & he appeared to have sense even in the hour of Death.

I have seen the solemn service performed by having him Decently entered in my grave yard. There to rest until the day of general Resorrection of the Dead. I cannot say that we are well for Moses is very sick and has been for about three weeks there is a great deal of sickness in this neighborhood at this time. Sally Broshar is sick at this time and has thought to be dangerous though a little better. Nothing more bur Remain Brother and Sister until Death.
Aaron Culver

Pennsylvania Archives, Series 3, Vol. 22, p. 722.
Effective Supply Tax for the County of Washington 1781

	Acres	Horses	Cattle	Sheep	Value
House, Levi	45	..	1	..	39

Register of the Kentucky Historical Society; Early Kentucky Tax Records; Clearfield Publishing, Baltimore, Md., 1999; p. 184.
A List of Taxable Property Within the District of Gabriel Slaughter, Commissioner of the County of Mercer for the Year 1795.

Persons Charged with the Tax	Horses	Cattle
House, Levy	3	5

Judge Lewis Collins; Franklin County, KY Revolutionary Soldiers, Compiled from Kentucky Pension Roll of 1835 & History of Kentucky; http://www.rootsweb.ancestry.com/~kyfrankl/revwar.htm.
The following is a listing of soldiers that once lived in Franklin County, Kentucky. This list does not suggest the soldiers applied for a pension or died in Franklin County, only that they once resided in this county. Name, rank, birth and or death dates, place of service, pension and or Bounty Land file numbers are included.
LEVI HOUSE, Pennsylvania & Virginia Line, R5265

Rejected or Suspended Applications for Revolutionary War Pensions; Reprinted for Clearfield Company Inc. by Genealogical Publishing Co., Inc., Baltimore, MD, 1998. p.412.
A list of persons residing in Indiana who have applied for pensions under the act of July 7, 1832, whose claims have been suspended; prepared in conformity with the resolution of the Senate of the United States, September 16, 1850.

Names	Residence	Reason for suspension
House, Levi	Madison, Jefferson	For proof of service by witnesses.

Census of Indiana Territory for 1807; Indiana Historical Society, 1980, p. 23.
A list of free males above the age of twenty one in Dearborn County in March 1807.

Persons Names	Number
Levi House	227

O'Byrne, comp. Mrs. Roscoe C., comp.; Roster of Soldiers and Patriots of the American Revolution Buried in Indiana, Vol. III; Indiana Daughters of the American Revolution, 1966, p. 26.
HOUSE, LEVI   Ripley County
Born – 1754 Pa.
Service – Enl. May 1777 in Capt. Hooks Calico Hunting Shirt CO. Also served under Lt. Adam Row, Col. Broadhead's Washington Co., Va. (now Pa.) on Ten Mile Creek.
Proof – Applied for pension Feb. 13, 1836 Jefferson Co., Ind. age 80. #R5265.

Died – Oct. 8, 1846. Buried Old Culver Cemetery, Delaware Twp., Ripley Co., Ind.
Married – Wife's name unknown.
Children – Levi P.; Cassandra b. Ky. d. Aug. 2, 1849 m. Aaron Culver; Susanna m. George Tumey; Simeon m. Nancy Phillis; Sally m. Edward Broshers; Rachel b. Jan. 30, 1812 m. Daniel Comingon; Elizabeth b. Aug. 14, 1785 m. John Hall; William; Ruth b. 1807 m. Henry Salyers; Molly/Polly m. Moses Lutz.
By Mrs. David Gibbs, RR #2, Box 82, Hopewell Road, Holton, Indiana 47023.

Gibbs, A.; Ripley County Historical Society Data on Revolutionary Soldiers, 1973 review.
Exact location of marker: marker & burial in Culver Cemetery; Delaware Tw. Ripley Co. Ind.; N.E. Corner Sec 34 T9 R11
Type of marker: Gov't
Date placed: 11 Oct 1977
Dedicated: 24 Oct 1977 – Veteran's Day
Placed by: Ross' Run Chapter Daughters of the American Revolution
Additional comments: b. cir. 1754-5; d. Oct. 8, 1846 Ripley Co. Ind.; enl. May 1777. Capt. James Hook's Calico Hunting Shirt Co., Va. Line, Lt. Adam Row, Col. Broadhead, Washington Co., Va. now Pa. on 10 Mile Creek; #R5265, p. 412
Wording on marker:

Levi House
Capt. Shirt's Co.
Va. Line
Rev. War
1754-1846

Tombstone Location: Culver Cemetery, Napoleon, Jackson Twp.,
Levi House Ripley Co., IN

Tombstone Inscription:

LEVI HOUSE
CAPT. SHIRT'S CO VA LINE
REVOLUTIONARY WAR
1754 - 1845

HOWLETT (HOWLETE), WILLIAM

Patriot: William Howlett
Birth: abt. 1767
Married Spouse 1: 29 Nov 1815   Ross Co., OH   Martha Jack (- 1853)
Service state(s): VT & Navy
Rank: Private
Proof of Service: Pension application
Pension application No.: R5305
Residences: Bennington Co., VT; Ross Co., OH; Jennings Co., IN
Died: 27 Aug 1852   Jennings Co., IN
Buried: Unknown
DAR Ancestor No.: None as of 7 Jun 2017.

Pension Application Abstracted from National Archives microfilm Series M804, Roll 1348, File R5305.
Pension abstract for – William Howlett
Service state(s): VT & Navy
Alternate spellings: War dept. had Hamlett, corrected 11 Mar 1833
Date: 26 Aug 1832
County of: Jennings   State of: IN
Declaration made before a Judge or Court: Circuit Court
Act of: 7 Jun 1832
Age: 75 yrs.   Record of age:
Where and year born:
Residence when he entered service: Bennington Co., VT
Residence(s) since the war: Bennington Co., VT; Ross Co., OH; Jennings Co., IN
Residence now: Jennings Co., IN
Volunteer, Drafted, or Substitute: Volunteered all tours
Rank(s): Private
Statement of service-

Period	Duration	Names of General and Field Officers
1776	3 mos.	Capt. John Facet, Lt. Rufus Perry, Col. Samuel Robinson
Again 1776	6 mos.	
1779	5/6 mos.	Capt. William Hutchinson
Mar 1780	9 mos.	Marine on ship Trumbull, a man-of-war

Battles: none
Clergyman: Philip Conner
Certificate of Pension issued the 25 Day of Nov 1832 and sent to Hardin, Versailles, Indiana.
&
Pension abstract for – Martha Howlett widow of William Howlett
Date: 15 Apr 1853
County of: Jennings   State of: IN
Declaration made before a Judge or Court: Notary Public
Act of: 3 Feb 1853
Age: 69 yrs.

Death of soldier: 27 Aug 1852   Jennings Co., IN
Wife's name before marriage: Martha Jacks
Marriage date and place: 29 Nov 1815   Ross Co., OH – certification provided
Proof of marriage: Certified by John Johnston, J.P., Ross Co., OH
Statement: Martha Howlett a resident of Decatur County in the State of Indiana, aged sixty nine; she is the widow of William Howlett who was a pensioner and drew a pension of seventy six dollars and sixty six and two third cents per yr.; she was lawfully married on 29 Nov 1815; her husband died 27 Aug 1852 in Jennings Co. IN.
&
On 27 May 1853, Martha Howlett appeared again before James Myers NP. She stated that deceased pensioner resided in Jennings Co., IN for 34 yrs. bef. d. and previously lived in Ripley Co., IN.

Revolutionary War Service Records; National Archives Publication number M881, Compiled service records of soldiers who served in the American Army during the Revolutionary War, 1775-1783.
https://www.fold3.com/image/21651824?terms=Howlett,%20William
Herrick's Regiment, Vermont Militia
William Howlett, Appears with the rank of -___ on a Pay Roll of Capt. Samuel Robinson's Company in Colo. Samuel Herrick's Regiment of Militia that went to Rutland on Otter Crick in the service of the United States of America to gard the frontiers under the Immediate Command of Lieut. Colo. Ebenezer Walbridge, June 15th, 1778, dated Bennington, Aug 8, 1778. When entered service – June 16, 17__; When discharge – July 9, 17__; Number of days in service – 24; Amount of Wages - £1-12; Number of miles and home – 110; At what per mile – d1; Amount of milage – s9-d2; Total amount of milage and wages £2-s1-d2.
&
Will'm Howlett, Appears with the rank of ____ on a Pay Roll of Captain Samuel Robinson's Company of Militia, Under the Command of Lieut. Colo. Eben'z Walbridge, for Twenty days service, Comme ssing 15th June, 1778, Ended 10 July, 1778, both days Included, dated - Dec 18, 1778; Wen Enter'd the Service – June 15, 1778; When Left the Service – July 9, 1778; Comm't of pay – June 15, 1778; No. of day paid – 24; Pay pr Month – 2-10-0; Whole amount of pay 2-0-0.

United States Revolutionary War Pension Payment Ledgers, 1818-1872, FamilySearch (https://familysearch.org/ark:/61903/1:1:Q24Q-PS7P : accessed 27 September 2016), William Howlett, 01 Mar 1849; citing Indiana, United States, NARA microfilm publication T718 (Washington D.C.: National Archives and Records Administration, 1962), roll 9; FHL microfilm 1,319,389.
Name: William Howlett
Event Type: Military Service
Event Date: 01 Mar 1849
Event Place: Indiana, United States
Death Date: Aug 1852
Page: 388
Affiliate Publication Title: Ledgers of Payments, 1818-1872, to U.S. Pensioners Under Acts of 1818 through 1858, from the Records of the Office of the Third

Auditor of the Treasury. Affiliate Film Number: 9; GS Film Number: 001319389; Digital Folder Number: 007196952; Image Number: 00325.

John E. Goodrich, comp. and ed.; *Rolls of the Soldiers in the Revolutionary War, 1775 to 1783*; pub by authority of the legislature; The Tuttle Company, Rutland, VT, 1904. p. 78, 81, 399, 603.

p. 78
Revolutionary War Rolls
A Pay Roll of Capt. Samuel Robinson's Company of Militia, under the command of Lt. Col. Eben'r Walbridge, for twenty days service, commencing 15th June, 1778 ending 10th July, 1778, both days included.

Names	When Entered service	When left service	Commence't of pay	No. of days paid	Pay per month	Total
[Listed as private]	1778	1778	1778			
William Howlit	June 15	July 9	June 15	25	2.10	2.0.0.

p. 81.
Revolutionary War Rolls
A Pay Roll of Capt. Samuel Robinson's Company in Col. Samuel Herrick's Regiment of Militia that went to Rutland on Otter Creek in the service of the United States of America, to guard the frontiers under the immediate command of Lt. Col. Ebenezer Walbridge, June 15, 1778.

Names	Entered	Discharged	Days	Per day	Amt wages	Miles	Pay per mile	Total
[Listed as private]								
William Howlett	June 16	July 9	24	1.4	1.12	110	0.0.1d	2.1.2

p. 399.
Revolutionary War Rolls
A Pay Roll of Capt. Bigelow Lawrence's Company in Col. Walbridge's Regiment for service done in the alarm at Cambridge and Saratoga in July, 1781.

Names	Days in service	Miles travel	Officers' rations	Amt. of wages, milage & rations
[Listed as private]				
Wm Howlett	4	50		1.2.0

p. 603.
Revolutionary War Rolls
A Pay Roll of Capt. Bigelow Lawrence's Company, Col. Walbridge's Regiment for services done in assisting the sheriff in Windham County, in Sept. 1782, said Comp'y commanded by Ensign Josiah Perry.

Names	No. days In service	Miles travel	Total
[Listed as private]			
Wm Howlett	5	3/pr day	1.10.0

Ohio, County Marriages, 1789-2013; vol. B p202; county courthouses, Ohio; accessed 11 April 2016 from https://familysearch.org/ark:/61903/1:1:XDGM-59Q
Name: William Howlette
Event Type: Marriage
Event Date: 29 Nov 1815
Event Place: Ross, Ohio, United States
Spouse's Name: Martha Jacks
Reference ID: vol B p202
GS Film Number: 281649
Digital Folder Number: 004016206; Image Number: 00225
FHL microfilm 281,649

Waters, Margaret R.; Indiana Land Entries Vol. 1 Cincinnati District, 1801-1840; Originally Published Indianapolis 1948, Second Reprint 1979 by The Bookmark, P.O. Box 74, Knightstown, In 46148. p. 5.
CINCINNATI DISTRICT – VOL. 1
Page 4.   T 3 N,   R 1 W of 1st P.M.   OHIO CO.
William Howlett   SE ¼ - S5; 3-10-1813

Mikesell, Shirley Keller, ed.; Early Settlers of Indiana's "GORE" 1803-1820; Heritage Books, Inc., 1995, p.17.
Dearborn County Original Land Entries Tract Book
Township 3, Range 1W
Format: Section –   Purchaser –   Year – page;
        5 -   William Howlett – 1813 – page 1

Berry, Ellen T. & Berry, David A., compilers; Early Ohio Settlers, Purchasers of Land in Southwestern Ohio, 1800-1840; Genealogical Publishing Co., Inc., Baltimore, MD, 1986. p. 154.

Purchaser	Year	Date	Residence	R	T	S
Howlett, William (B)	1813	March 16	Dearborn (Ind)	01	03	05

(B) Indiana Survey: Land lying west of a meridian drawn west of the Great Miami (known as the "Gore"). Switzerland, Dearborn, Franklin, Ohio, Union and Randolph Counties (all or only a part of each county) – all in Indiana.

The Pension Roll of 1835 Volume IV, The Mid-Western States, Indexed Edition, In Four Volumes; Genealogical Publishing Co., Inc., Baltimore, MD, Reprint 1968, p. 78.
Statement, &c. of Jennings county, Indiana.

INDIANA Names	Rank	Annual allowance.	Sums received	Description of service
William Howlett	Private	76.66	229 98	Vt. State troops

When placed on pension roll	Commencement of pension	Ages	Laws under which they were formerly placed on the pension roll; and remarks.
Nov 23, 1832	March 4, 1831	74	-

Ripley County Indiana, Recorder's Office, Tract Book 3, p. 39.
Howlett, William   20 Jun 1836   R11, T8, S13   40 acres

A Census of Pensioners for Revolutionary or Military Services with their Names, Ages, and Places of Residence Under the Act for Taking the Sixth Census in 1840; Genealogical Publishing Co., Inc., Baltimore, Maryland, 1965, p. 183.

Names of pensioners for revolutionary or military services.	Ages	Names of heads of families with whom pensioners re- Sided June 1, 1840.
INDIANA, JENNINGS COUNTY		
William Howlett	82	William Howlett

U.S. Department of Interior, Bureau of Land Management, General Land Office Records; Land Patent Search
Name: Howlett, William
Accession Nr. CV-0034-488; Document Type – Credit Volume Patent; Issue Date – 6/27/1817; Cancelled – No
Land Office – Cincinnati; Authority – April 24, 1820: Sale-Cash Entry (3 Stat. 566); Document Nr. 0; Total Acres – 0.00
Land Descriptions: State – IN; Meridian – 1stPM; Twp-Rng – 003N – 001W; Aliquots – SE1/4; Section – 5; County - Ohio
&
Name: Howlett, William
Accession Nr. IN0290_.409; Document Type – State Volume Patent; Issue Date – 9/9/1835; Cancelled – No
Land Office – Jeffersonville; Authority – April 24, 1820: Sale-Cash Entry (3 Stat. 566); Document Nr. 4920; Total Acres – 40.00
Land Descriptions: State – IN; Meridian –2ndPM; Twp-Rng – 008N – 009E; Aliquots – NE1/4NE1/4; Section – 1; County - Jennings
&
Name: Howlett, William
Accession Nr. IN2670_.268; Document Type – State Volume Patent; Issue Date – 8/2/1838; Cancelled – No
Land Office – Jeffersonville; Authority – April 24, 1820: Sale-Cash Entry (3 Stat. 566); Document Nr. 9810; Total Acres – 40.00
Land Descriptions: State – IN; Meridian – 2ndPM; Twp-Rng – 008N – 011E; Aliquots – NW1/4NE1/4; Section – 13; County - Ripley
&
Name: Howlett, William
Accession Nr. ; Document Type – State Volume Patent; Issue Date – 8/1/1838; Cancelled – No
Land Office – Jeffersonville; Authority – April 24, 1820: Sale-Cash Entry (3 Stat. 566); Document Nr. 10518; Total Acres – 40.00

Land Descriptions: State – IN; Meridian – 2ndPM; Twp-Rng – 008N – 009E; Aliquots – NW1/4NE1/4; Section – 1; County - Jennings

O'Byrne, Mrs. Roscoe C., comp. & ed.; <u>Roster Soldiers and Patriots of the American Revolution Buried in</u> Indiana; Published by Indiana Daughters of the American Revolution, 1938, Reprinted Genealogical Publishing Co., Baltimore MD, 1968, p. 185.

HOWLETT, WILLIAM   Jennings County

Born – About 1767.

Service – First enlistment under Capt. John Facet, Lieut. Rufus Perry.
        Second, under Col. Samuel Robinson, Col. Whitcomb, Maj. Wait, Capt. Wm. Buchanan, Lieut, Jacob Ferman n Vermont Militia.
        Third, 1779, under Capt. Huntington Col. Seth Warren. Was in the Battle of Bennington and at surrender of Burgoyne. 15 mos.
        Fourth enlistment, volunteered at New London, Conn., as mariner on "Trumbull," Capt. Nichols, Lieuts. Malby and Starr.

Proof – Pension claim R. 5305, rejected for insufficient proof.

Died - Aug. 27, 1852, Jennings County.

Married – 1815, Martha Jack.

HYATT, GIDEON

His name appears on the old "Bronze Tablet" at the Ripley County Court House. Gideon Hyatt did not serve in the American Revolution. No record of service has been located for him. He did not apply for pension.

Patriot: Gideon Hyatt
Birth: 1762 Prince George's County, MD
Married Spouse 1: Anne Ryan
Service state(s): Not applicable
Rank: X
Proof of Service: None
Pension application No.: None
Residences: Maryland; 1787, Huntingdon Co., PA; Ripley Co., IN
Died: aft. 1822
Buried: Hyatt Family Cemetery, Brown Twp., Ripley Co., IN
DAR Ancestor No.: None as of 7 Jun 2017.

Note: Violet Toph wrote to the War Department requesting records for this man. This is the response: There are no claims for pension on file based upon service of Aaron Osborne as described by you in the Revolutionary War, nor of Richard Hodges, Gideon Hyatt and John Signer for service therein. There is no claim for pension of file based upon service of Alexander Boyle and Gideon Hyatt in the War on 1812.

Gibbs, A.; Ripley County Historical Society Data on Revolutionary Soldiers, 1973 review.
Exact location of marker: not found; Brown Tw. Ripley Co. Ind.
Additional comments: on Court House tablet

> Ripley County Historical Society minutes Aug. 26, 1923
> p. 9 "Former congressman John S. Benham followed his brother's talk with an informing talk in which he said that Ripley County could furnish more Revolutionary soldiers than any other county in Indiana. The Gov't pension lists show thirty-seven soldiers of the Revolution in Ripley County. As no pensions were granted prior to 1816, it is probably that several from this County died before this list was furnished…at least six Revolutionary soldiers are buried in Brown Tw. (where the meeting of the day was being held). Thomas Johnson is buried at Friendship, Wycoff, Rutledge buried at Barth Cem., Hyatt buried in the Hyatt neighborhood, Geo. Buchanan buried near the Ripley-Jefferson Co. lines, and Bassett on the Thomas Shields farm (no first name given for Hyatt, Wycoff etc.)

JOHNSON, JAMES

Patriot: James Johnson
Birth: 1760 Scotland
Married Spouse 1: abt. 1785   Agnes Baker (1764-1845)
Service state(s): VA Continental
Rank: Private
Proof of Service: Pension application
Pension application No.: S36664 [a]
Residences: VA; Shelby Co., KY; Clark Co., IN; Ripley Co., IN
Died: 1850 Versailles, Ripley Co., IN
Buried: Cliff Hill Cemetery, Johnson Twp., Ripley
DAR Ancestor No.: A063326

[a] There was a second James Johnson of Shelby Co., KY who applied for pension. His application is #S35471.

Pension Application Abstracted from National Archives microfilm Series M804, Roll 1423, File S36664.
Pension abstract for – James Johnson
Service state(s): VA Continental
Date: 20 May 1818
County of: Fayette   State of: KY
Declaration made before a Judge or Court: Court of Common Law and Criminal Jurisdiction
Act of: 18 Mar 1818
Age: about 58 yrs.
Residence when he entered service: Not stated
Residence now: Shelby Co., KY
Volunteer, Drafted, or Substitute: Enlisted
Rank(s): Private
Statement of service-

Period	Duration	Names of General and Field Officers
Spring 1782- Abt. fall 1783	1 yrs. 6 mos.	VA Continental Line, [1st Dragoons] company under Lt. John Harris, commanded by Gen. Steuben
Abt. Fall 1783 - Close of War		VA Line under Col. White [1st Dragoons; transferred to Corps of Light Horse under Col. Wm. Washington

Discharge received: he together with about one hundred more of said Light Dragoon service came away from the State of Georgia without permission not designing to desert but knowing their times to have Expired according to the terms of their Enlistment and proceeded to Prince Edward County in Virginia at which place they surrendered to General [Daniel] Morgan and was marched from there to Winchester where he received a furlow from Capt. Murrow to return home and remained at home Two or three years and then received a honorable discharge signed by Lieutenant Harris in or about 1786.
&

Pension abstract for – James Johnson
Date: 30 Jun 1820
County of: Shelby   State of: KY
Declaration made before a Judge or Court: Circuit Court
Act of: 18 Mar 1818
Age: 60 yrs.
Residence now: Shelby Co., KY
Wife: Not named
Names and ages of children: he has a Wife and four children living with him one son about twelve years of age and three daughters one about thirty two years of age, one about nineteen years of age who is a cripple in her arm and one about seventeen years old and he has one granddaughter who is an orphan aged about fifteen months who is destitute and friendless.
&
Pension abstract for – James Johnson
Date: 3 Jul 1823
County of: Shelby   State of: KY
Declaration made before a Judge or Court: Court of Common Law
Act of: 18 Mar 1818 & 1 May 1820 & 1 May 1823
Age: 63 yrs.   Record of age:
Wife: Not named   Wife's age: abt. 59 yrs.
Marriage date and place:
Proof of marriage:
Names and ages of children: four children to wit one daughter named Mary 22 years old, one daughter named Sarah 35 years old, one daughter named Nancy 19 years old, and one son named Able 15 years old, and one Granddaughter named Lucy Johnson 4 years old.
&
Date: 21 Sep 1833
Document: Letter from William H. Todd attorney for James Johnson, addressed to the Honorable Secretary of War.
Dear Sir, I as the attorney in fact for James Johnson of Shelby County Kentucky acknowledge the receipt of a Military Land Warrant which issued to James Johnson on the 5th day of September in the year of Crist 1833 for one hundred acres of land for his Services as a private of Dragoons of the Virginia Line No of said Warrant 1963   Signed Leve Cass Secretary of War Register
&
Pension abstract for – James Johnson
Date: 31 Oct 1837
County of: Shelby   State of: KY
Declaration made before a Judge or Court: Justice of the Peace
Declaration: applied to transfer his pension to Clarke County, IN where he had moved for the following reason: "His children have most of them gone to Indiana & he wishes to be near them, that he may receive the assistance of his children in his present aged & Infirm Condition.
&
Pension abstract for – James Johnson
Date: 2 Jan 1843

County of: Ripley   State of: IN
Declaration made before a Judge or Court: Justice of the Peace
Declaration: that he was placed on the Pension Roll of the State of Kentucky from whence he has lately removed that he now resided in the County of Ripley & State of Indiana where he intends to remain and wishes his pension to be made payable at Madison in future, that being the nearest Pension Office to his place of residence.

Abstract of Final Payment Voucher; General Services Administration, Washington, DC
LAST   FINAL PAYMENT VOUCHER RECEIVED FROM
            THE GENERAL ACCOUNTING OFFICE
NAME   Johnson, James, 1st
AGENCY OF PAYMENT   INDIANA
DATE OF ACT   1818
DATE OF PAYMENT   March 1, 1850
DATE OF DEATH   -
GENERAL SERVICES ADMINISTRATION
National Archives and Records Service   NA-286
GSA-WASH DC 54-4891   November 1953

Gwathmey, John H.; *Historical Register of Virginians in the Revolution, Soldiers, Sailors, Marines, 1775-1783;* The Dietz Press, Richmond, VA, 1938, p. 422, 424.
p. 422.
Johnson, James, 5th Troop, 1st Light Dragoons.
Johnson, James, 2nd Troop, 1st Light Dragoons; awarded 100 acres.
Johnson, James (Johnston) 2CL [Continental Line], 4 CL, 4, 8 and 12 CL, 6 CL, 7 CL, 8 CL, 9 CL, 10 CL, 12 CL, 13 CL.
p. 424.
2CL, 4 CL, 4, 8 and 12 CL, 6 CL, 7 CL, 8 CL, 9 CL, 10 CL, 12 CL, 13 CL.

Revolutionary War Land Office Military Certificates; Records of the Executive Branch, Land Office (Record Group 4), microfilm reels 1-38; Library of Virginia, Richmond, VA.
In order to receive bounty lands for Revolutionary War service, a soldier or sailor must have served continuously for at least three years in a Virginia or Continental unit. Service in the militia did not count. The certificates were numbered 1-9926 and cover the period July 14, 1782-August 5, 1876. The warrant specified the amount of lands to be received and directed the surveyor of lands to set aside that quantity of land in the Virginia Military District in Kentucky and Ohio.
[There are three records – unable to determine which is for this man – mjm]
Johnson, James   Rank: Private   Military Certificate number: LO 8421
Johnson, James   Rank: Private   Military Certificate number: LO 6140
Johnson, James   Rank: Private   Military Certificate number: LO 3782

Virginia Military Records from the Virginia Magazine of History and Biography, the William and Mary College Quarterly, and Tyler's Quarterly; Genealogical

Publishing Co., Baltimore, MD, 1983, p. 427.
Va. Officers and Men in the Continental Line, from VMHB, Vol.II (1895), 241-258, 357-370; III (1895), 92.
Doc. No. 34, House of Delegates, 1833-34
A List of some Officers and Soldiers (of Virginia) of the Revolutionary Army.
Included in list of Privates – Johnson, James

Senate Documents, Vol.9, No. 988, 63rd Congress, 3d Session, Washington, 1915; "Register of Certificates Issued by John Pierce, Esquire, Paymaster General and Commissioner of Army Accounts for the United States, to Officers and Soldiers of the Continental Army Under Act of July 4, 1783"; Seventeenth report of the National Society of the Daughters of the American Revolution; Genealogical Publishing Co., Inc., Baltimore, MD, 1984. p. 275.
Men listed in this volume with the same name.

No. of Certificate	To whom issued	Amount
23010	Johnson, James	33.30
33593	Johnson, James	40.00
34296	Johnson, James	8.02
34447	Johnson, James	180.00
34799	Johnson, James	120.62
35087	Johnson, James	80.00
36201	Johnson, James	10.15
56975	Johnson, James	4.08
57361	Johnson, James	136.00
62984	Johnson, James	524.00
62985	Johnson, James	524.00
62986	Johnson, James	525.30
67618	Johnson, James	50.00
68155	Johnson, James	37.60
78519	Johnson, James	65.70
78520	Johnson, James	123.30
78656	Johnson, James	80.00
78790	Johnson, James	123.30
80304	Johnson, James	11.85

Clift, G. Glens, Assistant Secretary, Kentucky Historical Society, Comp.; "Second Census" of Kentucky – 1800, A Privately Compiled and Published Enumeration of Tax Payers Appearing in the 79 Manuscript Volumes Extant of

Tax Lists of the 42 Counties of Kentucky in Existence in 1800; *Genealogical Publishing Co., Baltimore, MD, 1966, p. 153, 154.*

Name	County	Tax List Date	
Johnson, James	Shelby	8/7	1800
Johnson, James	Shelby	8/25/	1800
Johnston, James	Shelby	8/29/	1800
Johnston, James	Shelby	8/29/	1800

Register of the Kentucky Historical Society; Early Kentucky Tax Records*; Clearfield Publishing, Baltimore, Md., 1999; p. 231.*
Department of State Archives – Shelby County Tax Lists, 1795.
A List of Taxable Property Taken and Returned by Thomas Shannon, Esquire, Commissioner of the Tax for Shelby County for the Year 1795.

Persons Named Charges with the Tax	Horses	Cattle	County	Water Course	Acres of Land
Johnston, James	-	8	Shelby	Beech Creek	69 ½

Quisenberry, Anderson Chenault; Revolutionary Soldiers in Kentucky*, containing a roll of the officers of Virginia line who received land bounties, a roll of the Revolutionary pensioners in Kentucky, a list of the Illinois regiment who served under George Rogers Clark in the Northwest campaign, also a roster of the Virginia Navy; Reproduction of the original which appeared in Sons of the American Revolution Kentucky Society Year Book, Louisville, 1896, Southern Book Co., Baltimore, MD, 1959. p.224.*
Shelby County
Pensioners under the Act of March 18, 1818.
Johnson, 1st. James, private   Virginia line
    January 6, 1819;   May 20, 1818; $96.   Age 80.

The Pension Roll of 1835 Volume IV, The Southeastern States*, Indexed Edition, In Four Volumes; Genealogical Publishing Co., Inc., Baltimore, MD, Reprint 1968, p. 247.*
Statement, &c. of Shelby county, Kentucky.

KENTUCKY Names	Rank	Annual allowance.	Sums received	Description of service
James Johnson, 1st	Private	96.00	965.40	Virginia Line

When placed on pension roll	Commencement of pension	Ages	Laws under which they were formerly placed on the pension roll; and remarks.
Jan 6, 1819	May 20, 1818	80	Suspended under act May 1, 1820. Restored, commencing, Nov. 30, 1824.

Pensioners of the Revolutionary War Struck Off the Roll with an Added Index to States*; Reprinted by Genealogical Publishing Co., Baltimore, MD for Clearfield Company, Inc., 1989. p. 93.*
Pensioners in Kentucky who have been dropped from the pension roll under the act of 1st May, 1820; prepared in conformity with the resolution of the House of Representatives of the 17th December, 1835.

Names	Acts under which restored	Remarks
Include in list –		
James Johnson, 1st	March 1, 1823	-

U.S. Department of Interior, Bureau of Land Management, General Land Office Records; Land Patent Search
Name: Johnson, James
Accession Nr. IN2790_.379; Document Type – State Volume Patent; Issue Date – 1/9/1841; Cancelled – No
Land Office – Jeffersonville; Authority – April 24, 1820: Sale-Cash Entry (3 Stat. 566); Document Nr. 15919; Total Acres – 80.00
Land Descriptions: State – IN; Meridian – 2ndPM; Twp-Rng – 008N – 011E; Aliquots – E1/2SE1/4; Section – 20; County - Ripley

Cowen, Janet C., comp; Jeffersonville Land Entries 1808-1818; McDowell Publications, Utica, NY, 1984, p. 118, 124, 146.
p. 118.
Receipt # 10349   Johnson   James   KY   Shelby   NE S14 T02 N01E   160
Date 1816 09 12 *p. 124*
Receipt # 10752   Johnson   James   KY   Shelby   NE S14 T02 N01E   160
Date 1816 10 17
p. 146.
Receipt # 12160   Johnson   James   KY   Shelby   NE s14 T02 N01E   160
Date 1817 04 05

Ripley County Indiana, Recorder's Office, Tract Book 3, p. 41.
Johnson, James   11 Sep 1838   R11, R8, S20   80 acres

Ripley County, Indiana Will Records vol. B, June 1839-May 1862; p. 92.
&
Ripley County Indiana Probate Order Book B, 8 May 1837-17 Aug 1843; p. 262, 271, 362, 363.
&
Ripley County Indiana Complete Probate Record Book Vol. F., June 1851- June 1852; p. 335-339.
Abstract of will and administration for: James Johnson
Date and place will was made: 5 Dec 1843   Ripley Co., IN
Witnesses to will: John Lewis, Isaiah W. Robinson
Names of executors: John Lewis
Administrator: court appointed Ebenezer S. Hawley
Date recorded: 13 May 1850
Bonded by: John W. Smith $250.00.
Names of heirs and others mentioned in will and relationship if shown: Wife Agnes; Sons James, Abel, Joshua, David, Richard's heirs; Daughter Mary Johnson, now Mary Griffith, Sally Johnson.
My estate to my daughter Sally Johnson to take care of my wife Agnes Johnson during her natural life.
Date of division & disbursement, or final return: 19 Jun 1859

O'Byrne, Mrs. Roscoe C., comp. & ed.; Roster Soldiers and Patriots of the American Revolution Buried in Indiana; Published by Indiana Daughters of the American Revolution, 1938, Reprinted Genealogical Publishing Co., Baltimore MD, 1968, p. 210.

JOHNSON, JAMES   Ripley County
Born – About 1760.
Service – Enlisted spring 1782 in Vir., in company of Lieut. John Harres of Vir. Cnt'l Line commanded by Gen. Steuben at Point Fort on James River. In same year he re-enlisted in Light Dragoon Service, under Col. Wm. Washington; continued in service until 1784. Received bounty land.
Proof – Pension claim S. 36664, B. L. Wt. 1963-100.
Died – After 1843. Buried Cliff Hill Cemetery, Johnson Twp., Ripley Co., on an Indian mound near center of cemetery (S.A.R. Records).
Children – Mary; Sarah; Nancy; Able.

O'Byrne, comp. Mrs. Roscoe C., comp.; Roster of Soldiers and Patriots of the American Revolution Buried in Indiana, Vol. III; Indiana Daughters of the American Revolution, 1966, p. 28.

JOHNSON, JAMES   Ripley County
Born – ca. 1750.
Service – Enl. in spring of 1782 serving until June 1783. Pvt. in Va. Regt. in Light Dragoons, Continental Line under Capt. Hughes, Green and Watts command.
Proof – Pension #S5203 issued 1819 through Ky. agency then transferred to Ind. Agency. Patriot Index, p. 370.
Died – Apr. 1850. Buried Cliff Hill Cemetery, Versailles, Ind., Ripley Co. Ross Run Chapter DAR marked grave in 1974.
Married – Agnes Baker.
Children – Sarah; Annie b. ca. 1830 Ky. m. James Connelly; Mary b. ca. 1801 m. William Griffith; Nancy b. ca. 1804; Abel b. ca. 1808; James; Joshua; David; Richard.
By Mrs. David L. Gibbs, RR #2, Box 82, Hopewell Road, Holton, Indiana 47023.

Gibbs, A.; Ripley County Historical Society Data on Revolutionary Soldiers, 1973 review.

Exact location of marker: S.A.R. records - Indian Mound in Cliff Hill Cemetery, and a big flat slab for the burial site but no name marks the spot today (1973).
Toph notes: buried west of the tree on the Indian Mound.
Type of marker: Gov't
Date placed: Dedicated 11 Nov 1974
Placed by: Ross' Run Chapter Daughters of the American Revolution
Additional comments: Ripley County Will Book B, p. 92; will dated 5 Dec 1843; probated 13 Au 1850; sons James, Abel, Joshua, David, Richard; dau. Mary Griffith, Sally Johnson; wife Agnes.
1850 Mortality Schedule (census) age 100 b. Va d. April 1850

Wording on marker: James Johnson
Virginia
Pvt. 1 Regt.
Lt. Dragoons
Continental Line
Revolutionary
War
1750-1850

Tombstone Location: Cliff Hill Cemetery, Johnson Twp., Ripley

Tombstone Inscription:

JAMES
JOHNSON
VIRGINIA
PVT 1 REGT
LT DRAGOONS
CONTINENTAL LINE
REVOLUTIONARY
WAR
1750   1850

JOHNSON, PHILIP

Patriot: Philip Johnston (Johnson)
Birth: 1758[a] Unknown - Scotland or VA
Married Spouse 1: abt. 1782 Susannah (1766-1834)
Service state(s): VA
Rank: Private
Proof of Service: Pension application
Pension application No.: S36657
Residences: Essex Co., VA; Madison Co., KY; Fayette Co., KY; Montgomery Co., KY; Jefferson Co., IN; Ripley Co., IN
Died: 11 Jul 1835 Ripley Co., IN
Buried: West Bank of Otter Creek (Matt Kibler farm), Jennings Co., IN[a]
DAR Ancestor No.: A063571

Pension Application Abstracted from National Archives microfilm Series M804, Roll 1427, File S36657.
Pension abstract for – Philip Johnson
Service state(s): VA Continental Line
Alternate spelling(s): Johnston
Date: 12 Sep 1818
County of: Montgomery   State of: KY
Declaration made before a Judge or Court: Circuit Court
Act of: 18 Mar 1818
Age: 60 yrs.
Residence when he entered service: Not stated
Residence(s) since the war: Not stated
Residence now: Madison Co., KY
Volunteer, Drafted, or Substitute: Enlisted at Hobb's Hole, Essex Co., VA
Rank(s): Matross
Statement of service-

Period	Duration	Names of General and Field Officers
Apr 1777 - Close of War	6 yrs.	VA Continental Line in Co. 1st Regt. Artillery, commanded by Capt. James Pendleton, Lt. Bohannon,

Battles: Monmouth, Stony Point, Gates Defeat, Peters Barg [prob. Petersburg]
Discharge received: at Old Town, Halifax Co., VA
What became of it?: Gave his discharge to Capt. Bohannan to draw the balance of his pay and has never seen it since.
Person now living who can testify to service: Affidavit, dated 23 Dec 1819, of William P. Smith, Richmond, Charlotte Co., VA, describing Philip Johnson's service.
&
Pension abstract for – Philip Johnson
Date: 5 Sep 1820
County of: Madison   State of: KY
Declaration made before a Judge or Court: Circuit Court
Declaration: He belonged to the 1st Regiment of Virginia Artillery and to

Capt. Pendleton's Company. He provided a schedule of property.
Act of: 18 Mar 1818
Age: 61 yrs.
Wife: Not mentioned
Names and ages of children: He has five children living with him: Berry, 18; Langston, 15; Clement, 10 who is a cripple. All of his children are able to maintain themselves by there own labour except Clement who is a cripple.
&
Pension abstract for – Philip Johnson
Alternate spelling(s): Johnson
Date: 21 Nov 1825
County of: Jefferson				State of: IN
Declaration made before a Judge or Court: Justice of the Peace
Declaration: A pension certificate was granted 25 Apr 1820; he was placed on the list of KY agency; he resided in Lexington, KY up to 4 Sep 1825; he now resides in Ripley County, IN and expects to reside there; he wishes to be transferred from the Agency of the State of Kentucky to the Agency of the State of Indiana.
&
Additional Government papers in his pension file show he was born 1742?; died 11 Jul 1835; he drew pension in Montgomery Co., KY

Abstract of Final Payment Voucher; General Services Administration, Washington, DC
FINAL PAYMENT VOUCHER RECEIVED FROM
THE GENERAL ACCOUNTING OFFICE
NAME					JOHNSON, PHILIP
AGENCY OF PAYMENT	INDIANA
DATE OF ACT			1818
DATE OF PAYMENT		1st Qr. 1836
DATE OF DEATH		July 11, 1835
GENERAL SERVICES ADMINISTRATION
National Archives and Records Service		NA-286
GSA-WASH DC 54-4891				November 1953

Wardell, Patrick G., comp.; *Virginia/West Virginia Genealogical Data From Revolutionary War Pension and Bounty Land Warrant Records, Vol. 1 ---Aaron through Cyrus*; Heritage Books, Inc., Bowie, MD, 1988, p. 29.
Johnson, Philip, esf. 1777 Hales Hollow, Essex Co., VA; PN ae 60 Montgomery Co., KY, 1818 occupation farmer; res there 1820 when had 5 ch liv with him, including Berry ae 19, Langston ae 15 & Clement ae 10, a cripple; mvd c1824 to Ripley Co, IN; dd 7/11/35; surname also spelled Johnston; QLF states sol b 1742; QLF states a Philip Johnson, dd 1788, md Elizabeth Bray, & was member/o RW Committee of Safety, James Co VA. F-S36657 R1427.

Gwathmey, John H.; *Historical Register of Virginians in the Revolution, Soldiers, Sailors, Marines, 1775-1783*; The Dietz Press, Richmond, VA, 1938, p. 422, 424.

p, 422
Johnson, Philip, from Essex, in Col. Harrison's Reg, of Artillery; county ref. Feb. 20, 1781.
Johnson, Philp, Fifer and Matross, 1st Artillery.
p, 424
Johnston, Philip, attested as soldier from Essex in 1780.

<u>Revolutionary War Land Office Military Certificates</u>; *Records of the Executive Branch, Land Office (Record Group 4), microfilm reels 1-38; Library of Virginia, Richmond, VA.*
In order to receive bounty lands for Revolutionary War service, a soldier or sailor must have served continuously for at least three years in a Virginia or Continental unit. Service in the militia did not count. The certificates were numbered 1-9926 and cover the period July 14, 1782-August 5, 1876. The warrant specified the amount of lands to be received and directed the surveyor of lands to set aside that quantity of land in the Virginia Military District in Kentucky and Ohio.
Johnson, Philip Rank: Private Military Certificate number: LO 6352
[Note: His is not a common name, he may have served as a Sergeant, if so this record could be for him – mjm]
Johnston, Philip Rank: Sergeant Military Certificate number: LO 3479

Senate Documents, Vol.9, No. 988, 63rd Congress, 3d Session, Washington, 1915; "Register of Certificates Issued by John Pierce, Esquire, Paymaster General and Commissioner of Army Accounts for the United States, to Officers and Soldiers of the Continental Army Under Act of July 4, 1783"; <u>Seventeenth report of the National Society of the Daughters of the American Revolution</u>; *Genealogical Publishing Co., Inc., Baltimore, MD, 1984. p. 276.*
Men listed in this volume with the same name.

No. of Certificate	To whom issued	Amount
20601	Johnson, Philip	38.00
22387	Johnson, Philip	15.50
78441	Johnson, Philip	74.60
21798	Johnson, Philip, 1st	17.00
20568	Johnson, Philip, jr.	80.00
20927	Johnson, Philip, jr.	80.00
21629	Johnson, Philip, jr.	27.81
22102	Johnson, Philip, jr.	40.60

Bockstruck, Lloyd DeWitt; <u>Revolutionary War Bounty Land Grants Awarded by State Governments</u>; *Genealogical Publishing Co., IN, Baltimore, MD, 1996, p. 278.*
Johnson, Philip. Va. Private. 23 Dec. 1819. 100 acres.

Wilson, Samuel L., comp.; <u>Year Book of the Society, Sons of the American Revolution in the Commonwealth of Kentucky, 1894-1913, and Catalogue of Military Land Warrants Granted by the Commonwealth of Virginia</u>; *Lexington, KY, 1913, p. 229.*

No. of Warrant	Name of Officer or Soldier	No. of Acres	Character of Service as Private or Officer, If Officer, what Grade	Department of Service: Continental or State Line or Navy
3479	Johnson, Phillip	200	Sergeant	Va. Cont. Line

No. of Years of Service	Date of Warrant
3 yrs.	Oct. 23, '84

Clift, G. Glens, Assistant Secretary, Kentucky Historical Society, Comp.; *"Second Census" of Kentucky – 1800, A Privately Compiled and Published Enumeration of Tax Payers Appearing in the 79 Manuscript Volumes Extant of Tax Lists of the 42 Counties of Kentucky in Existence in 1800*; Genealogical Publishing Co., Baltimore, MD, 1966, p. 154.

Name	County	Tax List Date
Johnson, Philip	Clark	1800

The Pension Roll of 1835 Volume III, The Mid-Western States, Indexed Edition, In Four Volumes; Genealogical Publishing Co., Inc., Baltimore, MD, Reprint 1968, p. 51.

A statement showing the names, rank, &c., or persons residing in Ripley county, in the State of Indiana, who have been inscribed on the pension list under the act of Congress passed March 18, 1818.

INDIANA Names	Rank	Annual allowance.	Sums received	Description of service
Philip Johnson	Private	96.00	1,486 09	Virginia line

When placed on pension roll	Commencement of pension	Ages	Laws under which they were formerly placed on the pension roll; and remarks.
Ap'l 25, 1820	Sep 12, 1818	76	Transferred from Montgomery County, Kentucky

Toph, Violet E.; *Peoples History of Ripley County, Indiana*; self-published, c. 1940, p. 125.

Revolutionary Soldiers Who Came to Ripley County
Philip Johnson (or Johnston) enlisted from Virginia in June, 1777 and served six years. He was born in 1742 and died in 1835. He was pensioned from Madison County, Ky. and later moved to Ripley County.

O'Byrne, Mrs. Roscoe C., comp. & ed.; *Roster Soldiers and Patriots of the American Revolution Buried in Indiana*; Published by Indiana Daughters of the American Revolution, 1938, Reprinted Genealogical Publishing Co., Baltimore

MD, 1968, p. 211.
JOHNSON, PHILIP   Jennings County
Born – 1758, in Scotland or Virginia.
Service – Enlisted at Hale's Hole, Essex Co., Vir., April, 1777, and served for 6 years as matross in Capt. James Pendleton's CO. In battles of Monmouth, Stony Point, Gate's Defeat, and Petersburg.
Proof – Pension claim S. 36657.
Died – July 11, 1835. Buried on West Bank of Otter Creek, in an old garden on farm now owned by Mat Kibler, Jennings Co.
Married – 1782, Susannah -------- (1766-1834). Ch. Jane, b. 1783; William M., b. 1786 (War of 1812); Giles, b. 1788; Elizabeth, b. 1791; James R., b. 1793; Lemmy S., b. 1795; Joel W., b. 1798; Mary, b. 1800; Berry, b. 1802; Lankston, b. 1804; Clement, b. 1807.
Collected by Mrs. L. E. Tranter, Franklin, Indiana.

Gibbs, A.; Ripley County Historical Society Data on Revolutionary Soldiers, *1973 review.*
Exact location of marker: Clarence and Josie Rahe notes: Philip J. Johnson, a Rev. soldier, is buried on the Fisse farm on the line between the Fisse farm and the Mort Gilliland farm on the Laughrey (Creek) south of Bethel church. To get there from Versailles, take the Vevay Rd. (Rt. 129) past the Curran Schoolhouse, past Charlie Hofferkamp's to the top of Signor Hill; go to the foot of the hill on a road that turns left and cross the creek to reach the Fisse farm. The slab of the Johnson grave is broken off…about 150 rods from old brick house are several other Johnsons buried.
Type of marker: Family
Additional comments: on Court House tablet
    O'Byrne (Indiana DAR) places this man in Jennings Co. Ind.
    Pension Roll 1835, vol. 4, p. 29. Pvt. Va. line; placed on pension roll Apr. 25, 1820; commencement of pension Sept. 12, 1818, age 76 (in 1835).

[a]Additional notes: Charles W. Miles & Lafayette A. Hand & others; Brief History and Genealogy of Philip Johnson Family from 1759-1935; publ. North Vernon Ind. 1936; in the possession of Otis Grinstead, Butlerville, Ind. in 1974.
    Johnson, Philip   b. – 1758   d. 11 July 1835
    m. Susannah ----   b. 13 June 1766   d. 14 Nov 1834
    both buried in Kibler farm cemetery, Jennings Co., Ind., west bank Big Otter Creek, cemetery.

JOHNSON, ROSWELL

His name appears on the old "Bronze Tablet" at the Ripley County Court House. No evidence has been located proving he served as a "Drummer Boy" in the American Revolution. Due to lack of evidence, his name will not be included on the new Memorial. A bronze plate is reserved for him should anyone be able to furnish proof of his service.

Patriot: Roswell Johnson
Birth: 14 Aug 1769 Montgomery Co., VA
Married Spouse 1: 8 Jan 1798, Montgomery Co., VA   Mary "Polly" Barnett
(1778 - aft Feb 1839)

Service state(s): VA
Rank: Drummer Boy (?)
Proof of Service: None
Pension application No.: None
Residences: Montgomery Co., VA; Ripley Co., IN
Died: 14 Jul 1837 Ripley Co., IN
Buried: Roswell Johnson Family Cemetery, (remains removed to Bethel Cemetery) Johnson Twp., Ripley Co., IN
DAR Ancestor No.: None as of 7 June 2017.

Summers, Lewis Preston; Annals of Southwest Virginia 1769-1800; Genealogical Publishing Co., Inc., 1996, p. 869.
Montgomery County
Aug. 1, 1797
Raswell Johnston appointed overseer of the road from the first bridge below Mrs. Kent's to the upper crossing of Roanoak.

Virginia, Marriages, 1785-1940; accessed 12 December 2015 from https://familysearch.org/ark:/61903/1:1:XR8J-Y9Y
Name: Roswell Johnson
Spouse's Name: Polly Barnett
Event Date: 08 Jan 1798
Event Place: Montgomery County, Virginia
Spouse's Father's Name: John Barnett
Indexing Project (Batch) Number: M86878-8; System Origin: Virginia-EASy; GS Film number: 32633; Reference ID:P 74
FHL microfilm 32,633

United States Census, 1810, U.S. National Archives and Records Administration (NARA), Affiliate Publication Number: M252; Affiliate Film Number: 70; GS Film Number:0181430; Digital Folder Number: 005157087; Image Number: 00113; FamilySearch (https://familysearch.org/ark:/61903/1:1:XH28-SCR: accessed 12 December 2015).
Name: Roswell Johnston
Event Type: Census
Event Date: 1810

Event Place:	Christiansburg, Montgomery, Virginia, United States
Note:	Page:	663

<u>U.S. Department of Interior, Bureau of Land Management, General Land Office Records; Land Patent Search</u>
Name: Johnson, Roswell & Crawford, James M C; Accession Nr. CV-0038-075; Document Type – Credit Volume Patent; Issue Date – 3/23/1818; Cancelled – No; Land Office – Jeffersonville; Authority – April 24, 1820: Sale-Cash Entry (3 Stat. 566); Document Nr. 0; Total Acres – 0.00; Land Descriptions: State – IN; Meridian – 2ndPM; Twp-Rng – 007N – 012E; Aliquots – NW1/4; Section – 29; County - Ripley
&
Name: Johnson, Roswell & Morris, Claburn; Accession Nr. CV-0077-165; Document Type – Credit Volume Patent; Issue Date – 12/2/1822; Cancelled – No; Land Office – Jeffersonville; Authority – April 24, 1820: Sale-Cash Entry (3 Stat. 566); Document Nr. 283; Total Acres – 80.00; Land Descriptions: State – IN; Meridian – 2ndPM; Twp-Rng – 007N – 012E; Aliquots – E1/2SW1/4; Section – 29; County - Ripley
&
Name: Smith, Samuel S. & Johnson, Roswell; Accession Nr. CV-0078-009; Document Type – Credit Volume Patent; Issue Date – 12/30/1822; Cancelled – No; Land Office – Jeffersonville; Authority – April 24, 1820: Sale-Cash Entry (3 Stat. 566); Document Nr. 673; Total Acres – 160.00; Land Descriptions: State – IN; Meridian – 2ndPM; Twp-Rng – 007N – 012E; Aliquots – NE1/4; Section – 20; County - Ripley
&
Name: Johnson, Roswell; Accession Nr. IN0210_.122; Document Type – State Volume Patent; Issue Date – 7/28/1823; Cancelled – No; Land Office – Jeffersonville; Authority – April 24, 1820: Sale-Cash Entry (3 Stat. 566); Document Nr. 628; Total Acres – 80.00; Land Descriptions: State – IN; Meridian – 2ndPM; Twp-Rng – 007N – 012E ; Aliquots – E1/2SW1/4; Section – 10; County – Ripley
&
Name: Johnson, Roswell; Accession Nr. CV-0086-520; Document Type – Credit Volume Patent; Issue Date – 1/4/1830; Cancelled – No; Land Office – Jeffersonville; Authority – April 24, 1820: Sale-Cash Entry (3 Stat. 566); Document Nr. 2430; Total Acres – 80.00; Land Descriptions: State – IN; Meridian – 2ndPM; Twp-Rng – 007N – 012E; Aliquots – E1/2SE1/4; Section – 19; County - Ripley
&
Name: Johnson, Roswell; Accession Nr. CV-0086-551; Document Type – Credit Volume Patent; Issue Date – 1/4/1830; Cancelled – No; Land Office – Jeffersonville; Authority – April 24, 1820: Sale-Cash Entry (3 Stat. 566); Document Nr. 2461; Total Acres – 80.00; Land Descriptions: State – IN; Meridian – 2ndPM; Twp-Rng – 007N – 012E; Aliquots – W1/4SE1/4; Section – 20; County - Ripley
&

Name: Johnson, Roswell; Accession Nr. IN0330_.412; Document Type – State Volume Patent; Issue Date – 3/15/1837; Cancelled – No; Land Office – Jeffersonville; Authority – April 24, 1820: Sale-Cash Entry (3 Stat. 566); Document Nr. 6936; Total Acres – 40.00; Land Descriptions: State – IN; Meridian – 2ndPM; Twp-Rng – 007N – 012E; Aliquots – NE1/4SE1/4; Section – 20; County - Ripley
&
Name: Johnson, Roswell; Accession Nr. IN0330_.413; Document Type – State Volume Patent; Issue Date – 3/15/1837; Cancelled – No; Land Office – Jeffersonville; Authority – April 24, 1820: Sale-Cash Entry (3 Stat. 566); Document Nr. 6937; Total Acres – 40.00; Land Descriptions: State – IN; Meridian – 2ndPM; Twp-Rng – 007N – 012E; Aliquots – SW1/4NE1/4; Section – 29; County - Ripley

Cowen, Janet C., comp; Jeffersonville Land Entries 1808-1818; McDowell Publications, Utica, NY, 1984, p. 147, 153, 159, 174.
p. 147. Receipt # 12247
Johnson Roswell IN Jefferson SE S19 T07 N12E   1817 04 21
p. 153. Receipt # 12598
Johnson Roswell IN Jefferson SE S19 T07 N12E 160 1817 05 29
p. 159. Receipt #13018
Johnson Roswell IN Ripley NE S20 T07 N12E 160 1817 07 19
p. 174. Receipt # 13975
Johnson Roswell IN Ripley E 1/2 SE S20 T07 N12E 80 1817 10 06

Ripley County Indiana, Recorder's Office, Tract Book 1, p. 37.
Johnson, Roswell   21 Apr 1817   R12. T7, S20   160acres

Ripley County, Indiana Deed Records Vol. A, 11 Aug 1818-29 Jan 1827
Page(s): 90-92.
Abstract of Deed/Patent for: Roswell Johnson and Polly (dower) his wife of
                               County of Ripley, State of Indiana.
Purchaser (Grantee) or Seller (Grantor)?: Seller
Sold to: Samuel Cole son-in-law of the said Roswell Johnson.
State & county where recorded: Ripley Co., Indiana
Date entered: 2 Aug 1823
Recorded: 5 Nov 1823
Description: Part of the east half of the southwest quarter of Section 29, of Township 7, and Range 12 East of the lands offered for sale at Jeffersonville.
Amount paid: In consideration of the natural love and affection which he the said Roswell Johnson and Polly his wife hath and bequeath unto their son-in-law Samuel Cole as also for the better maintaining and support of him.
Name(s) of Witnesses: William Laycock & Jon Jonson

Ripley County, Indiana Deed Records Vol. B., 29 Jan 1827-21 Sep 1832,
Page(s) 34-35.
Abstract of Deed/Patent for: Roswell Johnson and Polly (dower) his wife of the county of Ripley.
Purchaser (Grantee) or Seller (Grantor)?: Seller
Sold to: George Pate of Dearborn Co., IN
State & county where recorded: Ripley Co., Indiana
Date entered: 31 Mar 1827
Recorded: 2 Apr 1827
Description: Northwest quarter of Section 29, in Township 7, North Range 12 East in the district of lands offered at Jeffersonville, containing 160 acres; also, 20 acres of southwest quarter of Section 29, in Township 7, North Range 12 East; in all 180 acres.
Amount paid: One thousand dollars ($1,000.00).
Name(s) of Witnesses: John Johnson & James Davis

Ripley County, Indiana Deed Records Vol. C., 21 Sep 1832 - 4 Feb 1834,
Page(s) 165-166. [Note: Some of the page numbers were repeated in this volume. These pages are in the second grouping of page numbers.]
Abstract of Deed/Patent for: Roswell Johnson and Mary (dower) his wife.
Purchaser (Grantee) or Seller (Grantor)?: Seller
Sold to: Joseph Blair and Sarah Jane Blair
State & county where recorded: Ripley Co., Indiana
Date entered: 10 Sep 1831
Recorded: 31 Dec 1831
Description: East half of the southwest quarter of Section 10, in Township 7 East, Range 12, land sold at Jeffersonville land office.
Amount paid: One hundred dollars ($100.00).
Name(s) of Witnesses: Edward Pendergast & William Johnson

Ripley County, Indiana Deed Records Vol. C., 21 Sep 1832 - 4 Feb 1834,
Page 516-517.
Abstract of Deed/Patent for: Roswell Johnson (no dower)
Purchaser (Grantee) or Seller (Grantor)?: Seller
Sold to: John Johnson, Jr.
State & county where recorded: Ripley Co., Indiana
Date entered: 5 Jan 1834
Recorded: 29 Jan 1834
Description: Peace or parcel of Land to wit; the East half of the South East quarter of Section 9 North of Range 12 East; containing 80 acres.
Amount paid: One hundred dollars ($100.00)
Name(s) of Witnesses: E. L. Dunbar & David P. Shook

1820 U. S. Census, Ripley Co., IN, NARA Roll M33_15; EN 7 Aug 1820, p. 79, 4th line from bottom of page.
Roswell Johnson
Males <10=2, Males 10-15=1, Males 45>=1, Females <10=1, Females 10-15=2, Females 16-25=1, Females 26-44=1.

Ripley County, Indiana Complete Probate Book Vol. A., *12 May 1834-10 May 1842; p. 226-238.*
&
Ripley Co., IN Probate Order Book, Vol.1 Wills, Sep 1821-Apr 1839, p. 41.
Abstract of will and administration for: Roswell Johnson
Date and place will was made: 9 Apr 1837, Johnson Twp., Ripley Co., IN
Witnesses to will: M. Hyatt, Benjamin Tribble, James Henderson
Names of executors – John Johnson, Henry Pate, Goff W. Willson
Date recorded: 8 Aug 1837
Bonded by and amount of bond: M. Hyatt, James Davis, Beverly Blair; $2,000.00
Names of heirs and others mentioned in will and relationship if shown:
My beloved wife (not named); sons & daughters John Johnson; Elizabeth Cole; Elanor Baker; Sarah Jane Johnson; Rebecca Pate; William Johnson; Thomas Westley Johnson; Amanda Johnson & "son" Goff W. Willson.
Date of division & disbursement, or final return: 2 Feb 1838

Toph, Violet E.; *Peoples History of Ripley County, Indiana;* self-published, c. 1940, p. 131.
Revolutionary Soldiers Who Came to Ripley County
Roswell Johnson was born August 14, 1769 in Montgomery County, Va. He served three months as a Drummer boy in the Continental army in 1782. He died July 17, 1837. He is buried on the old Johnson farm south of Versailles which is owned by Dick Grey. It is near the old Bethel cemetery where the Johnson family markers are.

O'Byrne, Mrs. Roscoe C., comp. & ed.; *Roster Soldiers and Patriots of the American Revolution Buried in Indiana;* Published by Indiana Daughters of the American Revolution, 1938, Reprinted Genealogical Publishing Co., Baltimore MD, 1968, p. 211.
JOHNSON, ROSWELL   Ripley County
Born – Aug. 14, 1769, Montgomery Co., Virginia.
Service – Drummer boy with the Vir. Troops in the Continental Army for 3 mos. in 1782.
Proof – Family records furnished by Mrs. Otto F. Thum, 617 S. Sherman, Denver, Colo.
Died – July 14, 1837. Buried near Versailles, Ind. Stone and bronze tablet placed by Ripley Co. Historical Society.
Married – Polly Burnet. Had 17 children. These names obtained – Sarah Jane, m. Obed Wilson; John; Wesley J.; Eliza Baker; Bettie Cole; Betsey Pate; Amanda Blackwell.
Collected by Mrs. A. B. Wycoff, Batesville, Indiana.

Gibbs, A.; *Ripley County Historical Society Data on Revolutionary Soldiers,* 1973 review.
Exact location of marker: 1/2 mi. back off Cave Hill Rd. on 200S in overgrown grove on cliff overlooking Laughrey Creek. Bethel Cemetery; s. of Versailles; Johnson Tw. Ripley Co. Ind.
Type of marker: Family (broken top)

Roswell 　　　　　　　　　　Mary, consort of Roswell Johnson
died 　　　　　　　　　　　　died
July 17, 1837 　　　　　　　　Aug. 10, 1844
Aged 67yr 11mo 3da 　　　　aged 66yr 5mo 8da
Type of marker: Memorial
Date placed: The RCHS held a dedication for this marker in Oct. 1928.
Placed by: Ripley County Historical Society
Wording on marker: 　　　　Roswell Johnson
　　　　　　　　　　　　　　First Treasurer
　　　　　　　　　　　　　　　　　of
　　　　　　　　　　　　　　Ripley County, Ind.
　　　　　　　　　　　　　　1818-1822
Additional comments: on Court House tablet

Tombstone Location: 　　　Bethel Cemetery, Johnson Twp., Ripley Co., IN

Tombstone Inscription: 　　ROSWELL JOHNSON
　　　　　　　　　　　　　　　　　DIED
　　　　　　　　　　　　　　　July 14, 1837
　　　　　　　　　　　　　　　Aged 67 Yrs
　　　　　　　　　　　　　　11 Mos. & 3 Da.
　　　　　　　　　　　[Further remark is illegible – mjm]

Additional marker: 　　　　ROSWELL JOHNSON
　　　　　　　　　　　　　　FIRST TREASURER
　　　　　　　　　　　　　　　　　OF
　　　　　　　　　　　　　　RIPLEY COUNTY, INDIANA
　　　　　　　　　　　　　　　1818-1822

JOHNSTON, THOMAS

Patriot: Thomas Johnson
Birth: 1755
Married Spouse 1: XX
Married Spouse 2: 22 Nov 1793, Greenbrier Co., VA
                          Sarah "Sally" Foster (1777-1846)
Service state(s): PA Continental
Rank: Private, 2nd Lieutenant
Proof of Service: Pension application
Pension application No.: W10158
Residences: PA; Greenbrier Co., VA; Greenbrier Co., WV; OH;
               Ripley Co., IN; Dearborn Co., IN
Died: 26 May 1823   Dearborn Co., IN
Buried: at Friendship per Ripley County Historical Society minutes 26 Aug 1923
DAR Ancestor No.:None as of 7 Jun 2017.

Pension Application Abstracted from National Archives microfilm Series M804, Roll 1434, File W10158.
Pension abstract for – Thomas Johnston
Service state(s): PA Continental Line
Date: 18 Jul 1818
County of: Dearborn   State of: IN
Declaration made before a Judge or Court: Judge, Dearborn Circuit Court
Act of: 18 Mar 1818
Age: nearly 63 yrs.
Residence when he entered service: Not stated
Residence(s) since the war: Not stated
Residence now: Dearborn Co., IN
Volunteer, Drafted, or Substitute: Enlisted
Rank(s): Private
Statement of service-

Period	Duration	Names of General and Field Officers
Apr 1777 - 4 Oct 1777	6 mos.	PA Continental Line, Capt. Henry McKinley, Col. Cook. *[12th PA Regt., Company F, recruited Northumberland & Northampton Cos.; merged with 3rd PA Regt.]*
4 Oct 1777		At Germantown, where he was shot in the leg (which shattered the bone very much). He was removed to Bethlehem Hospital for upward of 3 mos.; then removed to Shavertown Hospital in Lancaster Co., PA; then to Lebanon in PA where he was employed in the service of the United States by preparing ammunition cartridges abt. 6 wks.; then Philadelphia where surgeon determine him not fit for field service.
- Thru Apr 1780		Transferred to Capt. *[John David]* Woelpper's Invalid Regiment.

Battles: Skirmish at Pascatanay [Punxsutawney] where he received a wound in his left arm by buckshot; Brandywine; Germantown.

Discharge received: Apr 1780 by enlisting a man to serve in his place until the end of the war.
What became of it?: Does not know where it is.
Statement is supported by –
Documentary proof: Has none
&
Pension abstract for – Thomas Johnston
Date: 20 Sep 1820
County of: Dearborn   State of: IN
Declaration made before a Judge or Court: Circuit Court
Declaration: stated service, and has received Pension Certificate number 12,572; & provides schedule of property.
Act of: 18 Mar 1818
Age: 65 yrs.
Wife: Not mentioned
Names and ages of children: Five children: Nancy, 20; Isaac, 15; James, 13; Wayne, 8; Nathaniel, 6.
&
Pension abstract for – Sarah Johnston widow of Thomas Johnston
Date: 4 Apr 1843
County of: Ripley   State of: IN
Declaration made before a Judge or Court: Justice of the Peace
Act of: 7 Jul 1838 & 3 Mar 1843
Age: 64 yrs.
Death of soldier: 6 May 1823 in Dearborn Co., IN
Marriage date and place: 22 Nov 1793 Greenbrier Co., VA
Proof of marriage: Certification of Marriage: Thomas Johnson was married to Sally Foster by the Rev. Jacob Cookon the 22nd of November 1793, as the record in my office will show it. John Mathews, Greenbrier Co., VA.
&
Pension abstract for – Isaac Johnston, administrator for Estate of Sarah Johnston
Date: 6 Oct 1851
County of: Ripley   State of: IN
Declaration made before a Judge or Court: Judge of Circuit Court
Declaration for: Arrearages of Pension
Act of: 7 Jul 1838; 3 Mar 1843; 17 Jun 1844; joint resolution 23 Jan 1845; 1 Jul 1848.
Death: 11 Nov 1846   Ripley Co., IN
Names of surviving children: Nancy Johnston; Thomas Johnston; Wain Johnston; Nathaniel Johnston; Isaac Johnston.
&
Additional document in file shows Sarah Johnston died 11 Jan 1846.
[Note: Sarah says Thomas died in Dearborn Co., IN, however other papers in file show he died in Ripley Co., IN.]

Letter in the Pension application for Adam Fox
Versailles Indiana September the 19th 1839

Dear Sir Thomas Johnson who was a soldier of the Revolutionary war and who resided at the time of his death in the County of Dearborn and State of Indiana and who drew a pension for many years before his death also Ning Bell and William Lippard and Henry Wilyard all of whom was soldiers of the Revolutionary War and resided in the county of Ripley and State of Indiana and was in the receipt of pensions at the time of their death. They have all left surviving widows to wit Sarah Johnson, Agnes Willyard, Christina Beall, and Mary Lippard all of whom wish to apply for pensions under and by Authority of the Act of Congress of the 4th of July 1836, and the 3rd of March 1837. The said Thomas Johnson, Ning Beall, William Lipperd and Henry Wilyard at the time of their deaths left a draw of pensions due and in order to obtain the same, sayeth widows, was requested to surrender the pension Certificates of their deceased husbands which said Certificated I suppose has been returned to the proper office. In order to enable the widows of deceased pensioner to identify themselves as the widows of the deceased it is necessary for them to set out the original pension certificate of their deceased husbands and as they must be on file in the office over which you preside please transfer to me at Versailles Indiana the original certificated of the said Johnson, Beall, Lipperd, and Wilyard if it is in accordance with the custom of your office. If not, please send me a Certified Copy of the same

I herewith send the papers of Mr. Adam Fox who claims a pension. If the papers are different please point out the deficiency to me.

Let me hear from you as soon as convenient.

Yours respectfully
Joseph Robinson

Abstract of Final Payment Voucher; General Services Administration, Washington, DC

   LAST   FINAL PAYMENT VOUCHER RECEIVED FROM THE GENERAL ACCOUNTING OFFICE

NAME	~~JOHNSON~~ JOHNSTON, THOMAS
AGENCY OF PAYMENT	INDIANA
DATE OF ACT	1818
DATE OF PAYMENT	2d Qr. 1823
DATE OF DEATH	May 26, 1823
GENERAL SERVICES ADMINISTRATION	
National Archives and Records Service	NA-286
GSA-WASH DC 54-4891	November 1953

Senate Documents, Vol.9, No. 988, 63rd Congress, 3d Session, Washington, 1915; "*Register of Certificates Issued by John Pierce, Esquire, Paymaster General and Commissioner of Army Accounts for the United States, to Officers and Soldiers of the Continental Army Under Act of July 4, 1783*"; *Seventeenth report of the National Society of the Daughters of the American Revolution*; Genealogical Publishing Co., Inc., Baltimore, MD, 1984. p. 277, 278.
Men listed in this volume with the same name.

No. of Certificate	To whom issued	Amount
p.277.		
13742	Johnson, Thomas	59.30
14190	Johnson, Thomas	13.45
15008	Johnson, Thomas	80.00
15457	Johnson, Thomas	80.00
15815	Johnson, Thomas	80.00
68966	Johnson, Thomas	73.30
69151	Johnson, Thomas	20.00
p. 278.		
68418	Johnston, Thomas	33.30
68664	Johnston, Thomas	33.30
71778	Johnston, Thomas	40.60
72029	Johnston, Thomas	80.00

West Virginia Marriages, 1780-1970; p. 63, county clerks, West Virginia; accessed 11 April 2016 from https://familysearch.org/ark:/61903/1:1:FRFT-FHH
[Note: At the time of this marriage Greenbrier Co. was in the state of VA. WV became a state in 1863. – mjm]
Name: Thos. Johnston
Spouse's Name: Sally Foster
Event Type: Marriage
Event Date: About 1793
Event Place: Greenbrier, West Virginia
Spouse's Previous Husband's Name:
GS Film number: 595040; Digital Folder Number: 4130778
Image Number: 30; Reference ID: p63
Affiliate Repository Type: County Records
FHL microfilm 595,040

Clark, Murtie June, Comp.; Index to U.S. Invalid Pension Records 1801-1815; Genealogical Publishing Co., Inc., 1991, p. 60.

		Pennsylvania	
Name	Rank	Page	Remarks
Johnson, Thomas	Lieutenant	42, 107	-

Bockstruck, Lloyd DeWitt; Revolutionary War Pensions Awarded by State Governments 1775-1874, the General and Federal Governments Prior to 1814, and by Private Acts of Congress to 1905; Genealogical Publishing Co., Baltimore, MD, 2011, p. 420.
Johnson, Thomas. Pa. 2nd Lt. He served in Col. Cunningham's Flying Camp. He was wounded by a musket ball in the thigh in Aug. 1776 at Flatbush, Long Island. He lived in Managhan, Pa. in 1794 [There is a Monaghan Twp. In York Co., PA]. His rate was $5 per month from 17 Apr 1807. He was on the 1813 pension list.

Clark, Murtie June, comp.; The Pension Lists of 1792-1795 With Other Revolutionary War Pension Records; Genealogical Publishing Co., Inc., Second printing 1996, p. 34.
List of certificates transmitted by the Judge of the District Court for the District of Pennsylvania, of invalid pensioners examined by him.

Name	Rank	Regiment or Company	Residence	Remarks
Johnson, Thomas	2nd Lieut	Colo. Cunningham's Flying Camp	Managhan	Wounded by a musket ball in the thigh at Flatbush, Long Island, Aug. 1776; no militia rolls in War Dept.

Clark, Murtie June; The Pension List of 1820 [U.S. War Department]Reprinted with an Index; Genealogical Publishing Co., Inc., Baltimore, 1991. Originally published 1820 as Letter from the Secretary of War, p. 657.
INDIANA
Names of the Revolutionary Pensioners which have been placed on the Roll of Indiana, under the Law of the 18th of March, 1818, from the passage thereof, to this day, inclusive of the Rank they held, and the Lines in which they served, viz: -

Names	Rank	Line
Included in the list –		
Thomas Johnston	private	Pennsylvania

The Pension Roll of 1835 Volume IV, The Mid-Western States, Indexed Edition, In Four Volumes; Genealogical Publishing Co., Inc., Baltimore, MD, Reprint 1968, p. 36.
Statement, &c. of Dearborn county, Indiana.

INDIANA Names	Rank	Annual allowance.	Sums received	Description of service
Thomas Johnston	Private	96.00	466 31	Pennsylvania line

When placed on pension roll	Commencement of pension	Ages	Laws under which they were formerly placed on the pension roll; and remarks.
July 22, 1818	July 18, 1818	68	Died May 26, 1823.

Ripley County Indiana, Recorder's Office, Tract Book 3, p. 56.

Johnson, Thomas	11 Sep 1838	R12. T7, S9	40 acres

Toph, Violet E.; Peoples History of Ripley County, Indiana; self-published, c. 1940, p. 130-131.
Revolutionary Soldiers Who Came to Ripley County
Thomas Johnson entered the service from Pennsylvania in 1777 under Captain Henry McKinley and served three years. He was born in 1755 and died in Dearborn County, Ind. May 6, 1823. He was pensioned from Dearborn County.

In 1793 he married Sarah Foster. Sarah Johnson applied from Ripley County for a pension in 1842.

O'Byrne, Mrs. Roscoe C., comp. & ed.; Roster Soldiers and Patriots of the American Revolution Buried in Indiana; Published by Indiana Daughters of the American Revolution, 1938, Reprinted Genealogical Publishing Co., Baltimore MD, 1968, p. 212.

JOHNSTON, THOMAS   Ripley or Dearborn County
Born – 1755.
Service – Enlisted April, 1777, in Capt. Henry McKinley's CO., Col. Cook's Regt., Penn. Line, on the Continental Establishment; was wounded in his left leg Oct. 4, 1777 while in the battle of Germantown, was moved to Bethlehem Hospital for 3 mos. then to Shavertown Hospital, Lancaster Co., Penn., for 3 mos., then to Lebanon, Penn., where he was employed in preparing ammunition cartridges. Discharged April, 1780.
Proof – Pension claim W. 10158.
Died – May, 1823. Buried either in Ripley or Dearborn Co. Soldier applied and received pension while living in Dearborn Co. Name is on bronze tablet in Versailles Court House.
Married – 1793, Sarah Foster (1777-1846). Ch. Nancy; Isaac; James; Wayne; Nathaniel; Thomas; Elizabeth Rider.
Collected by Mrs. A. B. Wycoff, Batesville, Indiana.

Gibbs, A.; Ripley County Historical Society Data on Revolutionary Soldiers, 1973 review.

Exact location of marker: no further information on grave site
Placed by: Ripley County Historical Society
Additional comments: Pa. Archives, Series 3, vol. 13, p. 575, places this man in
    Dearborn County, Ind. (Rev. War soldiers residing in Ind.)

LAMBERT, JAMES

Patriot: James Lambert
Birth: 25 Mar 1758 On Pipe Creek, near Hagerstown, MD
Married Spouse 1: Margaret X
Married Spouse 2: Jane X (formerly m. to John Neely, pri. NY)
Service state(s): VA
Rank: Private
Proof of Service: Pension application
Pension application No.: R6099
Residences: MD; Rockingham Co., VA; PA; KY; OH, Dearborn Co., IN
Died: 1847
Buried: per SAR – Dearborn Co., IN, cemetery unknown
DAR Ancestor No.:None as of 7 Jun 2017.

Pension Application Abstracted from National Archives microfilm Series M804, Roll 1515, File R6099.
Pension abstract for – James Lambert
Service state(s): VA
Date: 18 Nov 1841
County of: Dearborn   State of: IN
Declaration made before a Judge or Court: Probate Court
Act of: 7 Jun 1832 & several others
Age: [84 yrs.] Will be 85 yrs. on 25 Mar 1842
Where and year born: State of Maryland
Residence when he entered service: Drafted in Town of Augusta, VA
Residence(s) since the war: VA, MD, PA, OH, Dearborn Co., IN for 27 yrs.
Residence now: Dearborn Co., IN
Volunteer, Drafted, or Substitute: 1st tour – Drafted; 2nd tour - volunteered
Rank(s): Militia Man/Private
Statement of service-

Period	Duration	Names of General and Field Officers
1777 (age 19)	6 mos.	Militia Man under Maj. Guy Hamilton, Capt. Spencer, Sgt. John Washer, Sgt. Hilde Perry, Sgt. William Bryan, Col. Hilliard or Hilyard.
	2 yrs.	Same

Battles: Battle of Cowpens
Discharge received: Yes, on the Yadkin River
What became of it?: Lost
Person now living who can testify to service: Lemuel Hungerford, age 79 on 14 May last, of Ross Twp., Butler Co., OH, gives affidavit on 23 Jul 1841, "in the years 1779 and 1780 as near as I can recollect in the militia under Captain Spence at West Point and Captain Cary at Horse neck and Captain Adam Shapely at New London where I saw Mr. James Lambert who resides in Dearborn County Indiana and who I have this day met and conversed with him Hamilton County Ohio serving at the

above named place as a Militia Soldier in the revolutionary war at the time I was there serving as such myself".

&

Pension abstract for – James Lambert
Date: 13 May 1844
County of: Ripley   State of: IN
Declaration made before a Judge or Court: Probate Court
Act of: 7 Jun 1832
Age: 86 yrs. the 25 day of Mar 1844
Record of age: Family record in Bible of my father, in Nelson Co., KY
Where and year born: on Pipe Creek, near Hagerstown, MD   25 Mar 1758
Residence when he entered service: 1st tour - Wilson's Station, Tygart's Valley, [VA]; 2nd & 3rd tour – Rockingham Co., VA.
Residence(s) since the war: Rockingham Co., VA; KY, OH, Dearborn Co., IN.
Residence now: Dearborn Co., IN -
Volunteer, Drafted, or Substitute: 1st tour – Volunteered; 2nd tour – Drafted; 3rd tour – Substitute for Jacob Ellsworth; 4th tour – Volunteered.
Rank(s): Not stated
Statement of service-

Period	Duration	Names of General and Field Officers
1 Jun 1774 (or near that time)	3 mos.	Against the Indians under Col. Lewis, Maj. Hamilton, Capt. Skidmore, Lt. Col. Rafe Stewart, Ens. William White, First Sgt. James Stewart.
Jul 1775- Oct 1775	3 mos.	Col. Hillyard, Capt. Spence, 1st Lt. Hilldepeny, Capt. John Washer.
Dec 1775	6 mos.	Col. Hillyard, Maj. Hamilton (he thinks), Capt. Spencer, Ens. William Bryant, Sgt. Hilldepeny.
Spring 1779- May/Jun 1781	2 yrs.	Capt. Andre Johnson, transferred to Capt. Christman, under command of Gen. Gates, Gen, Greene aft fall 1780, more…

Battles: Kings Bridge, Battle of Cowpens, Battle of Guilford Court House.
Discharge received: Yes
Signed by: Col. Hillyard
What became of it?: Lost
Statement is supported by –
Documentary proof: Has none
Clergyman: John Ruby
&
In this Pension File there is a Power of Attorney, signed by Jane Lambert, dated 14 Mar 1854, for the purpose of prosecuting the Claim of her deceased husband. POA was filed in Dearborn Co., IN. However, there is no "widow's application" in the file.

Abstract of Final Payment Voucher; General Services Administration, Washington, DC
NAME   LAMBERT, JANE WIDOW OF JOHN NEELY

AGENCY OF PAYMENT INDIANA
DATE OF ACT 1853 1st Sect.
DATE OF PAYMENT ended Feb. 3, 1858 pd. 1st Qr. 1858
DATE OF DEATH -
FINAL PAYMENT VOUCHER RECEIVED FROM
THE GENERAL SERVICES ADMINISTRATION Form
General Services Administration GSA DC 70-7035 GSA DEC 69 7068

Rejected or Suspended Applications for Revolutionary War Pensions; Reprinted for *Clearfield Company Inc.* by Genealogical Publishing Co., Inc., Baltimore, MD, 1998. p.413.
A list of persons residing in Indiana who have applied for pensions under the act of July 7, 1832, whose claims have been suspended; prepared in conformity with the resolution of the Senate of the United States, September 16, 1850.

Names	Residence	Reason for suspension
Lambert, James	Wilmington, Dearborn	Not on any rolls – no proof of service.

Wardell, Patrick G., comp.; *Virginia/West Virginia Genealogical Data From Revolutionary War Pension and Bounty Land Warrant Records, Vol. 3 ---Iams through Myers*; Heritage Books, Inc., Bowie, MD, 1988, p. 90.
Lambert, James, b 3/25/1758 near Hagerstown, MD; res Rockingham Co, VA all during RW; esf 1774 in Tygert's Valley on Monongahela River against Indians; esf ae 19 Augusta Co, VA for RW; mvd to KY, thence OH, thence IN, where afp 1841 Dearborn Co when res there 27 years; PAR, insufficient proof / o sve; afp again 1844 Ripley Co, IN when res Dearborn Co, IN & PAR; dd 1847; md Jane, who gave power /o attorney 1854 at Dearborn Co, IN, to agent to afp; children mbnn 1850. F-R6099 R1515

History of Dearborn and Ohio Counties, Indiana: from their earliest settlement: containing a history of the counties, their cities, townships, towns, villages, schools, and churches, reminiscences, extracts, etc., local statistics, portraits of early settlers and prominent men, biographies, preliminary chapters on the history of the North-west Territory, the state of Indiana, and the Indians; F.E. Weakley & Co., Chicago, 1885; p. 312.
Squire Bartholomew's Docket
In this ancient record, which is yet in the possession of Richard Hubbartt, Esq., of Aurora, the earliest entry was made January 9, 1822, in a case entitled "Ebenezer Lange vs. Noah and James Lambert." It was a plea of debt to recover $10. On that date the plaintiff appeared and withdrew the suit, when the case was dismissed by the justice.

Margaret R. Waters; *Revolutionary Soldiers Buried in Indiana (1949) With Supplement (1954) Two Volumes in One*; Genealogical Publishing Company, Baltimore, MD, 1970, p. 61.
LAMBERT, JAMES   Dearborn
b. 3-25-1757, Md.; d. 5-13-1844; m. Jane -----. Pens. appl. on 11-18-1841, ae, 85 on 3-25-1842, Dearborn Co., Ind. After War, liv. Va.; Md.; Pa.; Ohio; Ind. Again

appl. 5-13-1844, Ripley Co., Ind., but a resident of Dearborn Co., Ind.; lives ca. 30 mi. from Lawrenceburg but only ca. 15 mi. from Versailles & it is better road. Affid. 7-25-1841, Hamilton Co., O., of Lemuel Hungerford, ae. 79 last May 14, res. of Ross Twp., Butler Co., O.; that he & Lambert were in service at same time in same places. P of A, 3-14-1854, Dearborn Co., Ind., of wid. Jane Lambert. Service: first enl. June 1774, Wilson's Station in Tiger Valley on Monongahela River, in his 17th yr.; retd. to father at Wilson's Sta.; again enl. first Sept. 1774 for 3 mo.; father moved to n Fork of Potomac in Rockingham Co., Va; drf. In July 1775; Col. Hillyard, Capt. Spencer; in first appl. he says drf. ae. 19, Augusta Co., Va., Mil; Capt. Spencer, Maj. Guy Hamilton. REF: Pens. R.6099 Va.; Susp. Pens. List (1852) p. 143—not on any rolls—no proof of service.

LEVI, ISAAC

Patriot: Isaac Levi
Birth: 1 Feb 1749 Hungary
Married Spouse 1: bef. 1780 Kentucky   Martha/Mary Dunn (1755-1791)
Married Spouse 2: 14 Nov 1841, Ripley Co., IN Mrs. Mary "Polly" Tucker
(b.1801/1803 - 1853)
Widow of John Tucker
(d. Nov 1840 in Ripley Co.)
Service state(s): VA
Rank: Private
Proof of Service: Pension application
Pension application No.: W773
Residences: Lexington, Kentucky Co., VA; Harrison Co., KY; OH; Switzerland Co., IN; Ripley Co., IN
Died: 21 Sep 1850 Delaware Twp., Ripley Co., IN
Buried: Stone at Myers Cemetery, near Osgood, Ripley Co., IN – Bronze tablet at Versailles Court House - Stone in Perseverance Cemetery says buried Levi Cemetery.
DAR Ancestor No.: A069676
Children of Wife #1, Mary Dunn:
    Abraham Levi (b. abt. 1787; d. 1830 Ripley Co., IN)
    Martin Levi (b. abt. 1805, Lexington, KY; d. Osgood, IN)
    Elizabeth Levi, (b. abt. 1780) w. of Thomas Ewing

Pension Application Abstracted from National Archives microfilm Series 805, Roll 524, File W773.
Pension abstract for – Isaac Levi   Service state(s): Virginia
Date: 18 September 1832
County of: Switzerland   State of: Indiana
Declaration made before a Circuit Court.
Recorded in Book F, pg. 87.
Age: 82 Record of age: No record – was 17 years old when he came to America.
Where and year born: In Hungary in February 1749
Residence when he entered service: Lexington, Virginia (now Kentucky)
Residence(s) since the war: Lived in Lexington and continued in KY for about 40 years, lived in Ohio for 5 or 6 years, in Indiana the balance of time.
Residence now: Switzerland Co., IN
Volunteer or Drafted or Substitute: Enlisted
Rank(s): Private
Statement of service-

Period	Duration	Names of General and Field Officers
June 1780	Upwards of 2 years	Company of Virginia Militia commanded by Capt. Robert Patterson

Battles: Several battles with the Indians in Ohio and Indiana Territory
Discharge received: at the Falls of the Ohio
Signed by: Gen. Clark
What became of it?: Lost it.

Statement is supported by – Has none, and know of no body now living who can prove same.
Person now living who can testify to service: Andrew C. Forbes, Joseph Hayes, Thomas Mounts.
Clergyman: John Pavy
Persons in neighborhood who certify character: Joseph Hayes
&
Mary Levi, late Mary Tucker, Application for Pension
She is the Widow of John Tucker, a pensioner who was a resident of Ripley Co., IN. He drew his pension at the agency in Madison, IN.
Date: 26 March 1853
County of: Jefferson   State of: Indiana
Declaration made before a Judge of the Circuit Court
Widow's age: 50 years
Widow's residence: Jefferson Co., IN
Persons in neighborhood who certify character:
Soldier, John Tucker, died 14 November 1840 in Ripley Co., IN
Marriage date and place: to John Tucker in Scott Co., KY in February 1833.
Reference made to 2 children of John & Mary Tucker.
&
Marriage record for (Mrs.) Polly (aka Mary) Tucker to Isaac Levi, Sr. is in this pension file.
Marriage date and place: 14 November 1841 at Versailles, Ripley Co., IN by R. B. Mitchell, J.P.
In the same year the couple moved to Ripley Co., IN
Soldier, Isaac Levi, died 21 September 1850 in Ripley Co., IN
She was allowed pension on account of the service of her husband Isaac Levi.
Application executed 26 March 1853. Mary (Polly) Levi died 14 October 1853. She left several children at her death "some of which are not of age".

Switzerland County, Indiana Civil Order Book Vol., A, Oct. 19, 1829-April 16, 1837, p. 178.
In the matter of Robert Ricketts, Thomas Mounts, Ebenezer Humphrey, Daniel Heath, William Coy and Isaac Levi, An application to obtain a pension.

   Personally appeared in open Court before the Switzerland Circuit Court now Sitting The above named applicants who being first duly Sworn doth in their several oaths make their several declarations in order to obtain the benefit of the Act of Congress of the 7th June Ad 1832 that they entered the Service of the United States under the Officers named in their several declarations (here insert them) And the said Court do hereby declare their opinion after the investigation of the matter and after putting the interrogations prescribed by the War Department that the above named applicants were Revolutionary Soldiers and Served as they have stated And the Court further certifies that is appears to them that John Pavy who signed the several Certificates is a Clergyman resident in Switzerland County and State of Indiana and the other persons who has also signed the same are credible persons and that their Statement is entitled to credit.

Abstract of Final Payment Voucher; General Services Administration, Washington, DC
LAST FINAL PAYMENT VOUCHER RECEIVED FROM
THE GENERAL ACCOUNTING OFFICE
NAME							Levi, Isaac
AGENCY OF PAYMENT			Indiana
DATE OF ACT					1832
DATE OF PAYMENT				1st Qr. 1851
DATE OF DEATH				Sept 21, 1850
GENERAL SERVICES ADMINISTRATION
National Archives and Records Service		NA-286
GSA-WASH DC 54-4891				November 1953
&
Abstract of Final Payment Voucher; General Services Administration, Washington, DC
NAME							Levi, Mary Widow of Isaac
AGENCY OF PAYMENT			Indiana
DATE OF ACT					1853 2d Sect
DATE OF PAYMENT				4th Qr. 1853
DATE OF DEATH				Oct 14, 1853
LAST FINAL PAYMENT VOUCHER RECEIVED FROM
THE GENERAL ACCOUNTING OFFICE		Form
General Services Administration		GSA DA 70-7035 GSA Dec 69 7068

Clark, Murtie June; *American Militia in the Frontier Wars, 1790-1796*; Genealogical Publishing Co., Inc., 1990. p. 23.
Kentucky Militia
Muster Roll of Mounted Volunteers from Kentucky under the Command of Captain John Hall, Lieut. Colo. Horation Hall's Regiment, in the service of the United States Commanded by Major General Charles Scott, Oct 30, 1793.

Nr	Rank	Name	Remarks
7	Sergeant	Levi, Isaac	enlisted Sept 22

Gwathmey, John H.; *Historical Register of Virginians in the Revolution, Soldiers, Sailors, Marines, 1775-1783*; The Dietz Press, Richmond, VA, 1938, p. 470.
Levi, Isaac, IP [The Illinois Papers. A collection of rolls of militia and regulars in the Illinois Department now in the State Library, indexed in the State Archives.]
Levi, Isaac, 75, Switzerland Co., Ind., mpl. [Militia Pension List. Compiled from a report of the Secretary of War in 1835]

Wardell, Patrick G., comp.; *Virginia/West Virginia Genealogical Data From Revolutionary War Pension and Bounty Land Warrant Records, Vol. 3 ---Iams through Myers*; Heritage Books, Inc., Bowie, MD, 1988, p. 118-119.
Levi, Isaac, b 2/1749 Hungary; to America aec 17; esf 1780 Lexington, KY Territory, in VA unit; res KY for c40 years, thence OH for 5-6 years, thence IN, where PN 1832 Switzerland Co; dd 9/21/50 Ripley Co, IN; md there 11/14/1841 Mary/Polly, wid of John Tucker (whom she md 2/1833 Scott Co, KY, & they

mvd to Ripley Co, IN, where he dd 11/14/1840); John Tucker RW sol from NC & PN 1818 ae 65 Scott Co, KY, & his s by Mary was ae 17 in 1820; Mary afp 3/1853 Jefferson Co, IN, ae 50 for svc/0 2nd h; dd 10/14/53 leaving several ch, some of whom not yet of legal ae; reference made 1854 to 2 of ch/o Mary & John Tucker; wid's surv ch gtd PN due her. F-W773 R1553

Clift, G. Glens, Assistant Secretary, Kentucky Historical Society, Comp.; "Second Census" of Kentucky – 1800, A Privately Compiled and Published Enumeration of Tax Payers Appearing in the 79 Manuscript Volumes Extant of Tax Lists of the 42 Counties of Kentucky in Existence in 1800; Genealogical Publishing Co., Baltimore, MD, 1966, p. 171.

Name	County	Tax List Date
Levy, Isaac	Harrison	1800

Mikesell, Shirley Keller, ed.; Early Settlers of Indiana's "GORE" 1803-1820; Heritage Books, Inc., 1995, p. 185.
Switzerland County: Original Land Entries Tract Book
Township 2, Range 2W
Format: Section – Purchaser –   year –   page;
        30 -   ISAAC LEVI –   1817 -   7

Riegel, Mayburt Stephenson, comp.; Early Ohioans' Residences From the Land Grant Records; Ohio Genealogical Society, Mansfield, OH, 1976, p. 8.
Land Grants Recorded by Residents of the Indiana Territory at the Cincinnati Land Office. The original Land Grant records are in the Archives of the Ohio Historical Society. They are from the Auditor of the State of Ohio Land Office.

NAME	DATE	SEC	TWP	RANGE	VOL	PG	RESIDENCE
LEVI, Isaac	9-19-1804	S29	T8	R1W	B	141	DN Dearborn

Waters, Margaret R.; Indiana Land Entries Vol. 1 Cincinnati District, 1801-1840; Originally Published Indianapolis 1948, Second Reprint 1979 by The Bookmark, P.O. Box 74, Knightstown, IN 46148. p. 18, 42.
p. 18
CINCINNNATI LAND DISTRICT – VOL. 1   FRANKLIN CO.
Page 14. T 8 N, R 1 W of 1st P.M.
Isaac Levi S ½ S29; 9-19-1804
p. 42.
CINCINNNATI LAND DISTRICT – VOL. 1   SWITZERLAND CO.
Page 40. Twp. 2 N, Range 2 W of 1st Principle Meridian
Isaac Levi W ½ - NW ¼ - S30; 9-8-1817.
-- Note: The tract books for the land offices in Indiana are deposited in the office of the Auditor of State, Indianapolis. They and are in the custody of the State Land clerk. --

Berry, Ellen T. & Berry, David A., compilers; Early Ohio Settlers, Purchasers of Land in Southwestern Ohio, 1800-1840; Genealogical Publishing Co., Inc., Baltimore, MD, 1986. p. 190.

Purchaser	Year	Date	Residence	R – T - S
Levi, Isaac (B)	1817	Sept. 08	Hamilton	02-02-30

(B) Indiana Survey: Land lying west of a meridian drawn west of the Great Miami (known as the "Gore"). Switzerland, Dearborn, Franklin, Ohio, Union and Randolph Counties (all or only a part of each county) – all in Indiana.

U.S. Department of Interior, Bureau of Land Management, General Land Office Records; Land Patent Search – *accessed 27 June 2012.*
Name: Levi, Issac; Accession Nr. CV-0016-108; Document Type – Credit Volume Patent; State – Indiana; Issued Date – 9/23/1812; Cancelled – No Names on Document: Jones, James; Levi, Isaac; Land Office – Cincinnati; Authority – April 24, 1820 Sale-Cash Entry (3 Stat. 566); Total Acres – 0.00 Land Descriptions: State – IN; Meridian –1st PM; Twp-Rng – 008N-001W; Aliquots – S1/2; Section – 29; County - Franklin
&
Accession Nr. CV-0069-192; Document Twp – Credit Volume Patent; State – Indiana; Issue Date – 11/10/1827; Cancelled – No; Names on Document: Jackson, Albion; Jackson, George A.; Levi, Isaac; Land Office – Cincinnati; Document Nr. 2163; Total Acres – 99.48; Land Descriptions: State – IN; Meridian – 1st PM; Twp-Rng – 002N-002W; Aliquots – W1/2NW1/4; Section – 30; County – Switzerland

Indiana Territory, Switzerland Circuit Court Records, Order Book, October Term 1814 to March Term 1815. p. 72.
He is listed in county records for the first time on 8 May 1820, as a defendant.
Author's note: There are entries in this volume that are not within the range of dates shown on the binder cover.

1830 U.S. Census, Indiana, Switzerland, No Twp., Series: M19 Roll: 32 Page: 51
Levi, Isaac age 70-79 *[b.1751-1760]*; others in household 1 male 20-30, 1 female 20-30, 1 female 60-70 *[b. 1760-1770].*

The Pension Roll of 1835 Volume IV, The Mid-Western States, Indexed Edition, *In Four Volumes; Genealogical Publishing Co., Inc., Baltimore, MD, Reprint 1968, p. 92.*
Statement, &c. of Switzerland county, Indiana.

INDIANA Names	Rank	Annual allowance.	Sums received	Description of service
Isaac Levi	Private	80.00	240 00	Virginia militia
When placed on pension roll	Commencement of pension	Ages		Laws under which they were formerly placed on the pension roll; and remarks.
Aug 26, 1833	Mar 4, 1831	75		-

McAllister, J.T.; *Virginia Militia in the Revolutionary War*; McAllister Publishing Co., Hot Springs, VA, 1913, p. 279.
Part V.
Alphabetical List of Pensioners Residing Outside of Virginia in 1835, whose Pensions were Granted for Services as Virginia Militiamen.
This list was compiled from a repot made by the Secretary of War in 1835. The ages are those given in that report, and are believed to be the ages of the pensioners in 1835. The names of the pensioners in what is now West Virginia are embraced under Part IV.
Levi, Isaac   75   Switzerland   Indiana

A Census of Pensioners for Revolutionary or Military Services with their Names, Ages, and Places of Residence Under the Act for Taking the Sixth Census in 1840; Genealogical Publishing Co., Inc., Baltimore, Maryland, 1965. p.184.

INDIANA, RIPLEY, JOHNSON Names of Pensioners for Revolutionary or Military services	Ages	Names of heads of families with whom pensioner resided June 1, 1840
Levi, Isaac	91	Martin Levi

Scott, Craig R.; *The "Lost" Pensions, Settled Accounts of the Act of 6 April 1838*; Willow Bend Books, Lovettsville, VA, 1996. p. 195.
An Act directing the transfer of money remaining unclaimed [for the term of eight months] by certain pensioners, and authorizing payment of the same at the Treasury of the United States.
Name – Levi, Mary; Pension Office - Ohio; Box - 73; Account - #12743.

United States Census, 1840; Johnson Twp., Ripley Co., IN; Roll: 92; p. 110, 111.
Isaac Levi, age 90-100 *[b. 1741-1750]* was enumerated in the household of his son Martin. He was listed as a Revolutionary War Pensioner age 91 on the following page.

United States Census, 1850; Delaware Twp., Ripley Co., IN; M432; Film No.169. House Number: 89; Family 89; Line:1; National Archives and Records Administration, Washington, D.C.

Household	Gender	Age	Birthplace
Isaac Levi	M	114	Hungary [b. 1749 = age 101]
Mary Levi	F	49	Virginia
Martha Green	F	22	Kentucky *[Mary's dau from m. to John Tucker]*
Benja. Tucker	M	14	Kentucky *[Mary's son from m. to John Tucker]*

Ripley County, Indiana Will Records vol. B, June 1839-May 1862; p. 100.
Ripley County, Indiana Probate Order Book Vol. E., 18 Jun 1849-25 Sep 1852;
    p. 197,199,203,207,232,240,266,301,336,351,356,380,493.
Ripley County, Indiana Probate Order Book Vol. 1, 40, 82, 85, 111, 112, 118,
    139, 140, 191, 217, 261, 262, 315, 346.
Abstract of will and administration for: Isaac Levi Sen'r
Date and place will was made: 20 Jul 1847

Witnesses to will: John S.S. Hunter, Henry P. Lipperd, Morton C. Hunter
Names of administrator: Martin Levi
Date of death: (if specifically mentioned): 21 Sep 1850
Book E., p. 240 In the matter of the death of Isaac Levi, Pensioner.
        And now at this day it appears to the satisfaction of the Court by the Oath of Francis Driver and Martin Levi that Isaac Levi was a pensioner of the United States at the rate of Eighty dollars per annum, was a resident of the County of Ripley, in the State of Indiana, and died in Delaware Township in the County and State aforesaid in the year 1850 on the 21st day of September, that he left a widow whose name is Mary Levi, all of which is ordered to be certified by the Clerk of this Court.
Place of death: Delaware Twp., Ripley Co., IN
Date recorded: 16 Jun 1851
Bonded by and amount of bond: Allen Burton $300.00
Names of heirs and others mentioned in will & estate and relationship if shown: widow, Mary Levi; Grandchildren: Elzeba Levi; Jackson Levi; Armington Levi; Margaret Levi; Eliza Levi; Judas Levi; and Calvin Levi, minor children of my beloved son Martin Levi begat upon the body of Martha Levi his first wife.
Date of division & disbursement, or final return: 1 May 1856

Toph, Violet E.; <u>Peoples History of Ripley County, Indiana</u>; self-published, c. 1940, p. 130.
Revolutionary Soldiers Who Came to Ripley County
Isaac Levi enlisted from Lexington, Virginia (now Kentucky) in 1780 and served two years. He was born in 1751 and died Sept. 21, 1850. He resided in Kentucky, Ohio and then in Indiana. He was pensioned from Switzerland County, Ind. He married Mary (Polly) Tucker widow of John Tucker November 14, 1841. The Ripley County Historical Society, assisted by Miss Pearl Roberts placed a Government marker at his grave on Mrs. Black's lot in the eastside of Osgood, Ind.

O'Byrne, Mrs. Roscoe C., comp. & ed.; <u>Roster Soldiers and Patriots of the American Revolution Buried in</u> Indiana; Published by Indiana Daughters of the American Revolution, 1938, Reprinted Genealogical Publishing Co., Baltimore MD, 1968, p. 235.
LEVI, ISAAC   Ripley County
Born – 1751, Germany
Service – While resident of Lexington, Ky., he enlisted in 1780. Pri. in Capt. Robert Patterson's and Benj. Harrison's CO., a troop on expedition against the Indians on Big Miami under Gen. George Rogers Clark. In the battle of Pickaway Town, defeated the Indians. Stationed at Post Vincennes. Served two years.
Proof – Pension claim W. 773.
Died – Sept. 21, 1850. Buried near Osgood, Ripley, Co. Bronze tablet at Versailles Court House.
Married – Last W. Mary Tucker (widow of John Tucker, a Rev. S.), m. Nov. 14, 1841. Descendants of former marriages settled about Osgood, Indiana.
Collected by Mrs. A. B. Wycoff, Batesville, Indiana.

Hill, Mary, compiler; Revolutionary Soldiers of Switzerland County; John Paul Chapter-Daughters of the American Revolution; January, 1958; http://www.ingenweb.org/inswitzerland/switzrevsoldiers.html- Viewed June 2012.
LEVI, ISAAC   Pension record: W.773
Isaac Levi was born in February, 1749 in Hungary, and when about seventeen years of age arrived in America. The names of his parents were not shown. While a resident of Lexington, "Kentucky" he enlisted sometime in June, 1780, served as a private in Captain Robert Patterson's and Benjamin Harrison's companies with the Virginia troops; went on a expedition against the Indians on the Big Miami under General Clark, was in a battle at Pickaway Town, where the Indians were defeated and the town burned, after which they were stationed for fifteen or eighteen months at Fort Vincent (later Vincennes, Indiana); then returned to the Falls of the Ohio, where he was discharged having served "upwards of two years."
He continued to reside in Kentucky for about forty years, then moved to Ohio and lived five or six years, thence to Indiana.
Isaac Levi was allowed pension on his application executed September 18, 1832, at which time he was living in Switzerland Co. Ind.
He married November 14, 1841, in Ripley County, Indiana Mrs. Mary (Polly) Tucker. She was the widow of John Tucker, to whom she was married in February 1836 in Scott County, Kentucky. In the same year they moved to Ripley County, Indiana, where John Tucker died November 14, 1840.
Isaac Levi died September 21, 1850 in Ripley County, Indiana. His widow, Mary Levi, was allowed pension on account of the services of her husband, Isaac Levi, on her application executed March 26, 1853, at which time she was aged fifty years and a resident of Jefferson County, Indiana. She died October 14, 1853. Reference was made in 1854 to two children of John & Mary Tucker, and it was stated that the widow, at her death, left several children, "some of which are not of age:. Names of children are not given.
Roster; Buried near Osgood, Ripley Co. John Tucker also served in Revolution.

Hatcher, Patricia Law; Abstract of Graves of Revolutionary Patriots (4 volumes); Pioneer Heritage Press, Dallas, TX, 1987. Vol. 3, p. 12.
This is an abstract and an index to information reported to the Daughters of the American Revolution and published in their annual reports to the Smithsonian Institution , printed as Senate Documents (1900-1974) and published annually in the DAR magazine (1978-1987).
Published 1972 (Senate Doc. 54)
LEVI, Isaac   Nr Osgood, Ripley Co IN

Gibbs, A.; Ripley County Historical Society Data on Revolutionary Soldiers, 1973 review.
Exact location of marker: Toph notes: placed on Black's lot in Osgood Greendale Cemetery, w. of Osgood, Ind., Center Twp. Ripley Co. Ind.
Type of marker: Gov't
Date placed: 1936?
Placed by: Ripley County Historical Society
Additional comments: on Court House tablet

1840 census Ripley Co. Ind. pension list, p. 218 Isaac Levi age 91.
1850 census Ripley Co. Ind., Delaware Tw., p. 411/206 Isaac Levi age 114 b. Hungary – a note at the bottom of the census page says that he died without an hour of sickness; entered the service 1776 at age 41; served 4 years; b. May 10, 1736; crossed Atlantic May 1, 1758.

United States Headstone Applications for U.S. Military Veterans, 1925-1949, database with images; (https://familysearch.org/ark:/61903/1:1:VHZ8-N63 : 17 May 2016); Affiliate Publication Number: M1916; Affiliate Publication Title: Applications for Headstones for U.S. Military Veterans, 1925-1941; Affiliate Film Number: 69; GS Film Number: 1878218; Digital Folder Number: 004832236; Image Number: 01233.
Application for Headstone; War Department O.Q.M.G. Form No. 623
Name: Levi, Isaac
Event Date: Sept. 2, 1935
Name of Cemetery: A lot in Osgood, Ind.
Located in or near: Osgood, Ind.
Death Date: Died in KY; Sept, 21, 1855
Enlistment Dates: 1780
Discharge Dates: served 2 years
Rank: Private
Company: Capt. Patterson's and Benj. Harrison's, Virginia Troops
To be shipped to: Miss Pearl Roberts at Osgood, Ripley Co., INd.
Whose post-office address is: Versailles, Ind.
This application is for the UNMARKED grave of a veteran. It is understood the stone will be furnished and delivered at the railroad station or steamboat landing above indicated, at Government expense, freight prepaid. I hereby agree to promptly accept the headstone at destination, remove it and properly place same at decedent's grave at my expense. Ripley Co. Historical Society, Applicant. No fee should be paid in connection with this application.
Applicant: Ripley Co. Historical Society, Versailles, Ind.

Tombstone Location: Perseverance Cemetery, Osgood, Center Twp., Ripley Co., IN

Tombstone inscription: ISAAC
LEVI
PVT
CONTINENTAL
LINE
REV WAR
FEB 1 1749
SEP 21 1850
BURIED IN LEVI CEM
CENTER TWP
RECORDED P PG 103

And -

Tombstone Location: Myers Cemetery (aka Levi Cemetery), Osgood, Center Twp., Ripley Co., IN

Tombstone inscription:

ISAAC
LEVI
PVT
CONTINENTAL
LINE
REV WAR
FEB 1 1749
SEP 21 1850

The Vevay Reveille-Enterprise; Vol. 122, No. 37, 22 Sep 1935, p. 7, col. 1.
Roster of Revolutionary Soldiers Who Resided in Switzerland County
By Mrs. Effa M. Danner
Isaac Levi – Pension certificate No. W773, granted 1834 in Switzerland County. Age 75 granted Va. Born February 1749 in Hungary, Europe, emigrated at the age of 17 to America. While a resident of Lexington, Ky., he enlisted in 1780 as private in Captain Robert Patterson's and Benj. Harrison's Co., of Virginia troops on expedition against Indians on Big Miama under Gen. George Roger Clark. He was in the battle of Pickaway Town, defeated the Indians. Stationed at Fort Vincennes (later Vencennes, Ind.) returned to the falls of the Ohio; served two years and was discharged.
Switzerland County land entry T2, R. 2W, Sect. 30, Sept. 8, 1817.
He is listed in Ripley County, 1840, age 91, guardian Martin Levi. Switzerland County census 1820 he had four boys and one girl.
Pension record, Isaac Levi married Nov. 14, 1841 in Ripley County, Ind., Mrs. Mary Tucker, widow of John Tucker to whom she was married February 1833 in Scot County, Ky. He died in Ripley County, November 14, 1840.
Isaac Levi died September 21, 1850, Ripley County, Ind. Widow, Mary Levi allowed pension March 26, 1856, she being 50 years old and residing in Jefferson County, Oct. 14, 1853. She died leaving minor children. Mary Levi must have been his second wife.

Tri-County Genealogical Society Newsletter; Batesville, IN; Oct. 2006, Vol. 14, Iss. 4, p. 6.
Mr. Isaac Levi Revolutionary War Pensioner
The following entry is found on the 1850 Census of Ripley Co., IN, Delaware Twp, p. 206 (House #89):

Isaac Levi,	114,	born in Hungary
Mary Levi,	49,	born in Virginia
Benjamin Tucker,	14,	born in Kentucky
Martha Green	22,	born in Kentucky

At the bottom of the page, the following is written:
Mr. Levi died Sept. 21, 1850, without an hour's sickness. He believed himself to be in his one hundred and fifteenth year. He said he was born in Hungary (Europe) May 10, 1736, crossed the Atlantic May 1758, enlisted in the

American Army August, 1776, in his 40th year, served 4 years therein and died as above. He was a pensioner.

If this information is correct, Mr. Levi may well have been the oldest living Revolutionary War pensioner in 1850. Does any reader have more information about Mr. Levi or the three people living in his household in 1850?

Contributed by Charlie Hessler

Author's note: A similar article appeared in the *Ripley County Indiana Historical Society Quarterly Bulletin; Versailles, IN; Jan 2006, Vol 27, Iss 1, p 2.*

LIPPERD, WILLIAM

Patriot: William Lipperd
Birth: 17 Jul 1760 Mecklenburg Co., NC
Married Spouse 1: 31 Dec 1784, Mecklenburg Co., NC Mary Cress (1766-prob 1855)
Service state(s): SC
Rank: Private
Proof of Service: Pension application
Pension application No.: W10199
Residences: Mecklenburg Co, NC; Indiana Territory; Ripley Co., IN
Died: 5 May 1834 Ripley Co., IN
Buried: Old Washington Church Cemetery, Washington Twp., Ripley Co., IN
DAR Ancestor No.: A069651
Children (shown in pension) John, Coderine, William.

Pension Application Abstracted from National Archives microfilm Series M804, Roll 1569, File W10199.
Pension abstract for – William Lippard
Service state(s): SC
Alternate spelling(s): Lipperd, Lepherd
Date: 23 Aug 1832; amended 11 Feb 1833
County of: Ripley State of: IN
Declaration made before a Judge or Court: Probate Court
Act of: 7 Jun 1832
Age: 72 yrs.
Where and year born: Mecklenburg Co., NC 17 Jul 1760
Residence when he entered service: Mecklenburg Co., NC. Enlisted in SC.
Residence(s) since the war: Mecklenburg Co., NC until 1813; Indiana Territory until a state; then to Ripley Co., IN.
Residence now: Ripley Co., IN
Volunteer, Drafted, or Substitute: Enlisted
Rank(s): Private
Statement of service-

Period	Duration	Names of General and Field Officers
Feb 1780 - Mar 1781	1 yr.	5th Regt. SC Line, Capt. Wood, Gen, Greene, Col. Dudley, Maj. White.
Mar 1781 - Mar 1782	1 yr.	3rd Regt. SC Line, Capt. Robinson's Light Horse, Gen. Sumpter, Col. Poke, Maj. Alexander.

Battles: Battle of Camden (SC), Battle of Eutaw Springs where he was wounded in the leg by a bayonet.
Discharge received: Rec'd 2 written discharges
Signed by: General Greene & General Sumter
What became of it?: Both consumed by fire at the house of my brother-in-law.
Statement is supported by –
Person now living who can testify to service: Jacob Micheler, of Butler Co., OH, and Sibble Shelhouse gave affidavits.

Clergyman: Michaek Hyatt
Persons in neighborhood who certify character: John McClain, Esq. David Wallace, John Stockwell, Stephen B. Irving, St. S. Harding, Henry B. Hukill.

&

Pension abstract for – Mary Lipperd widow of William
Date: 14 Nov 1839
County of: Ripley   State of: IN
Declaration made before a Judge or Court: Probate Court
Act of: 4 Jul 1836 & 3 Mar 1837
Age: 73 yrs.   Record of age:
Persons in neighborhood who certify character: Jacob Mitchellor has been acquainted with Mary & William Lipperd for 60 yrs.
Death of soldier: 5 May 1834
Marriage date and place: 1 Jan 1783   Mecklenburg, NC.
Proof of marriage: Jacob Michellor testified marriage occurred 1783, Mecklenburg, NC.

&

Pension abstract for – Mary Lipperd widow of William Lipperd
Date: 13 Oct 1842
County of: Ripley   State of: IN
Declaration made before a Judge or Court: Justice of the Peace
Act of: 7 Jul 1838
Widow's former name: Mary Cress (Crefs)
Marriage date and place: Dec 1784
Proof of marriage: She has no memorandum of marriage and no Family Record. On 24 Jun 1842, Jacob Michellor provides affidavit that he was acquainted with Mary Crefs now Mary Lipperd, that their marriage occurred some time in the month of December 1784
Names and ages of children: John, b. 17 Nov 1785; Coderine, b. 19 Sep 1787; 8 children since.

&

Pension abstract for – Mary Lipperd widow of William Lipperd
Date: 3 Nov 1849
County of: Ripley   State of: IN
Declaration made before a Judge or Court: Justice of the Peace
Act of: 2 Feb 1848
Age: 83 yrs.   Record of age:
Residence now: Washington, Ripley Co., IN
[Note: Mary testified on other occasions in order to obtain her pension.]

Letter in the Pension application for Adam Fox
Versailles Indiana September the 19th 1839
    Dear Sir Thomas Johnson who was a soldier of the Revolutionary war and who resided at the time of his death in the County of Dearborn and State of Indiana and who drew a pension for many years before his death also Ning Bell and William Lippard and Henry Wilyard all of whom was soldiers of the Revolutionary War and resided in the county of Ripley and State of Indiana and

was in the receipt of pensions at the time of their death. They have all left surviving widows to wit Sarah Johnson, Agnes Willyard, Christina Beall, and Mary Lippard all of whom wish to apply for pensions under and by Authority of the Act of Congress of the 4th of July 1836, and the 3rd of March 1837. The said Thomas Johnson, Ning Beall, William Lipperd and Henry Wilyard at the time of their deaths left a draw of pensions due and in order to obtain the same, sayeth widows, was requested to surrender the pension Certificates of their deceased husbands which said Certificated I suppose has been returned to the proper office. In order to enable the widows of deceased pensioner to identify themselves as the widows of the deceased it is necessary for them to set out the original pension certificate of their deceased husbands and as they must be on file in the office over which you preside please transfer to me at Versailles Indiana the original certificated of the said Johnson, Beall, Lipperd, and Wilyard if it is in accordance with the custom of your office. If not, please send me a Certified Copy of the same

I herewith send the papers of Mr. Adam Fox who claims a pension. If the papers are different please point out the deficiency to me.

Let me hear from you as soon as convenient.

Yours respectfully
Joseph Robinson

Abstract of Final Payment Voucher; General Services Administration, Washington, DC

FINAL PAYMENT VOUCHER RECEIVED FROM
THE GENERAL ACCOUNTING OFFICE
NAME	LIPPARD, WILLIAM
AGENCY OF PAYMENT	INDIANA
DATE OF ACT	1832
DATE OF PAYMENT	3rd Qr. 1834
DATE OF DEATH	May 5, 1834

GENERAL SERVICES ADMINISTRATION
National Archives and Records Service   NA-286
GSA-WASH DC 54-4891   November 1953

Abstract of Final Payment Voucher; General Services Administration, Washington, DC
NAME	Lippard, Mary widow of William
AGENCY OF PAYMENT	Madison, Ind.
DATE OF ACT	1848
DATE OF PAYMENT	Sept 1855
DATE OF DEATH	-

LAST   FINAL PAYMENT VOUCHER RECEIVED FROM
THE GENERAL ACCOUNTING OFFICE   Form
General Services Administration   GSA DC 70-7035   GSA DES 69 7068

Moss, Bobby Gilmer; <u>Roster of South Carolina Patriots in the American Revolution</u>; Genealogical Publishing Co., IN., Baltimore, MD, 1983, p. 572.
Lipperd, William   W10199

BLWt 26066-160-155
b.	17 July 1760, Mecklenburg County, N.C.
d.	5 May 1834
M.	Mary Cress (Creps), 1 January 1783
While residing in Mecklenburg County, North Carolina, he enlisted during February 1780 under Capt. Wood and Col. Dudley. He was in the battle at Camden. On March 1781, he enlisted under Capt. Robinson and Col. Polk of the light horse. He was in the battle at Eutaw Springs, where he was wounded in the leg by a bayonet. During March 1782, he was discharged. (Moved to Ind.)

Ervin, Sarah Sullivan; South Carolinians in the Revolution, With Service Records and Miscellaneous Data, also Abstracts of Wills, Laurens County (Ninety-Six District) 1775-1855; Genealogical Publishing Co., Baltimore, MD, 1971 (Originally published 1949), p. 121.
Soldiers of Other States, Including List of Many from South Carolina
South Carolina Soldiers to Indiana
[In this listing is] Lipperd, Wm.

Ripley County Indiana, Recorder's Office, Tract Book 1, p. 74.
Lipperd, William   28 Sep 1818   R13, T6, S7   160 acres

U.S. Department of Interior, Bureau of Land Management, General Land Office Records; Land Patent Search
Name: Lipperd, William & Lipperd, Moses
Accession Nr. CV-0087-415; Document Type – Credit Volume Patent; Issue Date – 9/6/1831; Cancelled – No
Land Office – Jeffersonville; Authority – April 24, 1820: Sale-Cash Entry (3 Stat. 566); Document Nr. 2665; Total Acres – 160.00
Land Descriptions: State – IN; Meridian – 2ndPM; Twp-Rng – 007N – 012E; Aliquots – NW1/4; Section – 7; County - Ripley
&
Name: Lipperd, William
Accession Nr. CV-0087-434; Document Type – Credit Volume Patent; Issue Date –9/6/1831; Cancelled – No
Land Office – Jeffersonville; Authority – April 24, 1820: Sale-Cash Entry (3 Stat. 566); Document Nr. 2683; Total Acres – 160.00
Land Descriptions: State – IN; Meridian – 2ndPM; Twp-Rng – 007N – 012E; Aliquots – SE1/4; Section – 1; County - Ripley

1820 U. S. Census, Ripley Co., IN, NARA Roll M33_15; EN 7 Aug 1820, p. 78, line 23.
William Lipperd
Males 10-15=2, Males 16-25=1, Males 26-44=2, Males 45>=1,
Females 16-25=2, Females 45?=1.

The Pension Roll of 1835 Volume IV, The Mid-Western States, Indexed Edition, In Four Volumes; Genealogical Publishing Co., Inc., Baltimore, MD, Reprint 1968, p. 87.
Statement, &c. of Ripley county, Indiana.

INDIANA Names	Rank	Annual allowance.	Sums received	Description of service
William Lippard	Private	80.00	200 00	Virginia militia

When placed on pension roll	Commencement of pension	Ages	Laws under which they were formerly placed on the pension roll; and remarks.
June 29, 1833	March 4, 1831	68	-

Ripley Circuit Court Civil Order Book Vol. C, April 1828-February 1835; Ripley County, Indiana; p. 378.
3 Aug 1834, August Term.
Mary Lippard widow of the Late William Leppard Deceased now Appeared in Court and proved to the satisfaction of the Court that she is the Widow of said deceased, And that he died on the fifth day of May AD. 1834, in order to procure the balance of A pension due her said husband to his death.

Scott, Craig R.; *The "Lost" Pensions, Settled Accounts of the Act of 6 April 1838*; Willow Bend Books, Lovettsville, VA, 1996, p. 198.
An Act directing the transfer of money remaining unclaimed [for the term of eight months] by certain pensioners, and authorizing payment of the same at the Treasury of the United States.
Lippard, Mary; Pension Office – Ind.; Box – 106; Account - #8413
Lippard, Mary; Pension Office – Ind.; Box – 99; Account – 3644
Lippard, Mary; Pension Office - INd.; Box – 122; Account - 8775

Toph, Violet E.; *Peoples History of Ripley County, Indiana*; self-published, c. 1940, p. 128.
Revolutionary Soldiers Who Came to Ripley County
William Lipperd enlisted from South Carolina in February, 1780 and was discharged in March, 1781. He re-enlisted in March 1781 and was discharged in March 1782. He was born in 1760 and died May 5, 1834. He was pensioned from Ripley County, Ind. and is buried in Old Washington Cemetery.
In July, 1936, the Ripley County Historical Society, aided by subscriptions from descendants of the five Revolutionary soldiers buried in Old Washington cemetery, Edward Pendergast, Ninian Beall, James Grimes, Joseph McDonald and William Lipperd enclosed the cemetery with a durable wove wire fence and placed Government markers for each of the five soldiers, thus making a notable Revolutionary Shrine for Washington Township.

O'Byrne, Mrs. Roscoe C., comp. & ed.; Roster Soldiers and Patriots of the American Revolution Buried in Indiana; Published by Indiana Daughters of the American Revolution, 1938, Reprinted Genealogical Publishing Co., Baltimore MD, 1968, p. 238.

LIPPERD, WILLIAM   Ripley County
Born – 1760.
Service – Enlisted from South Carolina in February, 1780. Discharged in March, 1781. Re-enlisted on same date; discharged in March, 1782.
Proof – Pension claim W-10199.
Died – May 5, 1834. Cliff Hill Cemetery, Versailles, Ripley Co., Ind. Bronze tablet in Versailles C. H. 1928, by Ripley Co., Ind. Historical Society.
Collected by Mrs. A. B. Wycoff, Batesville, Indiana.

[Note: the following citation differs from other records – mjm.]
Hatcher, Patricia Law, Comp.; Abstract of Graves of Revolutionary Patriots (4 volumes); Pioneer Heritage Press, Dallas, TX, 1987, Vol. 3, p. 26.
Lipperd William   Cliff Hill Cem, Versailles, Ripley Co IN 72

Gibbs, A.; Ripley County Historical Society Data on Revolutionary Soldiers, 1973 review.
Exact location of marker: out of Elrod on 525 to 50N, right to Thermon Boyd farm (1973); mile n.e. of house, going down across creek and up a hill; no road on path. Old Washington Cemetery north east out of Elrod, Washington Tw. Ripley Co. Ind.
O'Byrne (Indiana DAR) says: Bur. Cliff Hill Cem.
Toph note: pensioned from Ripley Co. (this does not appear in the Probate A Book up to 1837; he d. 1834.)
Type of marker: Gov't

Date placed: Oct. 1936 (minutes of R.C.H.S.
Placed by: Ripley County Historical Society
Additional comments: on Court House tablet
Wording on marker:

William Lipperd
Pvt. Wood's Co.
Dudley's S.C. Rgt.
May 5, 1834

United States Headstone Applications for U.S. Military Veterans, 1925-1949, database with images; (https://familysearch.org/ark:/61903/1:1:VHZ8-VVJ : 17 May 2016); Affiliate Publication Number: M1916; Affiliate Publication Title: Applications for Headstones for U.S. Military Veterans, 1925-1941; Affiliate Film Number: 70; GS Film Number: 1878219; Digital Folder Number: 004832237; Image Number: 00776.
Application for Headstone; War Department O.Q.M.G. Form No. 623

Name: Lippard, William
Event Date: May 34, 1934
Name of Cemetery: Old Washington
Located in or near: Milan, Ind.
Death Date: May 5, 1834
Enlistment Dates: Feb. 1780
Discharge Dates: March 1782
Rank: Private
Company: Capt. Wood's Co., Col. Dudley's S.C. Regt., South Carolina Line
To be shipped to: Ripley Co. Historical Society, Osgood, Ind., Ripley Co.
Whose post-office address is: Versailles, Ind.
This application is for the UNMARKED grave of a veteran. It is understood the stone will be furnished and delivered at the railroad station or steamboat landing above indicated, at Government expense, freight prepaid. I hereby agree to promptly accept the headstone at destination, remove it and properly place same at decedent's grave at my expense. Ripley Co. Historical Society, Applicant.
No fee should be paid in connection with this application.
Applicant: Ripley Co. Historical Society, Versailles, Ind.

Tombstone Location: Old Washington Church Cemetery, Washington Twp., Ripley Co., IN

Tombstone Inscription:

WILLIAM
LIPPERD
PRI IN WOOD'S CO.
DUDLEY'S S.C. REGT.
REV. WAR
MAY 5, 1834

LIVINGSTON (LEVINSTON), GEORGE

Patriot: George Livingston
Birth: cir 1754
Married Spouse 1: 22 Oct 1785, Albemarle Co., VA
Elizabeth Jopline (- 1838)
Service state(s): VA
Rank: Private
Proof of Service: Gwathmey's Historical Register of Virginians; Conquest of the Country Northwest of the River Ohio 1778-1783
Pension application No.: None
Residences: KY; Dearborn and/or Ripley Co., IN
Died: 1809-1820   Dearborn or Ripley Co., IN[a]
Buried: Unknown
DAR Ancestor No.: A008995

[a] *Evidence that George Livingston died bef. 1820 is that his wife, Elizabeth, was listed in the 1820 census, Ripley Co., IN; p. 76.*

Household	Males 16-25	2
	Females 10-15	2
	Females 45& over	1 Elizabeth

National Society Daughters of the American Revolution has accepted death as being between 1809 and 1820. Ripley Co. was formed in 1818, so depending on when he died would determine the death place. - mjm

Gwathmey, John H.; *Historical Register of Virginians in the Revolution, Soldiers, Sailors, Marines, 1775-1783*; The Dietz Press, Richmond, VA, 1938, p. 470, 479.
P. 470.
Levingston, George, Clark's Ill. Reg.
p. 479.
Livingston, George, Ky, Mil., C. [C—"Collins History of Kentucky", an accredited work.]

Virginia Military Records from the Virginia Magazine of History and Biography, the William and Mary College Quarterly, and Tyler's Quarterly; Genealogical Publishing Co., Baltimore, MD, 1983, p. 701.
The Illinois Regiment and the Northwestern Territory, from VMHB, Vol. I (1893), 127-141.
A List of Non-Commissioned Officers and Soldiers of the Illinois Regiment, and the Western Army, Under the Command of General George Rogers Clark.
Included in the list – Levinston, George Private

English, William Hayden; Conquest of the Country Northwest of the River Ohio 1778-1783; Bowen-Merril Co., 1895. Vol. II, p. 846, 1118.
p. 846.
Roll of Officers and Soldiers who were allotted Land in Clark's Grant (Indiana) for services under George Rogers Clark, "In the Reduction of the British Posts in

the Illinois." With the Quantity, and Descriptive Numbers of the Land Received by Each.
Levingston, George - 8 acres in 196 and 100 acres in 86.
p. 1118.
Alphabetical List of those Original Claimants who sold their Rights as Appeared by Assignments, Etc., produced to the Board of Commissioners previous to the 13th of December, 1785, with the names of the several assignees to whom the same right passed, as they stand arranged.
Livingston, George, private…D. Brodhead, whole claim, W. Davis, 100 acres.
[Note: these lands were located in the present state of Indiana across the river from Louisville, Kentucky. – mjm]

Ripley Co., IN Probate Order Book, Vol.1 Wills, Sep 1821-Apr 1839, p. 60.
Last Will & Testament of Elizabeth Livingston. Names children: Prudence Earheart, Patsey Livingston, Jane Ross, Nancy Purcell, Mary McCalla, George Livingston, Elizabeth Purcell, James Livingston, Sally Boswell, and Esther Dimick. James Livingston, exec.

Ripley Co., IN Probate Order Book, Vol. B. 8 May 1837-17 Aug 1843, p. 73, 79, 89, 98, 186, 247, 265, 284, 285, 287, 360, 392, 422.
Be it remembered that on the 20th day of October A.D. 1838 the Will of Elizabeth Livingston was duly Proven ……etc.

O'Byrne, Mrs. Roscoe C., comp.; Roster of Soldiers and Patriots of the American Revolution Buried in Indiana, Vol. II; Indiana Daughters of the American Revolution, 1980, p. 67-68..
p. 67.
LIVINGSTON, GEORGE   Dearborn of Ripley County
Service – Pvt. under George Rogers Clark. Enl. Mar. 4, 1778, Capt. Joseph
    Bowman's Co. Received land grant for service.
Proof – Conquest of Northwest, English, p. 839; Brumbaugh's, p. 206;
    Wayland's History of Shenandoah Co., Vir., p. 214; Collin's History of
    Ky., Vol. 1, p. 11.
Died – Before 1820. Prob. bur. In Dearborn or Ripley Co., Ind.
Married – Oct. 22, 1785, in Vir., to Elizabeth Jopline, d. 1838 (her Will in Ripley Co., Ind.). Ch. George, m. Sarah Prudence Connell; Elizabeth, m. John Purcell; Sarah, m. Garrison Boswell; Nancy, m. Benjamin Purcell; James, m. Polly Brown and Mary Curran; Esther, *p. 68* m. Adolphus Dimmiek; Prudence, m. --- Earheart; Jane, m. --- Ross; Mary, m. James McCalla; Patsey; Henry, m. Mahala Robinson.
By Mrs. Courtenay R. Livingston, 145 Mulberry Rd., Danville, Va. 24543.

O'Byrne, comp. Mrs. Roscoe C., comp.; Roster of Soldiers and Patriots of the American Revolution Buried in Indiana, Vol. III; Indiana Daughters of the American Revolution, 1966, p. 67.
LIVINGSTON, GEORGE   Roster II, p. 67   Ripley County
Proof – Probate Order Book A., p. 43 *[p. 60.]*, Ripley Co., Ind.; Will Book – Elizabeth Livingston's will probated Oct. 20, 1838.

LLOYD, INDIAN ROBIN (ROBERT)

His name appears in Ripley County, IN on the 1850 list of resected/suspended applications thus proving his ties to the county. He often interacted with the men of the county who he served with in the Revolutionary War.

Patriot: Robin Lloyd   aka Indian Robin
Birth: 1760   Dinwiddie Co., VA
Married Spouse 1:
Service state(s):   VA
Rank: Private
Proof of Service: Pension application
Pension application No.: R6501
Residences: VA; NC for 21 yrs.; Clark Co., IN; Jennings Co., IN; Ripley Co., IN
Died: aft 1850
Buried: Unknown
DAR Ancestor No.: None as of 7 Jun 2017.

Pension Application Abstracted from National Archives microfilm Series M804, Roll 1596, File R6501.
Pension abstract for – Robin Lloyd, a man of color   Service state(s): VA
Alternate spelling(s): aka Indian Robin, Robert Loyd
Date: 10 Nov 1834
County of: Jennings   State of: IN
Declaration made before Probate Court
Act of: 7 Jun 1832
Age: 64 years   Record of age: No record
Where and year born: 1760
Residence when he entered service: Dinwiddie Co., VA
Residence(s) since the war: Dinwiddie Co., VA; North Carolina for 21 yrs; Indiana Territory; Jennings Co., IN
Residence now: Jennings Co., IN
Volunteer, Drafted, or Substitute: Volunteer
Rank(s): Private
Discharge received: Yes, written.
Signed by: Capt. Jones, Capt. Powell
Statement of service-

Period	Duration	Names of General and Field Officers
Jun 1778-Jun/Jul 1779	1 yr.	Gen. Spencer, Gen. Ramsey, Col.. Bannister, Col. Gee, Maj. Hunt, Adj. Binge or Benge, Capt. John Jones, Capt. Ned Powell, Lieut. James Gee, Ensign Goodin Hunt, Sgt. Thomas Hill, Corp. Edward Walker.
Jan 1780-Jan 1781	1 yr.	Gen. Morgan, Col. Robert Walker, Maj. Clabon Cauder(?), Adj. Green Hill, Capt. Powell, Lieut. Thomas Giliam.
Feb 1781-Nov 1781	10 mos.	Gen. Green, Col. Dick, Maj. Cauder,

Capt. Richard Jones.
Battles: Cowpens, Guilford Courthouse, Yorktown
Discharge received: Yes, written.
Signed by: Capt. Jones, Capt. Powell, Capt. Richard Jones
What became of it?: Soon after the war a negro girl set fire to the house in which they were deposited.
&
Date: 12 Feb 1838
County of: Jennings   State of: IN
Declaration made before Probate Court
Act of: 7 Jun 1832
Age: 80 years   Record of age: No record
Where and year born: 1760
Residence when he entered service: Dinwiddie Co., VA
Residence(s) since the war: Dinwiddie Co., VA; North Carolina for 21 yrs; Indiana Territory; Jennings Co., IN
Residence now: Jennings Co., IN
Person now living who can testify to service: John Grimes, resident of Ripley
 Co., IN, testified that he frequently heard his father, James Grimes a Revolutionary soldier, talk of a Negro man by the name of Indian Robin; that Robin was a soldier, served as a footman and part of the time in a troop in a Light Horse line, was at the taking of Cornwallis at Yorktown. Robin was at my father's house a few day before my father's death.
 Bartholomew Turner a Revolutionary soldier, resident of Jennings Co., IN, testified he knew a Negro man named Robin who was in the service of the United States as a soldier in the Revolution. I saw him twice or three times on horseback armed for battle but what company he was attached I do not know; I believe this Negro man, now present, who goes by the name Indian Robin and sometime Robin Loyd is the same man who applied for pension.
Death of soldier: Not shown
Wife: None shown
&
Transcription of Stephen Hardin letter in Lloyd file –
Milan, Ind.   September 9th 1843
J. L. Edwards Esq.
 Commis'n of Pensions
Sir, The department over which you preside, will confer a great favor on me by giving me information on the following subjects, viz. –
<u>1 st the Condition of the application of Indian Robbin (alias Robin or Robert Lloyd) who applied for a pension some 9 or 10 years since, from Jennings Co., Ind. and the additional proof necessary in establishing his claim. I understand that Hon. Mr. Carr late a Representative in Congress has had something to do with the case, since I _____,
_____ engaged by applicant to make one more effort in the case.</u>
2 nd Will you be so good as to have a different search made _____ the _____ Military Rolls and see if the name of <u>Stacy</u> Wilson can be found. The case

is simply this – the widow of Stacy Wilson is about 84 years of age and is beyond a doubt in my mind, entitled to a pension under the Act of July 7th , 1838. She _____, is old and _____, that it is hardly possible to learn more from her, that that Mr. Wilson was an <u>enlisted</u> <u>soldier</u> in the Revolutionary War, for "during the War" and served about seven years. He died on the 6th of August 1807, and consequently in old age lady speaks wholly from memory. She cannot tell his immediate officers names – but that he enlisted at the breaking out of the war, in the Town of Winchester Virginia but by whom he was enlisted, she cannot tell. Stacy Wilson, was in the Battle of Brandywine, and at the taking of Charleston South Carolina, and was there taken a prisoner, and remained a prisoner for a year or 14 months – He was also in some other engagements which she cannot remember. He resided at Philadelphia, at the time of the breaking out of the war – whether his name can be found or on _____ remains to be seen – and it does, so appear, it will be impossible to make out the case, owing to the great lapse of time, and _____ in consequence of the old ladys incapacity. She however, is a most fit object of the Charity, and justice of the government and I hope you will cause a deliberate search to be made as above requested and answer me immediately on the subject.

3 rd   Will you be good enough to inform me on what evidence of the marriage of Bulah Robinson widow

[pg. 2]

of Winthrop Robinson of Indiana her certificate #97 64/__ was issued on the 13th day of June last, and sent to W. C. _____ of New York, Indiana. It is necessary to have your statement in the previous, in order that justice may be done for _____ _____, and money paid in processing papers ___ in the said case. I forwarded to the Department the affidavit of Mrs. Sawyer, together with two letters of Harrison Hurst Esq. Post master at Berlin [?]. Question – was the Certificate issued upon the testimony they offered, or on the testimony sent to the Department of Mr. _____. This may be out of your line of _____, but it is necessary that I should have your statements.

I am very Respectfully,
Stephen S. Hardin

<u>Journal of The House of Representatives of the United States being The First Session of the Twenty-Sixth Congress, begun and held At the City of Washington, December 2, 1839, In the sixty-fourth year of the Independence of the Said States</u>; Blair and Rives, Washington, DC, 1840, Vol. 362, p. 324.

Mr. Carr presented a declaration and papers of Robin Loyd, alias Indian Robin, of the county of Jennings, in the State of Indiana, in support of his claim for a pension.

<u>Rejected or Suspended Applications for Revolutionary War Pensions</u>; Reprinted for Clearfield Company Inc. by Genealogical Publishing Co., Inc., Baltimore, MD, 1998. p.413.

A list of persons residing in Indiana who have applied for pensions under the act of July 7, 1832, whose claims have been suspended; prepared in conformity with the resolution of the Senate of the United States, September 16, 1850.

Names	Residence	Reason for suspension
Lloyd, Robin	Versailles, Ripley	For further proof of service.

Wardell, Patrick G., comp.; Virginia/West Virginia Genealogical Data From Revolutionary War Pension and Bounty Land Warrant Records, Vol. 3 ---Iams through Myers; Heritage Books, Inc., Bowie, MD, 1988, p. 148.
Loyd, Robin (aka Robin, Indian); free man of color; b 1760 Dinwiddie Co, VA, where esf 1778; mvd to NC for 21 years, thence IN Territory, where afp Jennings Co, IN, 1834; afp again 1838 there; PAR both times. F-R6501 R1596

Grundset, Eric G., Ed.; Forgotten Patriots, African American and American Indian Patriots in the Revolutionary War; National Society Daughters of the American Revolution, 2008, p. 494, 521.
p. 494.
Virginia's American Indians during the Revolution
Robin Loyd of Dinwiddie County was known as "Indian Robin" to his fellow soldiers in the 5th Virginia Regiment. He fought at the Battle of Cowpens but could not prove the duration of his service when he filed a pension application in 1834, in Jennings County, Indiana. [60]
Footnote 60 – RWPF, R6501. (Revolutionary War Pension File R6501, Record Group 15, National Archives and Records Administration.)
p. 521.
LOYD, ROBIN, Indiana, R6501, Dinwiddie Co., also listed as INDIAN ROBIN

Margaret R. Waters; Revolutionary Soldiers Buried in Indiana (1949) With Supplement (1954) Two Volumes in One; Genealogical Publishing Company, Baltimore, MD, 1970, p. 67
LOYD, ROBIN   Jennings
(Also known as Indian Robin; negro). b. 1760, Dinwiddie Co. Va. Pens. Appl. 11-10-1834, ae. 74, Jennings Co., Ind, of Indian Robin, alias Robin Loyd. After War, to N.C. for 21 yr.; to Indiana Terr,; again appl. 2-12-1838, ae. 80, Jennings Co., Ind.; formerly res. In Clark Co. Ind.; in Ind. over 20 yr. Affid. 9-26-1838, Ripley Co., Ind. of James Grimes; that his father James Grimes, decd. ("Roster" p. 165) often spoke of Indian Robin as a Rev. sold. Service: enl. June 1778, Dinwiddie Co., Va; Col. Bannister, Lt.-Col. Gee, Maj. Junt, Capts. John Jones & Ned Powell. REF: Pens R.6501 Va.; Susp. Pens. List (1852) p.413—for further proof of service.

MARQUEST, SAMUEL

Patriot: Samuel Marquest
Birth: abt. 1759
Married Spouse 1: 30 Oct 1784, Cecil Co., MD Rachel Touchstone (- c. 1787)
Married Spouse 2: c. 1788, PA Catherine
Service state(s): MD
Rank: Public Service
 Signed Patriot's Oath 2 Mar 1778, Cecil Co., MD
Proof of Service: 1840 Census Pensioners
Pension application No.: None
Residences: Cecil Co., MD; Washington Co., PA; Ripley Co., IN
Died: aft. 1840 Ripley Co., IN
Buried: Unknown
DAR Ancestor No.: None as of 7 Jun 2017.

Peden, Henry C. Jr.; Revolutionary Patriots of Cecil County Maryland; Family Line Publications, Westminster, MD, 1991, p. 69.
List of men who served in the American Revolution in the 2nd, 18th and 20th Militia Battalions, and in the Maryland Continental Line, as well as those who rendered material aid and signed the Oath of Allegiance.
Oath of Allegiance administered by Justice David Smith, 2 Mar 1778.
Among those listed is-
Marquis, Saml [also listed are Marquis, John; Marquis, John Jr.; Marquis, Robert; Marquis, Robert Jr.]

Captain Jeremiah Baker Chapter Daughters of the American Revolution, comp,; Cecil County, Maryland Marriage Licenses 177-1840; originally published by The Captain Jeremiah Baker Chapter Daughters of the American Revolution, Elkton, MD, 1928, Reprinted Genealogical Publishing Co., Inc., Baltimore, MD, 1974, p. 6.

MAN	WOMAN	MINISTER
1784		
Oct. 30 Samuel Marquiss to	Rachel Touchstone	Thompson

Washington Co., PA Land Records; Deed Books, 1781-1886
2 April 1824, John Simanton and Elizabeth his wife of Washington Co. PA to John Duncan Junr. of afsd, for $700 paid, sell a tract of land on the waters of Kings Creek in Hanover Twp, Washington Co., contained by land of estate of James Simanton, by land of Jacob Speck, by land of James Simanton, by land of Jonas Potts, by land of James Simanton, containing 101 acres 140 perches strict measure, being part of a tract of land called Contention granted to Samuel Marques by patent 2 April 1799 in Patent Book No.35 page 293, the within part conveyed by Samuel Marquis to Robert Russell by indenture 17 May 1802

Creigh, Alfred; History of Washington County from its First Settlement to Present Time; Washington, PA, 1871, p. 8 in Appendix.
Appendix; Chapter IV; Whiskey Insurrection

2 Nov 1794, Oath of Allegiance taken before Joseph Vance of Smith Township Samuel Marquis is in this list.

Cowen, Janet C., comp; Jeffersonville Land Entries 1808-1818; McDowell Publications, Utica, NY, 1984, p. 33.
Receipt # 02083
Marques Samuel IN Jefferson FR S05 S06 T03 N11E 191.83 1812 10 03

A Census of Pensioners for Revolutionary or Military Services with their Names, Ages, and Places of Residence Under the Act for Taking the Sixth Census in 1840; Genealogical Publishing Co., Inc., Baltimore, Maryland, 1965. p. 184.

Names of pensioners for revolutionary or military services.	Ages	Names of heads of families with whom pensioners resided June 1, 1840.
RIPLEY COUNTY		
JOHNSON		
Samuel Marquest	81 [b. abt 1759]	Benjamin Richardson

Gibbs, A.; Ripley County Historical Society Data on Revolutionary Soldiers, 1973 review.

Exact location of marker: no further information on grave site. His wife perhaps buried at Ryker's Ridge.
Additional comments: on Court House tablet
    Toph: resided with Henry Wilson 1840 census Ripley Co. Ind. pension List, p. 230 Samuel Marquest age 81.

MATHEWS, AMOS V.

Patriot: Amos V. Mathews
Birth: 1759 Litchfield Co., CT
Married Spouse 1: 16 Jan 1825   Delila Wilson (abt 1793 -)
Service state(s): CT
Rank: Private
Proof of Service: Pension application
Pension application No.: W9537 & BLWt 75006-160-55
Residences: Litchfield, CT; Henry Co., KY; Ripley Co., IN; Gallatin Co., KY; Carroll Co., KY.
Died: 4 Aug 1844   Gallatin Co., KY
Buried: Unknown
DAR Ancestor No.: None as of 7 Jun 2017.

Pension Application Abstracted from National Archives microfilm Series M804, Roll 1651, File W9537, BLWt 75006-160-55.
Pension abstract for – Amos V. Mathews
Service state(s): CT
Date: 25 Aug 1833
County of: Henry   State of: KY
Declaration made before a Judge or Court: Justice of the Peace; unable, because of bodily infirmity and fear of cholera, to attend court.
Act of: 7 Jun 1832
Age: 74 yrs.   Record of age: None
Where and year born: Litchfield, CT   1759
Residence when he entered service: Watertown, Litchfield Co., CT
Residence(s) since the war: Litchfield, CT; KY, now Henry Co., KY
Residence now: Henry Co., KY
Volunteer, Drafted, or Substitute: 1st tour - Enlisted in Watertown, CT by Lt. Towbridge; 2nd tour – volunteered; 3rd tour – Drafted; 4th tour – Volunteered; 5th tour – Volunteered; 6th tour – Volunteered; 7th tour – Volunteered.
Rank(s): Private & Militia Man
Statement of service-

Period	Duration	Names of General and Field Officers
Apr 1775	6 mos.	Capt. [Benedict] Arnold, Col. Enos from Litchfield Co.
Jul 1775	3 mos.	Same officers
Jun 1776	3 mos.	Rendezvoused at Watertown, Capt. Edwards, then under Regt. of Col. Richards
Apr 1777	6 mos.	Rendezvoused at Watertown, Capt. Edwards
May 1778	3 mos.	Capt. Amos Bradley, Regt. of Col. Smith
Jul 1779	6 mos.	Rendezvoused at Watertown, Capt. Edwards, then under command of Col. Richards
Mar 1780	6 mos.	Rendezvoused at Watertown, Capt. Bradley, Regt. under command of of Col. Smith

Battles: Long Island
Discharge received: In writing for each tour; 3rd tour at North River.
What became of it?: Lost
Statement is supported by –
Persons in neighborhood who certify character: Affidavit of Daniel White and Wm. McCracken – they were well acquainted, and he was reputed to have served
&
Pension abstract for – Amos V. Mathews
Date: 17 Nov 1835
County of: Ripley   State of: IN
Declaration made before a Judge or Court: Justice of the Peace
Declaration: Makes request for transfer from the KY Pension Rolls to Indiana where he intends to remain. There was a small tract of Land in the State of Indiana that fell to his wife by heirship and no land in Kentucky & wishing to secure a home, he removed to aforesaid state [Indiana].
Statement of service: He is the same person who belonged to the company commanded by Benedict Arnold in the Regt. commanded by Col. Thompson formerly Maj. Thompson
&
Pension abstract for – Delila Mathews widow of Amos V. Mathews
Date: 2 Feb 1857 for Pension & 10 Sep 1857 for Bounty Land
County of: Jefferson   State of: IN
Declaration made before a Judge or Court: Justice of the Peace; Notary Public
Act of: 3 Feb 1853
Age: 84 yrs. (in Sep. she is 62 yrs.)
Residence now: Rockport, Spencer Co., IN
Death of soldier: 4 Aug 1844 Carroll Co., KY
Widow's former name: Delila Wilson
Marriage date and place: 16 Jan 1825   Gallatin Co., KY
Proof of marriage: Marriage Certificate
      & affidavit of John H. Taylor, a notary in Jefferson Co., has known Delila Mathews since before16 Jan 1825; her name before marriage was Delila Wilson; on 16 Jan 1825 she was lawfully married to Amos V. Mathews; at the time of marr. were both residents of Gallatin Co., KY.
      & affidavit of Samuel Carlisle same as above; also includes marriage took place in Gallatin Co., KY and soldier resided in house of affiant at the time of his death.
[Note: Notation in file indicates Delila Mathews died 18 Dec 1863.]

Abstract of Final Payment Voucher; General Services Administration, Washington, DC
NAME   MATHEWS, Amos. V.
AGENCY OF PAYMENT   INDIANA
DATE OF ACT   1832
DATE OF PAYMENT   4th qtr. 1844
DATE OF DEATH   Aug. 4, 1844
         FINAL PAYMENT VOUCHER RECEIVED FROM

THE GENERAL ACCOUNTING OFFICE Form
General Services Administration   GSA 70-7035   GSA DEC 69 7068

Adjutants-General, by the Authority of the General Assembly, comp.; Record of Service of Connecticut Men in the I. War of the Revolution; The Case, Lockwood & Brainard Company Printers and Binders, Hartford, CT, 1889, p. 41.
Continental Regiments – 1775
5th Company (This Company served at the Siege of Boston.)

Benedict Arnold	Captain	New Haven	Dis no serve with the Co.
Caleb Towbridge	Captain	New Haven	Com. May 1; disc. Dec. 10, '75 re-ent. Service in '76.
Jesse Curtiss	1st Lieut.	Waterbury	Com. May 1; disc. Dec. 20, '75
Nathaniel Edwards	2d Lieut	Waterbury	Com. May 1; disc. Dec. 20, '75
Elias Stillwell	Ensign	New Haven	Com. May 1; disc. Dec. 10' 75

Privates

Names and Rank	Time Enlisted	When Discharged, &c.
Amos Mathews	May 8	Dec. 20.

Quisenberry, Anderson Chenault; Revolutionary Soldiers in Kentucky, containing a roll of the officers of Virginia line who received land bounties, a roll of the Revolutionary pensioners in Kentucky, a list of the Illinois regiment who served under George Rogers Clark in the Northwest campaign, also a roster of the Virginia Navy; Reproduction of the original which appeared in Sons of the American Revolution Kentucky Society Year Book, Louisville, 1896, Southern Book Co., Baltimore, MD, 1959. p. 126. 149.
p. 126.
Carroll County (Formed after 1835.)
Revolutionary Pensioners Living in County in 1840. (Collins, Vol. 1, p.6.)
Matthews, Amos V.,   age 79.
p. 149.
Gallatin County
Pensioners Under the Act of June 7, 1832. (Began March 4, 1831.)
Matthews, Amos V., private   Virginia line
      September, 23, 1833; $80.   Age 75.

Margaret R. Waters; Revolutionary Soldiers Buried in Indiana (1949) With Supplement (1954) Two Volumes in One; Genealogical Publishing Company, Baltimore, MD, 1970, p. 35, 135.
p. 35.
MATTHEWS, AMOS V. & DELILA   Ripley & Spencer
He d. 8-4-1844, Carroll Co., Ky., but had liv. in Ripley Co., Ind., 1835. She liv. Rockport, Spencer Co., Ind., 1857, ae. 64. Pens.
&
p. 135.
The following 121 soldiers did not die in Indiana. Their widows later moved to Indiana. Of the 121 widows, there are pension files for 120. Since these are not Revolutionary soldiers who died in Indiana, I jotted down only the sketchiest of

data which may, however, help some reader. When known, Indiana residence is given for widow.

MATTHEWS, AMOS V. & DELILA   Ripley & Spencer
He d. 8-4-1844, Carroll Co., Ky., but had liv. in Ripley Co., Ind., 1835. She liv. Rockport, Spencer Co., Ind., 1857, ae. 64. Pens.

MAVITY, WILLIAM

Patriot: William Mavity
Birth: 1 Nov 1747 Ireland
Married Spouse 1: abt 1775, VA Mary Jones (1755 - 1825/30)
Service state(s): VA
Rank: Sergeant Major, Patriotic Service
Proof of Service: His diary
Pension application No.:
Residences: Ireland; Henry Co., VA (now Franklin Co., VA);
Ripley Co., IN (1824/5)
Died: 1832 Ripley Co., IN
Buried: Mavity family graveyard located on land that was once their family farm, Old Michigan Rd. near Rexville, Shelby Twp., Ripley Co IN., later the Hugh Black farm.
DAR Ancestor No.:A075769

Revolutionary Service: Sergeant Major, Henry Co., VA Militia,
2nd Battalion, 4th Regiment, Col. Waller;
Took Oath of Allegiance

Mavity, William; *Diary of William Mavity, Sergeant Major, 2nd Battalion, 4th Regiment, Virginia.*
Excerpts:
    p. 2   I was Discharged Oct. 25, 1781
    p. 8   Quartered before York Town , October 20, 1781
    William Mavity, Sergeant Major in my Battalion being unfit for duty is by order of General Lawson hereby discharged. Given under my hand, Geo. Waller, Major H.B.

William Mavity's Diary pertaining to the battle at Yorktown; this is a partial transcription.
"We arrived at Swanspoint on Saturday the 29th and in conjunction with the Bedford Troops our time began the 29th of Sept. 1781.
In Camp at Springfield, " 'Sept. 28, 1781. '" Our men marched down to York, and the Rifle men and French Infantry attacked the British outlines and took their works, which Deprived them, of Pasture and ocostined them to kill their Horses; and on the 29th our Riflemen Drove them into their main works, and General Washington with the Grand Army appeared before York and Pitched their camps in view of the Enemies' works about a mile Distant, and immediately Laid close siege to their whole Garison, both by sea and Land, and raised Bateries without firing a shot till the eight of Oct., when we had three Batteries opened and began to play furiously upon the Enemy and silenced their fire, which they kept continually Pouring upon our men, while they were firing their works; and one 14th, at night our men made an Attack on the Enemies' Redoubt, where they kept their Picket Guard and stormed them with a considerable loss and made a great Carnage with the Enemy and took fifty nine prisoners, wounded forty three, and took several stands of arms. We had one Colonel, two Captains and forty rank

and file killed, and one major and twenty wounded; and the 15th at night, our men made a Trench in conjunction with the Redoubt that they had taken from the Enemy within two hundred yards of the Enemies' lines, and raised three Bateries; and they began to mount their cannon; but the Enemy came upon our militia and Drove them out of the works, took possession of our Grand Batery and spiked six pieces of our cannon; but the front came up and Drove them off and killed several and took eight; and on the 16th we finished our works; and on the 17th our Grand Batery Began to play very Heavy, and the Enemy sent a flag for terms of Capitulation; and on the 18th the flag continues; and on the 19th they marched out with the honors of War."

[The diary also includes lists of men and substitutes as well as statistics of wounded and killed. Microfilm can be rented from the Church of Jesus Christ of Later-Day Saint. – mjm]

<u>1820 United States Federal Census; Franklin, Virginia</u>; Page: *156*; NARA Roll: *M33_136*; Image: *174, Line 21.*
Free white males 16-18=1; Free white males 16-25=4; Free white males 45 & over= 1 *[William Mavity]*; Free white females under 10=1; Free white females 26-44=2; Free white females 45 & over=1 *[Mary Mavity].*

<u>Ripley County Indiana, Recorder's Office, Tract Book 1</u>, *p. 28.*
Mavity, William Sr.   15 Aug 1825   R11, T6, S19   80 acres

Mavity , Norman Bloss, comp.; <u>The Mavity Family</u>*; Lithoprinted by Edwards Brothers, Inc., Ann Arbor, MI, 1951; p. 226.*
Land Records and Deed Records, Ripley County, Indian
Early land entries: (from certified copy taken from land office).
William Mavity, Sr. August 15, 1825, W1/2 SE1/4, Sec. 19, T. 6, R. 11

<u>1830 U. S. Census</u>, *Ripley County, IN; Series M19, Roll 32; p. 9, line 7.*
William Mavity
Free white males 30-39=1; Free white males 80-89=1 *[William Mavity]*; Free white females 15-19=1; Free white females 40-49=2.
[His sp. Mary was deceased before this census was taken.]

Toph, Violet E.; <u>Peoples History of Ripley County, Indiana</u>*; self-published, c. 1940, p. 120.*
Revolutionary Soldiers Who Came to Ripley County
William Mavity was born in Ireland about 1750. He was a sergeant-Major of the Fourth Regiment, commanded by Col. Waller of the Virginia Troops. It was his duty to make daily reports. These he set down in a pocket diary. Mr. E. B. Mavity of French Lick, Ind. has a copy of this book. His grave is on the Hugh Black farm near Rexville in Ripley County. He came to Indiana in 1824 and died in 1832. His wife was Mary Jones, They had seven sons, John, William, Jesse, James, David, Jones, Morton and Wesley Mavity. This data was furnished by Mrs. N. B. Mavity, of 223 Sumner Circle, French Lick, Ind.

O'Byrne, Mrs. Roscoe C., comp. & ed.; Roster Soldiers and Patriots of the American Revolution Buried in Indiana; Published by Indiana Daughters of the American Revolution, 1938, Reprinted Genealogical Publishing Co., Baltimore MD, 1968, p. 248.
MAVITY, WILLIAM   Ripley County
Born – About 1750, Ireland
Service – Sergeant-Major of 2nd Battalion, 4th Regt., Vir. Troops, under Col. Walker. It was his duty to make daily reports. These he set down in a pocket diary. This was in possession of a great-great-grand daughter, Mrs. Carrie Riggins of St. Helens, Cal, in 1922. This diary contains a description of the siege of Yorktown and the surrender of Cornwallis.
Died – 1832. Buried near New Marion, Ripley Co., Ind.
Married – Mary Jones. Ch. John; William; Jesse; James; David Jones; Morton; Wesley.
Collected by Mr. N. B. Mavity, 223 Summit Circle, French Lick, Indiana.

O'Byrne, Mrs. Roscoe C., comp.; Roster of Soldiers and Patriots of the American Revolution Buried in Indiana, Vol. II; Indiana Daughters of the American Revolution, 1980, p. 127.
Roster, Vol. 1, p. 248
MAVITY, WILLIAM   Ripley County
Born – Nov. 8, 1747, Ireland
Children – John, b. July 12, 1776, m. Dorothy Reel, June 25, 1795; William, b. 1780; Mary, m. Richard Beckett, April 19, 1810; Martha, m. Mathew L. Moore; Margret; Jesse, b. 1791, m. Susannah Riggs, March 1, 1819; James, b. 1794, m. Margaret Watts, Sept. 13, 185; David Jones, b. July 3, 1798, m. Lurana Blackman Davis, June , 1836; Morton, b. 1800, m. Charity Watts, Oct. 24, 1828; Wesley, b. 1803, m. Ellen ---.
By Mrs. Gail C. Lamson, Registrar, Julia Watkins Brass Chapter, 467 S. Court St., Crown Point, Ind.

Gibbs, A.; Ripley County Historical Society Data on Revolutionary Soldiers, 1973 review.
Exact location of marker: no further information on grave site. An 'ordered' was written on Ripley County materials of Revolutionary soldiers; was probably reference to purchasing a Govt. marker.

Mavity, Norman Bloss, comp.; The Mavity Family; Lithoprinted by Edwards Brothers, Inc., Ann Arbor, MI, 1951; p. Forward-vii.
"Records at the courthouse gave the location of his land on the Michigan Road south of Versailles, near Rexville. Here an elderly man was plowing in a field. He proved to be Mr. Hugh Black, owner of a part of the William Mavity farm. Upon inquiry as to a burial ground on the farm, Mr. Black pointed to a knoll about fifty feet from the east side of the road and said: "My father always said that was the Mavity family graveyard. It has never been disturbed."
The little group of graves had only rough stone markers without inscriptions, evidently brought from a shallow creek bed nearby. They stood in a

tangle of grass, surrounded by a wire fence in disrepair. Later investigation showed that those buried there, in addition to William Mavity and wife, were their son John and wife; Charity Watts Mavity and her mother, Deborah Riker Watts; Mary Mavity Beckett and her daughter, Martha Beckett Miles; and Margaret Mavity, daughter of William."

Gravesite location - On March 24, 2017, Ross' Run Chapter Daughters of the American Revolution member Marlene McDerment, Chapter Registrar (compiler of this book) with the assistance of Judy Kappes, Chapter Regent, located the Mavity graveyard by dowsing. The site has been graded through the years, and Michigan Road (U.S. 421) is now higher than the original knoll. A tree stands about in the middle of the graves which are approximately 50 feet from the road. The graves seem to run to the left and right and in front of the tree. There are no graves between the tree and the stream behind it. The stones that marked the graves are not visible. This site is across the road, and slightly north of the Honey Jug restaurant, 8782 U.S.421.

MAXWELL, DAVID

David Maxwell did not live in Ripley County. He died in ME, his wife Abigail came to Ripley County where she applied for the Widow's Pension.

Patriot: David Maxwell
Birth: abt 1757
Married Spouse 1: 17 Jul 1785, Wells, ME (dist. MA)   Abigail Whittum
(1766-1855)
Service state(s): MA Sea Service
Rank: Marine
Proof of Service: Pension application
Pension application No.: R7045
Residences: Yorkshire Co., MA (now York Co., ME); Kennebec Co., ME
Died: 21 Feb 1814   Augusta, Kennebec Co., ME
Buried: Unknown
DAR Ancestor No.: A206429

Pension Application Abstracted from National Archives microfilm Series M804, Roll 1657, File R7045.
Pension abstract for – Abigail Maxwell widow of David Maxwell
Soldier's Service state(s): Sea Service - MA
Date: 13 May 1844
County of: Ripley   State of: IN
Declaration made before a Judge or Court: Probate Court
Act of: 4 Jul 1838
Widow's Age: 79 yrs. on the 25th of March
Residence when Soldier entered service: Wells, Yorkshire Co., MA,
now York Co., ME
Soldier's Residence(s) since the war: Lived in Maine until his death.
Widow's Residence now: Ripley Co., IN
Volunteer, Drafted, or Substitute: Enlisted
Soldier's Rank(s): Marine
Statement of Soldier's service-

Period	Names of General and Field Officers
Sep 1778 - Peace in 1783	On board the Russel then lying in Boston, commanded by Capt. Joshua Trafton [?]; the Russel sailed to the West Indies twice

Battles: Captured by the British during second cruise & taken to the West Indies then to Portsmouth, England.
Statement of Soldier's Service is supported by –
Living witness, name(s): Nathaniel Leighton & James Parker gave affidavit they were acquainted with David Maxwell and understood he served as a Marine or Seaman from the time he was 21 yrs. of age until the Peace in 1783.
Soldier's birth place and year: 9 Nov 1757 – he was 21 y/o on 9 Nov 1778
Death of soldier: 21 Feb 1814 in Augusta, [Kennebec Co.] ME
Marriage date and place: 17 Aug 1785 Wells, Yorkhire Co., MA

(now York Co., ME)
Proof of marriage: None presented
Names and ages of children: None mentioned
[Note: on 2 Jun 1852, Abigail issued a Power of Attorney in order to obtain benefits that had been denied.]

Rejected or Suspended Applications for Revolutionary War Pensions; Reprinted for Clearfield Company Inc. by Genealogical Publishing Co., Inc., Baltimore, MD, 1998. p. 419.
A list of persons residing in Indiana who have applied for pensions under the act of July 7, 1838, whose claims have been suspended; prepared in conformity with the resolution of the Senate of the United States, September 16, 1850.

Names	Residence	Reason for suspension
Maxwell, Abigail, widow of David	Versailles, Ripley	For further proof.

Senate Documents, Vol.9, No. 988, 63rd Congress, 3d Session, Washington, 1915; "Register of Certificates Issued by John Pierce, Esquire, Paymaster General and Commissioner of Army Accounts for the United States, to Officers and Soldiers of the Continental Army Under Act of July 4, 1783"; *Seventeenth report of the National Society of the Daughters of the American Revolution;* Genealogical Publishing Co., Inc., Baltimore, MD, 1984. p.347.
. 347.
Men listed in this volume with the same name.

No. of Certificate	To whom issued	Amount
93400	Maxwell, David	51.50

Maine Marriages, 1771-1907; accessed 11 April 2016 from https://familysearch.org/ark:/61903/1:1:F46D-XWG
Name: David Maxell Jr.
Spouse's Name: Abigail Whittum
Event Date: 17 Jul 1785
Event Place: Wells, York, Maine
System Origin: Maine-EASy
GS Film number: 12622
Reference ID: pg 33
FHL microfilm 12,622
[Note: a second Family Search record shows the marriage date as 17 Nov 1785. DAR has accepted the date as 17 Aug 1785. – mjm]

Waters, Margaret R.; *Revolutionary Soldiers Buried in Indiana (1949) With Supplement (1954) Two Volumes in One;* Genealogical Publishing Company, Baltimore, MD, 1970, p.. 35, 135.
p. 35.
MAXWELL, DAVID & ABIGAIL   Ripley
He d. 2-21-1814, Augusta, Maine. Pens.

p. 135.
The following 121 soldiers did not die in Indiana. Their widows later moved to Indiana. Of the 121 widows, there are pension files for 120. Since these are not Revolutionary soldiers who died in Indiana, I jotted down only the sketchiest of data which may, however, help some reader. When known, Indiana residence is given for widow.

MAXWELL, DAVID & ABIGAIL   Ripley
He d. 2-21-1814, Augusta, Maine. Pens.

Toph, Violet E.; Peoples History of Ripley County, Indiana; self-published, c. 1940, p. 126.
Revolutionary Soldiers Who Came to Ripley County
Abigail Maxwell, widow of David Maxell, applied for a pension from Ripley County. David Maxwell entered the service from Massachusetts in 1778 in the Marine Service. He married Aug. 17, 1785. He was born in 1757 and died Feb. 21, 1814. Nothing was said about him ever being in Indiana.

Gibbs, A.; Ripley County Historical Society Data on Revolutionary Soldiers, 1973 review.
Comments: died Feb. 21, 1814 in Augusta, Maine
   His widow, Abigail Maxwell, on pension in Ripley Co. Ind.
   Toph: appl. for pension in Ripley Co. Ind.
   See 1850 census Ripley Co. Ind. Delaware Tw.

McCULLOUGH, JOHN

Patriot: John McCullough
Birth: abt 1760 Cumberland Co., PA
Married Spouse 1: 10 Dec 1787, Mercer Co., KY
                               Constant Kesiah Jones (abt 1770-1848)
Service state(s): NC Continental Line
Rank: Private, Public Service
Proof of Service: Pension application
Pension application No.: W9558
Residences: NC; Mercer Co., KY; Switzerland Co., IN; Ripley Co., IN
Died: 15 Jun 1823   Ripley Co., IN
Buried: Unknown
DAR Ancestor No.: A032513

Pension Application Abstracted from National Archives microfilm Series M804, Roll 1674, File W9558.
Pension abstract for – Constant McCullough widow of John McCullough
Service state(s): NC
Alternate spelling(s):
Date: 10 Mar 1840 & 14 Jun 1843
County of: Ripley   State of: IN
Declaration made before a Judge or Court: Circuit Court
Act of: 7 Jul 1838
Age: 70 yrs.
Residence when he entered service: Not stated
Residence(s) since the war: Not stated
Residence now: Ripley Co., IN
Volunteer, Drafted, or Substitute: Enlisted
Rank(s): Private
Statement of service-

Period	Duration	Names of General and Field Officers
8 Feb 1777	3 yrs.	4th Regt. NC Continental Line, Capt. Cole

Battles: Not stated
Discharge received: Not stated
Statement is supported by –
Living witness, name(s): Affidavit filed in Ripley Co., IN on 10 Mar 1840, of Benjamin Jones, of Decatur Co., IN, states he has known Constant McCullough, formerly Constant Jones since infancy to the present time; he was also acquainted with John McCullough from the year 1785 until his death in June 1823; saw them legally joined together at the home of John Jones, father of Constant, in Mercer Co., KY sometime in the month of Dec 1787; widow is now 70 yrs. of age; believes in the neighborhood where he resided to have been a soldier of the Revolution.

[Additional affidavits were filed when Constant made application again in 1843.]
Documentary proof: Certificate -
I William Hill, Secretary of State in and for the State of North Carolina do hereby Certify that it appears from the Muster Rolls of the Continental Line of this State in the Revolutionary War; that John McCullough enlisted as a Private Soldier in Caleb Cole's company of the 4th Regiment on the 8th day of February 1777 for the term of three years, that he was a prisoner on the 14th day of April 1779, and mustered again in November 1779.
Given under my hand this 28th day of November 1839.
[The same statement was provided again with this addition:]
It also appears of record in this Office, that he was allowed the quantity of land given a Soldier for three years services by the laws of this State. Warrant No. 1219.
Given under my hand this 28 April 1843.
Death of soldier: 15 Jun 1820 Ripley Co., IN
Marriage date and place: 10 Dec 1787
Proof of marriage: Marriage Bond, Mercer Co., KY, dated 28 Nov 1787
Names and ages of children: Not stated

Abstract of Final Payment Voucher; General Services Administration, Washington, DC
 LAST   FINAL PAYMENT VOUCHER RECEIVED FROM
        THE GENERAL ACCOUNTING OFFICE
NAME   McCULLOUGH, JOHN
AGENCY OF PAYMENT   INDIANA
DATE OF ACT   1832
DATE OF PAYMENT   Sept. 3, 1843
DATE OF DEATH   -
GENERAL SERVICES ADMINISTRATION
National Archives and Records Service   NA-286
GSA-WASH DC 54-4891   November 1953

Abstract of Final Payment Voucher; General Services Administration, Washington, DC
NAME   McCullough, Constant widow of John
AGENCY OF PAYMENT   INDIANA
DATE OF ACT   1848
DATE OF PAYMENT   Sept. 1852
DATE OF DEATH
  last   ~~FINAL~~ PAYMENT VOUCHER RECEIVED FROM
          THE GENERAL ACCOUNTING OFFICE   From
General Services Administration   GSA DC 70-7035   GSA DEC 69 7068

Thomas, Abishai & Catlin, Lynde & Mifflin, Benjamin; Roster of the North Carolina Troops in the Continental Army, Volume 16; The University of North Carolina at Chapel Hill, Chapel Hill, NC, 1791, p. 1111.
Roster of the Continental Line from North Carolina, 1783.

Names and Rank	Companies	Dates of Commissions and Enlistments.	Occurrences
McCullough, John, pt.	Cole's	1777, 8 Feb'y 3 yrs.	Pris. 14 Apl. '79, musd. Nov. '79.

North Carolina Daughters of the American Revolution, comp.; Roster of soldiers from North Carolina in the American Revolution with an appendix containing a collection of miscellaneous records.; North Carolina Daughters of the American Revolution, Durham, NC, 1934, p. 74.
Roster of the Continental Line from North Carolina
Reference: North Carolina State Records, Clark, Vol. XVI, 1782-1783
Copy of a Register showing the names alphabetically (in Regiments) rank, dates of commission and enlistment, periods of service, and occurrences, taken from the original muster and pay rolls of the North Carolina Line of the late Army of the United States.
1ST REGIMENT – COL. THOS. CLARK

Name and Rank	Company	Dates of Enlistment and Commission	Period of Service	Occurrences
McCullough, John, Pt.	Cole's	8 Feb '77	3 yrs.	Pris 14 Apr '79 Must'd Nov '79

U.S. Department of Interior, Bureau of Land Management, General Land Office Records; Land Patent Search
Name: McCullough, John & Marsh, William
Accession Nr. CV-0036-070; Document Type – Credit Volume Patent; Issue Date – 12/17/1817; Cancelled – No
Land Office – Cincinnati; Authority – April 24, 1820: Sale-Cash Entry (3 Stat. 566); Document Nr.   0; Total Acres – 0.00
Land Descriptions: State – IN; Meridian – 2ndPM; Twp-Rng – 002N – 002W; Aliquots – NE1/4; Section – 28; County - Switzerland

Ripley County Indiana, Recorder's Office, Tract Book 3, p. 29.
| McCullough, John | 20 Sep 1821 | R11, T6, S28 | 80 acres |

Waters, Margaret R.; Indiana Land Entries Vol. 1 Cincinnati District, 1801-1840; Originally Published Indianapolis 1948, Second Reprint 1979 by The Bookmark, P.O. Box 74, Knightstown, IN, p. 8.
CINCINNATI DISTRICT – VOL. 1
T 4 N, R 1 W of 1st P.M.   OHIO CO.
John McCollough   NW ¼ - S28; 2-5-1814

1820 U. S. Census, Ripley Co., IN, NARA Roll M33_15; EN 7 Aug 1820, p. 73, line 25.
John McCullough

Males 16-25=2, Males 26-44=1, Males 45>=1, Females <10=1, Females 10-15=1, Females 45>=1.

Waters, Margaret R.; <u>Revolutionary Soldiers Buried in Indiana (1949) With Supplement (1954) Two Volumes in One</u>; Genealogical Publishing Company, Baltimore, MD, 1970, p. 23.

McCULLOUGH, JOHN   Ripley Co.
d. 6-15-1823; m. 12-10-1787, Mercer Co., Ky., Constant Jones, b. 1769-1770, dau of John Jones; marr. bond. Iss. 11-28-1787; bondsmen James McCullough & Jeremiah Sallyers; wid. liv. Shelby Twp., Ripley Co. Enl. 2-4-1777. 4th Regt., N.C., Capt. Cole; 3 yr. REF-Pens. W.9558.

Gibbs, A.; <u>Ripley County Historical Society Data on Revolutionary Soldiers</u>, 1973 review.

Exact location of marker: no known marker; possibly Flat Rock Cem. Shelby Tw. Ripley Co. Ind.

Additional comments: dec'd by 4 Sept 1823 Court. Ripley Co. Ind. Probate Book A, p. 33, 53, 74, 111, 116; McCullough estate.

1850 census Ripley Co. Ind. Shelby Tw., p. 648 9/324-5 Constant McCullough with J. Salyers.

McDONALD (McDONIELDS), JOSEPH

Patriot: Joseph McDonald
Birth: 1760 Frederick Co. MD
Married Spouse 1: XX (- 15 Jun 1841)
Service state(s): PA Frontier
Rank: Private
Proof of Service: Pension application
Pension application No.: S33065
Residences: Frederick Co., MD; Bedford Co., PA; Nicholas Co., KY; Ripley Co., IN
Died: 15 Jun 1841 Ripley Co., IN
Buried: Old Washington Church Cemetery, Washington Twp., Ripley Co., IN
DAR Ancestor No.: A201907

Pension Application Abstracted from National Archives microfilm Series M804, Roll 1678, File S33065.
Pension abstract for – Joseph McDonield
Service state(s): PA
Date: 12 Aug 1833
County of: Ripley   State of: IN
Declaration made before a Judge or Court: Probate Court
Act of: 7 Jun 1832
Age: 73 yrs.
Record of age: None – what my parents told me
Where and year born: Frederick Co., MD   1706
Residence when he entered service: Bedford Co., PA
Residence(s) since the war: MD until 1796; KY 13 yrs.; Ripley Co., IN
Residence now: Ripley Co., IN
Volunteer, Drafted, or Substitute: 1st tour – Volunteered; 2nd tour – Substitute for Jared Francis [?]; 3rd tour – Substitute for Daniel O'Neal [?].
Rank(s): Private
Statement of service-

Period	Duration	Names of General and Field Officers
May 1779	3 mos.	Col. Ashman's PA Regt., Capt. Thomas Norton's company, Capt. Moore
1779	18 days	Col. Ashman's PA Regt., Capt. George Enslow's company
1780	1 mo.	Col. Ashman's PA Regt., Capt. George Enslow's company

Battles: None stated
Discharge received: Not stated
Clergyman: Meshack Hyatt
Persons in neighborhood who certify character: Ephraim E. Wilson
Wife: Not named
Marriage date and place: MD (aft. War) She d. bef. 12 Aug 1833
Names and ages of children: Not stated – there were heirs

Clift, G. Glens, Assistant Secretary, Kentucky Historical Society, Comp.; *"Second Census" of Kentucky – 1800, A Privately Compiled and Published Enumeration of Tax Payers Appearing in the 79 Manuscript Volumes Extant of Tax Lists of the 42 Counties of Kentucky in Existence in 1800*; Genealogical Publishing Co., Baltimore, MD, 1966, p. 185.

Name	County	Tax List Date
McDonald, Joseph	Nicholas	1800

Ripley County, Indiana Deed Records Vol. A, 11 Aug 1818-29 Jan 1827
Page(s): 151-153.
Abstract of Deed/Patent for: Joseph McDonald and Deborah (dower) his wife
Purchaser (Grantee) or Seller (Grantor)?: Purchaser
Purchased from: Samuel Webster
State & county where recorded: Ripley Co., Indiana
Date entered: 10 Nov 1824
Recorded: 1 Dec 1824
Description: South half of the northeast quarter of Section 12, in Township 7, North of Range 12 East in the district offered for sale at Jefferson, containing eighty acres.
Amount paid: One hundred and fifty dollars ($150.00).
Name(s) of Witnesses: William Hamilton & Stephen Austin

The Pension Roll of 1835 Volume IV, The Mid-Western States, Indexed Edition, *In Four Volumes;* Genealogical Publishing Co., Inc., Baltimore, MD, Reprint 1968, p. 87.
Statement, &c. of Ripley county, Indiana.

INDIANA Names	Rank	Annual allowance.	Sums received	Description of service
Joseph McDonald	Private	25.33	75 99	Va. State troops

When placed on pension roll	Commencement of pension	Ages	Laws under which they were formerly placed on the pension roll; and remarks.
Oct 1, 1833	March 4, 1831	82	-

Toph, Violet E.; *Peoples History of Ripley County, Indiana;* self-published, c. 1940, p. 123, 128.
Revolutionary Soldiers Who Came to Ripley County
[Please see record for James Grimes. James' son, John, married Mary, daughter of Joseph McDonald.]
p. 128.
In July, 1936, the Ripley County Historical Society, aided by subscriptions from descendants of the five Revolutionary soldiers buried in Old Washington cemetery, Edward Pendergast, Ninian Beall, James Grimes, Joseph McDonald and William Lipperd enclosed the cemetery with a durable wove wire fence and placed Government markers for each of the five soldiers, thus making a notable Revolutionary Shrine for Washington Township.

O'Byrne, Mrs. Roscoe C., comp. & ed.; *Roster Soldiers and Patriots of the American Revolution Buried in Indiana; Published by Indiana Daughters of the American Revolution, 1938, Reprinted Genealogical Publishing Co., Baltimore MD, 1968, p. 270.*

McDONALD (McDONIELDS), Joseph   Ripley County
Born – 1760, Frederick County, Maryland.
Service – Volunteered May, 1779, served on frontier of Penn. Under Ensign Joseph Sparks, Lieut. Johnson. From Aug. to Nov., 1779, served as substitute under Col. Ashmon, Capt. Thomas Norton. Total service 6 mos. and 18 days.
Proof – Pension claim S. 33065.
Died – June 15, 1841. Buried Old Washington Cemetery, Versailles, Ind. Government marker.
Daughter – Mary, m. John Grimes.
Collected by Mrs. A. B. Wycoff, Batesville, Indiana.

Gibbs, A.; *Ripley County Historical Society Data on Revolutionary Soldiers, 1973 review.*
Exact location of marker: east out of Elrod on 525 to 50N, right to Thermon Boyd farm (1973); mile n.e. of house, going down across creek and up a hill; no road or path. Old Washington Cemetery north east out of Elrod, Washington Tw. Ripley Co. Ind.
Type of marker: Gov't
Date placed: 1936 (R.C.H.S. minutes)
Placed by: Ripley County Historical Society
Additional comments: on Court House tablet
> Ripley Co. Ind. Probate A. p 138, appl. for pension Aug. 1833.
> Toph notes: speaker at dedication of Court House tablet, in 1928, Rev. Walter Grimes of Indianapolis, was a descendant of Joseph McDonald and James Grimes.

Wording on marker:

Joseph McDonald
Pvt. Clark's Co.
1 N.C. Rgt.
Rev. War
1840

United States Headstone Applications for U.S. Military Veterans, 1925-1949, database with images; (https://familysearch.org/ark:/61903/1:1:VHZ8-Y5D : 17 May 2016) Affiliate Publication Number: M1916; Affiliate Publication Title: Applications for Headstones for U.S. Military Veterans, 1925-1941; Affiliate Film Number: 73; GS Film Number: 1878222; Digital Folder Number: 004832240; Image Number: 02099.
Application for Headstone; War Department O.Q.M.G. Form No. 623
Name: McDonald, Joseph
Event Date: May 31, 1934
Name of Cemetery: Old Washington

Located in or near: Milan, Ind.
Death Date: 1840
Enlistment Dates: July 1, 1777
Discharge Dates: Served 3 years
Rank: Private
Company: Col. Thomas Clarke's 1st North Carolina Reg.
To be shipped to: Ripley Co. Historical Society, Osgood, Ind., Ripley Co.
Whose post-office address is: Versailles, Ind.
This application is for the UNMARKED grave of a veteran. It is understood the stone will be furnished and delivered at the railroad station or steamboat landing above indicated, at Government expense, freight prepaid. I hereby agree to promptly accept the headstone at destination, remove it and properly place same at decedent's grave at my expense. Ripley Co. Historical Society, Applicant. No fee should be paid in connection with this application.
Applicant: Ripley Co. Historical Society, Versailles, Ind.

Tombstone Location: Old Washington Church Cemetery, Washington Twp., Ripley Co., IN

Tombstone Inscription:

JOSEPH
McDONALD
PVT. [Illegible]
[Illegible]
[Illegible]

MacMILLEN (McMILLON), DANIEL

Patriot: Daniel MacMillen
Birth: 1757 Ireland
Married Spouse 1: 14 Feb 1780   Nelly Keenany (- 1810)
Married Spouse 2: 17 Jan 1811, Cumberland Co., KY Jane Sconce (1785-1855)
Service state(s):   MD Continental
Rank: Sergeant
Proof of Service: Pension application
Pension application No.: W6800
Residences: Cecil Co., MD; Monroe Co., KY 1806, Cumberland Co, KY;
             Jefferson Co., IN; Ripley Co., IN.
Died: 15/16 Aug 1838   Brown Twp., Ripley Co., IN
Buried: McMillen Cemetery on Everett Pickett farm near Correct,
          Johnson Twp., Ripley Co., IN
DAR Ancestor No.: A078254

Pension Application Abstracted from National Archives microfilm Series M804, Roll 1697, File W6800.
Pension abstract for – Daniel McMillen
Service state(s): MD
Alternate spelling(s): McMillin
Date: 23 Jun 1818 & 17 Apr 1819
County of: Jefferson   State of: IN
Declaration made before a Judge or Court: Circuit Court
Act of: 18 Mar 1818
Age: 60 yrs. in 1818; 61 yrs. in 1819
Residence now: State of Indiana [county not named]
Volunteer, Drafted, or Substitute: Enlisted in the Continental Service at the heads of the Elk in the State of MD.
Rank(s): Private & Sergeant
Statement of service-

Period	Duration	Names of General and Field Officers
In 1778-Dec 1778		6th MD Regt., commanded by Capt. Henry Dobsin.

Battles: Monmouth
&
Pension abstract for – Daniel McMillen
Date: 24 Oct 1821
County of: Jefferson   State of: IN
Declaration made before a Judge or Court: Circuit Court
Declaration: included schedule of property
Act of: 18 May 1818 & 1 May 1820
Age: 64 yrs.
Residence now: Jefferson Co., IN
Volunteer, Drafted, or Substitute: Enlisted
Statement of service-

Period	Duration	Names of General and Field Officers

1778 -   9 mos.   6th Regt. MD Line Continental Estab.,
   Dec 1778   Capt. Henry Dobson, Col. Otha H.
                                     Williams.
Dec 1778 - Mar 1779   *   Same company & officers.
   *Enlisted for 3 yrs., was crippled by the kick of a horse.
Discharge received: By reason of wound [see *], was unable to perform military
   service, he remained in a situation where he could not walk for nearly 2
   yrs. in which time he considered himself in service, if able liable to
   perform military duty & he never received a discharge.
Wife: Not named   Wife's age: Not stated
Names and ages of children: Julia Ann, age 6; Franklin, age 4; Stephen, age 2;
   Margaret, age 1 yr.
&

Pension abstract for – Daniel McMillen
Service state(s): MD
Date: 20 Aug 1832
County of: Ripley   State of: IN
Declaration made before a Judge or Court: Circuit Court
Act of: 7 Jun 1832
Age: 75 yrs.
Where and year born: Ireland   1757
Residence when he entered service: Cecil Co. MD
Statement of service-
Names of General and Field Officers: Capt. James Maxwell, Lt. William
   Johnson, Maj. John Neil, MD Troops.
Battles: Trenton, Brandywine, Germantown, Monmouth.
Discharge received: Yes
Signed by: Maj. Neil
What became of it?: Burned in his house in 1806.
Statement is supported by –
Living witness, name(s): Knows no person
Documentary proof: Only had discharge
Clergyman: Wesley Mavity
Persons in neighborhood who certify character: Richard Blair, Joshua Cenn
&

Pension abstract for – Jane McMillin widow of Daniel McMillin
Date: 1 May 1853
County of: Dearborn   State of: IN
Declaration made before a Judge or Court: Justice of the Peace
Declaration: In order to receive Bounty Land
Act of: 28 Sep 1850
Age: 68 yrs.
Residence now: Clay Twp., Dearborn Co., IN; formerly of Ripley Co., IN
Statement is supported by –
Person now living who can testify on widow's behalf: James Ross, of Ripley Co.,
   IN, and Johnson Waltz, of Dearborn Co, IN gave testimony confirming
   her statements, and that she must become a county charge unless she
   receives the bounty.

Death of soldier: Brown Twp., Ripley Co., IN   15 or 16 Aug 1838
Widow's former name: Jane Sconce
Marriage date and place: 17 Jan 1811   Cumberland Co., KY
Names and ages of children: Not stated
&
Additional notations in file –
Death of soldier: 15 Aug 1838   Ripley Co., IN
Service: Served 4 mos. as Sergeant in Capt. Basil William's company in 1777.
Widow's death: 23 Mar 1855.

Abstract of Final Payment Voucher; General Services Administration, Washington, DC
  LAST   FINAL PAYMENT VOUCHER RECEIVED FROM
          THE GENERAL ACCOUNTING OFFICE

NAME	McMILLEN, DANIEL
AGENCY OF PAYMENT	INDIANA
DATE OF ACT	1832
DATE OF PAYMENT	3d Qr. 1839
DATE OF DEATH	Aug. 1839

GENERAL SERVICES ADMINISTRATION
National Archives and Records Service   NA-286
GSA-WASH DC 54-4891   November 1953

Abstract of Final Payment Voucher; General Services Administration, Washington, DC
  LAST   FINAL PAYMENT VOUCHER RECEIVED FROM
          THE GENERAL ACCOUNTING OFFICE

NAME	McMILLAN, JANE WIDOW OF DANIEL
AGENCY OF PAYMENT	INDIANA
DATE OF ACT	1853 2d Sect.
DATE OF PAYMENT	per Act 6 APRIL (Aug. 1857)
DATE OF DEATH	March 21, 1855

       FINAL PAYMENT VOUCHER RECEIVED FROM
       THE GENERAL ACCOUNTING OFFICE   From
General Services Administration   GSA DC 70-7035   GSA DEC 69

Muster Rolls and other records of service of Maryland Troops in the American Revolution; Archives of Maryland, reprinted with permission by Genealogical Publishing Co., Inc., Baltimore, 1972. p. 230.
MUSTERS OF MARYLAND TROOPS, VOL. ll.
Sixth Regiment   Dobson's

| | | Time of Service | | |
Names	Rank	Enlisted	Discharged	Remarks
McMullin, Danl.	Sergt.	10 June 78	1 Apr 79	deserted
1st Muster, June 78				Rein. 22 Dec 78

Newman, Harry Wright; Maryland Revolutionary Records; Tuttle Publishing, Rutland, VT, 1928. p. 36, 119.

p. 36.

| Maryland Revolutionary Pensioners | | | | Misc. facts and |
Name of Veteran	Birth	Rank	Establishment	other State services
McMillen, Daniel*	1757	Sergt.	Maryland Line	Injured

* Indicates that the widow applied for pension

p. 119.

Marriage Records

Daniel MacMillen	Jane Sconce	Jan. 17, 1811	Cumb. Co., Ky.

The Pension Roll of 1835 Volume IV, The Mid-Western States, Indexed Edition, In Four Volumes; Genealogical Publishing Co., Inc., Baltimore, MD, Reprint 1968, p. 87.

Statement, &c. of Ripley county, Indiana.

| INDIANA | | Annual allow- | Sums re- | Description of |
Names	Rank	ance.	ceived	service
Daniel McMillen	Pri & Ser	86.66	259 98	Md. militia

When placed on pension roll	Commencement of pension	Ages	Laws under which they were formerly placed on the pension roll; and remarks.
June 15, 1833	March 4, 1831	75	-

U.S. Department of Interior, Bureau of Land Management, General Land Office Records; Land Patent Search

Name: McMillen, Daniel

Accession Nr. IN0290_.485; Document Type – State Volume Patent; Issue Date – 9/9/1835; Cancelled – No

Land Office – Jeffersonville; Authority – April 24, 1820: Sale-Cash Entry (3 Stat. 566); Document Nr. 4996; Total Acres – 80.00

Land Descriptions: State – IN; Meridian – 2ndPM; Twp-Rng – 007N – 011E; Aliquots – E1/2SE1/4; Section – 33; County - Ripley

Toph, Violet E.; Peoples History of Ripley County, Indiana; self-published, c. 1940, p. 126.

Revolutionary Soldiers Who Came to Ripley County

Daniel McMillan enlisted from Maryland in the spring of 1778 and was discharged in December 1781. He was born in 1757 and died on the 15th or 16th of August, 1838. He was pensioned from Jefferson County, Ind. but later moved to and died in Ripley County. He is buried on the Everett Pickett farm four miles south of Versailles.

O'Byrne, Mrs. Roscoe C., comp. & ed.; Roster Soldiers and Patriots of the American Revolution Buried in Indiana; Published by Indiana Daughters of the American Revolution, 1938, Reprinted Genealogical Publishing Co., Baltimore MD, 1968, p. 275.

MacMILLEN, DANIEL   Ripley County
Born – 1757, Ireland.

Service – Enlisted from Maryland in spring of 1778. Discharged Sept., 1781.
Proof – Pension claim W. 6800.
Died – April 15 or 16, 1838. Buried near Correct, Ind., on a farm, now owned by Everett Pickett. Government marker. Name on bronze tablet in Versailles Court House.
Married – 1811, Jane Sconce. Ch. Julia Ann b. 1814, m. 1st Edwin Johns, 2nd John Green; Franklin b. 1816, d. young; Stephen b. 1818, m. Eliza Wade; Margaret b. 1819, d. young.
Collected by Mrs. A. B. Wycoff, Batesville, Indiana.

Gibbs, A.; *Ripley County Historical Society Data on Revolutionary Soldiers*, 1973 review.
Exact location of marker: 2/10th mi. west off 421 south of Versailles, on 450S on Everett Pickett farm, right at roadside (south side) of 450S. He is buried way back in the corner of the property, just north of creek in corner of field; he and a little girl buried there; no markers..the old house was across the Little Graham Creek; stones of foundation still evident in 1973. West of Correct Ind, Johnson Tw. Ripley Co. Ind.
Type of marker: Gov't (lovingly tended by present farm owner)
Date placed: Nov. 14, 1938 (R.C.H.S. minutes)
Placed by: Ripley County Historical Society
Additional comments: on Court House tablet
 Pensioned from Jefferson Co. Ind.
Wording on marker:
Daniel McMillin
Sgt. Neil's Md. Troops
Rev. War
Aug. 15, 1838

United States Headstone Applications for U.S. Military Veterans, 1925-1949, database with images; (https://familysearch.org/ark:/61903/1:1:VHZD-SC6 : 17 May 2016); *Affiliate Publication Number: M1916; Affiliate Publication Title: Applications for Headstones for U.S. Military Veterans, 1925-1941; Affiliate Film Number: 75; GS Film Number: 1878224; Digital Folder Number: 004832242; Image Number: 02069.*
Application for Headstone; War Department O.Q.M.G. Form No. 623
Name: McMillan, Daniel
Event Date: June 21, 1938
Name of Cemetery: McMillan, Private on the Everett Pickett farm
Located in or near: Versailles, Ind.
Death Date: Aug. 15, 1838
Enlistment Dates: Spring of 1778
Discharge Dates: December, 1781
Rank: Private
Company: Do not know Co. or Reg., Maryland Troops
To be shipped to: Ripley Co. Historical Society, Osgood, Ind., Ripley Co.
Whose post-office address is: Versailles, Ind.

This application is for the UNMARKED grave of a veteran. It is understood the stone will be furnished and delivered at the railroad station or steamboat landing above indicated, at Government expense, freight prepaid. I hereby agree to promptly accept the headstone at destination, remove it and properly place same at decedent's grave at my expense. Ripley Co. Historical Society, Applicant. No fee should be paid in connection with this application.
Applicant: Ripley County Historical Society, Versailles, Ind.

MICHELLER (MITCHELLER), JACOB

Patriot: Jacob Micheller
Birth: 1764 Mecklenburg Co., NC
Married Spouse 1: XX
Married Spouse 2: Ripley Co., IN 3 Mar 1842 Mary Oliver (c. 1811–c. 1876)
Service state(s): NC
Rank: Private
Proof of Service: Pension application
Pension application No.: W25706
Residences: NC, Butler Co., OH, Ripley Co., IN, Butler Co., OH
Died: Fall 1844 Butler Co., OH (while visiting his daughter)
Buried: Unknown
DAR Ancestor No.: None as of 7 Jun 2017.

Pension Application Abstracted from National Archives microfilm Series M804, Roll 1719, File W25706.
Pension abstract for – Jacob Micheller
Service state(s): NC
Alternate spelling(s): Mitchellor
Date: 23 Feb 1833 & Amendment 11 Nov 1833
County of: Ripley   State of: IN
Declaration made before a Judge or Court: Circuit Court
Act of: 7 Jun 1832
Age: 69 yrs.
Record of age: a record made by my father at this time in OH
Where and year born: Mecklenburg Co., NC   1764
Residence when he entered service: Mecklenburg Co., NC
Residence(s) since the war: Mecklenburg Co., NC; 1807 to OH; Ripley Co., IN; Butler Co., OH; expect to shortly return to Ripley Co.
Residence now: Butler Co., OH, he intends shortly to move back to this county
Volunteer, Drafted, or Substitute: 1) Volunteer; 2) Volunteer;
Rank(s): Private
Statement of service-

Period	Duration	Names of General and Field Officers
Aug 1778-Sep 1778	1 mo.	NC Line, Col. Caleb [Phifer], Gen. Rutherford, Maj. White, Capts. Potts & Hise, Lt. Ross, Lt. Simeannor & Garver. Ens. Russell.
Jul 1779-Nov 1781	2 yrs. 2 mos.	NC Line, Col. Caleb [Phifer], Gen. Rutherford, Maj. White.

Additional remark: In the month of Sep 1781, when returning from States Borough to Charlotte, he was attacked and robbed by a Tory (he supposes) of $600 in specic of his own money that he was taking to his residence in Mecklenburg Co. The villain assaulted him with a sword and gave him a severe wound on the head which so disabled him that he was insensible to what transpired for a considerable time. He obtained permission from his officers to go home for a few days.

Battles: None stated
Discharge received: 1) Yes 2) Verbally by Maj. White
Statement is supported by –
Living witness, name(s): Affidavits from William Lippard and Delpha Lewis
Person now living who can testify to service: Eugene J. Davis, P. Shooker, Stephen J. Harring, Minot S. Craig, John Lewis
Wife: Not stated
&
Pension abstract for – Mary Micheller widow of Jacob Micheller
Alternate spelling: Mitchter or Muorgtchler
Date: 25 Jan 1854 and 25 Apr 1855 and 18 Nov 1868
County of: Ripley					State of: IN
Declaration made before a Judge or Court: Common Pleas Court
Act of: 3 Feb 1853; 28 Feb 1855 Bounty Land; 27 Jul 1868
Age: 42 yrs. (1853)l 57 (1868)
Residence now: Milan, Ripley Co., IN
Persons in neighborhood who certify character: David Wallace, Samuel Harper
Death of soldier: In or near Rossville, Butler Co., OH in 1844.
	[Pension paid to 4 Sep 1844; deposition by grandson, states d. Apr 1844]
Marriage date and place: 3 Mar 1842   Ripley Co.. IN
	He left his residence in Ripley Co. for the purpose of visiting his daughter, and drawing his pension, and there died.
Proof of marriage: James Meyers, Justice of the Peace, Certified he performed the rights of matrimony between Jacob Mitchler and Mary Oliver on the 3 Mar 1842.
Names and ages of children: A daughter residing in Butler Co., OH in 1844. [this dau. would have been a child of a marr. prev. to Mary Oliver].
Widow's death: aft. 4 Mar 1876; dropped from rolls 4 Feb 1880 because pension was unclaimed for 3 yrs.

Abstract of Final Payment Voucher; General Services Administration, Washington, DC
  LAST   FINAL PAYMENT VOUCHER RECEIVED FROM
			THE GENERAL ACCOUNTING OFFICE
NAME				MICHELLER, MARY WIDOW OF JACOB
AGENCY OF PAYMENT		INDIANA
DATE OF ACT			1853 2d Sect
DATE OF PAYMENT		March 1862
DATE OF DEATH			-
  Last   ~~FINAL~~ PAYMENT VOUCHER RECEIVED FROM
			THE GENERAL ACCOUNTING OFFICE		From
General Services Administration		GSA DC 70-7035 GSA DEC 69 7068

The Pension Roll of 1835 Volume IV, The Mid-Western States, Indexed Edition, In Four Volumes; Genealogical Publishing Co., Inc., Baltimore, MD, Reprint 1968, p. 87.
Statement, &c. of Ripley county, Indiana.

INDIANA Names	Rank	Annual allowance.	Sums received	Description of service
Jacob Micheller	Private	60.00	-	N.C. State troops

When placed on pension roll	Commencement of pension	Ages	Laws under which they were formerly placed on the pension roll; and remarks.
Feb 7, 1833	March 4, 1831	71	-

1840 U. S. Census, Jackson Twp., Ripley County, IN; Roll 92; p. 98, line 7.
Jacob Mitchaton
Males 70-79=1.

Toph, Violet E.; *Peoples History of Ripley County, Indiana;* self-published, c. 1940, p. 128.
Revolutionary Soldiers Who Came to Ripley County
Jacob Mitchellor enlisted from North Carolina August, 1778 and was discharged in September, 1778 and re-enlisted in July. 1779 and was discharged in November 1781. He was pensioned from Ripley County, but later moved to Cincinnati, and then moved back to Ripley County. He died in the Fall of 1844.

Daughters of the American Revolution of the State of Ohio, comp. Official Roster III, Soldiers of the American Revolution Who Lived in the State of Ohio; Painesville Publishing, Painesville, OH, 1959, p. 236.
MICHELLER (Mecheller), JACOB - - ? Co
Pvt drew pens in Ind, Cert No 25,598, Apr 7, 1834. To O Sept 2, 1835. Widow, Mary, drew pens in Ind. Cert No 3987, Aug 5, 1854. Cert No 3987, Jan 7, 1869.
Ref: DAR Magazine, Oct, 1949, p 856; Nov 1949, p 933.

O'Byrne, Mrs. Roscoe C., comp. & ed.; *Roster Soldiers and Patriots of the American Revolution Buried in Indiana;* Published by Indiana Daughters of the American Revolution, 1938, Reprinted Genealogical Publishing Co., Baltimore MD, 1968, p. 257.
MITCHELLER (MICHELLER), JACOB   Ripley County
Service – Enlisted from N. C. in Aug. 1778. Discharged Sept. 1778. Re-enlisted July, 1779. Discharged Nov., 1781.
Proof – Pension claim W. 25706.
Died – 1844. Name on bronze tablet in Versailles Court House.
Collected by Mrs. A. B. Wycoff, Batesville, Indiana.

Margaret R. Waters; *Revolutionary Soldiers Buried in Indiana (1949) With Supplement (1954) Two Volumes in One;* Genealogical Publishing Company,

Baltimore, MD, 1970, p. 128.
The following 55 soldiers at one time lived in Indiana but moved to other states where they presumably may have died. With one exception they all have pension files. Since the soldiers did not die in Indiana, I did not abstract the pension files but jotted down only the briefest of notes. I made no particular effort to ascertain the Indiana county of residence but have given it if I found it easily. No references are given since full data can be obtained from the pension files. These 55 men are not listed in the "Roster", pages 404-405.

MITCHELLER, JACOB   Ripley
To Ohio, 9-2-1835.

Gibbs, A.; Ripley County Historical Society Data on Revolutionary Soldiers, 1973 review.
Exact location of marker: no further information on grave site
Additional comments: on Court House tablet
> Enl. from N.C. Aug. 1778; disch. Sept. 1778 and re-enl July 1779, disch. Nov. 1781; date of birth not given, d. in fall of 1844; pensioned from Ripley Co. Ind. but later moved to Cincinnati Ohio; and then moved back to Ripley Co. #W25706.

MYERS, HENRY

Patriot: Henry Myers
Birth: 1756 VA
Married Spouse 1: abt 1776 Hannah Deitch (abt 1756-1830/32)
Service state(s): PA
Rank: Private
Proof of Service: Pension application
Pension application No.: S31876
Residences: VA; Montgomery Co., PA; OH; (prob. Montgomery Co.) KY; Ripley Co., IN
Died: 20 Dec 1842 Ripley Co., IN
Buried: Meyers Family Cemetery, Brown Twp., Ripley Co., IN
DAR Ancestor No.: A083804

Pension Application Abstracted from National Archives microfilm Series M804, Roll 1798, File S31876.
Pension abstract for – Henry Myers
Service state(s): PA
Date: 10 Feb 1834
County of: Ripley   State of: IN
Declaration made before a Judge or Court: Probate Court
Act of: 7 Jun 1832
Age: 78 yrs.
Record of age: None; speak from what I have been told by my parents
Where and year born: So. branch of Potomac River in VA   1756
Residence when he entered service: Not stated
Residence(s) since the war: Montgomery Co., PA; mouth of Muskingum River in OH; KY; his son's home in Ripley Co., IN.
Residence now: Ripley Co., IN
Volunteer, Drafted, or Substitute: 1st tour – Enlisted; 2nd tour – Substitute for his brother Frederick Myers; 3rd tour - Enlisted
Rank(s): Private
Statement of service-

Period	Duration	Names of General and Field Officers
1 Mar 1778 - 1 Oct or Nov 1779	1 yr. 9 mos.	Capt. Michael Catt's company, Col. George Wilson's PA Regt.
Apr 1780	3 mos.	Capt. John Bingaman's [?Bingham] company, Col. Crawford's Regt.
Oct 1780	5 mos.	Capt. John Slover's company, Col. John Gibson

Battles: Sandusky Plains, Yellow Creek Station, Pricket's Fort.
Discharge received: Yes, all 3 tours
Statement is supported by –
Living witness, name(s): On 6 Jun 1834, Newton H. Tapp, age 72 yrs, gave testimony to a JP in Switzerland Co. that from the year 1774 he has been acquainted with Myers; that in 1778, 1780, 1781, he resided in Montgomery Co., PA; knows Myers enlisted; he has no hesitation in

saying Myers was a soldier in the Revolution.
&
On 15 Dec 1833, Elijah Piles, age 80, of Decatur Co., IL gave similar testimony.
Evidence: Traditionary
Clergyman: Meshack Hyatt
Persons in neighborhood who certify character: Zebulon Brinden
Death of soldier: 20 Dec 1842

Senate Documents, Vol.9, No. 988, 63rd Congress, 3d Session, Washington, 1915; "Register of Certificates Issued by John Pierce, Esquire, Paymaster General and Commissioner of Army Accounts for the United States, to Officers and Soldiers of the Continental Army Under Act of July 4, 1783"; <u>*Seventeenth report of the National Society of the Daughters of the American Revolution*</u>*; Genealogical Publishing Co., Inc., Baltimore, MD, 1984. p. 351, 370.*
Men listed in this volume with the same name.

No. of Certificate	To whom issued	Amount
p. 351		
38042	Meyer, Henry	19.30
p. 370		
50044	Myers, Henry	15.25
65233	Myers, Henry	80.00
65879	Myers, Henry	40.60
66440	Myers, Henry	73.30
66976	Myers, Henry	30.02

[In his pension application he stated he had lived in KY, but did not say where. He might have been either of the men on the following list. – mjm]

Clift, G. Glens, Assistant Secretary, Kentucky Historical Society, Comp.; <u>*"Second Census" of Kentucky – 1800, A Privately Compiled and Published Enumeration of Tax Payers Appearing in the 79 Manuscript Volumes Extant of Tax Lists of the 42 Counties of Kentucky in Existence in 1800*</u>*; Genealogical Publishing Co., Baltimore, MD, 1966, p. 213.*

Name	County	Tax List Date	
Myers, Henry	Montgomery	8/22/	1800

<u>*U.S. Department of Interior, Bureau of Land Management, General Land Office Records; Land Patent Search*</u>
Name: Myers, Henry
Accession Nr. IN0220_.589; Document Type – State Volume Patent; Issue Date –6/20/1828; Cancelled – No
Land Office – Jeffersonville; Authority – April 24, 1820: Sale-Cash Entry (3 Stat. 566); Document Nr. 1498; Total Acres – 80.00
Land Descriptions: State – IN; Meridian – 2ndPM; Twp-Rng – 007N – 012E; Aliquots – E1/2SW1/4; Section – 23; County - Ripley

Ripley County Indiana, Recorder's Office, Tract Book 2, p. 31.
Myers, Henry   19 May 1828   R11, T7, S13   80 acres

Ripley County, Indiana Deed Records Vol. C., 21 Sep 1832 - 4 Feb 1834,
Page 326-327.
Abstract of Deed/Patent for: Henry Myers and Martha (dower) his wife.
Purchaser (Grantee) or Seller (Grantor)?: Seller
Sold to: Allen Wykoff
State & county where recorded: Ripley Co., Indiana
Date entered: 13 Nov 1832
Recorded: 21 Jan 1833
Description: Tract of land being the west half of the South west quarter of Section 23 Township 7 North of Range 11 East; and the east half of the South west quarter of Section 23, Township 7 North of Range 11 East.
Amount paid: Four hundred fifty dollars ($450.00)

The Pension Roll of 1835 Volume IV, The Mid-Western States, Indexed Edition, In Four Volumes; Genealogical Publishing Co., Inc., Baltimore, MD, Reprint 1968, p. 87.
Statement, &c. of Ripley county, Indiana.

INDIANA Names	Rank	Annual allowance.	Sums received	Description of service
Henry Myers	Private	80.00	-	Penn. Cont'l line

When placed on pension roll	Commencement of pension	Ages	Laws under which they were formerly placed on the pension roll; and remarks.
July 12, 1834	March 4, 1831	87	-

Scott, Craig R.; The "Lost" Pensions, Settled Accounts of the Act of 6 April 1838; Willow Bend Books, Lovettsville, VA, 1996, p. 238.
An Act directing the transfer of money remaining unclaimed [for the term of eight months] by certain pensioners, and authorizing payment of the same at the Treasury of the United States.
Myers, Henry; Pension Office – Ind..; Box – 127; Account - #4563 card
Myers, Henry; Pension Office – Madison, Ind.; Box 19; Account #4563

A Census of Pensioners for Revolutionary or Military Services with their Names, Ages, and Places of Residence Under the Act for Taking the Sixth Census in 1840; Genealogical Publishing Co., Inc., Baltimore, Maryland, 1965. p. 184.

Names of pensioners for revolutionary or military services.	Ages	Names of heads of families with whom pensioners resided June 1, 1840.
RIPLEY COUNTY JACKSON		
Henry Myers	93	Lewis Myers

Toph, Violet E.; Peoples History of Ripley County, Indiana; self-published, c. 1940, p. 126.
Revolutionary Soldiers Who Came to Ripley County
Henry Myres entered the service from Pennsylvania in 1778 under Col. George Wilson and served two years and five months. He was pensioned from Ripley County.

O'Byrne, Mrs. Roscoe C., comp. & ed.; Roster Soldiers and Patriots of the American Revolution Buried in Indiana; Published by Indiana Daughters of the American Revolution, 1938, Reprinted Genealogical Publishing Co., Baltimore MD, 1968, p. 264.
MYERS, HENRY   Ripley County
Born 1747, Pennsylvania.
Service – Enlisted from Penn. In 1778 under Col. George Wilson. Served 2 yrs, 5 mos.
Proof – Pension claim S. 31876. Family records in Ripley Co., Ind. and Montgomery Co., Ky.
Died – Dec. 20, 1842. Buried Myers Cemetery, W. of Cross Plains. Stone. Government marker placed by Ripley Co. His. Society.
Children – Lewis; George; Daniel; Rebecca, m. Jacob Overturf. Probably others.
Collected by Mrs. A. B. Wycoff, Batesville, Indiana.

Gibbs, A.; Ripley County Historical Society Data on Revolutionary Soldiers, 1973 review.
Exact location of marker: 1974 notes – Sec. 25, T6, R12E. Take 900S west of Cross Plains, Brown Tw. Ripley Co. Ind. to 50E, turn south. There is a lake on this corner property; private property; gate at south end is locked. Cross the dam at south end of lake. At east side of dam, the dirt road turns and follows lake. Do not turn, but follow straight ahead, bearing slightly to left. This takes one down and over a creek bed (runway or spillway from dam goes here) maybe 1/8 mile from where western edge of dam is. There is a fence sometimes visible – it leads easterly (briefly) to the enclosed and very overgrown cemetery. The Henry Myers stone is at western edge of cemetery, by the fence, facing towards the lake but under no circumstances visible from lake or crest of hill. Marker is about a half mile or more from 50E.
Additional comments: on Court House tablet
   1840 census Ripley Co. Ind. pension list, p. 172 Henry Myers age 93. Ent. service from Pa. 1778, under Col. Geo. Wilson; served 2yr 5mo; #S31-876.
   Pa. Archives Series 3 Pennsylvanians residing in Ripley Co. Ind. Henry Myers pr. PL July 12, 1834 age 87.

United States Headstone Applications for U.S. Military Veterans, 1925-1949, database with images; (https://familysearch.org/ark:/61903/1:1:VHZD-TJC : 17 May 2016); Affiliate Publication Number: M1916; Affiliate Publication Number: M1916; Affiliate Publication Title: Applications for Headstones for U.S. Military

Veterans, 1925-1941; Affiliate Film Number: 85; GS Film Number: 1878234; Digital Folder Number: 004832252; Image Number: 01815.
Application for Headstone; War Department O.Q.M.G. Form No. 623
Name: Meyers (Myers), Henry
Event Date: Sept. 2, 1935
Name of Cemetery: Myers Private
Located in or near: Cross Plains, Ind.
Death Date: Dec. 20, 1842
Enlistment Dates: 1778
Discharge Dates: Served 2 years 5 months
Rank: Private
Company: Capt. Catt's Co., & more.
To be shipped to: Ripley Co. Historical Society, Osgood, Ind., Ripley Co.
Whose post-office address is: Versailles, Ind.
This application is for the UNMARKED grave of a veteran. It is understood the stone will be furnished and delivered at the railroad station or steamboat landing above indicated, at Government expense, freight prepaid. I hereby agree to promptly accept the headstone at destination, remove it and properly place same at decedent's grave at my expense. Ripley Co. Historical Society, Applicant. No fee should be paid in connection with this application.
Applicant: Mrs. Eva Hunter, Versailles, Ind.

Tombstone Location: Meyers Cemetery, Brown Twp., Ripley Co., IN

Tombstone Inscription:

HENRY
MYERS
INDIANA
PVT. GIBSON'S PA MIL.
REV. WAR
DECEMBER 20, 1842

NEWCOMER, PETER

Patriot: Peter Newcomer
Birth: 20 May 1758 Lancaster Co., PA
Married Spouse 1: Catherine A.
Service state(s): PA
Rank: Private
Proof of Service: Pension application
Pension application No.: S32412
Residences: Lancaster Co. PA; Northampton Co., PA; Hamilton Co., OH;
　　　　　Ripley Co., IN.
Died: 15 May 1836 Ripley Co., IN
Buried: Unknown
DAR Ancestor No.: A082740

Pension Application Abstracted from National Archives microfilm Series M804, Roll 1810, File S32412.
Pension abstract for – Peter Newcomer
Service state(s): PA
Date: 23 Aug 1833
County of: Ripley　　　　　　　　　　State of: IN
Declaration made before a Judge or Court: Circuit Court
Act of: 7 Jun 1832
Age: 75 yrs.　　　　　　　　　　　　Record of age: None
Where and year born: Lancaster Co., PA　　20 May 1758
Residence when he entered service: Northampton or Northumberland Co., PA
Residence(s) since the war: Northampton Co., PA; Hamilton Co., OH;
　　　　　Ripley Co., IN, 32 yrs..
Residence now: Ripley Co., IN
Volunteer, Drafted, or Substitute: Volunteered all tours
Rank(s): Private
Statement of service-

Period	Duration	Names of General and Field Officers
1 Nov 1778	2 mos.	Capt. William Wisey's company, Col. Weiser's PA Regt.
1779	4 mos.	Capt. John Black's company, Col. Clark's PA Regt.
1780	4 mos.	Capt. John Black's company, Col. John Cole's PA Regt.
1781	3 mos.	Capt. John Black's company, Col. John Cole's Regt.
1782	5 mos.	Same company & regt.

Battles: None stated
Discharge received: Never received a discharge
&
Other notations in file –
Death of soldier: 15 May 1836
Wife: Miss Houser

Abstract of Final Payment Voucher; General Services Administration, Washington, DC
  LAST FINAL PAYMENT VOUCHER RECEIVED FROM
           THE GENERAL ACCOUNTING OFFICE
NAME   NEWCMER, PETER
AGENCY OF PAYMENT   INDIANA
DATE OF ACT   1832
DATE OF PAYMENT   3rd Qr. 1836
DATE OF DEATH   May 15, 1836
GENERAL SERVICES ADMINISTRATION
National Archives and Records Service   NA-286
GSA-WASH DC 54-4891   November 1953

Revolutionary War Service Records; National Archives Publication number M881, Compiled service records of soldiers who served in the American Army during the Revolutionary War, 1775-1783.
https://www.fold3.com/image/21353539
Pennsylvania, 3 Battalion (Northumberland Co. Militia)
Capt. John Black's Company of Col. Hosterman's Battalion of Noth'd County Militia in the service of the United States.
Newcomer, Peter – Private –Appears on the Company Pay Roll; Sep 1 to Nov 4, 79; Time of entrance – Oct 12, 17--; When discharged – Nov 4, 17__; Pay for time of service - £1-18s-4d.

Riegel, Mayburt Stephenson comp.; *Early Ohioans' Residences from the Land Grant Records;* Ohio Genealogical Society, Mansfield, OH, 1976, p. 10.
Land Grants Recorded by Residents of the Indiana Territory at the Cincinnati Land Office. The original Land Grant records are in the Archives of the Ohio Historical Society. They are from the Auditor of the State of Ohio Land Office.
NAME   DATE   SEC TWP RANGE VOL PG   RESIDENCE
NEWCOMER, Peter 10-24-1804 S9   T4   R1E   B   178   HL Hamilton
                                                                                                       Co., OH

Mikesell, Shirley Keller, ed.; *Early Settlers of Indiana's "GORE" 1803-1820;* Heritage Books, Inc., 1995, p. 28.
Dearborn County: Original Land Entries Tract Book
Township 6, Range 3W
  Format: Section – Purchaser –   Year – page;
               27 –   PETER NEWCOMER –   1818 – 47

Waters, Margaret R.; *Indiana Land Entries Vol. 1 Cincinnati District, 1801-1840;* Originally Published Indianapolis 1948, Second Reprint 1979 by The Bookmark, P.O. Box 74, Knightstown, IN, p. 76.
CINCINNATI DISTRICT – VOL. 1   DEARBORN CO.
        Page 72. T 6 N, R 3 W of 1st P.M.
Peter Newcomer   NW ¼ - S27; 9-12-1818

Berry, Ellen T. & Berry, David A., compilers; <u>Early Ohio Settlers, Purchasers of Land in Southwestern Ohio, 1800-1840</u>; Genealogical Publishing Co., Inc., Baltimore, MD, 1986. p. 239.

Purchaser	Year	Date	Residence	R – T - S
Newcomer, Peter(B)	1818	Sep 12	Hamilton	03 06 27

(B) Indiana Survey: Land lying west of a meridian drawn west of the Great Miami (known as the "Gore"). Switzerland, Dearborn, Franklin, Ohio, Union and Randolph Counties (all or only a part of each county) – all in Indiana.

<u>U.S. Department of Interior, Bureau of Land Management, General Land Office Records; Land Patent Search</u>
Name: Newcomer. Peter
Accession Nr. CV-0053-406; Document Type – Credit Volume Patent; Issue Date – 12/29/1820; Cancelled – No
Land Office – Cincinnati; Authority – April 24, 1820: Sale-Cash Entry (3 Stat. 566); Document Nr.   0; Total Acres – 160.06
Land Descriptions: State – IN; Meridian – 2ndPM; Twp-Rng – 006N – 003W; Aliquots – NW1/4; Section – 27; County - Dearborn
&
Name: Newcomer, Peter & Inchminger, John
Accession Nr. CV-0082-232; Document Type – Credit Volume Patent; Issue Date – 4/7/1825; Cancelled – No
Land Office – Jeffersonville; Authority – April 24, 1820: Sale-Cash Entry (3 Stat. 566); Document Nr. 1145; Total Acres – 160.00
Land Descriptions: State – IN; Meridian – 2ndPM; Twp-Rng – 009N – 010E; Aliquots – SW1/4; Section – 28; County - Ripley

<u>1830 U. S. Census</u>, Ripley County, IN; Series M19, Roll 32; p. 20, 5th line from bottom of page.
Peter Neweamore
Males 20-29=1, Males 30-39=1, Males 80-89=1, Females 40-49=1, Females 70-79=1.

<u>Ripley County, Indiana Deed Records Vol. C., 21 Sep 1832 - 4 Feb 1834,</u>
Page 509-510.
Abstract of Deed/Patent for: Peter Newcomer and Catherine (dower) his wife/
Purchaser (Grantee) or Seller (Grantor)?: Seller
Sold to: Samuel Tucker
State & county where recorded: Ripley Co., Indiana
Date entered: 6 Dec 1833
Recorded: 20 Jan 1834
Description: All that certain tract or parcel of land; the est half of the south east quarter of Section 28, Township 9 North of Range 10 East; in the district of lands subject to sale at Jeffersonville; containing 80 acres.
Amount paid: One hundred thirty dollars ($130.00)
Name(s) of Witnesses: Thomas Moffett & Robert Wingate

The Pension Roll of 1835 Volume IV, The Mid-Western States, Indexed Edition, In Four Volumes; Genealogical Publishing Co., Inc., Baltimore, MD, Reprint 1968, p. 87.
Statement, &c. of Ripley county, Indiana.

INDIANA Names	Rank	Annual allowance.	Sums received	Description of service
Peter Newcomer	Private	61.66	184 98	Va. State troops

When placed on pension roll	Commencement of pension	Ages	Laws under which they were formerly placed on the pension roll; and remarks.
Oct 29, 1833	March 54, 1831	77	-

Ripley Co., IN Probate Order Book, Vol. A, 19 Nov 1818-Feb. 1837, p. 243, 245.
On the Application of Jacob Newcomer & Samuel Glasgow Leters of Administration was granted to them on the Estate of Peter Newcomer late of Ripley County Ind Dec'd on the 30 day of May 1836, who filed their Bond in the Penal Sum of Eight Hundred Dollars, with Ephraim Glasgow as their Security. 245.
Also was filed in the Clerks office by Jacob Newcomer & Saml. Glasgow Admrs. of Peter Newcomer Dec'd on the 8th day of August 1836 and Inventory of the Personal goods etc of sd. Dec'd which amounts to the Sum of $213.50
                    Notes & accounts Entered on Inventory is   156.18
                                             Total $369.68
The amount taken at the Appraised value by <u>Catherine Newcomer widow</u> of Dec'd is $120.50. Also another Amount of the sum of $99.87. Total Taken by Widow $220.37.

Toph, Violet E.; *Peoples History of Ripley County, Indiana;* self-published, c. 1940, p. 126.
Revolutionary Soldiers Who Came to Ripley County
Peter Newcomer, Private, in Captain John Black's company, Colonel Hosterman's 3rd Battalion, Northumberland County, Pennsylvania Militia, entered the service Oct. 12, 1779 and was discharged Nov. 4, 1779.

O'Byrne, Mrs. Roscoe C., comp. & ed.; *Roster Soldiers and Patriots of the American Revolution Buried in Indiana;* Published by Indiana Daughters of the American Revolution, 1938, Reprinted Genealogical Publishing Co., Baltimore MD, 1968, p. 278.
NEWCOMER, PETER   Ripley County
Service – Pri. in Capt. John Black's Company. Col. Hasterman's 3rd Battalion, Northumberland Co., Penn. Militia. Entered service Oct. 12, 1779, and was discharged on Nov. 4, 1779.
Proof – Pension records in War Department. Bronze tablet in Versailles Court House.
Collected by Mrs. A. B. Wycoff, Batesville, Indiana.

Gibbs, A.; Ripley County Historical Society Data on Revolutionary Soldiers, 1973 review.
Exact location of marker: no further information on grave site.
Additional comments: on Court House tablet
    In 1830 census Ripley Co. Ind. age 70-80.
    Probate Book A., p. 24, 243. Dec'd by 30 May 1836 Court; widow Catherine.

O'NEAL, JOHN

Patriot: John O'Neal
Birth: 1760   Essex Co., VA
Married Spouse 1: 10 Feb 1789, Culpeper Co., VA
                      Phoebe Scott (1764-1832)
Married Spouse 2: XX
Service state(s): VA & VA Continental Line
Rank: Private
Proof of Service: Pension application
Pension application No.: S32422
Residences: Essex Co., VA; Culpeper Co., VA; Franklin Co., KY; Ripley Co., IN
Died: 7 Nov 1832   Ripley Co., IN
Buried: Unknown
DAR Ancestor No.: A084080
Children: Henry; James; Jane, m. Murphy

Pension Application Abstracted from National Archives microfilm Series M804, Roll 1845, File S32422.
Pension abstract for – John O'Neal
Service state(s): VA
Date: 23 Aug 1832
County of: Ripley   State of: IN
Declaration made before a Judge or Court: Circuit Court
Act of: 7 Jun 1832
Age: 72 yrs.   Record of age: None
Where and year born: Essex Co., VA   1760
Residence when he entered service: Culpeper Co., VA
Residence(s) since the war: Culpeper Co., VA; Franklin Co., KY;
                              Ripley Co., IN.
Residence now: Ripley Co., IN
Volunteer, Drafted, or Substitute: Volunteered 1st tour, Substitute 2nd & 3rd tour
Rank(s): Private
Statement of service-

Period	Duration	Names of General and Field Officers
Jun 1777 - Nov 1777	5-6 mos.	Col. Pendleton, Maj. Roberts, Capt. Yancy
1 Oct 1780 – 20 Mar 1781		Gen. Stevens, Col. Barker, Capt. Terrel
Apr/May 1781	2 mos.	Gen. Muhlenberg, Col. Slaughter, Capt. Browning.

Battles: affair at Yadkin River; Battle of Petersburg
Discharge received: Yes
Signed by: Lt. Brown
What became of it?: cannot tell what has become of it
Statement is supported by –
Documentary proof: Has no documentary evidence
Person now living who can testify to service: Knows of no person.

Clergyman: Meshack Hyatt
Persons in neighborhood who certify character: James Behnam, Jesse Markland, William Harris, Thomas Hinton, William Holman, etc.
&
Other notations in file –
Death of soldier: 11 Feb 1833, heirs make deposition that soldier d.7 Nov 1832
Wife: Mahala Scott, did not survive him.
Marriage date and place: Not stated
Names and ages of children: Henry; James; Jane, m. Murphy.

Abstract of Final Payment Voucher; General Services Administration, Washington, DC
   L[ast] FINAL PAYMENT VOUCHER RECEIVED FROM
       THE GENERAL ACCOUNTING OFFICE
NAME   O'NEAL, JOHN
AGENCY OF PAYMENT   INDIANA
DATE OF ACT   1832
DATE OF PAYMENT   1st Qr. 1834
DATE OF DEATH   Nov. 7, 1832
GENERAL SERVICES ADMINISTRATION
National Archives and Records Service   NA-286
GSA-WASH DC 54-4891   November 1953

Revolutionary War Land Office Military Certificates; Records of the Executive Branch, Land Office (Record Group 4), microfilm reels 1-38; Library of Virginia, Richmond, VA.
In order to receive bounty lands for Revolutionary War service, a soldier or sailor must have served continuously for at least three years in a Virginia or Continental unit. Service in the militia did not count. The certificates were numbered 1-9926 and cover the period July 14, 1782-August 5, 1876. The warrant specified the amount of lands to be received and directed the surveyor of lands to set aside that quantity of land in the Virginia Military District in Kentucky and Ohio.
O'Neal, John   Rank: Private   Military Certificate number: LO 2314

Wilson, Samuel L., comp.; Year Book of the Society, Sons of the American Revolution in the Commonwealth of Kentucky, 1894-1913, and Catalogue of Military Land Warrants Granted by the Commonwealth of Virginia; Lexington, KY, 1913, p. 245.

No. of Warrant	Name of Officer or Soldier	No. of Acres	Character of Service as Private or Officer, If Officer, what Grade	Department of Service: Continental or State Line or Navy
2314	Oneal, John	200	Private	Va. Cont. Line

	No. of Years of Service	Date of Warrant		
	war	Jan. 29, '84		

Virginia Military Records from the Virginia Magazine of History and Biography, the William and Mary College Quarterly, and Tyler's Quarterly; Genealogical Publishing Co., Baltimore, MD, 1983, p. 713.
List of State Pensioners (1785), from W &MCQ, 1st Series, Vol. XX (1911), 11-15.
A List of Pensioners
Included in this list -   O'Neal, John   £24 0 0

Wardell, Patrick G., comp.; Virginia/West Virginia Genealogical Data From Revolutionary War Pension and Bounty Land Warrant Records, Vol. 4 – Nabors through Rymer; Heritage Books, Inc., Bowie, MD, 1988, p. 41.
O'Neal, John, b 1760 Essex Co, VA; esf 1777 Culpeper Co, VA, where res, in VA regiment; res after RW Franklin Co, KY, then to IN where PN 8/1832 Ripley Co; dd 11/7/32 leaving ch Henry, James, & Jane Murphy; w dd before sol; QLF says sol b Ireland, came to VA before RW, md Phoebe Scott in VA, & their 7 ch included James who dd 1879 Dupont, IN; QLF says sol b 1753 or 1754, mvd to KY before 1815 & md Mahala Scott. F-S32422 R1845

Bockstruck, Lloyd DeWitt; Revolutionary War Bounty Land Grants Awarded by State Governments; Genealogical Publishing Co., IN, Baltimore, MD, 1996, p. 399.
Oneal, John.   Va.   Private.   29 Jan 1784. 200 acres.

Abercrombie, Janice L. and Slatten, Richard, comp. & trans.; Virginia Revolutionary Publick Claims in three volumes; Iberian Publishing Co., Athens, GA, 1992, Vol. I, p. 256, 258 .
Culpeper County
p.256.
John Oneil   Dec. 1781   500# beef.
p.258.
John Oneil   Dec. 1781   for 200# beef.

Virginia Marriages, 1785-1940; accessed 11 April 2016 from https://familysearch.org/ark:/61903/1:1:XRHJ-2YQ
Name: John Oneals
Spouse's Name: Phoebe Scott
Event Date: 10 Feb 1789
Event Place: Culpeper, Virginia
Indexing Project (Batch) Number: M86874-4
System Origin: Virginia-EASy
GS Film number: 30927; Reference ID: P 71
FHL microfilm 30,927

Clift, G. Glens, Assistant Secretary, Kentucky Historical Society, Comp.; "Second Census" of Kentucky – 1800, A Privately Compiled and Published Enumeration of Tax Payers Appearing in the 79 Manuscript Volumes Extant of

Tax Lists of the 42 Counties of Kentucky in Existence in 1800; Genealogical Publishing Co., Baltimore, MD, 1966, p. 220.

Name	County	Tax List Date	
O'Neal, John	Franklin	8/7/	1800

Berry, Ellen T. & Berry, David A., compilers; *Early Ohio Settlers, Purchasers of Land in Southwestern Ohio, 1800-1840*; Genealogical Publishing Co., Inc., Baltimore, MD, 1986. p. 243.

Purchaser	Year	Date	Residence	R – T – S
O'Neal, John K.(B)	1816	Nov. 05	Kentucky	02 02 02

(B) Indiana Survey: Land lying west of a meridian drawn west of the Great Miami (known as the "Gore"). Switzerland, Dearborn, Franklin, Ohio, Union and Randolph Counties (all or only a part of each county) – all in Indiana.

Ripley County, Indiana Deed Records Vol. A, 11 Aug 1818-29 Jan 1827
Page(s): 270-271.
Abstract of Deed/Patent for: John O'Neal & William Bassett, Deacons of the regular Baptist church known by the name Middle Fork Church.
Purchaser (Grantee) or Seller (Grantor)?: Purchaser
Purchased from: James Benham and Mary (dower) his wife of Ripley Co., IN.
State & county where recorded: Ripley Co., Indiana
Date entered: 6 May 1826
Recorded: 10 May 1826
Description: Part of the southeast quarter of Section 12, Township 6, Range 11 East, of the lands offered for sale at Jeffersonville, containing nearly one acre
Amount paid: Sixteen dollars ($16.00)
Name(s) of Witnesses: Jesse Marklin & Joseph McINtosh

Ripley County Indiana, Recorder's Office, Tract Book 1, p. 54.

O'Neil (O'Neal), John	02 Jul 1831	R11, T9, S17	80 acres

The Pension Roll of 1835 Volume IV, The Mid-Western States, Indexed Edition, In Four Volumes; Genealogical Publishing Co., Inc., Baltimore, MD, Reprint 1968, p. 87.
Statement, &c. of Ripley county, Indiana.

INDIANA Names	Rank	Annual allow-ance.	Sums re-ceived	Description of service
John O'Neal	Private	46.66	76 30	Va. State troops

When placed on pension roll	Commencement of pension	Ages	Laws under which they were formerly placed on the pension roll; and remarks.
Oct 18, 1833	March 4, 1831	74	Died November 7, 1832

Toph, Violet E.; *Peoples History of Ripley County, Indiana*; self-published, c. 1940, p. 129.
Revolutionary Soldiers Who Came to Ripley County

John O'Neal entered the service from Virginia in June, 1777 and served one year, one month and twenty days. He was born in Essex Co. Virginia in 1760 and died Nov. 7, 1832. After the Revolution he resided in Franklin Co. Ky. and from there moved to Ripley County, Ind. He was pensioned in Ripley Co.

O'Byrne, Mrs. Roscoe C., comp. & ed.; Roster Soldiers and Patriots of the American Revolution Buried in Indiana; Published by Indiana Daughters of the American Revolution, 1938, Reprinted Genealogical Publishing Co., Baltimore MD, 1968, p. 281.
O'NEAL, JOHN   Ripley County
Born 1760 in Essex Co., Virginia.
Service – Enlisted June, 1777, from Virginia. Served 1 yr., 1 mo., 20 days.
Proof – Pension claim S. 32422.
Died – Nov. 7, 1832. Name appears on bronze tablet in Versailles Court House.
Collected by Mrs. A. B. Wycoff, Batesville, Indiana.

Gibbs, A.; Ripley County Historical Society Data on Revolutionary Soldiers, 1973 review.
Exact location of marker: no further information on grave site
Additional comments: on Court House tablet
       Appl. for pension Feb. 1833

OVERTURF (OBERDORF), MARTIN (ROGER MARTIN)

Patriot: Martin Overturf
Birth: 1756 Fayette Co., PA
Married Spouse 1: 3 Jul 1783 Catherine Deitch (1753-1833)
Service state(s): PA
Rank: Private, Patriotic Service
Proof of Service: PA Archives, Series 3, Vol. 23, p. 219.
Pension application No.:
Residences: Washington Co., PA; Montgomery Co, KY; Ripley Co., IN
Died: 1843 Ripley Co., IN
Buried: Overturf Family Cemetery (aka Glaze Cemetery),
    Benham, Brown Twp., Ripley Co., IN
DAR Ancestor No.:A085154

Pennsylvania Archives, Series 3, Volume XXIII, p. 219.
Soldiers of the Revolution
List of Soldiers Who Served As Rangers on the Frontiers 1778-1783.
Rangers on the Frontiers – 1778-1783
Washington County
[Included in list]   Martin Overtwiff

Pennsylvania Archives, Series 5, Vol. 4, p. 415.
Soldiers of the Revolution
Soldiers Who Received Depreciation Pay as Per Cancelled Certificates on File in the Division of Public Records, Pennsylvania State Library. (c.)
Washington County Militia (c.)
[Included in list]
Overturf, Martin, private

Pennsylvania Archives, Series 5, Vol. 4, p. 723.
Soldiers of the Revolution
List of "Soldiers of the Revolution who received pay for their services." Taken - from Manuscript Record having neither date nor title, but under "Rangers on the Frontiers, 1778-1783" was published in Vol. XXIII, Penna. Archives, Third Seried by the Former Editor. (c.)
Washington County (c.)
Overtwiff, Martin, private

Register of the Kentucky Historical Society; Early Kentucky Tax Records; Clearfield Publishing, Baltimore, Md., 1999; p. 205.
Montgomery County Tax Lists – 1797
William Thompson, Commissioner of the Tax for the Year 1797, Book for the Auditor, George Madison, Esq.

Persons chargeable with the tax	Acres of land
Oberturf, Martin	-

Clift, G. Glens, Assistant Secretary, Kentucky Historical Society, Comp.; "Second Census" of Kentucky – 1800, A Privately Compiled and Published Enumeration of Tax Payers Appearing in the 79 Manuscript Volumes Extant of Tax Lists of the 42 Counties of Kentucky in Existence in 1800; Genealogical Publishing Co., Baltimore, MD, 1966, p. 221.

Name	County	Tax List Date	
Overturf, Martin	Montgomery	8/22/	1800

Ripley County Indiana, Recorder's Office, Tract Book 3, p. 29.
Overturf, Martin of Montgomery Co., KY
       10 Dec 1813   R11, T6, S26

Ripley County, Indiana Deed Records Vol. A, 11 Aug 1818-29 Jan 1827
Page(s): 23.
Abstract of Deed/Patent: US Land Patent signed by President James Madison
               for Martin Overturf.
Purchaser (Grantee) or Seller (Grantor)?: Purchaser
Purchased from: The United States of America
State & county where recorded: Ripley Co., Indiana
State & county where agreement was made: Montgomery Co., KY
Date granted: 15 Mar 1814
Recorded: in Ripley Co. on 6 Feb 1820.
Description: Northeast quarter of Section 26, Township 6, North of the base line
          in Range 11 East of the second meridian, directed to be sold at
          Jeffersonville by the act of Congress in the Territory northwest of the
          Ohio and above the mouth of the Kentucky River.
Amount paid: Not shown. Statement – Full payment has been made.
Name(s) of Witnesses: Edward Tiffin, Commissioner of the General Land Office.

Cowen, Janet C., comp; Jeffersonville Land Entries 1808-1818; McDowell Publications, Utica, NY, 1984, p. 46.
p. 46.
Receipt #
02914 Overturf Martin KY Montgomery NE S26 T06 N11E 160 1813 12 10
Receipt #
02921 Overturf Martin KY Montgomery NE S26 T06 N11E 160 1813 12 10

1820 U. S. Census, Ripley Co., IN, NARA Roll M33_15; EN 7 Aug 1820, p. 75, line 5.
Martin Overturf
Males <10=1, Males 45>=1, Females 10-15=1, Females 26-44=1,
Females 45>=1.

O'Byrne, Mrs. Roscoe C., comp. & ed.; Roster Soldiers and Patriots of the American Revolution Buried in Indiana; Published by Indiana Daughters of the American Revolution, 1938, Reprinted Genealogical Publishing Co., Baltimore MD, 1968, p. 283.
OVERTURF, MARTIN   Ripley County

Born – 1756.
Service – Pri. in Continental Line, Washington Co., Penn., Militia.
Proof – Penn. Archives, 5th Series, vol. 4, pp. 415 and 723.
Died – About 1850. Buried Old Whitham Cemetery, Brown Twp. Government marker placed by Ripley Co. Historical Society.
Married – Catherine Deitch. Ch. Jacob b. 1785, m. Rebecca Myers; Samuel b. 1787, m. Sarah Cole; Catharine b. 1789, m. George Myers; Conrad b. 1791, m. Pelina Steele.
Collected by Mrs. A. B. Wycoff, Batesville, Indiana.

[The following citation shows he is buried in Old Whitham Cemetery; other sources show he was buried in the Overturf Family Cemetery, Brown Twp., Ripley Co. The government marker is placed in Glaze Cemetery. Are these cemetery names interchangeable? – mjm]

Hatcher, Patricia Law, Comp.; <u>Abstract of Graves of Revolutionary Patriots (4 volumes)</u>; Pioneer Heritage Press, Dallas, TX, 1987, Vol. 3, p. 138.
Overturf Martin   Old Whitham Cem, Brown Twp, Ripley Co IN 72

Gibbs, A.; <u>Ripley County Historical Society Data on Revolutionary Soldiers</u>, 1973 review.
Exact location of marker: Overturf Cemetery, Shelby Tw. Ripley Co. Ind.; off 421 south, turn left on 925S, rt. on 350W, left on 1025S, rt. on 300W. Cemetery is on knoll on left, visible from road.
Type of marker: Gov't
Date placed: 1936
Placed by: Ripley County Historical Society
Additional comments: from the "Osgood Journal', Aug. 6, 1936: "Within the last year Ripley Ind. Historical Society had located and placed Government markers at the graves of the following Rev. War soldiers who are buried in Ripley Co. Ind......Martin Overturf whose data is not at hand as this is being typed."
Wording on marker: not provided on this document.

<u>*United States Headstone Applications for U.S. Military Veterans, 1925-1949, database with images*</u>*; (https://familysearch.org/ark:/61903/1:1:VHZ6-WB2 : 17 May 2016); Affiliate Publication Number: M1916; Affiliate Publication Title: Applications for Headstones for U.S. Military Veterans, 1925-1941; Affiliate Film Number: 89; GS Film Number: 1878238; Digital Folder Number: 004832256; Image Number: 02020.*
Application for Headstone; War Department O.Q.M.G. Form No. 623
Name: Overturf, Martin
Event Date: May 31, 1934
Name of Cemetery: Glaze Cemetery
Located in or near: Versailles, Ind.
Death Date: 1850
Enlistment Dates: not shown
Discharge Dates: not shown

Rank: Private
Company: Washington Co. PA Militia, Continental Line
To be shipped to: Ripley Co. Historical Society, Osgood, Ind., Ripley Co.
Whose post-office address is: Versailles, Ind.
This application is for the UNMARKED grave of a veteran. It is understood the stone will be furnished and delivered at the railroad station or steamboat landing above indicated, at Government expense, freight prepaid. I hereby agree to promptly accept the headstone at destination, remove it and properly place same at decedent's grave at my expense. Ripley Co. Historical Society, Applicant.
No fee should be paid in connection with this application.
Applicant: Ripley Co. Historical Society, Versailles, Ind.

PARR, JOHN

Patriot: John Parr
Birth: 14 Jun 1759 Roxbury Twp., Morris Co., NJ
Married Spouse 1: XX
Service state(s): NJ
Rank: Private
Proof of Service: Pension application
Pension application No.: S17617
Residences: Morris Co., NJ; Wilkes Co., NC; Roane Co., TN;
 Shelby Co., IN; Johnson Co., IN
Died: 7 Sep 1850 Johnson Co., IN
Buried: Nolin Cemetery, Greenwood, Johnson Co., IN
DAR Ancestor No.:A088045
Children: David, Matthias, Moses, and Mary Jones

Pension Application Abstracted from National Archives microfilm Series M804, Roll 1879, File S17617.
Pension abstract for – John Parr
Service state(s): NJ
Date: 27 Jun 1818
County of: Roane State of: TN
Declaration made before a Judge or Court: Second Judicial Court of TN
Act of: 18 Mar 1818
Age: about 59
Residence when he entered service: Morris Co., NJ
Residence(s) since the war: Not stated
Residence now: Roane Co., TN
Volunteer, Drafted, or Substitute: 1st tour – Enlisted; 2nd tour - Enlisted
Rank(s): Private
Statement of service-

Period	Duration	Names of General and Field Officers
1)1776	12-13 mos.	3rd Regiment, Capt. Thomas Redding
2)	abt 9 mos.	2nd Regiment, Capt. Henry Luce.
Also 1780	abt 2 mos.	Capt. Abraham Dickerson

Battles: Monmouth; Battle of Springfield (with Dickerson's company)
Discharge received: 1st tour at Elizabethtown, NJ; 2nd tour at Newark, NJ
What became of it?: Both discharges were lost.
&
Date: 12 Nov 1832
County of: Johnson State of: IN
Declaration made before a Judge or Court: Probate Court
Act of: 7 Jun 1832
Age: 73 years
Where and year born: Roxbury Twp., Morris Co., NJ 14 Jun 1759
Residence when he entered service: Roxbury Twp., Morris Co., NJ
Residence(s) since the war: Morris Co., NJ; Wilkes Co., NC for 20 yrs.;

Roane Co., TN; Shelby Co., IN; Johnson Co., IN in 1833.
Residence now: Johnson Co., IN
Volunteer, Drafted, or Substitute: Enlisted/Volunteered
Rank(s): Private
Statement of service- [See amendment dated 13 May 1833]

Period	Duration	Names of General and Field Officers
Feb 1776	12-13 mos.	Capt. Thomas Reading's company, Col. Elias Dayton's NJ Regt.
1777	2 mos.	Capt. Abraham Dickerson
Summer 1778	9 mos.	Capt. Henry Luce, Col. Shreve's NJ Regt
1780	1 mo.	Capt. Israel Lane, NJ troops

Battles: skirmish at Greenwich; Battle of Monmouth; Battle of Springfield.
&
Date: 13 May 1833
County of: Johnson   State of: IN
Declaration: Amendment to statements made 12 Nov 1832; he was on the pension roll but was dropped thence for amount of property.
Declaration made before a Judge or Court: Probate Court
Act of: 7 Jun 1832
Statement of service-

Period	Duration	Names of General and Field Officers
	1 yr.	3rd Regiment, Col. Elias Dayton, Lieut. Col. White, Maj. Francis Banter [?], Lieut. Ballard, Capt. Thomas Redding.
	9 mos.	Not stated

Statement is supported by –
Documentary proof: Affidavit of Matthias Parr who served one year with him in the 3rd Regiment NJ Militia Line. *[Matthias appears to be John's brother as their service and residences coincide. Relationship not stated in either of their pension applications. – mjm]*
Clergyman: William G. Eaton
&
Additional notations in file:
Death of soldier: 7 Sep 1850, in letter from W. W. Parr, 352 Ripley St., city illegible, MO
Other correspondence indicates he died 7 Sep 1850, in Johnson Co., IN, age 92.

Abstract of Final Payment Voucher; General Services Administration, Washington, DC
  LAST   FINAL PAYMENT VOUCHER RECEIVED FROM
             THE GENERAL ACCOUNTING OFFICE
NAME   PARR, JOHN
AGENCY OF PAYMENT   INDIANA
DATE OF ACT   1832
DATE OF PAYMENT   4th Qr. 1850

DATE OF DEATH   Sept. 7, 1850
GENERAL SERVICES ADMINISTRATION
National Archives and Records Service   NA-286
GSA-WASH DC 54-4891   November 1953

Revolutionary War Service Records; National Archives Publication number M881, Compiled service records of soldiers who served in the American Army during the Revolutionary War, 1775-1783.
https://www.fold3.com/image/19193773?terms=Parr,%20John%20nj
2 New Jersey Regiment – Copied from Rolls; Luse's Company; Col. Israel Shreve.
Parr, John – Private; Date of appointment – June 1, 78; Term enlisted for – 9 mos.; Discharged – Mar 5, 79.

William S. Stryker, Adjutant General, Compiled Under Orders of His Excellency Theodore F. Randolph, Governor; <u>Official Register of the Officers and Men of New Jersey in the Revolutionary War</u>; by Printed by the Authority of the Legislature; Wm. T. Nicholson & Co., Printers, Trenton, NJ, 1872, Facsimile Reprint by Heritage Books, Inc., Bowie, MD, 1993; p. 263, 712.
p. 263.
PARR, JOHN.   Captain Luce's company, Second Battalion, Second Establishment; also militia.
p. 712.
PARR, JOHN.   "Western Battalion," Morris; also State troops; also Continental Army.

Armstrong, Zela; <u>Twenty-Four Hundred Tennessee Pensioners, Revolution – War of 1812</u>; Genealogical Publishing Co., Inc., Baltimore, MD, 1975, p. 87.
Parr, John; 1818 list age 75; served in NJ line; drew pension in Roane Co.

Clark, Murtie June; <u>The Pension List of 1820 [U.S. War Department]</u>Reprinted with an Index; Genealogical Publishing Co., Inc., Baltimore, 1991. Originally published 1820 as Letter from the Secretary of War, p. 622.
EAST TENNESSEE
Names of the Revolutionary Pensioners which have been placed on the Roll of East Tennessee, under the Law of the 18th of March, 1818, from the passage thereof, to this day, inclusive of the Rank they held, and the Lines in which they served, viz: -

Names	Rank	Line
Included in the list –		
John Parr	private	New Jersey

<u>The Pension Roll of 1835 Volume IV, The Mid-Western States,</u> Indexed Edition, In Four Volumes; Genealogical Publishing Co., Inc., Baltimore, MD, Reprint 1968, p. 87.
Statement, &c. of Ripley county, Indiana.

INDIANA Names	Rank	Annual allowance.	Sums received	Description of service
John Parr	Private	80.00	240 00	Penn. cont'l line

When placed on pension roll	Commencement of pension	Ages	Laws under which they were formerly placed on the pension roll; and remarks.
Aug 26, 1833	March 4, 1831	69	-

Pensioners of the Revolutionary War Struck Off the Roll with an Added Index to States; Reprinted by Genealogical Publishing Co., Baltimore, MD for Clearfield Company, Inc., 1989. p. 100.

Pensioners in the Tennessee who have been dropped from the pension roll under the act of the 1st of May, 1820; prepared in conformity with the resolution of the House of Representatives of the 17th of December, 1835.

Names	Acts under which restored	Remarks
Include in list –		
John Parr	June 7, 1832	-

A Census of Pensioners for Revolutionary or Military Services with their Names, Ages, and Places of Residence Under the Act for Taking the Sixth Census in 1840; Genealogical Publishing Co., Inc., Baltimore, Maryland, 1965, p. 183.

Names of pensioners for revolutionary or military services.	Ages	Names of heads of families with whom pensioners resided June 1, 1840.
INDIANA, JOHNSON COUNTY		
John Parr	81	Abraham Jones

Toph, Violet E.; *Peoples History of Ripley County, Indiana*; self-published, c. 1940, p. 127.
Revolutionary Soldiers Who Came to Ripley County
John Parr enlisted from New Jersey in February, 1776 and served thirteen months, then re-enlisted and afterwards volunteered four times. His service ranging from two month – nine months – four months respectively. He was born in 1760 and died Sept. 7, 1852. *[1850]*

O'Byrne, Mrs. Roscoe C., comp. & ed.; *Roster Soldiers and Patriots of the American Revolution Buried in Indiana*; Published by Indiana Daughters of the American Revolution, 1938, Reprinted Genealogical Publishing Co., Baltimore MD, 1968, p. 285.
PARR, JOHN   Johnson County
Born – June 14, 1759, Morris Co., New Jersey.

Service – Enlisted middle of Feb., 1776, as a pri. in Capt. Thomas Reading's CO., Col. Elias Dayton's N. J. Regt., for 12 or 13 mos. Served 2 mos. under Capt. Abraham Dickerson. In summer of 1778, 9 mos. in Capt. Henry Luce's CO., Col. Shreves' N. J. Regt. 1 mo. In 1780, under Capt. Isreal Luce. In battles of Monmouth and Springfield.
Proof – Pension claim S. 17617.
Died – Sept. 7, 1850. Buried in Nolin Cemetery near Greenwood, Ind. Stone.
Children – David; Matthias; Moses; Mary.
Collected by Mrs. I. E. Tranter, Franklin, Indiana.

Gibbs, A.; Ripley County Historical Society Data on Revolutionary Soldiers, 1973 review.7
Exact location of marker: no further information on grave site.
Additional comments: on Court House tablet
  Pa. Archives Series 3, Pennsylvanians residing in Ripley Co. Ind., pr.
  PL 26 Aug 1833 age 69
  b. 1760 d Sept. 1852 #s17617

Tombstone Location: Nolin Cemetery, Greenwood, Johnson Co., IN

Tombstone Inscription: Original stone illegible

Tombstone Inscription – placed by DAR:
      JOHN
      PARR
      PVT
     CONTINENTAL
      LINE
     REV WAR
    JUN 14, 1759
    SEP 7, 1850

Additional note: His brother, Matthias S17001, made the same moves ending in Johnson Co., IN. - mjm

PENDERGAST, EDWARD

Patriot: Edward Pendergast
Birth: 1765, Winchester, Frederick Co., VA
Married Spouse 1: Mary (- 1840/1850)
Service state(s): PA
Rank: Private
Proof of Service: Pension application
Pension application No.: S16505
Residences: Winchester, VA; Cumberland Co., PA; Nicholas Co., KY; Ripley Co., IN
Died: *1850 (aft. 28 Aug)Ripley Co, IN
Buried: Old Washington Church Cemetery, Washington Twp., Ripley Co., IN
DAR Ancestor No.: A088316

*There is confusion about his date of death. It seems that Violet Toph, Ripley County Historical Society, shows death in 1843. She apparently misread a notation in Edward's pension papers and used that date to order the government tombstone.
He was clearly still living in 1850 as he was listed in the census in the household of his son William (see abstract below). And, he continued to receive a pension until 1850 (see abstract below). National Society Daughters of the American Revolution has accepted "p1850". - mjm

Pension Application Abstracted from National Archives microfilm Series M804, Roll 1906, File S16505.
Pension abstract for – Edward Pendergast
Service state(s): PA
Date: 25 Aug 1832
County of: Ripley   State of: IN
Declaration made before a Judge or Court: Circuit Court
Act of: 7 Jun 1832
Age: 67 yrs.
Record of age: No written evidence, only speak from what I heard my parents say
Where and year born: Winchester, VA 1765
Residence when he entered service: Carlisle, Cumberland Co., PA
Residence(s) since the war: Carlisle, Cumberland Co., PA; KY for near 20 yrs.; Ripley Co., IN.
Residence now: Ripley Co., IN
Volunteer, Drafted, or Substitute: Enlisted with Thomas Brown, a recruiting Sgt.
Rank(s): Private
Statement of service-

Period	Duration	Names of General and Field Officers
1779	1 yr.	PA Line, Maj. Wilson, Capt. Samuel Postlethwaite, Lt. Holmes.

Battles: Not stated
Discharge received: Written discharge
Signed by: Capt. Postlethwaite

What became of it?: Does not know but suppose it is lost
Statement is supported by –
Person now living who can testify to service: Affidavit from his brother Sidney Pendergast (Carlisle, PA); Affidavit of his sister Mary Quigley.
Clergyman: Meshack Hyatt
Death of soldier: Pension Benefit paid to 4 Mar 1843
Wife: Not stated
Names and ages of children: Not stated [family referred to, but not named]

Abstract of Final Payment Voucher; General Services Administration, Washington, DC.

LAST FINAL PAYMENT VOUCHER RECEIVED FROM THE GENERAL ACCOUNTING OFFICE	
NAME	GAST PENDER~~GOST~~, EDWARD
AGENCY OF PAYMENT	INDIANA
DATE OF ACT	1832
DATE OF PAYMENT	March 1, 1850
DATE OF DEATH	-
GENERAL SERVICES ADMINISTRATION	
National Archives and Records Service	NA-286
GSA-WASH DC 54-4891	November 1953

Ripley County, Indiana Deed Records Vol. C., 21 Sep 1832 - 4 Feb 1834,
Page(s) 27-28.
Abstract of Deed/Patent for: Edward Pendergast and Mary (dower) his wife.
Purchaser (Grantee) or Seller (Grantor)?: Seller
Sold to: Robert Pendergast
State & county where recorded: Ripley Co., Indiana
Date entered: 7 Dec 1830
Recorded: 7 Dec 1830
Description: Parcel of land lying in the southwest quarter of Section 15, in
       Township 7 North of Range 12 East, of the Jeffersonville district,
       containing sixty acres.
Amount paid: One hundred dollars ($100.00).
Name(s) of Witnesses: Jas. Steele & James Wright

Ripley County, Indiana Deed Records Vol. C., 21 Sep 1832 - 4 Feb 1834,
Page(s) 28-30.
Abstract of Deed/Patent for: Edward Pendergast and Mary (dower) his wife.
Purchaser (Grantee) or Seller (Grantor)?: Seller
Sold to: William Pendergast
State & county where recorded: Ripley Co., Indiana
Date entered: 7 Dec 1830
Recorded: 7 Dec 1830
Description: Parcel of land lying in the southwest quarter of Section 15,
       Township 7 North of Range 12 East, of the Jeffersonville district,
       containing fifty acres.

Amount paid: One hundred dollars ($100.00).
Name(s) of Witnesses: Jas. Steele & James Wright

Ripley County, Indiana Deed Records Vol. C., 21 Sep 1832 - 4 Feb 1834,
Page 492.
Abstract of Deed/Patent for: Edward Pendergast
Seller (Grantor)?: Assign over and transfer mortgage
to Jesse L. Hollman, Commissioner of the School lands & his survivors; for
    the use of Congressional Township 7 North in Range 11 East.
State & county where recorded: Ripley Co., Indiana
Date entered: 7 Nov 1833
Recorded: 9 Nov 1833
Description: Fifty acres lying in the South East corner of the South West quarter of Section 15, Township 7 North and Range 12 East.
Amount paid: Mortgage of twenty five dollars in three years from date with ten
    percent interest payable in advance annually.

The Pension Roll of 1835 Volume IV, The Mid-Western States, Indexed Edition, In Four Volumes; Genealogical Publishing Co., Inc., Baltimore, MD, Reprint 1968, p. 87.
Statement, &c. of Ripley county, Indiana.

INDIANA Names	Rank	Annual allowance.	Sums received	Description of service
Edward Pendergrast	Private	40.00	120 00	Virginia militia

When placed on pension roll	Commencement of pension	Ages	Laws under which they were formerly placed on the pension roll; and remarks.
June 29, 1833	March 4, 1831	70	-

A Census of Pensioners for Revolutionary or Military Services with their Names, Ages, and Places of Residence Under the Act for Taking the Sixth Census in 1840; Genealogical Publishing Co., Inc., Baltimore, Maryland, 1965. p. 184.

Names of pensioners for revolutionary or military services.	Ages	Names of heads of families with whom pensioners resided June 1, 1840.
RIPLEY COUNTY JACKSON		
Edward Pendergast	70	Edward Pendergast

National Archives and Records Administration ; *United States Census, 1850,* Edward Pendergast in household of William Pendergast, enumerated 28 August 1850, Washington Twp., Ripley, Indiana, United States; citing family 38, household 38, line 7. NARA microfilm publication M432, Washington, D.C.
Name: Edward Pendergast
Age: 85

Race: White
Birth Year (Estimated): 1765
Birthplace: Pennsylvania

Toph, Violet E.; Peoples History of Ripley County, Indiana; self-published, c. 1940, p. 124, 128.
Revolutionary Soldiers Who Came to Ripley County
Edward Pendergast enlisted from Carlisle, Cumberland County, Penn. in 1779 and served one year under Major Wilson and Lieut Holmes. He was born in 1765 and died in 1843. He was pensioned from Ripley County. His burial was in Old Washington Cemetery.
p. 128.
In July, 1936, the Ripley County Historical Society, aided by subscriptions from descendants of the five Revolutionary soldiers buried in Old Washington cemetery, Edward Pendergast, Ninian Beall, James Grimes, Joseph McDonald and William Lipperd enclosed the cemetery with a durable wove wire fence and placed Government markers for each of the five soldiers, thus making a notable Revolutionary Shrine for Washington Township.

O'Byrne, Mrs. Roscoe C., comp. & ed.; Roster Soldiers and Patriots of the American Revolution Buried in Indiana; Published by Indiana Daughters of the American Revolution, 1938, Reprinted Genealogical Publishing Co., Baltimore MD, 1968, p. 290.
PENDERGAST, EDWARD   Ripley County
Born – 1765 Winchester, Virginia.
Service – Enlisted from Carlisle, Cumberland Co., Penn., in 1779. Served 1 yr. under Maj. Wilson and Lieut. Holmes, Capt. Samuel Postlewait.
Proof – Pension claim S. 16505.
Died – 1843. Buried Old Washington Cemetery, Versailles, Ind. Government marker and name on bronze table in Versailles Court House by the Ripley Co. Historical Society.
Collected by Mrs. A. B. Wycoff, Batesville, Indiana.

Gibbs, A.; Ripley County Historical Society Data on Revolutionary Soldiers, 1973 review.
Exact location of marker: east out of Elrod on 525 to 50N, right to Thermon Boyd farm (1973), mi. n.e. of house, going down across creek and up a hill, no road or path. Old Washington Cemetery, northwest out of Elrod, Washington Tw. Ripley Co. Ind.
Type of marker: Gov't
Date placed: Oct 1936 (minutes of R.C.H.S.)
Placed by: Ripley County Historical Society
Additional comments: on Court House tablet; 1840 census Ripley Co. Ind. pension list, p. 158; Edw. Pendergast age 70; 1850 census, Ripley Co. Ind. Washington Tw., p. 620; Edw. Pendergast age 85, b. Pa (which makes the tombstone data in error); Ripley Co. Ind. Probate Book A, p. 135, appl. for pension Feb. 1833.
Wording on marker:

Edward Pendergast
Pvt.
Postlethwaite's Co.
Wilson's Pa. Troops
Rev. War
1843

<u>United States Headstone Applications for U.S. Military Veterans, 1925-1949;</u> <u>database with images</u>; *https://familysearch.org/ark:/61903/1:1:VHZ6-DN2 : 17 May 2016); Affiliate Publication Number: M1916; Affiliate Publication Title: Applications for Headstones for U.S. Military Veterans, 1925-1941; GS Film Number: 1878241; Digital Folder Number: 004832259; Image Number: 00725*
Application for Headstone; War Department O.Q.M.G. Form No. 623
Name: Edward Pendergast
Event Date: 08/29/1934
Name of Cemetery: Old Washington
Located in or near: Milan, , Indiana, United States
Death Date: 1843
Enlistment Dates: 1779
Discharge Dates   1780
Rank: Private
Company: Capt. Samuel Postlethwaite's Co. under Maj. Wilson
   & Lt. Holmes, PA Troops
To be shipped to: Ripley Co. Historical Society, Osgood, Ind., Ripley Co.
Whose post-office address is: Versailles, Ind.
This application is for the UNMARKED grave of a veteran. It is understood the stone will be furnished and delivered at the railroad station or steamboat landing above indicated, at Government expense, freight prepaid. I hereby agree to promptly accept the headstone at destination, remove it and properly place same at decedent's grave at my expense. Ripley Co. Historical Society, Applicant. No fee should be paid in connection with this appliction.
Applicant: Ripley Co. Historical Society, Versailles, Ind.

Tombstone Location: Old Washington Church Cemetery, Washington Twp.,
   Ripley Co., IN

Tombstone Inscription:
EDWARD
PENDERGAST
PVT
POSTLETHWAITE'S CO
WILSON'S PA TROOPS
REV WAR
1843

PENNETENT (PENMETENT), JOHN

Patriot: John Pennetent (Penmetent)
Birth: abt. 1748
Married Spouse 1: Catherine (- 1837)
Service state(s): VA
Rank: Private
Proof of Service: Pension application
Pension application No.: S35554
Residences: VA; Switzerland Co., IN; Ripley Co., IN; Widow to McDonald Co., SW Missouri
Died: 24 Oct 1821 Ripley Co., IN
Buried: prob. Ripley Co., IN
DAR Ancestor No.: None as of 7 Jun 2017.

Pension Application Abstracted from National Archives microfilm Series 805, Roll644, File S35554.
Pension abstract for – John Pennetent   Service state(s): VA
Date: 3 September 1818
County of: Switzerland   State of: Indiana
Declaration made before a Court.
Age: Abt. 70
Where he entered service: 1. Staunton, Augusta Co., VA
                            2. Botetourt Co., VA
Volunteer or Drafted or Substitute: Volunteered
Statement of service-

Period	Duration	Names of General and Field Office
1. 1776	18 months	Lieut. Samuel Bell; 16th Regt. commanded by Col. Graceham of General Scott's brigade.
2. ----	18 months	Capt. Porter, Lieut. Thomas Bell, & Ensign Green.

Battles: Monmouth, NJ; Guilford, NC; at the taking of Ft. Friday in SC; at the Siege of Ninety-Six in SC. He was wounded severely at the Siege of Ninety-Six.
Discharge received: 1. Yes
                       2. Yes
Signed by: 1. Col. Graceham, written by Col. James Woods of the 8th Regiment
           2. Adj. Gen. Williams at the Highlands of Santee in South Carolina
What became of it?: Does not have papers and certificates.
Statement is supported by – He has Scars and is indigent.
Documentary proof: None
Persons in neighborhood who certify character: William Cotton, Associate Judge &
Date: 6 June 1821
County of: Switzerland   State of: IN
Declaration made before a Court
Age: 73 or 74
Statement of service-

Period	Duration	Names of General and Field Officers
	For 3 years	Company commanded by Capt. John McGuire in The 16th Virginia Regiment, Commanded by Col.William Griegan in the Virginia Line.

Statement is supported by – His original Certificate for Pension , No. 11,999
Wife: Not named   Wife's age: Abt. 41
&
Heirs (Inquiry) Application for Pension – by Catherine Pennetent
Date: 15 June 1854
County of: McDonald   State of: Southwest Missouri
Declaration made before a Court.
Death of soldier: the year 1821
Death of spouse: Catherine   June 1837
Author's note: Application Rejected – Not married before 1894.
Catherine Pennetent d. 22 Jun 1837.

<u>Switzerland County, Indiana Civil Order Book 4, 1820 – 1823</u>, June 1821,
<u>Switzerland County Courthouse</u>; pg. 192.
John Penmetent, Revolutionary soldier and U.S. pensioner---$184.12 1/2

Gwathmey, John H.; <u>Historical Register of Virginians in the Revolution, Soldiers, Sailors, Marines, 1775-1783</u>; *The Dietz Press, Richmond, VA, 1938, p. 615.*
Penetant, John, Pvt., WD.

Brumbaugh, Gaius Marcus, M.D, M.s., Litt.D; <u>Revolutionary War Records – Virginia, Virginia Army and Navy Forces with Bounty Land Warrants for Virginia Military District of Ohio, and Virginia Military Script, from Federal and State Archives</u>; *Genealogical Publishing Co., Inc., Baltimore, 1995, p. 608*
A List of the Men's Names in Dunmore County Militia Under the Command of Capt. John Holeman.
Penneitt (Pinnett?), John

Wardell, Patrick G., comp.; <u>Virginia/West Virginia Genealogical Data From Revolutionary War Pension and Bounty Land Warrant Records, Vol. 4 – Nabors through Rymer</u>; *Heritage Books, Inc., Bowie, MD, 1988, Vol. 4, p. 91.*
Pennetent, John, esf 1776 Staunton, Augusta Co, VA, in 16th VA Regiment; ON aec 70 Switzerland Co, IN, 1818; res there in 1820 ae 73-74 when had w mbnn aec 46; res 1821 Ripley Co, IN. F-S3554 R1907

<u>Ripley County Indiana, Recorder's Office, Tract Book 1</u>, p. 41.
Penitent, John   05 Apr 1816   R12, T8, S19   160 acres

Cowen, Janet C., comp; <u>Jeffersonville Land Entries 1808-1818</u>;*McDowell Publications, Utica, NY, 1984, p. 146.*
Receipt #
12159 Pennitent John IN Ripley NE S19 T08 N12E 160 1817 04 05

Clark, Murtie June; *The Pension List of 1820 [U.S. War Department]Reprinted with an Index; Genealogical Publishing Co., Inc., Baltimore, 1991. Originally published 1820 as Letter from the Secretary of War, p. 658.*
INDIANA
Names of the Revolutionary Pensioners which have been placed on the Roll of Indiana, under the Law of the 18th of March, 1818, from the passage thereof, to this day, inclusive, with the Rank they held, and the Lines in which they served, viz.

Names	Rank	Line
Included in the list -		
John Pennetent	private	Virginia

Pensioners of the Revolutionary War Struck Off the Roll with an Added Index to States; Reprinted by Genealogical Publishing Co., Baltimore, MD for Clearfield Company, Inc., 1989. p.100.
Pensioners in Indiana who have been dropped under the act of 1st May, 1820; prepared in conformity with a resolution of the House of Representatives of the United States of the 17th December, 1835.

Names	Acts under which restored	Remarks
John Pennetent	March 1, 1823	

The Pension Roll of 1835 Volume IV, The Mid-Western States, Indexed Edition, In Four Volumes; Genealogical Publishing Co., Inc., Baltimore, MD, Reprint 1968, p. 55.
Statement, &c. of Switzerland county, Indiana.

INDIANA Names	Rank	Annual allowance.	Sums received	Description of service
John Pennetent	Private	96.00	277 67	Virginia line

When placed on pension roll	Commencement of pension	Ages	Laws under which they were formerly placed on the pension roll; and remarks.
June 17, 1819	Dec 3, 1818	73	Died October 24, 1821.

Ripley Co., IN Probate Order Book, Vol. A, 19 Nov 1818-Feb. 1837, p. 20
May the 20th 1832
Letters of administration were this day granted to Catherine Penitent in the estate of John Penitent Deceased and William Stewart and William Bogard are accepted of a Security.

Gibbs, A.; *Ripley County Historical Society Data on Revolutionary Soldiers,* 1973 review.
Exact location of marker: no further information on grave site.
Additional comments: Ripley Co. Ind. Probate Book A, Court of May, 1822; adm. Catherine Pennitent.

O'Byrne, Mrs. Roscoe C., comp. & ed.; Roster Soldiers and Patriots of the American Revolution Buried in Indiana; Published by Indiana Daughters of the American Revolution, 1938, Reprinted Genealogical Publishing Co., Baltimore MD, 1968, p. 290

PENNETENT, JOHN   Ripley County
Born – About 1748.
Service – Pri. in Regt. commanded by Cols. Bluford and Haws of Vir. Line, 18 mos. service.
Proof – Pension claim S. 35554.
Died – Oct. 24, 1821, Ripley Co.
Married – Catherine _____ d. 1834. *[should be 1837]*

The Vevay Reveille-Enterprise; Vol. 122, No. 37, 22 Sep 1935, p. 7, col. 3-4.
Roster of Revolutionary Soldiers Who Resided in Switzerland County
By Mrs. Effa M. Danner
John Pennetent – S35554. Switzerland County, May 22, 1819. Served in Company under Capt. John McQuire who resigned at Valley Forge, enlisted, Winchester, Virginia – 15th Reg. Gen. Scott's brigade in May or June, 1780. Discharged by Col. Gracehemp of Gen. Scott's Brigade. Col. James Wood wrote discharge. Enlisted in Boutetort Co., Vir., attached to Capt. Thos. Bell's Co., at Staunton, Augusta Co., Virginia. Reg. attached to Col. Bluford's line in Hillsboro, N.C. Served 18 months and discharged at highlands of Santee (Col. Thompson's plantation, Oct. 31, 1781) signed by Adj. Gen. Williams. December 3, 1819, about 70 years of age. In battles of Monmouth, Guilford, Camden, Fort Friday in S.C., Siege of 96. Mentions wife about 41 has rheumatic pains. Died October 24, 1821 in Ripley Co.
Loomesville, McDonald Co., S.W. Mo., July 3, 1850 letters written in relation to claim of Catherine Pennetent's heirs (none named). ~~Widow~~ died June 22, 1834. Ind. Cert. 11999, John P., private in Regiment of Cols. Bluford and Haws of Virginia line, 18 months, inscribed on rolls of Indiana at rate of $8.00 per a. to commence Dec. 3, 1819. Cert. issued June 17, 1819, sent to Wm. Keen, Vevay, Jefferson Township, Indiana.
No records here.

PENMETENT, JOSEPH

His name is on the old "Bronze Tablet" at the courthouse. There is no record of a man by this name associated with the Revolutionary War. The given name is probable incorrect. It should have been John.

There is a record for a man named John Pennetent (Penmetent) who lived in Switzerland County and died in Ripley County. See his record on the preceding pages.

PRATT, JONATHAN

Patriot: Jonathan Pratt
Birth: 8 Mar 1764 Needham, MA
Married Spouse 1: 1798/1799 Elizabeth aka Betsey (1775-1849)[a]
Service state(s): MA
Rank: Private
Proof of Service: Pension application
Pension application No.: S40290
Residences: MA; ME; Geauga Co., OH (1833); Warren Co., OH (1835); Ripley Co., IN.
Died: 13 Jan 1850 Prattsburg, Ripley Co., IN
Buried: Prattsburg Cemetery, Prattsburg, Delaware Twp., Ripley Co., IN
DAR Ancestor No.: A092482
Children: in 1820 – Lucy ag 18; Samuel ag 15; Dyer ag 12; Jonathan ag 9; Eben ag 5; Elijah ag 3.

[a] It has not been determined if Jonathan was married once or twice. Family records indicate one wife, Elizabeth, born 1775. In his 1818 pension application he states he had a family of ten and an aged mother; he does not claim a wife. In the 1820 pension application he names his wife Betsey, aged 45 and his aged mother.

Pension Application Abstracted from National Archives microfilm Series M804, Roll 1967, File S40290.
Pension abstract for – Jonathan Pratt
Service state(s): MA Continental
Date: 22 Apr 1818
County of: Somerset State of: ME
Declaration made before a Judge or Court: Josiah Stebbins, Esq., Judge of the Circuit Court of Common Pleas, for the Second Eastern Circuit of Massachusetts, comprising the Counties of Lincoln, Kennebec and Somerset.
Act of: 18 Mar 1818
Age: 55 yrs.
Where and year born: Needham, MA
Residence when he entered service: Enlisted at Templeton, MA
Residence now: Phillips, Somerset Co., ME
Residence since the war: Not stated
Volunteer, Drafted, or Substitute: Enlisted
Rank(s): Private
Statement of service-

Period	Duration	Names of General and Field Officers
Mar 1781 - Oct 1783	3 yrs.	Capt. Lunt's company, Col. Tupper's 10th MA Regt. for 2 yrs.; at discharge was in Col. Vose's 1st MA Regt.

Battles: King's Bridge
Discharge received: Yes, at West Point
What became of it?: Sold it to Caleb Parker, for a mere trifle, being poor, &

thinking it of no value.

Statement is supported by –
Person now living who can testify to service: Benjamin Dolber, of Freeman, ME, provided affidavit that Jonathan Pratt was a native of Nedham with me, and I was with him in the Army, that he did duty abt. 3 yrs.
Names and ages of children: a family of ten children dependent on me for support, also an aged mother. *[This might indicate that his wife, mother of these ten children was deceased; or was his wife one of the family of ten?]*
&
Pension abstract for – Jonathan Pratt
Date: 16 Jun 1820
County of: Kennebec   State of: ME
Declaration made before a Judge or Court: Circuit Court of Common Pleas
Declaration: Schedule of Property
Act of: 1 May 1820
Age: 56 yrs.
Residence now: Strong, Sommerset Co., ME
Wife: Betsy   Wife's age: 45 yrs.
Names and ages of children: Lucy, ag. 18; Samuel, ag. 15; son Dyer, ag. 12; Jonathan, ag. 9; Eban, ag. 5; Elijah ag. 3 yrs. He is also supporting his aged mother.
&
Pension abstract for – Jonathan Pratt
Date: 27 Apr 1833
County of: Geauga   State of: OH
Declaration made before a Judge or Court: Justice of the Peace
Declaration: Application for Transfer - He was previously placed on the Pension Roll of district of Maine, (now State); he now resides in Ohio where he intends to remain.
Reason for removal: climate being more mild he thought health would be better
&
Pension abstract for – Jonathan Pratt
Date: 17 Aug 1835
County of: Warren   State of: OH
Declaration made before a Judge or Court: Justice of the Peace
Declaration: Application for Transfer
Reason for removal: in hopes he might be able to do better for his family
&
Notation in file shows he died 3 Jul 1850, in Ripley Co., IN.

<u>Massachusetts Soldiers and Sailors of the Revolutionary War, A Compilation from the Archives</u>; prepared and published by the Secretary of the Commonwealth in accordance with Chapter 100, Resolves of 1891, Vol. XII; Wright & Potter Printing co., State Printers, Boston, MA, 1904. p. 697.
PRATT, JONATHAN.   Receipt dated Templeton, March 3, 1781, for bounty paid said Pratt by Jonathan Holman and others, on behalf of Class No. 7

of the town of Templeton, to serve in the Continental Army for the term of 3 years; also Private, Col. Benjamin Tupper's (10th) regt.; service from Jan. 15, 1781, 23 mos. 17 days.

Senate Documents, Vol.9, No. 988, 63rd Congress, 3d Session, Washington, 1915; "Register of Certificates Issued by John Pierce, Esquire, Paymaster General and Commissioner of Army Accounts for the United States, to Officers and Soldiers of the Continental Army Under Act of July 4, 1783"; Seventeenth report of the National Society of the Daughters of the American Revolution; Genealogical Publishing Co., Inc., Baltimore, MD, 1984. p. 410.

Men listed in this volume with the same name.

No. of Certificate	To whom issued	Amount
16960	Pratt, Jonathan	21.04
29766	Pratt, Jonathan	19.35
30698	Pratt, Jonathan	38.80
32691	Pratt, Jonathan	67.80
33349	Pratt, Jonathan	80.00
34133	Pratt, Jonathan	28.52
36521	Pratt, Jonathan	21.54
37543	Pratt, Jonathan	81.60
38090	Pratt, Jonathan	80.00
38634	Pratt, Jonathan	44.66

Clark, Murtie June; The Pension List of 1820 [U.S. War Department]Reprinted with an Index; Genealogical Publishing Co., Inc., Baltimore, 1991. Originally published 1820 as Letter from the Secretary of War, p. 97.

MAINE

Names of the Revolutionary Pensioners which have been placed on the Roll of Maine, under the Law of the 18th of March, 1818, from the passage thereof, to this day, inclusive of the Rank they held, and the Lines in which they served, viz:

Names	Rank	Line
Included in the list –		
Jonathan Pratt	private	Massachusetts

The Pension Roll of 1835 Volume IV, The Mid-Western States, Indexed Edition, In Four Volumes; Genealogical Publishing Co., Inc., Baltimore, MD, Reprint 1968, p. 186.

Statement, &c. of Geauga county, Ohio.

OHIO Names	Rank	Annual allow-ance.	Sums re-ceived	Description of service
Jonathan Pratt	Private	96.00	1,523 46	Mass. continental

When placed on pension roll	Commencement of pension	Ages	Laws under which they were formerly placed on the pension roll; and remarks.
Jan 28, 1819	Ap'l 22, 1818	71	Transferred from Maine.

1840 U. S. Census, Johnson Twp., Ripley County, IN; Roll 92; p. 109, line 7.
Johnathan Pratt
Males <5=1, Males 20-29=2, Males 30-39=1, Males 70-79=1, Females 30-39=1, Females 60-69=1.

Toph, Violet E.; Toph Papers; collected during her lifetime 1878-1956, p. 999.
Excerpt from "Pratt History by Miss Bessie Pratt, Jan, 14, 1936".
    Jonathan Pratt was born in Needham. Mass. March 8, 1764. He came to Ripley County, Ind. and died Jan. 13, 1850. His wife Elizabeth was born March 9, 1775 and died June 13, 1849. They are buried in the Prattsburg Cemetery in Delaware Township, Ripley County, Indiana.
    He enlisted in the Revolutionary War in March 1781 from Massachusetts and served until October 1785 as a private under the officers, Capt. Daniel Lunt, Col. Tupper, and Col. Vose. He applied for pension April 22, 1818 from Phillips, Somerset County, Maine. He had ten children but we have the names of only nine, Lucy, Samuel, Diah, Jonathan. Jr., Eben and Elijah, Phoebe, Sarah, Mary.
[His 1818 pension application states he has a family of ten. It is unclear as to whether he had 10 children, or 9 children and his wife.]

Toph, Violet E.; Peoples History of Ripley County, Indiana; self-published, c. 1940, p. 131.
Revolutionary Soldiers Who Came to Ripley County
Jonathan Pratt enlisted in March 1781. His length of service was until October 1785. He was a private and served under Captain Daniel Lunk, Col. Tupper and Col. Voss from Massachusetts. His residence at time of enlistment was Templeton, Mass. He applied for a pension April 22, 1818 which was allowed. His residence then was Phillips, Somerset Co. Maine, and his age 55. Later he moved to Ripley County, Ind. and is buried in the Prattsburg cemetery. Ripley County Historical Society placed a Government Marker at his grave July 13, 1936.

O'Byrne, Mrs. Roscoe C., comp. & ed.; Roster Soldiers and Patriots of the American Revolution Buried in Indiana; Published by Indiana Daughters of the American Revolution, 1938, Reprinted Genealogical Publishing Co., Baltimore MD, 1968, p. 299.
PRATT, JONATHAN   Riley County
Born – 1764, Needham, Massachusetts.
Service – Enlisted in March, 1781, served to Oct. 1785, as a pri. Enlisted at Templeton, Mass. Served under Capt. Daniel Lunk, Col. Tupper, Col. Vose.
Proof – Pension record.
Died – Jan. 19, 1850. Prattsburg, Ripley Co. Government marker placed by Hist. Society.
Married – Betsey -----, 1775-1849. Ch. Lucy b. 1802; Samuel b. 1805; Dyer b. 1808; Jonathan b. 1809; Eben b. 1815; Elijah b. 1817.
Collected by Mrs. A. B. Wycoff, Batesville, Indiana.

Gibbs, A.; Ripley County Historical Society Data on Revolutionary Soldiers, 1973 review.
Exact location of marker: turn east off Delaware Rd. on 650; cemetery between 400E and 575N; near Franklin-Delaware Tw. line. Prattsburg Cemetery, visible from road; n.e. from Delaware, Delaware Tw. Ripley Co. Ind.
Type of marker: Gov't and family
Date placed: Gov't (no date) and at time of death by family
Additional comments: Toph says: pensioned from Maine.
    On 1850 Census Mortality Schedule age 86.
    Family marker: Elizabeth b. Mar. 9, 1775 d. June 13, 1849.

United States Headstone Applications for U.S. Military Veterans, 1925-1949, database with images; (https://familysearch.org/ark:/61903/1:1:VHZ6-WB2 : 17 May 2016); Affiliate Publication Number: M1916; Affiliate Publication Title: Applications for Headstones for U.S. Military Veterans, 1925-1941; Affiliate Film Number: 89; GS Film Number: 1878238; Digital Folder Number: 004832256; Image Number: 02020.
Application for Headstone; War Department O.Q.M.G. Form No. 623
Name: Pratt, Jonathan
Event Date: May 31, 1934
Name of Cemetery: Prattsburg
Located in or near: Delaware, Ind.
Death Date: Jan. 13, 1850
Enlistment Dates: March 1781
Discharge Dates: 178 5 Oct.
Rank: Private
Company: Capt. Lunt's Co., Col. Tupper's 10 Mass Regt.
To be shipped to: Ripley Co. Historical Society, Osgood, Ind., Ripley Co.
Whose post-office address is: Versailles, Ind.
This application is for the UNMARKED grave of a veteran. It is understood the stone will be furnished and delivered at the railroad station or steamboat landing above indicated, at Government expense, freight prepaid. I hereby agree to promptly accept the headstone at destination, remove it and properly place same at decedent's grave at my expense. Ripley Co. Historical Society, Applicant.
No fee should be paid in connection with this application.
Applicant: Ripley Co. Historical Society, Versailles, Ind.

Tombstone Location: Prattsburg Cemetery, Prattsburg, Delaware Twp., Ripley Co., IN

Tombstone Inscription (old stone):
JONATHAN PRATT
BORN
March 8, 1764
DIED
January 13, 1850
Aged 85 years 10
Months & 5 days.

Tombstone Inscription (new stone):
JONATHAN
PRATT
PVT. LUNT'S CO.
10 MASS REGT.
REV WAR
JANUARY 13, 1850

PROTHERO (PROTHEN), THOMAS

Thomas Prothero did not have ties to Ripley County, Indiana. His wife, Hannah, resided in Ripley County, Indiana where her pension was rejected/suspended in 1850.

Patriot: Thomas Prothero
Birth:
Married Spouse 1: Bond- 19 Aug 1785, Botetourt Co. VA
Marr - 25 Aug 1786, Botetourt Co., VA
Hannah Miles (1762 - 1864)
Service state(s): NC
Rank: Private
Proof of Service: Widow's pension application
Pension application No.: R8501
Residences: NC; Botetourt Co., VA; Franklin Co., VA; TN; Shelby Co., KY
Died: 28 Jun 1817   Shelby Co., KY
Buried: Unknown
DAR Ancestor No.: None as of 7 Jun 2017.

Pension Application Abstracted from National Archives microfilm Series M804, Roll 1981, File R8501.
Pension abstract for – Hannah Prothero widow of Thomas Prothero
Service state(s): NC
Date: 23 Aug 1845
County of: Jefferson   State of: IN
Declaration made before a Judge or Court: Circuit Court
Act of: 7 Jul 1838 & 3 Mar 1842
Age: 83 yrs.
Widow's residence now: Jefferson Co., IN
Rank(s): Private
Statement of service-
>She heard him say but cannot remember about the time her husband entered the Service not the place nor cannot remember the officers named..he was under Gen. Green, she does not know the length of each tour but thinks his service was rendered in NC.

Battles: She heard her husband say he was at Battle of Guilford Court House and Battle at Ramsour's Mill. Burke or Lincoln Co., NC
Death of soldier: 28 Jun 1817
Marriage date and place: 25 Aug 1786 Botetourt Co., VA
Proof of marriage: Marriage Bond dated 19 Aug 1785, Botetourt Co., VA
Persons in neighborhood who certify character: Isaac Miles of Shelby Co., KY, gave deposition 11 Jan 1845 in Ripley Co., IN, that he was present at the marriage of Hannah Miles to Thomas Prothero; Evan Miles of Ripley Co., IN, gave testimony that he knew Hannah and Thomas Prothero, that they lived together as man and wife as early as 1786, he thinks Thomas died in 1818.
Names and ages of children: Not stated
[Hannah's application for pension was Rejected. The reason is not shown.]

Virginia Marriages, 1785-1940; accessed 11 April 2016 from https://familysearch.org/ark:/61903/1:1:XRC3-THW.
Name: Thomas Prothers Or Pludrough
Spouse's Name: Hannah Miles
Event Date: 19 Aug 1785
Event Place: Botetourt, Virginia
Spouse's Father's Name: Bartholamew Miles
Indexing Project (Batch) Number: M86871-7
System Origin: Virginia-EASy
GS Film number: 30734; Reference ID: pg 26
FHL microfilm 30,734

Rejected or Suspended Applications for Revolutionary War Pensions; Reprinted for Clearfield Company Inc. by Genealogical Publishing Co., Inc., Baltimore, MD, 1998. p. 419.
A list of persons residing in Indiana who have applied for pensions under the act of July 7, 1838, whose claims have been suspended; prepared in conformity with the resolution of the Senate of the United States, September 16, 1850.

Names	Residence	Reason for suspension
Prothen, Hannah, widow of Thomas	Versailles, Ripley	For proof of service.

Toph, Violet E.; Peoples History of Ripley County, Indiana; self-published, c. 1940, p. 126.
Revolutionary Soldiers Who Came to Ripley County
Hannah Protheroe, widow of Thomas Protheroe, having married him in Virginia Aug. 19, 1785, applied for a pension from Ripley County in 1845.

Margaret R. Waters; Revolutionary Soldiers Buried in Indiana (1949) With Supplement (1954) Two Volumes in One; Genealogical Publishing Company, Baltimore, MD, 1970, p. 83.
PROTHERO, THOMAS   Jefferson
d. 6-28-1817; m 8-19-1785 (bond dated; 8-25-1786 according to wid.'s affid.), Botetourt Co., Va., Hannah Miles, b. 1762; chn.: poss. son Evan Prothero (in 1830 Cens., Jefferson Co., Ind. Affid. 1-11-1845, Ripley Co. Ind., but a res, of Shelby Co., Ky., of Isaac Miles (rel. not given); that he knew they were mar.; she nee Miles; she will be 83 next Mar.; she liv. Jefferson Co., Ind. Same affid. 8-30-1845, Ripley Co., Ind., of Evan Miles (rel. not given). Service N.C. service. REF: Pens. R.8501 N.C.; Susp. Pens. List (1852) p. 419—for proof of service; this gives wid. as of Ripley Co., Ind.; 1830 Cens., Jefferson Co., Ind., v.?, p. 274.

Gibbs, A.; Ripley County Historical Society Data on Revolutionary Soldiers, 1973 review.
Comments: Widow Hannah, having married him in Va. 19 Aug 1785, applied for pension in Ripley Co. Ind. in 1845 #R8501.
Samuel Protherow Sr. b. 1761 d. 1840 Rev. War
Samuel J. died Delaware Ind. 1871.

RASOR (RESOR), PETER

Peter was not a resident of Ripley County, IN. Some of his children settled in Ripley County which seems to be the reason his name appears, in memorial, on the old "Bronze Tablet" at the courthouse.

Patriot: Peter Rasor
Birth: 1 Oct 1758 poss. Sussex Co., NJ
Married Spouse 1: VA 17 Oct 1786 Frances "Frankie" Adair (1759-1852)
Service state(s): VA
Rank: Private
Proof of Service: Pension application
Pension application No.: R8600
Residences: Culpeper Co., VA; Abbeville Dist., SC; Jefferson Co., KY; Spencer Co., IN
Died: 4 Nov 1831 Spencer Co., IN
Buried: Hackleman Graveyard, Rockport, Spencer Co., IN
DAR Ancestor No.: A093824
Child: Semeon b. 1 Sep 1787; Elizabeth b. 10 Apr 1788
Note: Peter's father, George Raysor, furnished supplies for the Revolutionary War cause. He is a recognized patriot. DAR Ancestor No. A133598.

Pension Application Abstracted from National Archives microfilm Series M804, Roll 2003, File R8600.
Pension abstract for – Frances Rasor widow of Peter Rasor
Service state(s): VA
Date: 18 Mar 1843
County of: Spencer State of: IN
Declaration made before a Judge or Court: Probate Court
Act of: 7 Jul 1838
Age: 84 yrs.
Residence when he entered service: Not stated
Residence(s) since the war: Culpeper Co., VA; Spencer Co., IN
Residence now: Spencer Co., IN
Volunteer, Drafted, or Substitute: Drafted
Rank(s): Private
Statement of service-

Period	Duration	Names of General and Field Officers
1781	2 mos.	Culpeper Co., VA Militia under Capt. Clork [Clark], Maj. Groves
1781	2 mos.	Same
1781-1783	Other tours	She believes under Col. Barber

Battles: Cornwallis defeat
Statement is supported by –
Living witness, name(s): Peter Rasor's brother, Christian Rasor appears before a magistrate and makes this statement -
South Carolina Abbeville District: December the 28th 1842

Dear Sir I received yours of the 3rd of this Instant respecting my knowledge of my brother Peter Rasor's Services in the Revolutionary war – none knowledge is that he served 2 tours in the year 1781 2 months each. I believe he was dismissed on account of his being sick before Wallace was taken prisoner the last tour he was under Captain Clark of Culpeper Virginia and was attached to Major Graves Battalion, he was a private militia Soldier drafted each time for 2 months as to the 1st tour I was not with him but I feel confident he did serve that tour.

Death of soldier: 4 Nov 1831

Widow's name before marriage: Not stated

Marriage date and place: Oct 17--; she cannot recollect the year in which she was married but knows very well that it was before the year 1794.

Proof of marriage: On March 18, 1843 in Spencer County Indiana, Simeon Rasor gave testimony that Peter Rasor died November 4, 1831 leaving Frances Rasor his widow who has remained unmarried ever since the death of Peter; that attached is a family record in the handwriting of Christian Rasor; that said record has been in the possession of Peter and Frances Rasor for it at least the last 40 years.

Family Record: "Peter Rasor was Borned 1st day of October 1758
    my Son Semeon Born the 1 day of Saptamber 1787
    my dauther Elezabath Born the 10 day of abrel 1788"

[Note: the claim was not allowed as it was not proven he served six months.]
&

Letter in the pension file for Peter Rasor: Rockport, Ind., June 25, 1928
Bureau of Pensions, Washington, D.C.

Dear Sir: - The information I desire about Peter Rasor, is in the above department somewhere but I do not know where to tell you to look for it. About two years ago, Viola Root Cameron Rasor called at the Bureau of Pensions and got Peter Rasor's revolutionary record, but it was misplaced. Peter Rasor – and two brothers, enlisted from Virginia, served in Revolutionary war. Peter afterward married Frankie Adair, moved to Spencer Cp., Indiana in 1808, spent the remainder of his life here, after his death, his widow Frankie Adair Rasor applied for a pension, which was not granted.

These are the facts that I have, thanking you in advance for the desired facts, I am Respectfully, Grace H. Pattie

U.S. Department of Interior, Bureau of Land Management, General Land Office Records; Land Patent Search – accessed

Name: RASOR, PETER

Accession Nr. CV-0043-370; Document Type – Credit Volume Patent; State - Indiana; Issue Date – 3/1-1819; Cancelled – No; Land Office – Vincennes; Authority – April 24, 1820: Sale-Cash Entry (3 Stat. 566); Document Nr. 0; Total Acres – 0.000; Land Descriptions: State – IN; Meridian – 2nd PM; Twp-Rng – 007S-006W; Aliquots – E ½ NE 1/4; Section – 5; County - Spencer

Rejected or Suspended Applications for Revolutionary War Pensions; Reprinted for Clearfield Company Inc. by Genealogical Publishing Co., Inc., Baltimore, MD, 1998. p. 419.
A list of persons residing in Indiana who have applied for pensions under the act of July 7, 1838, whose claims have been suspended; prepared in conformity with the resolution of the Senate of the United States, September 16, 1850.

Names	Residence	Reason for suspension
Rasor, Francis, widow of Peter	LaFayette, Spencer	Six month' service not in proof.

Wardell, Patrick G., comp.; *Virginia/West Virginia Genealogical Data From Revolutionary War Pension and Bounty Land Warrant Records, Vol. 4 – Nabors through Rymer*; Heritage Books, Inc., Bowie, MD, 1988, p. 184.
Rasor, Peter, b 6/10/1758; esf 1781 Culpeper Co, VA; dd 11/4/1831 Spencer Co, IN; md Frances in month of October before 1794 who afp ae 84 Spencer Co, IN, 1843, & PAR; s Simeon b 9/1/1787; d Elizabeth b 4/10/1788; sol wid decd when s Simeon gave power of attorney there 1855 to agent to afp, & PAR; QLF says sol 2 bro's also VA RW sol's, he md Frankie Adair & mvd to Rockport, Spencer Co, IN, in 1808, where sol dd. F-R8600 R2003

Clift, G. Glens, Assistant Secretary, Kentucky Historical Society, Comp.; *"Second Census" of Kentucky – 1800, A Privately Compiled and Published Enumeration of Tax Payers Appearing in the 79 Manuscript Volumes Extant of Tax Lists of the 42 Counties of Kentucky in Existence in 1800*; Genealogical Publishing Co., Baltimore, MD, 1966, p. 242.

Name	County	Tax List Date
Razor, Peter	Jefferson	1800

U.S. Department of Interior, Bureau of Land Management, General Land Office Records; Land Patent Search
Name: Rasor, Peter
Accession Nr. CV-0043-370; Document Type – Credit Volume Patent; Issue Date – 3/1/1819; Cancelled – No
Land Office – Vincennes; Authority – April 20, 1820: Sale-Cash Entry (3 Stat. 566); Document Nr. 0; Total Acres – 0.00
Land Descriptions: State – IN; Meridian – 2ndPM; Twp-Rng – 007S – 006W; Aliquots – E1/2NE1/4; Section – 4; County - Spencer

Toph, Violet E.; *Peoples History of Ripley County, Indiana*; self-published, c. 1940, p. 120.
Revolutionary Soldiers Who Came to Ripley County
Peter Reson, or Rasor, entered service from Virginia in 1781. He died Nov. 4, 1831. His wife Mrs. Frances Resor applied for a pension from Spencer Co., Ind. in 1843. He was a relative of the McGuires at Friendship, Ind.

O'Byrne, Mrs. Roscoe C., comp. & ed.; Roster Soldiers and Patriots of the American Revolution Buried in Indiana; Published by Indiana Daughters of the American Revolution, 1938, Reprinted Genealogical Publishing Co., Baltimore MD, 1968, p. 306.

RASOR, PETER   Ripley County
Born – Oct., 1758, Culpeper Co., Virginia.
Service – Enlisted from Culpeper Co., Virginia, as pri. in Vir. Militia. Served several tours of duty in 1781, under Capt. Clark and Maj. Groves. Present at surrender of Cornwallis.
Proof- Pension claim R. 8600. Rejected for lack of 6 mos. service.
Died – Nov. 11, 1831. Buried Hackleman graveyard, Rockport, Ind. Stone.
Married – Frances Adair. Ch. Simeon b. 1787; Elizabeth b. 1788; George; Anne.
Collected by Miss Laura M. Wright, Rockport, Indiana.

Gibbs, A.; Ripley County Historical Society Data on Revolutionary Soldiers, 1973 review.
Exact location of marker: no further information of grave site.
Comments: Toph notes: a relative of McGuire's of Friendship, Ind.
    Entr. Service from Va. 1781; date of birth not given; d. Nov. 4, 1831; wife Frances Raser applied for pension from Spencer Co. Ind. in 1843. #R 8600.
    Ripley County Historical Society Minutes Mar. 9, 1942: Marking of graves of soldiers was discussed and Miss Toph as chairman of this committee was authorized to secure a Govt. marker for the grave of Mr. Resor in the Olive Branch Cemetery if possible.
    The only known Olive Branch Cem is in Switzerland Co. Ind. and the only Resor marker there (1973) was for Zella, dau. of Wm. And R. Reser. This cemetery is east of Friendship.

United States Headstone Applications for U.S. Military Veterans, 1925-1949, database with images; (https://familysearch.org/ark:/61903/1:1:VHZ6-RWV : 17 May 2016); *Affiliate Publication Number: M1916; Affiliate Publication Title: Applications for Headstones for U.S. Military Veterans, 1925-1941; Affiliate Film Number: 97; GS Film Number: 1878246;*
Digital Folder Number: 004832264; Image Number: 01545.
Application for Headstone; War Department O.Q.M.G. Form No. 623
Application Number: 56823
Name: Peter Rasor
Event Date: April 21, 1930
Name of Cemetery: Hackelman
Located in or near: Rockport, Indiana
Death Date: Nov. 4th 1831
Enlistment Dates: not identified
Discharge Dates: not identified
Rank: Private
Company: Virginia Militia
To be shipped to: J. A. Huffman
At: Rockport, Indiana; Spencer County

This application is for the UNMARKED grave of a veteran. It is understood the stone will be furnished and delivered at the railroad station or steamboat landing above indicated, at Government expense, freight prepaid. I hereby agree to promptly accept the headstone at destination, remove it and properly place same at decedent's grave at my expense. Ripley Co. Historical Society, Applicant. No fee should be paid in connection with this application.
Applicant: J. A. Huffman

Tombstone Location: Hackleman Graveyard, Rockport, Spencer Co., IN
                GPS: N 37 Degrees 57.996'   W 87 Degrees 05.493'

Tombstone Inscription: PETER RASOR
                                      VA. MIL.
                                      REV. WAR
                                      10. – 1758
                                      11. – 1831

ROBBINS, EPHRAIM

Patriot: Ephraim Robbins
Birth: 11 Dec 1759 Killingly, Windham Co., CT
Married Spouse 1: Lucina Webster (- 1843)
Service state(s): CT
Rank: Private
Proof of Service: Pension application
Pension application No.: S17052
Residences: Windham Co., CT; NY; Ripley Co., IN
Died: 16 Jun 1844 Rising Sun, Ohio Co., IN
Buried: Old Rising Sun Cemetery or Cedar Hedge Cemetery,
Rising Sun, Ohio Co. IN
DAR Ancestor No.: A096682

Pension Application Abstracted from National Archives microfilm Series M804, Roll 2054, File S17052.
Pension abstract for – Ephraim Robbins
Service state(s): CT
Date: 13 Nov 1832
County of: Ripley State of: IN
Declaration made before a Judge or Court: Probate Court
Act of: 7 Jun 1832
Age: 73 yrs.
Record of age: No record, only what my parents told me.
Where and year born: Killingly, Windham Co., CT 11 Dec 1759
Residence when he entered service: Brooklyn, Windham Co., CT
Residence(s) since the war: Brooklyn, Windham Co., CT; NY; Ripley Co., IN.
Residence now: Ripley Co., IN
Volunteer, Drafted, or Substitute: Volunteer
Rank(s): Private
Statement of service-

Period	Duration	Names of General and Field Officers
Apr 1775	3 mos.	Gen. Putman, Lt. Robbins, Capt. Abner Adam's company
Dec 1777	3 mos.	CT Line, Col. Ely, Capt. Beet's comp.
Aug 1778	abt. 2 mos.	Capt. Samuel Williams company
Again 1778	2 mos.	Capt. Daniel Tyler's company
1779	2 mos.	Capt. Shelden's company
Fall of 1780	abt. 2 mos.	officers not recollected

Battles: Black's Point, Rhode Island – wounded in the leg
Discharge received: Only one from Capt. Beets
What became of it?: Lost
&
Proceedings in the matter of Pension of Ephraim Robbins, deceased
Date: 16 Aug 1844
County of: Ohio State of: IN
Proceedings before a Judge or Court: Probate Court

Death of soldier: 16 Jun 1844   Ohio Co., IN
Wife: "left no widow"
Names and ages of children: Only heirs –
Rhoda Merrell, intermarried with Morris Merrell of Ohio Co., IN;
Claressa Porter, intermarried with Elhanan Porter of Marion Co., IN;
Daniel Robbins & Newman Robbins, who have not been heard of for 5 or 6 yrs.

Abstract of Final Payment Voucher; General Services Administration, Washington, DC
LAST   FINAL PAYMENT VOUCHER RECEIVED FROM
           THE GENERAL ACCOUNTING OFFICE
NAME   ROBBINS, EPHRAIM
AGENCY OF PAYMENT   INDIANA
DATE OF ACT   1832
DATE OF PAYMENT   3d Qr. 1844
DATE OF DEATH   June 16, 1844
GENERAL SERVICES ADMINISTRATION
National Archives and Records Service   NA-286
GSA-WASH DC 54-4891   November 1953

Senate Documents, Vol.9, No. 988, 63rd Congress, 3d Session, Washington, 1915; "Register of Certificates Issued by John Pierce, Esquire, Paymaster General and Commissioner of Army Accounts for the United States, to Officers and Soldiers of the Continental Army Under Act of July 4, 1783"; <u>Seventeenth report of the National Society of the Daughters of the American Revolution</u>; *Genealogical Publishing Co., Inc., Baltimore, MD, 1984. p. 432.*
Men listed in this volume with the same name.
No. of Certificate   To whom issued   Amount
2787   Robins, Ephraim   3.79

Bockstruck, Lloyd DeWitt; <u>Revolutionary War Bounty Land Grants Awarded by State Governments</u>; *Genealogical Publishing Co., IN, Baltimore, MD, 1996, p. 448.*
Robbins, Ephraim. Conn. Sufferer. Fairfield. 106.14.10.

Ripley County, Indiana Deed Records Vol. A, 11 Aug 1818-29 Jan 1827
Page(s): 116-117.
Abstract of Deed/Patent for: Warrantee deed – Ephraim J. Robins
Purchaser (Grantee) or Seller (Grantor)?: Purchaser
Purchased from: Robert Carnahan
State & county where recorded: Ripley Co., Indiana
Date entered: 13 Feb 1824
Recorded: 22 Mar 1824
Description: East half of the southeast quarter of Section 20, Township 9, North Range 12 East in the district of land directed to be sold by the act of Congress at Jeffersonville

Amount paid: Five hundred dollars ($500.00).
Name(s) of Witnesses: John Borden
References to other files - book & page no. (orphans, minors, inventories,

The Pension Roll of 1835 Volume IV, The Mid-Western States, Indexed Edition, In Four Volumes; Genealogical Publishing Co., Inc., Baltimore, MD, Reprint 1968, p. 87.
Statement, &c. of Ripley county, Indiana.

INDIANA Names	Rank	Annual allowance.	Sums received	Description of service
Ephraim Robbins	Private	46.66	139 98	Conn. militia

When placed on pension roll	Commencement of pension	Ages	Laws under which they were formerly placed on the pension roll; and remarks.
April 9, 1833	March 4, 1831	75	-

Toph, Violet E.; *Peoples History of Ripley County, Indiana*; self-published, c. 1940, p. 124.
Revolutionary Soldiers Who Came to Ripley County
Ephraim Robbins entered service from Connecticut in 1775 and served fourteen months under Gen Putman and Lieut. Robbins, He was born in 1759 and died in 1836.

O'Byrne, Mrs. Roscoe C., comp. & ed.; *Roster Soldiers and Patriots of the American Revolution Buried in Indiana*; Published by Indiana Daughters of the American Revolution, 1938, Reprinted Genealogical Publishing Co., Baltimore MD, 1968, p. 314.
ROBBINS, EPHRAIM   Ohio County
Born – 1759, Kellingly, Connecticut.
Service – Entered service from Connecticut in 1775 and served 14 months under Gen. Putnam and Lieut. Robbins.
Proof – Pension claim S. 17052; Conn. Hist. Collections, vol. 12, p. 128 (1775-83).
Died – 1836. Buried Rising Sun, Ind. Stone. Name on bronze tablet in Versailles Court House. (Ripley Co.)
Married – Lusina Webster, Ch. Rhoda 1790-1859, m. Morris Merrill.
Collected by Mrs. A. B. Wycoff, Batesville, Indiana.

O'Byrne, Mrs. Roscoe C., comp.; *Roster of Soldiers and Patriots of the American Revolution Buried in Indiana, Vol. II*; Indiana Daughters of the American Revolution, 1980, p. 132.
Additional Data on some of the soldiers listed in Volume I.
Roster, Vol. I, p. 314
ROBBINS, EPHRAIM   Ohio County
Soldier died June 16, 1844. Wife died about 10 months before.

O'Byrne, comp. Mrs. Roscoe C., comp.; Roster of Soldiers and Patriots of the American Revolution Buried in Indiana, Vol. III; Indiana Daughters of the American Revolution, 1966, p. 74.
Additional data and/or corrections received since 1966 to the records of the soldiers and patriots listed in Rosters I and II.
ROBBINS, EPHRIAM   Roster I, p. 314   Ohio County
From Ohio Co. Court House Clerk's office, Rising Sun, Ind. Probate Order Book I, p. 1, the following heirs are listed: Rhoda m. Morris Merrill; Dau. Clarissa m. Elkannon Poeter (living in Marion Co., Ind.) and two sons, Daniel and Newman. By Mrs. A. G. Charlton, 310 Sunnyside Avenue, Aurora, Indiana 47001.

Hatcher, Patricia Law, Comp.; Abstract of Graves of Revolutionary Patriots (4 volumes); Pioneer Heritage Press, Dallas, TX, 1987, Vol. 3, p. 222.
Robbins Ephraim Old Cem, Rising Cem, Ohio Co IN 78

Gibbs, A.; Ripley County Historical Society Data on Revolutionary Soldiers, 1973 review.
Exact location of marker: no further information on grave site.
Additional comments: on Court House tablet
    Toph states: Buried at Rising Sun, Ohio Co. Ind.
    Ripley Co. Ind. Probate Book A, p. 135. Appl for pension Nov. 1832.

ROLLF (ROLFF), JAMES

Patriot: James Rolff
Birth: 1764
Married Spouse 1: Lucy (abt 1760 -)
Service state(s): NH Continental
Rank: Private
Proof of Service: Pension application
Pension application No.: S36876
Residences: Hollis, [Hillsborough Co.], NH; Windsor VT; Ripley Co., IN
Died: 6 Jun 1837   IN
Buried: Unknown
DAR Ancestor No.:None as of 7 Jun 2017.
Children: in 1820 – Joseph ag 23; Levi ag 20; Polly ag 25
Grandchildren: in 1820 – Ebenezer Hayden age 10; John Lathrop age 5.

Pension Application Abstracted from National Archives microfilm Series M804, Roll 2078, File S36876.
Pension abstract for – James Rolff
Service state(s): NH
Alternate spelling(s): Rolff
Date: 20 Apr 1818
County of: Windsor   State of: VT
Declaration made before a Judge or Court: County Court
Act of: 18 Mar 1818
Age: 54 yrs.
Residence when he entered service: Entered service in Hollis, NH
Residence now: Windsor Co., VT
Volunteer, Drafted, or Substitute: Enlisted both tours
Rank(s): Private
Statement of service-

Period	Duration	Names of General and Field Officers
Mar 1781	abt. 1 yrs.	NH Line, 2nd Regt., Col Reed, Capt. Jeremiah Fogg.
Mar 1782-Jun 1783	more than 1 yr.	Same corps

Discharge received: 8 Jun 1783 at Newburgh, NY
What became of it?: Lost
Statement is supported by –
Documentary proof: Has no evidence
&
Pension abstract for – James Rolff
Date: 31 Jul 1820
County of: Windsor   State of: VT
Declaration made before a Judge or Court: Supreme Court of Judicature
Declaration: includes schedule of property
Act of: 1 May 1820
Age: 56 yrs.
Residence now: Pomfret, Windsor Co., VT

Volunteer, Drafted, or Substitute: Enlisted at Hollis, NH

Statement of service-
Period	Duration	Names of General and Field Officers
Apr 1781 - 8 Jun 1783	2 yrs. 3 mos.	Company commanded by Capt. Jeremiah Fogg, Col. Reed, 2nd NH Regt, Continental Establishment.

Discharge received: 8 Jun 1783 at Newburgh, NH
Wife: Lucy   Wife's age: 58 yrs. - sickley
Names and ages of children: Joseph, 23 – of age; Levi, 2? – not perfectly healthy; Polly, 2? – her health bad; grandchildren Ebenezer Hagan [?], 10; John Lotrop [?], 5.
&
Additional notations in file –
Letter in file: Addressed to Commissioner of Pensions from E.D. Johnston, Dearborn Branch, 19 Sep 1837, advises James Rolph, pensioner, died 6 Jun 1837, two days after his semiannual payment became due.

Abstract of Final Payment Voucher; General Services Administration, Washington, DC

FINAL PAYMENT VOUCHER RECEIVED FROM
THE GENERAL ACCOUNTING OFFICE
NAME	ROLLF, James
AGENCY OF PAYMENT	INDIANA
DATE OF ACT	1818
DATE OF PAYMENT	1st Qr. 1838
DATE OF DEATH	Sept. 6, 1837
GENERAL SERVICES ADMINISTRATION	
National Archives and Records Service	NA-286
GSA-WASH DC 54-4891	November 1953

Revolutionary War Service Records; *National Archives Publication number M881, Compiled service records of soldiers who served in the American Army during the Revolutionary War, 1775-1783.*
https://www.fold3.com/image/18505230?terms=Rolf,%20James%20NH
New Hampshire 2d Regiment; Capt. Jeremiah Fogg's Co., commanded by Lieut. Col. George Reid.
Rolf, James – Private – Appears on the Company Muster Roll; Feb, Mar, Apr 1781, New Hampshire Villages, enlisted Mar 1, 81, term of enlistment – 3 years; Jan 82; Feb 82; Mar, Apr, May 82, term of enlistment - War; Jun, Jul, Aug Sep 82; Oct 82; Nov 82; Dec 82; Jan 83; Mar 83; Apr 83.

Senate Documents, Vol.9, No. 988, 63rd Congress, 3d Session, Washington, 1915; "Register of Certificates Issued by John Pierce, Esquire, Paymaster General and Commissioner of Army Accounts for the United States, to Officers and Soldiers of the Continental Army Under Act of July 4, 1783"; Seventeenth report of the

National Society of the Daughters of the American Revolution; Genealogical Publishing Co., Inc., Baltimore, MD, 1984. p. 436.
Men listed in this volume with the same name.

No. of Certificate	To whom issued	Amount
19015	Rolf, James	21.13
19698	Rolf, James	80.00
20975	Rolf, James	80.00
22151	Rolf, James	40.60

Clark, Murtie June; *The Pension List of 1820 [U.S. War Department]* Reprinted with an Index; Genealogical Publishing Co., Inc., Baltimore, 1991. Originally published 1820 as Letter from the Secretary of War, p. 329.
VERMONT
Names of the Revolutionary Pensioners which have been placed on the Roll of Vermont, under the Law of the 18th of March, 1818, from the passage thereof, to this day, inclusive of the Rank they held, and the Lines in which they served, viz:

Names	Rank	Line
Included in the list –		
James Rollf	private	New Hampshire

U.S. Department of Interior, Bureau of Land Management, General Land Office Records; Land Patent Search
Name: Rollf, James
Accession Nr. IN0280_.313; Document Type – State Volume Patent; Issue Date – 10/8/1834; Cancelled – No
Land Office – Jeffersonville; Authority – April 24, 1820: Sale-Cash Entry (3 Stat. 566); Document Nr. 4327; Total Acres – 40.00
Land Descriptions: State – IN; Meridian – 2ndPM; Twp-Rng – 009N – 011E; Aliquots – SE1/4SE1/4; Section – 8; County - Ripley

Ripley County Indiana, Recorder's Office, Tract Book 1, p. 52.
Rolf, James   28 Mar 1833   R11, T8, S8   40 acres

The Pension Roll of 1835 Volume III, The Mid-Western States, Indexed Edition, In Four Volumes; Genealogical Publishing Co., Inc., Baltimore, MD, Reprint 1968, p. 51.
Statement, &c. of Ripley county, Indiana.

INDIANA Names	Rank	Annual allow-ance.	Sums re-ceived	Description of service
James Rolf	Private	96.00	1,524 76	New Hamp. line

When placed on pension roll	Commencement of pension	Ages	Laws under which they were formerly placed on the pension roll; and remarks.
June 7, 1819	Ap'l 17, 1818	80	Transferred from Windsor County, Vermont

Toph, Violet E.; Peoples History of Ripley County, Indiana; self-published, c. 1940, p. 124.
Revolutionary Soldiers Who Came to Ripley County
James Rolff entered service from Vermont in 1781 and served two years. He moved to Indiana in 1822. He was born in 1764 and died in September 1837.

O'Byrne, Mrs. Roscoe C., comp. & ed.; Roster Soldiers and Patriots of the American Revolution Buried in Indiana; Published by Indiana Daughters of the American Revolution, 1938, Reprinted Genealogical Publishing Co., Baltimore MD, 1968, p. 317-318.
ROLFF, JAMES   Ripley County
Born – 1764.
Service – Entered from Vermont in 1781. Served 2 yrs.
Proof – Pension claim S. 36876.
Died – September, 1837. Name on bronze marker in Versailles Court House.
Many descendants still living in Ripley County, Indiana.
Collected by Mrs. A. B. Wycoff, Batesville, Indiana.

Gibbs, A.; Ripley County Historical Society Data on Revolutionary Soldiers, 1973 review.
Exact location of marker: no further information on grave site.
Additional comments: on Court House tablet
    O'Byrne (Indiana DAR) notes: Sept. 1837, Probate A Ripley Co. Ind., p. 111, 116. Dec'd by Jan. 1831 Court; admin Hazen Rolph (Rolf).

RUTLEDGE, PETER

Patriot: Peter Rutledge
Birth: 16 Feb 1760   Baltimore, MD
Married Spouse 1: Baltimore, MD
    Miriam (1765/70 – 1816)
Married Spouse 2: 10 Jun 1816, Harrison Co., KY
    Ruth Robinson (1782-)
Service state(s): MD
Rank: Private
Proof of Service: Pension application
Pension application No.: R9115
Residences: Baltimore, MD; Harrison Co., KY; Ripley Co., IN
Died: 29 May 1844   Ripley Co., IN
Buried: Old Middlefork (Benham Methodist), Benham, Brown Twp., Ripley
DAR Ancestor No.: A098750
Children of Ruth and Peter: Sarah, America Ann & Benjamin (twins), Eliza.

Pension Application Abstracted from National Archives microfilm Series M804, Roll 2106, File R9115.
Pension abstract for – Peter Rutledge
Service state(s): MD
Date: 13 May 1844
County of: Ripley   State of: IN
Declaration made before a Judge or Court: Probate Court
Act of: 7 Jun 1832
Age: 84 yrs.
Record of age: There is no Record, it was set down in a Bible but it is worn out.
Where and year born: Baltimore, MD   16 Feb 1760
Residence when he entered service: Baltimore, MD
Residence(s) since the war: Baltimore, MD; KY; last 24 yrs. IN, now Ripley Co.
Residence now: Ripley Co., IN
Volunteer, Drafted, or Substitute: Volunteered both tours
Rank(s): Private
Statement of service-

Period	Duration	Names of General and Field Officers
Jun 1776- abt 2 wks. bef. Christmas	6 mos.	Capt. Joshua Miles MD company
Last of Aug 1781	16 days	Col. Cockey Owen, Capt. John Talbot, Lt. John Demock, 1st Sgt. Joseph Sutton, was guarding military stores in Baltimore

Battles: No battles, some skirmishes with Tories
Discharge received: Written discharge from both tours
Signed by: 1st tour – Capt. Miles; 2nd tour – Capt. Talbot
What became of it?: they were destroyed by a Negro girl
Statement is supported by –
Clergyman: Meshack Hyatt
Persons in neighborhood who certify character: Jesse Holman

&

Pension abstract for – Ruth Rutledge widow of Peter Rutledge
Date: 12 Jan 1854
County of: Ripley   State of: IN
Declaration made before a Judge or Court: Justice of the Peace
Declaration: Her husband made a Declaration a few days before his death of his
    service, which is on file at Washington; she had papers showing his -
    service but his house was robbed at one time and they were stolen with
    other articles, and the thief burned them to prevent detection.
Act of: 7 Jul 1838 & 3 Feb 1853 & all other applicable acts
Age: 72 yrs.
Residence now: Ripley Co., IN
Statement is supported by –
Living witness, name(s): Sally [illegible surname], of Jefferson Co., IN, testified
    she knew Peter & Ruth, was present at their marriage, verified widow's
    statements.
Death of soldier: 29 May 1844   Ripley Co., IN   was 88 yrs. old
Widow's former name: Ruth Robinson
Marriage date and place: Jun 1816   Harrison Co., KY
Names and ages of children: Sarah Rutledge, age. 36; America & Benjamin
(twins), 34; Eliza, 31.
[Claim(s) denied because of lack of proof of service.]

Newman, Harry Wright; Maryland Revolutionary Records; Tuttle Publishing, Rutland, VT, 1928. p. 45, 122.
p. 45.

Maryland Revolutionary Pensioners

Name of Veteran	Birth	Rank	Establishment	Misc. facts and other State services
Rutledge, Peter	1760	Pvt.	Militia	-

p. 122.
Marriage Records

Peter Rutledge	Ruth Robinson	June 1816	Harrison Co., Ky.

Peden, Henry C., Jr., M.A.; Revolutionary Patriots of Baltimore Town and Baltimore County Maryland 1775-1783; Family Line Publications, Silver Spring, Md., 1988, p. 234, 332.
p. 234.
RUTLEDGE, PETER, Private in Col. Aquila Hall's Baltimore County Regiment in 1777. (TTT-13)
p. 332.
Colonel Aquila Hall's Baltimore County Regiment, 1776-1777
Captain Elijah Rutledge; Lieutenant Nathaniel Standiford; Lieutenant Robert Gwynn; Ensign Samuel Standifer; Sergeants Samuel Richardson, Thomas Gudgeon, Richard Jones.
Privates
[Included in list]   Peter Rutledge

[Peter did not mention living in Bourbon Co., KY, however his name is not common so it is possible he is the man in the following record. He was married in Harrison Co. which is adjacent to Bourbon Co. – mjm]

Clift, G. Glens, Assistant Secretary, Kentucky Historical Society, Comp.; <u>"Second Census" of Kentucky – 1800, A Privately Compiled and Published Enumeration of Tax Payers Appearing in the 79 Manuscript Volumes Extant of Tax Lists of the 42 Counties of Kentucky in Existence in 1800</u>; Genealogical Publishing Co., Baltimore, MD, 1966, p. 256.

Name	County	Tax List Date
Rutledg, Peter	Bourbon	7/23/ 1800

<u>Kentucky, County Marriages, 1797-1954</u>; Harrison, Kentucky, United States, Madison County Courthouse, Richmond; accessed 11 April 2016 from https://familysearch.org/ark:/61903/1:1:V5Z8-S2C.
Name: Peter Rutledge
Event Type: Marriage
Event Date: 10 Jun 1816
Event Place: Harrison, Kentucky, United States
Spouse's Name: Ruth Robinson
GS Film number: 000216880
Digital Folder Number: 004542900; Image Number: 00527
FHL microfilm 216,880

<u>Rejected or Suspended Applications for Revolutionary War Pensions</u>; Reprinted for Clearfield Company Inc. by Genealogical Publishing Co., Inc., Baltimore, MD, 1998. p.413.
A list of persons residing in Indiana who have applied for pensions under the act of July 7, 1832, whose claims have been suspended; prepared in conformity with the resolution of the Senate of the United States, September 16, 1850.

Names	Residence	Reason for suspension
Rutledge, Peter	Versailles, Ripley	For proof from the records of Annapolis.

<u>Ripley County Indiana, Recorder's Office, Tract Book 3</u>, p. 62.
Rutledge, Peter	14 May 1836	R12, T7, S31	40 acres

<u>U.S. Department of Interior, Bureau of Land Management, General Land Office Records; Land Patent Search</u>
Name: Rutledge, Peter
Accession Nr. IN2660_.136; Document Type – State Volume Patent; Issue Date – 8/2/1838; Cancelled – No
Land Office – Jeffersonville; Authority – April 24, 1820: Sale-Cash Entry (3 Stat. 566); Document Nr. 9180; Total Acres – 40.00
Land Descriptions: State – IN; Meridian – 2ndPM; Twp-Rng – 007N – 012E; Aliquots – NE1/4SE1/4; Section – 31; County - Ripley

1840 U. S. Census, Twp. not stated, Ripley County, IN; Roll 92; p. 127, 7th line from bottom of page.
Peter Rutledge
Males 15-19=1, Males 80-89=1, Females 15-19=1, Females 20-29=2, Females 50-59=1.

Toph, Violet E.; Peoples History of Ripley County, Indiana; self-published, c. 1940, p. 131.
Revolutionary Soldiers Who Came to Ripley County
Peter Rutledge entered the service from Maryland in 1776 under Captain Joshua Miles and served six months and sixteen days. He was born in 1756 and died May 29, 1844 in Ripley County. He married in 1816 Ruth somebody. He applied for a pension from Ripley County.

O'Byrne, Mrs. Roscoe C., comp. & ed.; Roster Soldiers and Patriots of the American Revolution Buried in Indiana; Published by Indiana Daughters of the American Revolution, 1938, Reprinted Genealogical Publishing Co., Baltimore MD, 1968, p. 321.
RUTLEDGE, PETER   Ripley County
Born – 1756.
Service – Entered service from Maryland in 1776 under Capt. Joshua Miles, served 6 mos. and 16 days.
Proof – Pension claim R-9115.
Died – May 29, 1844. Buried near Olean, Brown Twp. Name on Bronze tablet in Versailles Court House.
Married - 1818, Ruth -----. Ch. Sarah; America and Benjamin (twins); Elijah.
Collected by Mrs. A. B. Wycoff, Batesville, Indiana.

O'Byrne, Mrs. Roscoe C., comp.; Roster of Soldiers and Patriots of the American Revolution Buried in Indiana, Vol. II; Indiana Daughters of the American Revolution, 1980, p. 134.
Additional Data on some of the soldiers listed in Volume I.
Roster, Vol. I, p. 321.
RUTLEDGE, PETER   Ripley County
Born – Jan. 18, 1760/1.
Married – 1st, 1785, Mary E. Sanford, b. 1761, d. 1812, Harrison Co., Ky.
Ch. Abraham, b. 1786, m. Mary E. Huffman; Peter; Edward; James; John; Pollyanna.

Gibbs, A.; Ripley County Historical Society Data on Revolutionary Soldiers, 1973 review.
Exact location of marker: Barth Cemetery, Brown Tw. Ripley Co. Ind.
Comments: on Court House tablet
    Age 80-90 in 1840 census Ripley Co. Ind.

Tombstone Location: Old Middlefork (Benham Methodist), Benham, Brown Twp., Ripley

Tombstone Inscription:
PETER
RUTLEDGE
PVT
STATE MILITIA
REV. WAR
FEB 16 1760
MAY 29 1844

RYAN, GEORGE

Patriot: George Ryan
Birth: 1756
Married Spouse 1:
Service state(s): VA Continental Line
Rank: Private
Proof of Service: Pension Application
Pension application No.: S36879
Residences: VA; NW Territory; Dearborn Co., IN; Switzerland Co., IN; Ripley Co., IN
Died: 10 Mar 1831   Ripley Co., IN
Buried: Unknown
DAR Ancestor No.: None as of 7 Jun 2017.

Pension Application Abstracted from National Archives microfilm Series M804, Roll 106, File S36879.
Pension abstract for – George Ryan
Service state(s): VA Continental Line
Date: 4 Nov 1819
County of: Dearborn   State of: IN
Declaration made before a Judge or Court: Circuit Court
Act of: 18 Mar 1818
Age: 64 yrs.
Rank(s): Private
Statement of service-

Period	Duration	Names of General and Field Officers
1776	2 yrs.	VA 8th Regt. of Infantry Continental Establishment, Capt. Clarke, commanded by Col. Muhlenberg
	3 yrs.	VA 4th Regt. Continental Establishment, company commanded by Capt. Abraham Kirkpatrick, Col. John Neville & different colonels.

Battles: White Plains, Brandywine, Germantown, Monmouth, taken prisoner at Siege of Charleston.
Discharge received: Yes, 2nd tour
Signed by: Col. Buford at Charlotte
What became of it?: Lost
&
Pension abstract for – George Ryan
Date: 30 Oct 1820
County of: Switzerland   State of: IN
Declaration made before a Judge or Court: Circuit Court
Declaration: Served 5 yrs. in the VA Line of the Continental Establishment, files will be found in War Dept. office; Virginia Land Patent granted to VA Line of Continental Establishment, recorded in General Land Office, Vol. 8, p. 14, dated 30 Aug 1816, No. 6071.

Act of: 1 May 1820
Statement is supported by – See declaration
&
Pension abstract for – George Ryan
Date: 31 Oct 1820
County of: Jefferson				State of: IN
Declaration made before a Judge or Court: Circuit Court
Declaration: Provides schedule of assets & testimony of service.
Act of: 1 May 1820
Residence now: Ripley County
Rank(s):
Statement of service-

Period	Duration	Names of General and Field Officers
1776	2 yrs.	Under Capt. Jonathan Clark, 8th VA Regt., commanded by Col. Peter Muhlenberg.
	3 yrs.	Under Capt. John Steed, commanded by Capt. Abraham Kirkpatrick, then under Capt. James Curry.

Wife: Not named, cripple caused by cancer		Wife's age: 52 yrs.
Names and ages of children: Not named – Son age 18; Son age 14; Daughter age 16; Daughter, a widow with one child.
&
Pension abstract for – George Ryan
Date: 21 Jan 1825
County of: Switzerland				State of: IN
Declaration made before a Judge or Court: Justice of the Peace
Declaration: He was placed on the Pension Roll in the State of Indiana, he received a certificate of that fact on 5 Mar 1824 near Versailles, the same was trampled and buried in the wet ground near that place as he was returning home.
&
Additional notation in file: Soldier died 10 March 1831, place not stated.

Abstract of Final Payment Voucher; General Services Administration, Washington, DC

FINAL PAYMENT VOUCHER RECEIVED FROM
THE GENERAL ACCOUNTING OFFICE
NAME				RYAN, GEORGE
AGENCY OF PAYMENT		INDIANA
DATE OF ACT			1818
DATE OF PAYMENT		2nd Qr. 1833
DATE OF DEATH			died in 1831
GENERAL SERVICES ADMINISTRATION
National Archives and Records Service		NA-286
GSA-WASH DC 54-4891				November 1953

Revolutionary War Service Records; National Archives Publication number M881, Compiled service records of soldiers who served in the American Army during the Revolutionary War, 1775-1783.
https://www.fold3.com/image/23239879;
8 Virginia Regiment
Ryan, George – Private/Corporal
4 Virginia Regiment
Ryan, George – Corporal/Corporal
https://www.fold3.com/image/22206945?terms=ryan,%20george%20va
8th Battalion, Capt. Richard Campbell's company, commanded by Col. Abraham Bowman.
Ryan, George – Private – Muster Roll for May-Jun 77; Jul 77; Aug 77.
4 Virginia Regiment, Capt. Abraham Kirkpatrick's Co., commanded by John Nevill.
Ryan, George – Private – Muster Roll for Sep 78; Oct-Nov 78; Dec 78.
Roll of Capt. Abraham Kirkpatrick's Company of the 4, 8, 12 Virginia Regt. of Foot, commanded by Col. James Wood.
Ryan, George – appears with the rank of Colonel, time of service – 3 years; 4, 8 & 12 Regt., Nov, Dec 77, Jan, Feb, Mar, Apr, May, Jun 78; Jan, Feb, Mar, Apr, May, Jun, Jul, Aug, Sep, Oct, Nov 79.

Revolutionary War Land Office Military Certificates; Records of the Executive Branch, Land Office (Record Group 4), microfilm reels 1-38; Library of Virginia, Richmond, VA.
In order to receive bounty lands for Revolutionary War service, a soldier or sailor must have served continuously for at least three years in a Virginia or Continental unit. Service in the militia did not count. The certificates were numbered 1-9926 and cover the period July 14, 1782-August 5, 1876. The warrant specified the amount of lands to be received and directed the surveyor of lands to set aside that quantity of land in the Virginia Military District in Kentucky and Ohio.
Ryan, George   Rank: Private   Military Certificate number: LO 2974

Wardell, Patrick G., comp.; Virginia/West Virginia Genealogical Data From Revolutionary War Pension and Bounty Land Warrant Records, Vol. 4 – Nabors through Rymer; Heritage Books, Inc., Bowie, MD, 1988, p. 285.
Ryan, George, esf 1776 in 8th VA Regiment; VA BLW6071 issued 8/30/1816 (land in OH); PN ae 64 Dearborn Co, IN, 1819; res there 1820, occupation farmer, with w ae 52, s ae 18, s ae 4, d ae 16, & widowed d (ae not given) and her ch; sol dd 3/10/31. F=S36979 [should be S36879] R2106

Bockstruck, Lloyd DeWitt; Revolutionary War Bounty Land Grants Awarded by State Governments; Genealogical Publishing Co., IN, Baltimore, MD, 1996, p. 462.
Ryan, George, Va., Private. 9 Dec. 1783. 100 acres.

Ripley County, Indiana Deed Records Vol. A, 11 Aug 1818-29 Jan 1827
Page(s): 186-189.
Abstract of Deed/Patent for: George Ryan

Purchaser (Grantee) or Seller (Grantor)?: Purchaser
Purchased from: William Jolly and Betsy (dower) his wife of Ripley Co.
State & county where recorded: Ripley Co., Indiana
Date entered: 2 Jul 1825   Recorded: 2 Jul 1825
Description: More or less being part of the northeast quarter of Section 8,
    Township 6, North of Range 12 East, containing one hundred acres.
Amount paid: Five hundred dollars ($500.00).
Name(s) of Witnesses: William Laycock, Henry Boalman, Absalom Laycock.

The Pension Roll of 1835 Volume IV, The Mid-Western States, Indexed Edition, *In Four Volumes; Genealogical Publishing Co., Inc., Baltimore, MD, Reprint 1968, p. 42.*
Statement, &c. of Jefferson county, Indiana.

INDIANA Names	Rank	Annual allow-ance.	Sums re-ceived	Description of service
George Ryan	Private	96.00	1,089 78	Virginia line

When placed on pension roll	Commencement of pension	Ages	Laws under which they were formerly placed on the pension roll; and remarks.
Dec 29, 1820	Nov 4, 1819	75	Died March 10, 1831.

Ripley Co., IN Probate Order Book, Vol. A, 19 Nov 1818-Feb. 1837, p. 128.
The Clerk of this Court now lay before the Court and inventory of the Personal goods of George Ryan deceased, filed by John Ryan Administrator of the said deceased in the Clerks office May 10 th 1832. Which amounted to Ninety one Dollars Eighty one & 1/4 cents--- $91.81-1/4.

Mrs. Roscoe C. O'Byrne, comp.; *Roster of Soldiers and Patriots of the American Revolution Buried in Indiana, Vol. I;* Indiana Daughters of the American Revolution, 1981, p. 321-322.
p. 321
RYAN, GEORGE   Jefferson County
Born – 1756.
Service – Served on Continental Establishment about 5 yrs. Enlisted in 1776,
    Capt. Jonathan Clark, 8th Vir. Regt., Col. Peter Muhlenburg. Served 2
    yrs. Enlisted under John Steed for 3 yrs. Capt. Abraham Kirkpatrick,
    Capt.. James Curry. Discharged by Col. Bluford at Charlotte, S.C.
Proof – Oath of service, Jeff. Co. Records, Order bk. B-352.
p.322
Died – March 10, 1831.
Married – Had wife, and four ch. in 1820.
Collected by John Paul Chapter D.A.R.

Mrs. Roscoe C. O'Byrne, comp.; Roster of Soldiers and Patriots of the American Revolution Buried in Indiana, Vol. III; Indiana Daughters of the American Revolution, 1966, p. 74.

RYAN, GEORGE   Roster I. pp. 321-322   Ripley County instead of
                                                                    Jefferson County

Proof – Ripley Co., Ind. Probate Book C, Minutes, p. 203 dated Feb. 23, 1832
    Shows that George Ryan died in Ripley Co. leaving no widow. Probate Minutes also gives the following children and heirs: John Ryan, Elijah Ryan; Abraham Ryan; Isaac Ryan; Seth Low and wife; Isaac Hull and wife; Isaac Dowers and wife; Joel Robins and wife.

Died – Place and burial unknown.

By Mrs. David Gibbs, RR #2, Box 56, Holton, Indiana 47023.

STEPHENS (STEVENS), SAMUEL

Patriot: Samuel Stephens
Birth: Jun 1758 Carlisle, Cumberland Co., PA
Married Spouse 1: 26 Aug 1779, Headwaters Peter's Creek, VA
                                          Mary X (1760-prob 1846)
Service state(s): PA
Rank: Private, Patriotic Service
Proof of Service: Pension application
Pension application No.: W22332
Residences: Cumberland Co., PA; Washington Co., PA (was then VA); Mercer Co., KY; IL; Ripley Co., IN; Montgomery Co., IN
Died: 21 Jul 1834   Montgomery Co., IN
Buried: Unknown
DAR Ancestor No.: A109127

Pension Application Abstracted from National Archives microfilm Series M804, Roll 2280, File W22332.
Pension abstract for –
Service state(s): PA
Alternate spelling(s): Stevens
Date: 12 Aug 1833
County of: Ripley   State of: IN
Declaration made before a Judge or Court: Probate Court
Act of: 7 Jun 1832
Age: 75 yrs. last June
Record of age: Has no record, speak from what my parents told me.
Where and year born: Carlisle, PA   Jun 1758
Residence when he entered service: Washington Co., PA
Residence(s) since the war: Head waters of Peter's Creek (then VA, now PA); Mercer Co., KY; State of Illinois; Ripley Co., IN.
Residence now: Ripley Co., IN
Volunteer, Drafted, or Substitute: 1st tour – Drafted; 2nd tour – Substitute for Anthony Boli; 3rd tour - Drafted
Rank(s): Private
Statement of service-

Period	Duration	Names of General and Field Officers
Mar 1777 - Jul 1777	3 mos.	Col. James Cannon, Maj. Gabriel Cox, Capt. James Wright, 1st Lt. William Stevens in the PA Line.
Late 1777	2 mos.	Same officers
May – Jul 1778	2 mos.	Former officers with some changes
Not stated	2 mos.	Same

Battles: No battles
Discharge received: Not written
Statement is supported by –
Evidence: Traditionary
Documentary proof: None

Person now living who can testify to service: Ephraim Wilson – affidavit given.
Clergyman: Meshack Hyatt
Persons in neighborhood who certify character: John McClain
&
Pension abstract for – Mary Stephens widow of Samuel Stevens
Date: 17 Jul 1840
County of: Montgomery   State of: IN
Declaration made before a Judge or Court: Circuit Court
Act of: 7 Jul 1838
Age: 80 yrs.
Residence now: Montgomery Co., IN
Death of soldier: 21 Jul 1834
Marriage date and place: 26 Aug 1779 Headwaters of Peter's Creek, VA, then the backwoods.
Proof of marriage: She does not believe there is any record except as kept by Mr. Heway the minister of the Church of England who married them; she * has no family record nor can she recollect what became of the record of her children's ages.
Names and ages of children: Mary Stephens b. 3 Aug 1780, marr. Joseph Harber; [probably others].
&
Pension abstract for – Mary Stephens
Date: 18 Nov 1846 & 21 Jul 1848
County of: Schuyler   State of: IL
Declaration made before a Judge or Court: Justice of the Peace
Declaration: Request transfer to Roll of State of Illinois
Act of: 5 Mar 1843
Age: 86 yrs.in 1846 & 88 in 1848.
Residence now: Schuyler Co., IL

Abstract of Final Payment Voucher; General Services Administration, Washington, DC

LAST   FINAL PAYMENT VOUCHER RECEIVED FROM
          THE GENERAL ACCOUNTING OFFICE
NAME   Stephens, Samuel
AGENCY OF PAYMENT   INDIANA
DATE OF ACT   1832
DATE OF PAYMENT   3d Qr. 1834
DATE OF DEATH   July 21, 1834
GENERAL SERVICES ADMINISTRATION
National Archives and Records Service   NA-286
GSA-WASH DC 54-4891   November 1953

Senate Documents, Vol.9, No. 988, 63rd Congress, 3d Session, Washington, 1915; "Register of Certificates Issued by John Pierce, Esquire, Paymaster General and Commissioner of Army Accounts for the United States, to Officers and Soldiers of the Continental Army Under Act of July 4, 1783"; Seventeenth report of the

National Society of the Daughters of the American Revolution; Genealogical Publishing Co., Inc., Baltimore, MD, 1984. p. 482.
Men listed in this volume with the same name.

No. of Certificate	To whom issued	Amount
16669	Stevens, Samuel	18.70

Stemmons, John D and E. Diane (comp);*Pennsylvania in 1780, A Statewide Index of Circa 1780 Pennsylvania Tax Lists*, Self- published, 1978, p. 174.

STEVENS	SAMUEL	CUMB:CR [Carlisle Twp.]

Register of the Kentucky Historical Society; Early Kentucky Tax Records; Clearfield Publishing, Baltimore, Md., 1999; p. 186.
Mercer County Tax List – 1789
List of Taxable property within the District of Wm. Green commissioner for the county of Mercer for the year, '89.

Persons Charged With The Tax	Horses	Cattle
Stephens, Samuel	-	-

Clift, G. Glens, Assistant Secretary, Kentucky Historical Society, Comp.; *"Second Census" of Kentucky – 1800, A Privately Compiled and Published Enumeration of Tax Payers Appearing in the 79 Manuscript Volumes Extant of Tax Lists of the 42 Counties of Kentucky in Existence in 1800*; Genealogical Publishing Co., Baltimore, MD, 1966, p. 281.

Name	County	Tax List Date
Stephens, Samuel	Mercer	1800

[This record may be for Samuel who may have been in Dearborn County, IN as early as 1807. – mjm]
Census of Indiana Territory for 1807; Indiana Historical Society, 1980, p. 26.
A list of free males above the age of twenty one in Dearborn County in March 1807.

Persons Names	Number
Samuel Stevens	488

The Pension Roll of 1835 Volume IV, The Mid-Western States, Indexed Edition, In Four Volumes; Genealogical Publishing Co., Inc., Baltimore, MD, Reprint 1968, p. 87.
Statement, &c. of Ripley county, Indiana.

INDIANA Names	Rank	Annual allowance.	Sums received	Description of service
Samuel Stephens	Private	30.00	90 00	Va. State troops

When placed on pension roll	Commencement of pension	Ages	Laws under which they were formerly placed on the pension roll; and remarks.
Oct 1, 1833	March 4, 1831	69	-

Toph, Violet E.; <u>Peoples History of Ripley County, Indiana</u>; self-published, c. 1940, p.124.
Revolutionary Soldiers Who Came to Ripley County
Samuel Stephens (or Stevens) entered service from Pennsylvania in 1777 and served nine months. He died in 1834.

O'Byrne, Mrs. Roscoe C., comp. & ed.; <u>Roster Soldiers and Patriots of the American Revolution Buried in</u> Indiana; Published by Indiana Daughters of the American Revolution, 1938, Reprinted Genealogical Publishing Co., Baltimore MD, 1968, p. 343.
STEVENS (STEPHENS), SAMUEL   Ripley County
Born – June, 1768, Carlisle, Pennsylvania.
Service – Drafted March, 1777. Marched against Shawnees and Wyandottes under Col. John Cannon, 3 mos. Served 3 mos. from July, 1777, as substitute for Anthony Boll under same officers. May, 1778, served 3 mos. at Meutuers Bottom. Total of 9 mos.
Proof – Pension claim W. 22332.
Died – July 1, 1834. Name on bronze tablet in Versailles Court House.
Married – Mary ----- b. 1760. Ch. Mary b. 1780, m. Joseph Harber; other Ch.
Collected by Mrs. A. B. Wycoff, Batesville, Indiana.

Gibbs, A.; <u>Ripley County Historical Society Data on Revolutionary Soldiers</u>, 1973 review.
Exact location of marker: no further on grave site.
Additional comments: on Court House tablet
        Ripley Probate Book A., p. 138, Appl. for pension Aug. 1833.

STEWART (STEWARD), CHARLES

Patriot: Charles Steward
Birth: 1759 VA
Married Spouse 1: Ann X *[see note 1.]*
(b. abt. 1760/1762 VA, d. 5/7 Nov 1837 Ripley Co., IN)
Service state(s): VA
Rank: Private, Marine
Proof of Service: Pension application
Pension application No.: S16261
Residences: Spotsylvania Co., VA; KY; Switzerland Co., IN; Ripley Co., IN
Died: 4 or 6 Feb 1845 Switzerland Co., IN
Buried: Cross Plains Methodist Church Cemetery, Cross Plains,
Brown Twp., Ripley Co., IN
DAR Ancestor No.: A135172

[Note: National Society Daughters of the American Revolution has accepted his wife as being Ann X (surname unknown). <u>Roster of Soldiers and Patriots of the American Revolution Buried in Indiana, Vol. I</u> by O'Byrne shows wife is Nancy Ann Beckley. His son, Charles, married Marian (Mary Ann) Beckley on 20 Mar 1826 in Switzerland Co., IN. Did O'Byrne confused the wife of the son with the wife of the patriot? – mjm]

<u>Pension Application Abstracted from National Archives microfilm Series M804, Roll 2289, File S16261</u>.
Pension abstract for – Charles Steward
Service state(s): VA
Alternate spelling(s):
Date: 13 Aug 1832
County of: Ripley   State of: IN
Declaration made before a Judge or Court: Probate Court
Act of: 7 Jun 1832
Age: 73 years
Where and year born: Not stated
Residence when he entered service: Spotsylvania Co., VA
Residence(s) since the war: Not stated
Residence now: Ripley Co., IN
Volunteer, Drafted, or Substitute: Enlisted with Lieut. Stubblefield
Rank(s): Private, Marine
Statement of service-

Period	Duration	Names of General and Field Officers
1775		VA Line, 1st Regt. (he thinks), Lieut. Stubblefield, Capt. Gabriel Jones, Col. Gibson.
	18 mos.	Marine Service in neighboring capes & bays.
20 Dec 1776	3 yrs.	Aforesaid regt., under Lieut. Stubblefield.

Capt. G. Jones, Co. Gibson. To Georgetown, MC where he was taken sick & received a furlough. Recovered, returned, sick again, received a furlough to return home. Did not join army again.

Battles: None stated
Discharge received: Furloughed
Signed by: Peter Stubblefield
Documentary proof: Certification from S/Peter Stubblefield: "This is to Certify that the Bearer Charles Steward a soldier Colonel Geo. Gibsons Regiment from Virginia Listed with me the 20th day of December 1776 for the term of 3 years."
&
Certification from S/Peter Stubblefield, Off., Colo. Gibson' Regiment: "George Town in Maryland 18th October 1777 – The Bearer hereof Charles steward a Soldier in my Company not being able to do Duty by having a Dropsical Disorder on him I have given him leave to Return home and there to Stay till he gets able to do duty at which time he is to join me."
&
Letter from War Dept. in Pension File – Charles Steward

Mrs. Iva Hisle	March 6, 1936
410 East Main Street	Charles Steward – S.16261
Madison, Indiana	BA-J/AWF

Dear Madam:
    Reference is made to your letter in which you request the Revolutionary War record of Charles Stewart, who was pensioned in 1832, while living in Indiana.

    The data furnished herein were obtained from the papers on file in the pension claim, S.16261, based upon the service of Charles Steward in the Revolutionary War.

    The date and place of birth of this soldier are not given, nor are the names of his parents stated.

    Charles Steward (as the name is found in the claim), while residing in Spotsylvania County, Virginia, enlisted in 1775 and marched down to Hobbs Hole under Lieutenant Stubblefield, and there went into the marine service and served eighteen months. He enlisted December 20, 1776, for three years, served in Captain Gabriel Jones' company, Colonel George Gibson's Virginia regiment, was furloughed, May 17, 1779 on account of sickness.

    He was allowed pension on his application executed August 13, 1833, then aged seventy-three years and living in Ripley County, Indiana.

    The papers in this claim contain no reference to the family of Charles Steward.

                                  Very truly yours
                                      A.D. HILLER
                    Executive Assistant to the Administrator

Abstract of Final Payment Voucher; General Services Administration, Washington, DC
      FINAL PAYMENT VOUCHER RECEIVED FROM
      THE GENERAL ACCOUNTING OFFICE
NAME   Stewart, Charles
AGENCY OF PAYMENT   Indiana
DATE OF ACT   1832
DATE OF PAYMENT   4th Qr. 1845
DATE OF DEATH   Feb 6, 1845
GENERAL SERVICES ADMINISTRATION
National Archives and Records Service   NA-286
GSA-WASH DC 54-4891   November 1953

Revolutionary War Service Records; National Archives Publication number M881, *Compiled service records of soldiers who served in the American Army during the Revolutionary War, 1775-1783.*
https://www.fold3.com/image/21895250
1 Virginia State Regiment; Capt. John Camp's company, commanded by Col. George Gibson.
Steward, Charles – Private – Muster Roll taken to 12 Oct, 12 Nov 77, to 1 Dec 1777; Jan, Feb, Mar, Apr, May, Jun 1778.

Gwathmey, John H.; Historical Register of Virginians in the Revolution, Soldiers, Sailors, Marines, 1775-1783; The Dietz Press, Richmond, VA, 1938, p. 741.
Steward, Charles (Stuart) 1 CL, 1 Va. State Reg., 1 and 10 CL, 3 and 4 CL, 7 CL, 15 CL.
Stewart, Charles, (Stuart) 1 CL, 1 Va. State Reg., 1 and 10 CL, 3 CL, 3 and 4 CL, 5 CL, 5 and 9 CL, 15 CL.

Revolutionary War Land Office Military Certificates; Records of the Executive Branch, Land Office (Record Group 4), microfilm reels 1-38; Library of Virginia, Richmond, VA.
In order to receive bounty lands for Revolutionary War service, a soldier or sailor must have served continuously for at least three years in a Virginia or Continental unit. Service in the militia did not count. The certificates were numbered 1-9926 and cover the period July 14, 1782-August 5, 1876. The warrant specified the amount of lands to be received and directed the surveyor of lands to set aside that quantity of land in the Virginia Military District in Kentucky and Ohio.
Stewart, Charles   Rank: Private   Military Certificate number: LO 4768
Stewart, Charles   Rank: Ensign   Military Certificate number: LO 6308

Bockstruck, Lloyd DeWitt; Revolutionary War Bounty Land Grants Awarded by State Governments; Genealogical Publishing Co., IN, Baltimore, MD, 1996, p. 505.
Stewart, Charles, Va. Private. 6 Feb 1797 100 acres.

Brumbaugh, Gaius Marcus, M.D, M.s., Litt.D; Revolutionary War Records – Virginia, Virginia Army and Navy Forces with Bounty Land Warrants for

Virginia Military District of Ohio, and Virginia Military Script, from Federal and State Archives; Genealogical Publishing Co., Inc., Baltimore, 1995, p. 116.
List of Officers of the Army and Navy, Who Have Received Lands from Virginia for Revolutionary Services; The Quantity Received, The Time of Service for which each Officer Received Land, &c. Down to September, 1833.
Stewart, Charles   Ensign   Cont'l   2666-2/3 Apr. 10, 1819   3 years
p. 503
Virginia Military Land Warrants, Virginia District of Ohio, Granted for Revolutionary War Services, State Continental Line, Beginning August 8, 1872.

Number	Warrantees	Rank & Service	
4768	Stewart, Charles	Soldier	3 years

p. 617
Original Bounty Land Warrants Located in Virginia Military District in Ohio
Stewart, Charles

Pennsylvania Archives, Series 3, Volume XXIII. p. 597.
Muster Rolls of the Navy and Line, Militia and Rangers, 1775-1783 with <u>List of Pensioners, 1818-1832.</u>
Statement Showing the Names of Pennsylvanians Residing in the State of Indiana, Who Have Been Inscribed on the Pension List under the Act of Congress Passed June 7th, 1832.
Dearborn County   Reamer, David, artificer P.M., July 30, 1833; 80.

Senate Documents, Vol.9, No. 988, 63rd Congress, 3d Session, Washington, 1915; "Register of Certificates Issued by John Pierce, Esquire, Paymaster General and Commissioner of Army Accounts for the United States, to Officers and Soldiers of the Continental Army Under Act of July 4, 1783"; <u>Seventeenth report of the National Society of the Daughters of the American Revolution</u>; Genealogical Publishing Co., Inc., Baltimore, MD, 1984. p. 483.
Men listed in this volume with the name Charles Steward & Charles Stewart & Charles Stuart.
<u>Author's note:</u> Due to the large number of men with this name they are not listed here. "Pierce's Register" is available in most large libraries.

U.S. Department of Interior, Bureau of Land Management, General Land Office Records; Land Patent Search – accessed 27 June 2012.
STEWART, CHARLES
Accession Nr. CV-0022-487; Document Type – Credit Volume Patent; State - Indiana; Issue Date – 10/3/1814; Cancelled – No
Names on Document: Stewart, Charles; Lane, Joseph
Land Office – Jeffersonville; Authority – April 24, 1820 Sale-Cash Entry (3 Stat. 566); Total Acres – 0.00
Land Description: State - IN; Meridian – 2nd PM; Aliquots – 005N-011E; Section - 19; County - Jefferson
&
Accession Nr. CV-0040-205; Document Type – Credit Volume Patent; State - Indiana; Issue Date – 7/15/1818; Cancelled – No
Names on Document: Stewart, Charles; Lander, John

Land Office – Jeffersonville; Authority – April 24, 1820 Sale-Cash Entry (3 Stat. 566); Total Acres – 0.00
Land Description: State - IN; Meridian – 2nd PM; Aliquots – 005N-012E; Section - 9; County - Switzerland
&
Accession Nr. CV-0040-207; Document Type – Credit Volume Patent; State - Indiana; Issue Date – 7/15/1818; Cancelled – No
Names on Document: Stewart, Charles; Lander, John
Land Office – Jeffersonville; Authority – April 24, 1820 Sale-Cash Entry (3 Stat. 566); Total Acres – 0.00
Land Description: State - IN; Meridian – 2nd PM; Aliquots – 005N-012E; Section - 4; County - Switzerland
&
Accession Nr. CV-0053-362; Document Type – Credit Volume Patent; State - Indiana; Issue Date – 12/6/1820; Cancelled – No
Land Office – Jeffersonville; Authority – April 24, 1820 Sale-Cash Entry (3 Stat. 566); Total Acres – 160.00
Land Description: State - IN; Meridian – 2nd PM; Aliquots – 006N-012E; Section - 21; County - Ripley

Ripley County Indiana, Recorder's Office, Tract Book 3, p. 55.
Stewart, C.   27 Jul 1820   R12, T6, S21   160 acres

Ripley County, Indiana Deed Records Vol. C., 21 Sep 1832 - 4 Feb 1834,
Page 407
Abstract of Deed/Patent for: Charles Stewart senior and Ann (dower) his wife
Purchaser (Grantee) or Seller (Grantor)?: Seller
Sold to: John Copelin
State & county where recorded: Ripley Co., Indiana
Date entered: 26 Nov 1832
Recorded: 29 May 1833
Description: Tract of parcel of land; North west quarter of Section 21, Township 6 North of Range 12 East; containing 160 acres; patented in the name of Charles Stewart assignee of James F. Hukill; land sold at Jeffersonville; patent dated at the city of Washington 6 December 1828, signed by James Monroe, President of the United States.
Amount paid: One hundred twenty five dollars ($125.00)
Name(s) of Witnesses: James Witham & William Cullough

A Census of Pensioners for Revolutionary or Military Services with their Names, Ages, and Places of Residence Under the Act for Taking the Sixth Census in 1840; Genealogical Publishing Co., Inc., Baltimore, Maryland, 1965. p.185.

INDIANA, SWITZERLAND, PLEASANT Names of Pensioners for Revolutionary or Military services	Ages	Names of heads of families with whom pensioner resided June 1, 1840
Charles Steward	82	Charles Steward

1840 U.S. Census, Indiana, Switzerland, Pleasant Twp., National Archives, Series: M704 Roll: 95 Pg: 131.
Charles Stewart age 80-90; others in household 1 male under 5, 2 males 5-10, 1 male 10-15, 1 male 30-40, 1 female 10-15, 1 female 30-40.
Pensioners for Revolutionary or Military Services Included in the Foregoing

Names	Age
Charles Steward	82

Ripley County, Indiana Will Records vol. B, June 1839-May 1862; p. 59-60.
Abstract of will and administration for: Charles Stewart Sen'r
Date and place will was made: 7 Mar 1843   Ripley Co., IN
Witnesses to will: Samuel Copeland, James Lowell
Names of executors: son-in-law John Copeland, son John Stewart
Place of death: Ripley Co., IN
Date recorded: 11 Aug 1845
Names of heirs and others mentioned in will and relationship if shown: Heirs of my daughter Sally Copeland dec'd; son-in-law John Copeland; daughter Rebecca Hukill; son-in-law James Hukill; son John Stewart; Charles Stewart;

Ripley County Indiana Complete Probate Record Book Vol. C., Feb. 1846- Nov. 1846; p. 237-243.
Abstract of will and administration for: Charles Stewart, Senior
Place will was made: Ripley County
Witnesses to will: Samuel Copeland & James Laswell, a resident of Henry Co. IN
Names of executors: son-in-law John Copeland & son John Stewart
Place of death: Ripley Co., IN
Date recorded: 11 Aug 1845
Bonded by and amount of bond: William Bassett $500.00.
Names of heirs and others mentioned in will and relationship if shown: Heirs of
    oldest daughter Sally Copeland, deceased; their father John Copeland;
    heirs of daughter Rebecca Hukill, their father James F. Hukill; son
    Charles Stewart; son John Stewart
Date of division & disbursement, or final return: 13 Aug 1846

O'Byrne, Mrs. Roscoe C., comp. & ed.; Roster Soldiers and Patriots of the American Revolution Buried in Indiana; Published by Indiana Daughters of the American Revolution, 1938, Reprinted Genealogical Publishing Co., Baltimore MD, 1968, p. 343.
STEWART, CHARLES   Jefferson County
Born - 1759
Service – While residing in Spotsylvania Co., Vir., enlisted in 1775, marched to Hobbs Hole under Lt. Stubblefield, went into the marine service, served 18 mos. Enlisted Dec. 20, 1776, for 3 yrs. served in Capt. Gabriel Jones' CO., Col. George Gibson's Regt. Was furloughed May 17, 1779, on account of sickness, Proof – Penn. Archives, Series 2, vol. 10, p. 637. Pension claim S16261.
Died – 1840, in Switzerland Co. May be buried across the line in Ripley or Switzerland.   Married – Ann ------.
Collected by John Paul Chapter D.A.R., Madison, Indiana.

O'Byrne, Mrs. Roscoe C., comp. & ed.; *Roster Soldiers and Patriots of the American Revolution Buried in Indiana; Published by Indiana Daughters of the American Revolution, 1938, Reprinted Genealogical Publishing Co., Baltimore MD, 1968, p. 343.*
Stewart, Charles
b. 1759; d. 1840, Switzerland Co., IN; may be bur. across the line in Ripley or Switzerland Co; m. Ann ____.

O'Byrne, Mrs. Roscoe C., comp.; *Roster of Soldiers and Patriots of the American Revolution Buried in Indiana, Vol. I; Indiana Daughters of the American Revolution, 1980, p. 76.*
From a Roster of Revolutionary Ancestors of the Indiana Daughters of the American Revolution, Vol. 1, p. 608.
STEWART, CHARLES   Roster 1, p. 343   Ripley County
Proof – Ripley Co., Ind. Probate C:375 dated Nov. 3, 1845.
Died – Feb. 4, 1845 age 85 yrs., 3 mos. Buried Methodist Church, Cross Plains, Ripley Co., Ind.
Married – Nancy Ann Beckley d. Nov. 7, 1837 age 77.   *[See Note 1.]*
Children – Sally m. John Copeland; Rebecca m. James Hukill; Charles; John d. Oct. 8, 1852 age 50; Levi d. Mar. 5, 1847 age 18.
By Mrs. David Gibbs, RR #2, Box 58, Holton, Indiana 47023.

Gibbs, A.; *Ripley County Historical Society Data on Revolutionary Soldiers, 1973 review.*
Exact location of marker: Cross Plains United Methodist Church, on east side of R. 129 in Sec 28 T6 R12, Brown Tw. Ripley Co. Ind.
Type of marker: Gov't
Date placed: Sept. 1980
Placed by: Ross' Run Chapter Daughters of the American Revolution
Additional comments: listed in Indiana [DAR] Roster as of Jefferson Co. Ind., but he was buried in Ripley Co.

Tombstone Location: Cross Plains Methodist Church Cemetery,
                           Cross Plains, Brown Twp., Ripley Co., IN

Tombstone inscriptions of - Charles Stewart (Senior) & wife

Newer tombstone –	*Original tombstone -*	
CHARLES	CHARLES STEWART	NANCY STEWART
STEWART	SEIGNOR	Consort of
PVT	died February	Charles Stewart
REGT VA LINE	4th, 1845	died
REV WAR	Aged 85 Years & ?	November 5th 1847
FEB 4 1845	months	Aged 75 Years

THOMAS, HENRY

Patriot: Thomas Henry
Birth: 3 May 1756   Tulpehocken, [Berks Co.], PA
Married Spouse 1: 1780/1781   Mary Abernathy (1760-1851)
Service state(s): PA
Rank: Private
Proof of Service: Pension application
Pension application No.: W9851
Residences: Berks Co., PA; Northumberland Co., PA; *[Blount Co.]* TN; OH; Ripley Co., IN, Rush Co., IN
Died: 4 Sep 1836
Buried: Connell Cemetery, Brown Twp., Ripley Co., IN
DAR Ancestor No.: None as of 7 Jun 2017.

Pension Application Abstracted from National Archives microfilm Series M804, Roll 2368, File W9851.
Pension abstract for – Henry Thomas
Service state(s): PA
Date: 13 Sep 1833
County of: Ripley   State of: IN
Declaration made before a Judge or Court: Circuit Court
Act of: 7 Jun 1832
Age: 77 yrs.   Record of age:
Where and year born: 3 May 1756   Tulpehocken, [Berks Co.] PA
Residence when he entered service: Northumberland Co., PA
Residence(s) since the war: PA; TN for 26 yrs.; OH; Ripley Co., IN.
Residence now: Ripley Co., IN
Volunteer, Drafted, or Substitute: Drafted
Rank(s): Private & Orderly Sergeant
Statement of service-

Period	Duration	Names of General and Field Officers
Sep 1781-Mar 1782	7 mos.	Capt. John Ingram's PA company

Battles:
Discharge received: Verbal
Statement is supported by –
Person now living who can testify to service: Knows of no one
Clergyman: Meshack Hyatt
Persons in neighborhood who certify character: Michael Castater
&
Pension abstract for – Mary Thomas widow of Henry Thomas
Date: 21 Jul 1843
County of: Rush   State of: IN
Declaration made before a Judge or Court: Justice of the Peace
Act of: 7 Jul 1838
Age: above 76 yrs.; in 1848 she gave her age as 84 yrs.
Residence now: Rush Co., IN

Persons in neighborhood who certify character: Margaret Mull & Eli Hill testify knows her to be the widow of Henry Thomas; is acquainted with some of the children.
Death of soldier: 14 Sep 1836 "late of the county of Rush, IN"
Marriage date and place: Month of June 62 or 63 yrs. ago. [1780/1781]
Proof of marriage: Bible record lists births of children.
Names and ages of children: Jacob b. 1784; Henery b. 1786; Peggy b. 1787; Elizabeth b. 1790; Barbary b. 1792; Mary b. 1795; George b. 1798; Susanah b. 1802; Ana Elizabeth b. 1802.

Abstract of Final Payment Voucher; General Services Administration, Washington, DC

NAME	THOMAS, MARY
AGENCY OF PAYMENT	INDIANA
DATE OF ACT	1843
DATE OF PAYMENT	2nd QUARTER 1851
DATE OF DEATH	
LAST FINAL PAYMENT VOUCHER RECEIVED FROM THE GENERAL ACCOUNTING OFFICE From	
General Services Administration	GSA DC 70-7035 GSA DEC 69 7068

Abstract of Final Payment Voucher; General Services Administration, Washington, DC

LAST FINAL PAYMENT VOUCHER RECEIVED FROM THE GENERAL ACCOUNTING OFFICE	
NAME	Thomas, Mary widow of Henry
AGENCY OF PAYMENT	INDIANA
DATE OF ACT	1848
DATE OF PAYMENT	March 1851
DATE OF DEATH	
Last ~~FINAL~~ PAYMENT VOUCHER RECEIVED FROM THE GENERAL ACCOUNTING OFFICE From	
General Services Administration	GSA DC 70-7035 GSA DEC 69 7068

Senate Documents, Vol.9, No. 988, 63rd Congress, 3d Session, Washington, 1915; "Register of Certificates Issued by John Pierce, Esquire, Paymaster General and Commissioner of Army Accounts for the United States, to Officers and Soldiers of the Continental Army Under Act of July 4, 1783"; Seventeenth report of the National Society of the Daughters of the American Revolution; Genealogical Publishing Co., Inc., Baltimore, MD, 1984. p. 501.
Men listed in this volume with the same name.

No. of Certificate	To whom issued	Amount
56420	Thomas, Henry	73.30
57026	Thomas, Henry	32.38
57612	Thomas, Henry	40.60
58147	Thomas, Henry	80.00

Ripley County Indiana, Recorder's Office, Tract Book 1, p. 42.
Thomas, Henry   25 Sep 1807   R12, T8, S30   160 acres

1820 U. S. Census, Ripley Co., IN, NARA Roll M33_15; EN 7 Aug 1820, p. 72, line 26.
Henry Thomas
Males 45>=1, Females 16-25=1, Females 45>=1.

The Pension Roll of 1835 Volume IV, The Mid-Western States, Indexed Edition, In Four Volumes; Genealogical Publishing Co., Inc., Baltimore, MD, Reprint 1968, p. 87.
Statement, &c. of Ripley county, Indiana.

INDIANA Names	Rank	Annual allowance	Sums received	Description of service
Henry Thomas	Private	23.33	69 99	Penn. militia

When placed on pension roll	Commencement of pension	Ages	Laws under which they were formerly placed on the pension roll; and remarks.
Dec 21, 1833	March 4, 1831	65	-

Scott, Craig R.; *The "Lost" Pensions, Settled Accounts of the Act of 6 April 1838*; Willow Bend Books, Lovettsville, VA, 1996, p. 325.
An Act directing the transfer of money remaining unclaimed [for the term of eight months] by certain pensioners, and authorizing payment of the same at the Treasury of the United States.
Thomas, Henry; Pension Office – Ind.; Box – 49; Account - #5296 card
Thomas, Henry; Pension Office – a/o, Ky; Box – 69; Account - #10928
Thomas, Henry, w/o; Pension Office – Ind.; Box – 50; Account - #5637
Thomas, Henry, w/o; Pension Office – Ind.; Box – 25; Account - #5296

Toph, Violet E.; *Peoples History of Ripley County, Indiana*; self-published, c. 1940, p.124.
Revolutionary Soldiers Who Came to Ripley County
Henry Thomas entered the service from Pennsylvania in September 1781 and served seven months. He was born in 1766 and died in 1836.

O'Byrne, Mrs. Roscoe C., comp. & ed.; *Roster Soldiers and Patriots of the American Revolution Buried in Indiana*; Published by Indiana Daughters of the American Revolution, 1938, Reprinted Genealogical Publishing Co., Baltimore MD, 1968, p. 353.
THOMAS, HENRY   Rush County
Born – May 3, 1756, Tulpehocken, Penn.
Service – Enlisted Sept., 1781, in Northumberland Co., Penn.; served 7 mos. as orderly-sergeant in Capt. John Ingram's Penn. CO.

Proof – Pension claim W. 9851.
Died – Sept. 4, 1836.
Married – 1780 or 1781, Mary -----. Ch. Jacob, b. 1784; Henry, b. 1786; Margaret, b. 1787; Elizabeth, b. 1790 (?); Barbara, b. 1792; Mary, b. 1795; George, b. 1798; Susannah and Anna E., b. 1802.
Collected by Mrs. A. B. Wycoff, Batesville, Indiana.

Gibbs, A.; Ripley County Historical Society Data on Revolutionary Soldiers, 1973 review.
Exact location of marker: no further information on grave site.
Additional comments: on Court House tablet
Pa. Archives, Series 3, Pennsylvanians residing in Ripley
    Co. Ind. pr PN 21 Dec 1833 age 65.
    May be buried in Rush Co. Ind.

Burial location: Connell Cemetery, Brown Twp., Ripley Co., IN

Tombstone: Not located
              He is buried with his wife, Mary (Abernathy) Thomas

Revolutionary War Memorial, located in the Rush County Indiana Courthouse, includes HENRY THOMAS. Memorial dedicated by the Rushville Chapter Daughters of the American Revolution, 1981.

TUCKER, JOHN

Patriot: John Tucker
Birth: abt 1753
Married Spouse 1: XX 1758-bef 1833
Married Spouse 2: Feb 1833, Scott Co., KY
    Mary (Polly) X (b. 1801/1803, d. 14 Oct 1853)
    She then married Isaac Levi 14 Nov 1841
Service state(s): NC & NC Continental Line
Rank: Private
Proof of Service: Pension application
Pension application No.: S. *[no number; reference made to Certificate No. 12, dated 17 Nov 1818, in application]*
Residences: NC; Scott Co., KY; Jefferson Co., IN; Ripley Co., IN
Died: 31 Nov 1840   New Marion, Ripley Co., IN
Buried: Unknown
DAR Ancestor No.: None as of 7 Jun 2017.

Pension Application Abstracted from National Archives microfilm Series M804, Roll 2420, File S-----.
Pension abstract for – John Tucker
Service state(s): NC Continental Line
Date: 17 Apr 1818
County of: Scott   District of Kentucky
Declaration made before a Judge or Court: Circuit Judge
Act of: 18 Mar 1818
Age: 65 yrs.
Residence now: Scott County
Rank(s): Private
Statement of service-

Period	Duration	Names of General and Field Officers
Jun 1782 - Jul 1783	18 mos.	Company commanded by Capt. Brenkle; transferred to Capt. Coleman at Ashley Hill, Regt. commanded by Col Arch Lette, in gen Green's brigade.

Discharge received: at Charles Town, SC
Evidence: None
&
Pension abstract for – John Tucker
Date: 12 Jun 1820
County of: Scott   District of Kentucky
Declaration made before a Judge or Court: Circuit Court
Act of: 18 Mar 1818 & 1May 1820
Age: 65 yrs.
Volunteer, Drafted, or Substitute: Enlisted in NC
Statement of service-

Period	Duration	Names of General and Field Officers

1782 - 18 mos. NC Line, Continental Establishment,
  Until general peace Capt. John Coleman, Regt. commanded
    by Col. Archibald Lytle.
Battles: Skirmish at James Island near Ft. Johnson; Battle of Eutaw Springs
Discharge received: at Charleston, SC
Wife: not named Wife's age: 62 yrs
Names and ages of children: Son, not named, age 17 yrs.
&
Pension abstract for – John Tucker
Date: 19 Sep 1839
County of: Jefferson State of: IN
Declaration made before a Judge or Court: Notary Public
Declaration: Application for Transfer from KY to IN; that he resides in State of Indiana and intends to remain, and wishes his pension to be there payable in future.
Reason for Removing: that he would be near his son, and that he could obtain a piece of land with more ease than in Kentucky.
Names of General and Field Officers: Capt. Coleman, Regt. commanded by Col. Archibald Little.
Documentary proof: Testimony of James Stanley that John Tucker is the identical person named in the Certificate which he has exhibited before me [Notary Public] numbered 12 and dated at the War Office on 17 Nov 1818, and signed by J. C. Calhoun Secretary of War.
Person who certifies: James Stanley
&
Additional notations in file indicate:
   Letter from J. L. Edwards, Esq. 1839, enclosed the application for transfer, & states Mr. Tucker resides in Ripley Co., IN and may be addressed at New Marion, Ripley Co., IN.
   &
   John Tucker died 20 Dec 1840; pension paid to his death; Madison Roll.

Abstract of Final Payment Voucher; General Services Administration, Washington, DC
  LAST FINAL PAYMENT VOUCHER RECEIVED FROM THE GENERAL ACCOUNTING OFFICE
NAME TUCKR, JOHN
AGENCY OF PAYMENT INDIANA
DATE OF ACT 1818
DATE OF PAYMENT 1st Qr. 1841
DATE OF DEATH Dec. 20, 1840
GENERAL SERVICES ADMINISTRATION
National Archives and Records Service NA-286
GSA-WASH DC 54-4891 November 1953

Senate Documents, Vol.9, No. 988, 63rd Congress, 3d Session, Washington, 1915; "Register of Certificates Issued by John Pierce, Esquire, Paymaster General and Commissioner of Army Accounts for the United States, to Officers and Soldiers of the Continental Army Under Act of July 4, 1783"; <u>Seventeenth report of the National Society of the Daughters of the American Revolution</u>; *Genealogical Publishing Co., Inc., Baltimore, MD, 1984. p. 512.*
Men listed in this volume with the same name.

No. of Certificate	To whom issued	Amount
90561	Tucker, John	55.22
91006	Tucker, John	76.60

Quisenberry, Anderson Chenault; <u>Revolutionary Soldiers in Kentucky</u>, *containing a roll of the officers of Virginia line who received land bounties, a roll of the Revolutionary pensioners in Kentucky, a list of the Illinois regiment who served under George Rogers Clark in the Northwest campaign, also a roster of the Virginia Navy; Reproduction of the original which appeared in Sons of the American Revolution Kentucky Society Year Book, Louisville, 1896, Southern Book Co., Baltimore, MD, 1959. p. 221.*
Scott County
Pensioners Under the Act of March 18. 1818.
Rucker, John, private   North Carolina line
    November 17, 1818; April 17, 1818; $96.   Age 81.

Clark, Murtie June; <u>The Pension List of 1820 [U.S. War Department]</u>*Reprinted with an Index; Genealogical Publishing Co., Inc., Baltimore, 1991. Originally published 1820 as Letter from the Secretary of War, p. 616.*
KENTUCKY
Names of the Revolutionary Pensioners which have been placed on the Roll of Kentucky, under the Law of the 18th of March, 1818, from the passage thereof, to this day, inclusive of the Rank they held, and the Lines in which they served, viz: -

Names	Rank	Line
Included in the list –		
John Tucker	private	North Carolina

<u>The Pension Roll of 1835 Volume III, The Southeastern States,</u> *Indexed Edition, In Four Volumes; Genealogical Publishing Co., Inc., Baltimore, MD, Reprint 1968, p. 246.*
Statement, &c. of Scott county, Kentucky

KENTUCKY Names	Rank	Annual allow-ance.	Sums re-ceived	Description of service
John Tucker	Private	96.00	64 28	N.C. Line

When placed on pension roll	Commencement of pension	Ages	Laws under which they were formerly placed on the pension roll; and remarks.
Nov 17, 1818	Apr 17, 1818	81	-

A Census of Pensioners for Revolutionary or Military Services with their Names, Ages, and Places of Residence Under the Act for Taking the Sixth Census in 1840; Genealogical Publishing Co., Inc., Baltimore, Maryland, 1965. p. 184.

Names of pensioners for revolutionary or military services.	Ages	Names of heads of families with whom pensioners re-sided June 1, 1840.
RIPLEY COUNTY		
JACKSON		
John Tucker	80	John Tucker

Ripley Circuit Court Civil Order Book Vol. E, March 1841-August 1843; Ripley County, Indiana; p. 35.
4 March 1841
Ordered by the Court that the Clerk of this Court Certify that Polly Tucker Widow of John Tucker late of said County deceased on this day appeared in open Court and proved to the satisfaction of the Court that she is the Widow of John Tucker a Revolutionary pensioner who was the identical person named in an original Certificate which was produced to the Court and which is set out in her affidavit which she produced in Court And further that the said John Tucker departed this life on the 31st day of November 1840.

Toph, Violet E.; *Peoples History of Ripley County, Indiana;* self-published, c. 1940, p 128.
Revolutionary Soldiers Who Came to Ripley County
John Tucker entered the service from North Carolina in 1782 and served under John Coleman. He was pensioned in Scott County, Ky. and moved to Ripley County in 1839 near New Marion. He was born in 1754 and died in 1840.

O'Byrne, Mrs. Roscoe C., comp. & ed.; *Roster Soldiers and Patriots of the American Revolution Buried in Indiana;* Published by Indiana Daughters of the American Revolution, 1938, Reprinted Genealogical Publishing Co., Baltimore MD, 1968, p. 360.

TUCKER, JOHN, SR.   Ripley County
Born – About 1753.
Service – Enlisted June, 1782, as pri. in Capt. Brinkley's and John Coleman's CO., Col. Archibald Lytle's N. C. Regt. Battles of Eutaw Springs and James Island. Discharged July, 1783.
Died – Dec. 20, 1840. Buried near *[New]* Marion. Name on bronze tablet in Versailles Court House.
Married – First W. unknown. Second W., 1833, Mary -----. Had 2 sons.
Collected by Mrs. A. B. Wycoff, Batesville, Indiana.

Gibbs, A.; Ripley County Historical Society Data on Revolutionary Soldiers, 1973 review.
Exact location of marker: no further information on grave site.
Additional comments: on Court House tablet
    Pensioned from Scott Co. Ky. moved later (1839) to near New Marion in Shelby Tw. Ripley Co. Ind.
    1840 census Ripley Co. Ind. pension list, p. 158. John Tucker age 80.

VanBIBBER, PETER

Patriot: Peter VanBibber
Birth: 5 Aug 1757   Botetourt Co., VA
Married Spouse 1: 22 Jul 1785   Sarah Yolkecome (- bef. 1838)
Service state(s): VA
Rank: Private
Proof of Service: Pension application
Pension application No.: S32566
Residences: Botetourt Co., VA; Greenbrier Co., VA; Greenbrier Co., WV; NW Territory; OH; Ripley Co., IN; Vanderburgh Co., IN
Died: 8 Oct 1838 [pension file]   Place not stated
Buried: His name on plaque in the Vanderburgh County, IN Courthouse
DAR Ancestor No.: None as of 7 Jun 2017.
Children: Jacob, only heir

Pension Application Abstracted from National Archives microfilm Series M804, Roll 2440, File S32566.
Pension abstract for – Peter Vanbibber
Service state(s): VA
Date: 11 Nov 1833; Amendment 19 Dec 1833
County of: Ripley   State of: IN
Declaration made before a Judge or Court: Probate Court
Act of: 7 Jun 1832
Age: 76 yrs.
Record of age: None, speak from what my parents have told me
Where and year born: Botetourt Co., VA   5 Aug 1757
Residence when he entered service: Greenbrier Co., VA
Residence(s) since the war: Greenbrier Co., VA; OH many years; Ripley Co., IN
Residence now: Ripley Co., IN
Volunteer, Drafted, or Substitute: 1st tour – Volunteered; 2nd tour – Substitute for John Dixon; 3rd tour - Drafted
Rank(s): 1st tour – Private; Indian Spy part of 1st tour
Statement of service-

Period	Duration	Names of General and Field Officers
Oct 1775 - Jun 1777	1 yr. 18 mos.	Col. James Henderson, Maj. Thomas Quirk, Capt. Matthew Arbuckle.
Nov 1780 - Sep 1781	10 mos.	Col. Luke Boyer, Capt. James Grimes, Lt. John Hall, Ens. Samuel Campbell.
Jul 1782 - Dec 1782	5 mos.	Col. Luke Boyer, Maj. Thomas Quirk, Capt. James Grimes, Lt. Montgomery, Ens. Armstrong.

Battles: Point Pleasant, Donlay's Fork, Cornwallis' Surrender.
Discharge received: Verbal by my commanding officers. They told me that there orders to me were sufficient.
Statement is supported by –
Person now living who can testify to service: James Montgomery, John

Campbell, Samuel Gaskins, Arnold Peckham.
Clergyman: Meshack Hyatt
Persons in neighborhood who certify character: Samuel Gookins
&
Additional notations in file: Death of soldier: 8 Oct 1838

Gwathmey, John H.; Historical Register of Virginians in the Revolution, Soldiers, Sailors, Marines, 1775-1783; The Dietz Press, Richmond, VA, 1938, p. 790.
Vanbiber, Peter, Scout, Greenbrier Mil, T-GV1P239.[Purporting to be all of the manuscripts in the State Library pertaining to George Rogers Clark, photostated and bound, but not indexed. Serial letters, volume numbers and page numbers given. Thus T-CV1P239 means Serial C, Volume 1, Page 239.]
Vanbiber, Peter, Spy. Northwest Territory.

Abercrombie, Janice L. and Slatten, Richard, comp. & trans.; Virginia Revolutionary Publick Claims in three volumes; Iberian Publishing Co., Athens, GA, 1992, Vol. I, p. 419, 421.
Greenbrier County
p. 419.
Peter Vanbibber for 142 do [rations] State £7-2.
Peter Vanbibber Junr. For 71 do [rations] State £3-11.
p. 421.
Peter Vanbibber for same [scouting] 35 days.

Summers, Lewis Preston; Annals of Southwest Virginia 1769-1800; Genealogical Publishing Co., Inc., 1996, p. 201, 220, 221.
p. 201.   Botetourt County
At a court continued & held for Botetourt County the 13th day of August, 1773.
[Peter Vanbebber was on the jury.]
p. 220 & 221.   Botetourt County
At a court continued & held for Botetourt County the 15th day of April 1774.
[Peter Vanbebber was on the jury.]

Bentley, Elizabeth Petty, indexer; Virginia Marriage Records 1700-1850, From the Virginia Magazine of History and Biography, the William and Mary College Quarterly, and Tyler's Quarterly; Genealogy Publishing Co., Inc., 1984, n.p.
July the 22, 1785--Peter VenBebber with Sarah Yolkecome.

Johnston, Ross C., Comp.; West Virginians in the American Revolution, Excerpted from West Virginia History Vol. I (Oct 1939), and Vol. IX (Oct. 1947); Genealogical Publishing Co., Inc., Baltimore, MD, 1990, p. 18.
Van Bibber, John and Peter (Captains)
    John and Peter Van Bibber were of Dutch ancestry and lived in Pennsylvania and Maryland before coming to the Greenbrier Valley, Botetourt County, about 1771. John made an early exploration of Kentucky, passing down the Ohio and the Mississippi to New Orleans. In 1773, he was one of the

surveyors who explored the Great Kanawha, and left his name on a cliff below Kanawha Falls, still known as "Van Bibber's Rock." Both brothers took part in the Point Pleasant campaign in 1774, where a third brother, Isaac, was killed.

Both served as captains of militia. Peter had a blockhouse on Wolf Creek, which was an important frontier outpost. John wrote from Fort Greenbrier near Lowell, Summers County, in 1777. About 1781, the two brothers moved into the Kanawha Valley. Peter died at Point Pleasant in 1796 and John in 1821. Peter's sons, Matthias and Jacob, were noted in border warfare, and his daughter married a son of Daniel Boone.

Toph, Violet E.; Peoples History of Ripley County, Indiana; self-published, c. 1940, p. 127.
Revolutionary Soldiers Who Came to Ripley County
Peter Vanbibber enlisted from Virginia in October, 1775 and was discharged June, 1777. His service being one year and eight months, re-enlisted in November, 1780 and was discharged in September 1781. In July he was drafted for six months and was discharged in December, 1782 after serving five months. He was born in 1757.

O'Byrne, Mrs. Roscoe C., comp. & ed.; Roster Soldiers and Patriots of the American Revolution Buried in Indiana; Published by Indiana Daughters of the American Revolution, 1938, Reprinted Genealogical Publishing Co., Baltimore MD, 1968, p. 364-365.
VAN BIBBER, PETER   Ripley County
Born – 1757.
Service – Enlisted from Vir. in Oct., 1775. Discharged in June, 1777. 1 yr. 8 mos. Re-enlisted Nov., 1780. Discharged Sept., 1781. Drafted July, 1782, for 6 mos. Discharged Nov., 1782.
Proof – Pension claim S. 32566.
Children – Sarah, m. John Yocum; Rachel, m. Samuel Kincart.
Collected by Mrs. A. B. Wycoff, Batesville, Indiana.

O'Byrne, comp. Mrs. Roscoe C., comp.; Roster of Soldiers and Patriots of the American Revolution Buried in Indiana, Vol. III; Indiana Daughters of the American Revolution, 1966, p. 78.
Additional data and/or corrections received since 1966 to the records of the soldiers and patriots listed in Rosters I and II.
VAN BIBBE, PETER   Roster I, p. 364.   Vanderburgh County
Died – Oct. 8. 1838.
Married – In Vanderburgh Co. instead of Ripley Co.
Proof – Pension payment given to his son, Jacob, in 1838 and in Order Book B., p. 231 Probate Court Nov. term A.D. 1838 estate of Peter Van Bibber and also p. 276 August term 1839 Vanderburgh Co., Ind.
Children – Jacob was the only son.
By Mrs. Zella Davidson, 206 Gough Avenue, Boonville, Indiana 47601.

Gibbs, A.; <u>Ripley County Historical Society Data on Revolutionary Soldiers</u>, *1973 review.*
Exact location of marker: perhaps buried in Vanderburg Co. Ind.
Additional comments: on Court House tablet
      Ripley Co. Probate A, p. 141, appl for pension Nov. 1833.

WARD, JOHN

Patriot: John Ward
Birth: 1760 NC
Married Spouse 1: Hannah Pedry
Service state(s): NC
Rank: Private
Proof of Service: Pension application
Pension application No.: S16284
Residences: Rowan Co., NC; Surry Co., NC; KY; TN; Ripley Co., IN; Marion Co., IN
Died: 1845 Hendricks Co., IN
Buried: near Brownsburg, Hendricks Co., IN (per DAR)
DAR Ancestor No.: A210910

Pension Application Abstracted from National Archives microfilm Series M804, Roll 2488, File S16284.
Pension abstract for – John Ward
Service state(s): NC
Date: 23 Aug 1832
County of: Ripley   State of: IN
Declaration made before a Judge or Court: Circuit Court
Act of: 7 Jun 1832
Age: 72 yrs.
Record of age: No record, only statement of my parents
Where and year born: NC   1760
Residence when he entered service: Surry Co., NC
Residence(s) since the war: KY; TN; Ripley Co., IN in abt. 1826.
Residence now: Ripley Co., IN
Volunteer, Drafted, or Substitute: First tour – Volunteer;
Second tour – Substitute for his brother;
Third tour - Volunteer.
Rank(s): Private
Statement of service-

Period	Duration	Names of General and Field Officers
Nov 1777 - Apr 1778	5 mos.	NC Militia, Gen, Rudderford, Col. Bernard, Capt. Henry Smith.
1778	3 mos.	Gen. Rutherford, Col. Isaacs, Capt. Bostick, Lt. Umphries.
1778	short time	Light infantry, Col. Little, Maj. Nelson.

Battles: Battle of Ashe's [Nashes?] defeat in GA at Briar Creek; Battle of Camden in SC.
Discharge received: Written
Signed by: Col. Alexander
What became of it?: It was in his waistcoat pocket and in washing it destroyed the same.
Statement is supported by –

Living witness, name(s): Knows of no one
Documentary proof: Has none
Evidence: Traditionary
Clergyman: William Laycock
Persons in neighborhood who certify character: Jesse Murkland
&
Letter in pension file:

Genealogy
The Indianapolis Star
Editorial Room
Salem, Sept. 24, 1928

Bureau of Pensions
Rev. & 1812 War Section
Washington, D.C.

Reference M.E.E

    I wish to thank you for the fine data sent to me in Aug. and ask you to give me a record of another Rev. soldier for Indiana. The data you sent for Mathias Lemon, helped to clear this record for the State, as many errors seem to be recorded concerning this man.
    The record I need now is that of John Ward, Sr. a pensioner on the 1840 List, for Hendricks Co., Ind. He died in 1845, and is buried near Brownsburg, Hendricks Co. His wife Hannah Pedry. Thought to have enlisted in S.C. in 1776, and served seven years. The record from your office, with data of last voucher, and to show to whom paid, with any family data recorded, will help us to clear this record. I thank you for any data you may send, and would appreciate an early reply.
Very truly,
Mrs. Harvey Morris

Revolutionary War Service Records; National Archives Publication number M881, Compiled service records of soldiers who served in the American Army during the Revolutionary War, 1775-1783.
https://www.fold3.com/image/21081177?terms=Ward,%20John%20nc
4 North Carolina Regiment, Nelson's company.
Ward, John – Private – Commissioned or enlisted 16 May 1776, Term – 3 years.

Thomas, Abishai & Catlin, Lynde & Mifflin, Benjamin; Roster of the North Carolina troops in the Continental Army, Volume 16
The University of North Carolina at Chapel Hill, Chapel Hill, NC, 1791, p. 1190.
Roster of the Continental Line from North Carolina, 1783.

Names and Rank	Companies	Dates of Commissions and Enlistments.	Occurrences
Ward, Jno., pt.	Lytle's	1781. W [War]	-

North Carolina Daughters of the American Revolution, comp.; Roster of soldiers from North Carolina in the American Revolution with an appendix containing a

collection of miscellaneous records.; North Carolina Daughters of the American Revolution, Durham, NC, 1934, p. 237.
Military Land Warrants, Continental Line (Part 1)
A list of warrants for lands granted the officers and soldiers in the Continental Line out of the Secretary's Office.

No.	To whom granted And rank	No. Acres	Service in months	Location and to whom deeded and date of warrant. Within the limits of the lands allotted the officers and soldiers of the Continental Line, by Law, 1783, Oct. 14
205.	John Ward, Privt.	640	84	Oct. 24

Clark, Murtie June, Comp.; *Index to U.S. Invalid Pension Records 1801-1815*; Genealogical Publishing Co., Inc., 1991, p. 98.

		Tennessee	
Name	Rank	Page	Remarks
Ward, John	Private	133	began Nov 30, 1814

Bockstruck, Lloyd DeWitt; *Revolutionary War Bounty Land Grants Awarded by State Governments*; Genealogical Publishing Co., IN, Baltimore, MD, 1996, p. 553.
Ward, John. NC. Private. 24 Oct. 1783. 640 acres.

Senate Documents, Vol.9, No. 988, 63rd Congress, 3d Session, Washington, 1915; "Register of Certificates Issued by John Pierce, Esquire, Paymaster General and Commissioner of Army Accounts for the United States, to Officers and Soldiers of the Continental Army Under Act of July 4, 1783"; *Seventeenth report of the National Society of the Daughters of the American Revolution*; Genealogical Publishing Co., Inc., Baltimore, MD, 1984. p. 527.
There are too many men by the name of John Ward to be listed in this work.

[In his pension application he stated he lived in KY, but did not state what county. He may be one of the men in the following list. – mjm]

Clift, G. Glens, Assistant Secretary, Kentucky Historical Society, Comp.; *"Second Census" of Kentucky – 1800, A Privately Compiled and Published Enumeration of Tax Payers Appearing in the 79 Manuscript Volumes Extant of Tax Lists of the 42 Counties of Kentucky in Existence in 1800*; Genealogical Publishing Co., Baltimore, MD, 1966, p. 309.

Name	County	Tax List Date	
Ward, John	Bourbon	7/23	1800
Ward, John	Clark		1800
Ward, John	Franklin	8/10/	1800
Ward, John	Harrison		1800
Ward, John	Harrison		1800
Ward, John	Mason		1800
Ward, John	Washington		1800

The Pension Roll of 1835 Volume IV, The Mid-Western States, Indexed Edition, In Four Volumes; Genealogical Publishing Co., Inc., Baltimore, MD, Reprint 1968, p. 87.
Statement, &c. of Ripley county, Indiana.

INDIANA Names	Rank	Annual allowance.	Sums received	Description of service
John Ward	Private	26.66	66 65	N.C. militia

When placed on pension roll	Commencement of pension	Ages	Laws under which they were formerly placed on the pension roll; and remarks.
Nov 20, 1832	March 4, 1831	74	-

Scott, Craig R.; The "Lost" Pensions, Settled Accounts of the Act of 6 April 1838; Willow Bend Books, Lovettsville, VA, 1996, p. 342.
An Act directing the transfer of money remaining unclaimed [for the term of eight months] by certain pensioners, and authorizing payment of the same at the Treasury of the United States.
Name – Ward, John, w/o; Pension Office – Ind.; Box – 27; Account - #19089

A Census of Pensioners for Revolutionary or Military Services with their Names, Ages, and Places of Residence Under the Act for Taking the Sixth Census in 1840; Genealogical Publishing Co., Inc., Baltimore, Maryland, 1965, p. 182.

Names of pensioners for revolutionary or military services.	Ages	Names of heads of families with whom pensioners reSided June 1, 1840.
INDIANA, HENDRICKS COUNTY		
John Ward	90	John Ward

Toph, Violet E.; Peoples History of Ripley County, Indiana; self-published, c. 1940, p. 127.
Revolutionary Soldiers Who Came to Ripley County
John Ward enlisted from North Carolina in November, 1777 and was discharged in April 1778. He was born in 1760 and lived for some time in Versailles, Ind.

O'Byrne, Mrs. Roscoe C., comp. & ed.; Roster Soldiers and Patriots of the American Revolution Buried in Indiana; Published by Indiana Daughters of the American Revolution, 1938, Reprinted Genealogical Publishing Co., Baltimore MD, 1968, p. 371-372, 403.
p. 371-372.
WARD, JOHN   Ripley County
Born – 1760, North Carolina.
Service – While living in Surry Co., N.C., entered service Nov., 1777, for 3 mos. as a substitute. Served short time as volunteer in N.C. Militia under Gen.

Rutherford, Col. Bernard, Capt. Henry Smith, Col. Isaac, Capt. Bostick, Col. Little. In battle of Camden, S. C.
Proof – Pension claim S. 18284. Since Rev., resided in Ky. and Tenn. and Ripley Co., Ind.
Buried – Near Versailles, Ind. Name on bronze tablet Versailles Court House.
Collected by Mrs. A. B. Wycoff, Batesville, Indiana.
p. 403.

WARD, JOHN   Hendricks County
Buried in private cemetery-the only grave. Inscription on stone reads "John Ward-U.S. Soldier-Revolutionary War".
Collected by Mrs. J. Harold Grimes, Danville, Indiana.

Gibbs, A.; Ripley County Historical Society Data on Revolutionary Soldiers, 1973 review.
Exact location of marker: no further information on grave site
Comments: on Court House tablet
      Toph note: he lived in Versailles, Ind.

WAY, ISAAC

Patriot: Isaac Way
Birth: 1763 Shenandoah Co., VA
Married Spouse 1: Sarah
Service state(s): VA
Rank: Private
Proof of Service: Pension application
Pension application No.: S16568
Residences: Shenandoah Co., VA; Fauquier Co., VA; Indiana Territory;
              Ripley Co., IN
Died: 5 May 1835 Ripley Co., IN
Buried: Dearborn Co., IN (per History of Dearborn & Ohio Counties, p. 199)
DAR Ancestor No.: None as of 7 Jun 2017.

Pension Application Abstracted from National Archives microfilm Series M804, Roll 2510, File S16568.
Pension abstract for – Isaac Way
Service state(s): VA
Date: 24 Aug 1832; Amendment 11 Feb 1833
County of: Ripley   State of: IN
Declaration made before a Judge or Court: Circuit Court;
                        amendment in Probate Court
Act of: 7 Jun 1832
Age: 70 yrs.
Record of age: No record, only speak from what my father told me
Where and year born: Shenandoah Co., VA   17 Mar 1763
Residence when he entered service: Fauquier Co., VA
Residence(s) since the war: VA 20 yrs.; Ripley Co., IN
Residence now: Johnson Twp., Ripley Co., IN
Volunteer, Drafted, or Substitute: Enlisted
Rank(s): Private
Statement of service-

Period	Duration	Names of General and Field Officers
1780	1 yr.	Gen. Morgan, Col. Howard, Maj. Brooks, Capt. Francis Triplett, Lt. John Derrian

Battles: Battle of Cowpens where he was engaged in the Battle and was severely wounded on the side, back, arms, head and in the face by the cut of the sword of a British dragoon; when he asked Colonel Edmonds if he could not go down to Little York with his Regiment, that the Colonel came up to him and removed the bandage then around his head and face, and told him that he was too disabled to serve as a Soldier, that there are already too many such man in the service
Discharge received: Colonel Edmonds actually gave him a discharge, and that the same was destroyed by fire together with some other papers about twenty years since in the house of one James Way.
Statement is supported by –

Documentary proof: The said Isaac Way has no documentary evidence
Person now living who can testify to service: he knows of but two persons living who can testify to his services. The affidavits of George Cheek, Dearborn Co., IN, on 1 Jan 1833, and Ralph Weathers, Dearborn Co., IN made in the amendment.
Clergyman: Meshack Hyatt
Persons in neighborhood who certify character: Capt. Shook, David P. Shook, Dr. Connett, Jacob Lodwich, etc.

Gwathmey, John H.; *Historical Register of Virginians in the Revolution, Soldiers, Sailors, Marines, 1775-1783*; The Dietz Press, Richmond, VA, 1938, p. 812.
Way, Isaac, Ind. pens.

The Pension Roll of 1835 Volume IV, The Mid-Western States, Indexed Edition, In Four Volumes; Genealogical Publishing Co., Inc., Baltimore, MD, Reprint 1968, p. 87.
Statement, &c. of Ripley county, Indiana.

INDIANA Names	Rank	Annual allowance.	Sums received	Description of service
Isaac Way	Private	40.00	120 00	Va. cont'l line

When placed on pension roll	Commencement of pension	Ages	Laws under which they were formerly placed on the pension roll; and remarks.
June 29, 1833	March 4, 1831	85	-

Ripley Co., IN Probate Order Book, Vol. A, 19 Nov 1818-Feb. 1837, p. 174.
11 May 1835
Sarah May Widow of the Late Isaac Way Deceased now appeared in open couth and Proved to the satisfaction of the Court that she is the Widow of the deceased and that he died on the 5th day of May 1835.

Toph, Violet E.; *Toph Papers*; collected during her lifetime 1878-1956, p. 1468.
Notes by Mrs. Erma (Anderson) Huntington.
    Isaac Way, a Revolutionary Soldier, lived in the same house on Falling Timber Creek, long before the Spragues came from the east and occupied the same house.
    He was drowned in Laughery Creek and his body washed out on what was once the Steinbetz field but in 1944 is Versailles State Park land. He had two bench legged Fiste dogs which went home and roused the family in the night. The family followed the dogs and found the body.

Toph, Violet E.; *Peoples History of Ripley County, Indiana*; self-published, c. 1940, p. 127.
Revolutionary Soldiers Who Came to Ripley County

Isaac Way enlisted from Virginia in the spring of 1780, served one year and left service in the spring of 1781. He was born in 1762.

O'Byrne, Mrs. Roscoe C., comp. & ed.; Roster Soldiers and Patriots of the American Revolution Buried in Indiana; Published by Indiana Daughters of the American Revolution, 1938, Reprinted Genealogical Publishing Co., Baltimore MD, 1968, p. 374.

WAY, ISAAC   Dearborn or Ripley County
Born – 1763.
Service – Enlisted from Vir. in spring of 1780. Served 1 yr., left the service in 1781.
Proof – Pension claim S. 16568.
Buried – Either in Ripley or Dearborn County. Name on bronze tablet, Versailles Court House.
Collected by Mrs. A. B. Wycoff, Batesville, Indiana.

Gibbs, A.; Ripley County Historical Society Data on Revolutionary Soldiers, 1973 review.
Exact location of marker: no further information on grave site
Comments: In 1830 census age 60-70.
    Probate A wife said he d. 5 May 1835.
    Probate A Ripley Co. Ind. p. 135, appl. for pension Feb. 1833.
Additional comment: Revolutionary soldier lived in the same house on Falling Timber Creek long before the Spragues came from the east and occupied the same house. He was drowned in Laughrey Creek and his body washed out on what is now Steinmetz field. He had two bench-legged feisty dog which went home and roused the family in the night. The family followed the dogs and found the body. Perhaps he is buried in Pleasant Hill Cemetery.

WELCH (WELSH), DANIEL

Patriot: Daniel Welch
Birth: Jan 1763
Married Spouse 1: 29 Nov 1827, Dearborn Co., IN
                                             Nancy Hancock Davis
Service state(s): CT & CT Continental
Rank: Private
Proof of Service: Pension application
Pension application No.: S36841 & BLWt 919-100
Residences: CT; NY; Dearborn Co., IN; Ripley Co., IN
Died: 1835   Final Pension Payment 1 Mar 1845
Buried: Mt. Sinai Cemetery, Aurora, Dearborn Co., IN
DAR Ancestor No.:None as of 7 Jun 2017.

Pension Application Abstracted from National Archives microfilm Series M804, Roll 2524, File S36841, BLWt 919-100.
Pension abstract for – Daniel Welch
Service state(s): CT Continental
Alternate spelling(s): Welsh
Date: 12 Jun 1819 & 28 Apr 1820 for Bounty Land & 28 Sep 1820
      & miscellaneous notations from file
County of: Dearborn   State of: IN
Declaration made before a Judge or Court:
Act of: 18 Mar 1818; 1 May 1820
Age: 58 yrs, in 1820
Where and year born: Place not stated   Jan 1763
Residence when he entered service: Enlisted at Sandy Hill, Fort Edward, NY
Residence(s) since the war: Not stated
Residence now: Dearborn Co., IN
Volunteer, Drafted, or Substitute: Not stated
Rank(s): Private
Statement of service-

Period	Duration	Names of General and Field Officers
Jun 1778	1 yr.	Capt. Burrough, Col. Warner's Continental Regiment.
1779 - Close of War	3 yrs.	Capt. Converse, Col. Swift's Continental Regiment.

Battles: Taking of Fort George, Battle of Valentine's Hill, Cornwallis' Defeat
Death of soldier: between 1827-1835   Dearborn Co., IN
Wife: mentioned in 1820, not named; notations in file indicate she was
      Nancy Hancock Davis Welch.
Marriage date and place: 29 Nov 1827
Names and ages of children: "a girl" aged 5 in 1820, relationship not stated

Abstract of Final Payment Voucher; General Services Administration, Washington, DC

LAST FINAL PAYMENT VOUCHER RECEIVED FROM
       THE GENERAL ACCOUNTING OFFICE
NAME   WELSH, DANIEL
AGENCY OF PAYMENT   INDIANA
DATE OF ACT   1818
DATE OF PAYMENT   March 1, 1845
DATE OF DEATH   -
GENERAL SERVICES ADMINISTRATION
National Archives and Records Service   NA-286
GSA-WASH DC 54-4891   November 1953

Revolutionary War Service Records; National Archives Publication number M881, Compiled service records of soldiers who served in the American Army during the Revolutionary War, 1775-1783.
https://www.fold3.com/image/14709854?terms=Welch,%20Daniel%20ct
Connecticut 2nd formation, Converse's company, Col. Heman Swift's Regt. arrangement 1781.
Welch, Daniel – Date of appointment or enlistment – Jan 1, 1781; Muster Roll Mar, Apr, May, Jun, Jul 1781; Mar, Apr, May, Jun, Jul, Aug, Sep, Oct, Nov, Dec 1782; Jan, Feb, Mar, Apr 1783.

Adjutants-General, by the Authority of the General Assembly, comp.; Record of Service of Connecticut Men in the I. War of the Revolution; The Case, Lockwood & Brainard Company Printers and Binders, Hartford, CT, 1889, p. 259, 324, 361, 627, 646.
p. 259.
Additional Infantry, 1777-1781.
Col. Seth Warner's Regiment, 1777-81.
Officers and Men from Connecticut.
(This regiment was recruited under resolution of Congress in the fall of "76. Not credited to any State "Line" nor included among the "additional." It was raised at large. Men enlisted from the Hampshire Grants, Mass., and Conn. The regiment served in the Northern Dept., as at Bennington and Saratoga, and was stationed for some time at Forts Anne and George. In Oct., 1780, the enemy approached these forts by way of Lake Champlain. Capt. Chipman, commanding at Ft. George, sent 'his force to offer resistance but his men were overwhelmed and nearly all killed or taken prisoners. The following roster represents the Conn. Quota in the regt. as it stood in 1780, when it had been considerably reduced by discharges and casualties. The command was disbanded Jan. 1, 1781.)
Officers –

Major	Elisha Painter	New Haven
Surgeon	Azel Washburn	-
Quartermaster	David Bates	Stamford
	James Coon	Salisbury
Paymaster	William Sherman	New Haven
Captains	Giles Wolcott	-
	John Chipman	Salisbury

351

	William Moulton	Windham	
	David Bates	Stamford	
	Tomas Sill	Hartford	
Names and Rank	Residence	Date of Enlistment	Terms of Service
Daniel Welch	-	Dec. 5, '79	Cont. to '81

p. 324.
Captain Converse's Company

Captain	Thomas Converse	Goshen	Cont. from '77-'81; ret. By consolidations Jan. 1, '83.
Lieutenant	Ebenezer Tanner	Cornwall	

Non-Commissioned Officers and Privates.

Names and Rank	Paid from	Paid to
Daniel Welch	Jan. 1, '81	Dec. 31, '81

p. 361.
Second Regiment "Connecticut Line"
Formation of Jan. – June, 1783.
(Second Regiment, in third formation of the "line", Jan. –June, 1783. Composed of Second Regt. of previous formation and the Fifth. Remained in Camp at West Point and vicinity from Jan. 1, 1783, until early in June when by Washington's orders it was disbanded with the greater portion of the army. A certain number of men were retained for the regiment of the last formation.)
Company Rolls. – Size Roll of Captain Richard's Company, Feb. 1, 1783.

Names and Rank	Residences	When Enlisted	Term
Daniel Welch	Skeensb'ough	Jan 1, "80	War

p. 627.
Miscellaneous Rolls.
Men from Co. Warner's Regt., who joined the 2d Conn. Continental Regt.

Names and Rank	Residence	Date of enlistment
Daniel Welch	Windham	Dec. 5, '79

p. 646.
Connecticut Pensioners, Act of 1818, Residing in South Carolina, Georgia, Kentucky, East Tennessee, Indiana, Michigan, Missouri, and District of Columbia.

Daniel Welch	Priv.	Ind.

Indiana Marriages, 1811-2007; various county clerk offices, Indiana; accessed 11 April 2016 from https://familysearch.org/ark:/61903/1:1:XXTL-W9W
Name: Daniel Welch
Event Type: Marriage Registration
Event Date: 29 Nov 1827
Event Place: Dearborn, Indiana, United States
Gender: Male
Marriage License Date: 16 Nov 1827   Marriage Place: Dearborn, Indiana
Spouse's Name: Nancy Davis
Spouse's Gender: Female

Officiator's Name: Nath Richmond
Page: 6; Record Number: 27
GS Film Number: 001313295; Digital Folder Number: 004476631; Image Number: 00086; FHL microfilm 1,313,295.

Clark, Murtie June; The Pension List of 1820 [U.S. War Department]Reprinted with an Index; Genealogical Publishing Co., Inc., Baltimore, 1991. Originally published 1820 as Letter from the Secretary of War, p. 659.
INDIANA
Names of the Revolutionary Pensioners which have been placed on the Roll of Indiana, under the Law of the 18th of March, 1818, from the passage thereof, to this day, inclusive of the Rank they held, and the Lines in which they served, viz:
-

Names	Rank	Line
Included in the list –		
Daniel Welch	private	Connecticut

The Pension Roll of 1835 Volume IV, The Mid-Western States, Indexed Edition, In Four Volumes; Genealogical Publishing Co., Inc., Baltimore, MD, Reprint 1968, p. 36.
Statement, &c. of Dearborn county, Indiana.

INDIANA Names	Rank	Annual allow- ance.	Sums re- ceived	Description of service
Daniel Welch	Private	96.00	1,350 09	Connecticut line

When placed on pension roll	Commencement of pension	Ages	Laws under which they were formerly placed on the pension roll; and remarks.
July 29, 1819	June 12 1819	72	-

A Census of Pensioners for Revolutionary or Military Services with their Names, Ages, and Places of Residence Under the Act for Taking the Sixth Census in 1840; Genealogical Publishing Co., Inc., Baltimore, Maryland, 1965. p. 184.

Names of pensioners for revolutionary or military services.	Ages	Names of heads of families with whom pensioners re- sided June 1, 1840.
RIPLEY COUNTY		
DELAWARE		
Daniel Welch	77	Esau King

Senate Documents, Vol.9, No. 988, 63rd Congress, 3d Session, Washington, 1915; "Register of Certificates Issued by John Pierce, Esquire, Paymaster General and Commissioner of Army Accounts for the United States, to Officers and Soldiers of the Continental Army Under Act of July 4, 1783"; Seventeenth report of the National Society of the Daughters of the American Revolution; Genealogical Publishing Co., Inc., Baltimore, MD, 1984. p. 535.

Men listed in this volume with the same name.

No. of Certificate	To whom issued	Amount
41793	Welch, Daniel	16.52
42270	Welch, Daniel	56.54
51386	Welch, Daniel	73.22

Toph, Violet E.; <u>Peoples History of Ripley County, Indiana</u>; self-published, c. 1940, p. 128-129. Revolutionary Soldiers Who Came to Ripley County
Daniel Welch (or Welsh) entered service from Connecticut and enlisted at Sandy Hill, Fort Edwards, New York State with Captain Burris, in June, 1778 and served four years. He was born in 1763 and died in Dearborn County. He married Nancy Hancock Davis Welch Nov. 23, 1827 and was pensioned from Dearborn County.

O'Byrne, Mrs. Roscoe C., comp. & ed.; <u>Roster Soldiers and Patriots of the American Revolution Buried in</u> Indiana; Published by Indiana Daughters of the American Revolution, 1938, Reprinted Genealogical Publishing Co., Baltimore MD, 1968, p. 375-376.
WELCH, Daniel   Dearborn County
Born – 1763.
Service – Entered service from Conn. Enlisted at Sandy Hill, Fort Edwards, N. Y. State, with Capt. Burris, June, 1778, and served 4 yrs.
Proof – Pension claim S. 36841; B. L. Wt. 919-100.
Buried – Mt. Siani. Government marker placed by Col. Archibald Lochry Chapter D. A. R.
Married – 1827, Nancy Hancock Davis.
Collected by Mrs. Walter Kerr, Aurora, Indiana, and Mrs. A. B. Wycoff, Batesville Indiana.

Gibbs, A.; <u>Ripley County Historical Society Data on Revolutionary Soldiers</u>, 1973 review.
Exact location of marker: no further information on grave site.
Comments: Pensioned Dearborn Co. Ind.
       1840 census Ripley Co. Ind. pension list, p. 204. Daniel Welch age 77.

Tombstone Location: *Mt. Sinai Cemetery, Aurora, Dearborn Co., IN*

Tombstone Inscription:

DANIEL WELCH
WARNER'S
CONTL
TROOPS
REV. WAR
BORN JAN. 1763

WHITSTONE (WHETSTONE), DANIEL

Patriot: Daniel Whetstone
Birth: 1750 Funkstown, Frederick Co., MD
Married Spouse 1: Martha Bund
Service state(s): MD & NC
Rank: Private
Proof of Service: Pension application
Pension application No.: S32591
Residences: Funkstown, MD; Lincoln Co., NC, OH for 10-12 yrs;
 Dearborn Co., IN for 7 yrs.
Died: 1837 Caesar Creek, Dearborn Co., IN
Buried: Unknown
DAR Ancestor No.: None as of 7 Jun 2017.

Pension Application Abstracted from National Archives microfilm Series M804, Roll 2547, File S32591.
Pension abstract for – Daniel Whetstone
Service state(s): MD & NC
Date: 12 Nov 1832
County of: Dearborn State of: IN
Declaration made before a Judge or Court:
Act of: 7 Jun 1832
Age: 82 yrs.
Record of age: No, has no record
Where and year born: Andover [?], MD 1750
Residence when he entered service: 1st tour-Funkstown, MD;
 2nd tour–Lincoln Co., NC
Residence(s) since the war: Funkstown, MD; OH for 10-12 yrs.;
 Dearborn Co., for 7 yrs.
Residence now: Dearborn Co., IN
Volunteer, Drafted, or Substitute: 1st tour – not stated; 2nd tour - volunteered
Rank(s): Private
Statement of service-

Period	Duration	Names of General and Field Officers
1778	3 mos.	MD Militia, Gen. Washington, Col. Davis, Maj. Charles [illegible], Capt. Jacob Sharer, Lt. John Lunk
Feb 1780	6 mos.	NC under Gen. Rutherford, Col. William Grimes, Capt. John Dellinger, Lt. Mike Hostetler.

Discharge received: Yes
Signed by: Capt. Sharer
What became of it?: worn out, lost
Statement is supported by –
Person now living who can testify to service: no one living near him; but if
 Abraham Bayer were now here, who sometimes in OH, could

establish service by him
Clergyman: Robert Ray

Revolutionary War Service Records; National Archives Publication number M881, Compiled service records of soldiers who served in the American Army during the Revolutionary War, 1775-1783.
https://www.fold3.com/image/17265289?terms=Whetstone,%20Daniel%20md
Sarer's company, Washington County, Maryland Militia.
Whetstone, Daniel – 2 Class – Appears on Capt. Jacob Sarer's Militia 1777.

Clements, S. Eugene and Wright, F Edward; The Maryland Militia in the Revolutionary War; *Family Line Publications, Westminster, MD 21157, 1987, p. 248.*
Muster Rolls and Other Lists – Washington County
A List of Capt. Jacob Sarers Compy. As no Classd.
Capt. Jacob Sarer; 1 Lietn. George Sarer; 2 Lietn. John Funk; Ensign John Bowlen; 1 Sergnt. Joseph Price; 2. Do. Isaac Shater; 3 do. Baustin Baker; 4 do. John Monninger; 4 do. Thomas Brooke Junr.
2 Class – [In this listing is] Daniel Whetstone

Newman, Harry Wright; Maryland Revolutionary Records; *Tuttle Publishing, Rutland, VT, 1928. p. 54, 154.*
p. 54.
Maryland Revolutionary Pensioners   Misc. facts and
Name of Veteran   Birth   Rank   Establishment   other State services
Whetstone, Daniel 1750   Pvt.   Militia   N.C. Service
p. 154.
Miscellaneous Lists Other States
Whetstone, Daniel   Virginia

Ripley County Indiana, Recorder's Office, Tract Book 3, p. 77.
Whetstone, Daniel   01 Jul 1837   R12, T10, Lot C

U.S. Department of Interior, Bureau of Land Management, General Land Office Records; Land Patent Search – accessed
Name: WHETSTONE, DANIEL
Accession Nr.; IN2670_.427; Document Type – State Volume Patent; Issue Date – 8/2/1838; Cancelled – No; Land Office – Jeffersonville; Authority – April 24, 1820: Sale-Cash Entry (3 Stat. 566); Document Nr. 9971; Total Acres – 38.57; Land Descriptions: State – IN; Meridian – 2nd PM   ; Twp-Rng – 010N-012E; Aliquots – SW 1/4; Section – 19; County – Franklin/Ripley
Certificate No. 9971: To all whom these Presents shall come, Greeting: Whereas Daniel Whetstone of Ripley County Indiana….

The Pension Roll of 1835 Volume IV, The Mid-Western States, Indexed Edition, In Four Volumes; Genealogical Publishing Co., Inc., Baltimore, MD, Reprint 1968, p. 66.

Statement, &c. of Dearborn county, Indiana.

INDIANA Names	Rank	Annual allowance.	Sums received	Description of service
Daniel Whetstone	Private	29.76	79 28	Maryland State tr[oops]

When placed on pension roll	Commencement of pension	Ages	Laws under which they were formerly placed on the pension roll; and remarks.
Oct 21, 1833	March 4, 1831	81	-

O'Byrne, Mrs. Roscoe C., comp. & ed.; Roster Soldiers and Patriots of the American Revolution Buried in Indiana; Published by Indiana Daughters of the American Revolution, 1938, Reprinted Genealogical Publishing Co., Baltimore MD, 1968, p. 379.

WHETSTONE, DANIEL   Dearborn County
Born – 1750, near Hagerstown, Md.
Service – Pvt. in CO. commanded by Capt. Shearer, Regt. of Col. Davis, Md. Line, for 8 mos. 28 days.
Proof – Pension claim S.32591.

WILSON, EPHRAIM

Patriot: Ephraim Wilson
Birth: 18 Jul 1756 Essex Co., DE
Married Spouse 1: abt 1778, prob PA Catherine Krebs/Crabb (1760-1819) [a]
Married Spouse 2: Elizabeth Wilson (1780-)
Service state(s): PA
Rank: Private
Proof of Service: Pension application
Pension application No.: S32609
Residences: Sussex Co., DE; Washington Co., PA (then VA); Bourbon Co., KY; Ripley Co., IN
Died: 22 Mar 1850 Ripley Co., IN
Buried: Wilson Family Cemetery, Johnson Twp., Ripley Co., IN
DAR Ancestor No.: A127336

(a) Catherine's father, Henry Crabb, served in the Revolutionary War.
  DAR Ancestor No. A027129.

Pension Application Abstracted from National Archives microfilm Series M804, Roll 2605, File S32609.
Pension abstract for – Ephraim Wilson
Service state(s): PA
Date: 13 May 1833
County of: Ripley State of: IN
Declaration made before a Judge or Court: Probate Court
Act of: 7 Jun 1832
Age: 77 yrs. the 18 day of next July
Record of age: Record at home, one that my parents gave me.
Where and year born: Sussex Co., DE 18 Jul 1756
Residence when he entered service: Washington Co., PA then in VA.
Residence(s) since the war: Washington Co., PA until 1795; [Bourbon Co.] KY for 22 yrs.; Ripley Co., IN.
Residence now: Ripley Co., IN
Volunteer, Drafted, or Substitute: Tour 1 & 4 Volunteered; 2 & 5 Drafted; 3 Substitute for Daniel Brooks.
Rank(s): Private
Statement of service-

Period	Duration	Names of General and Field Officers
1776	2 mos. 16 days	Capt. Richard Johnson
May 1778	1 mo.	Capt. Zadock Wright
1778	1 mo.	Capt. Mayhany Irving
Mar 1779	1 mo.	Capt. David Richy, Col. John Cannon
Jun 1779	2 mos.	Capt. Sparks, Col. Daniel Brodhead
Mar 1780	2 mos.	Capt. Nathan Ellis

Battles: Not stated
Discharge received: Not stated

Statement is supported by –
Evidence: Traditionary
Person now living who can testify to service: Edward Pendergast
Clergyman: Mishack Hyatt
Wife: not stated
Additional papers in file indicate he died 22 March 1850, Ripley Co., IN.

Abstract of Final Payment Voucher; General Services Administration, Washington, DC
LAST   FINAL PAYMENT VOUCHER RECEIVED FROM
        THE GENERAL ACCOUNTING OFFICE
NAME   WILSON, EPHRAIM
AGENCY OF PAYMENT   INDIANA
DATE OF ACT   1832
DATE OF PAYMENT   March 1, 1850
DATE OF DEATH   -
GENERAL SERVICES ADMINISTRATION
National Archives and Records Service   NA-286
GSA-WASH DC 54-4891   November 1953

Clift, G. Glens, Assistant Secretary, Kentucky Historical Society, Comp.; "Second Census" of Kentucky – 1800, A Privately Compiled and Published Enumeration of Tax Payers Appearing in the 79 Manuscript Volumes Extant of Tax Lists of the 42 Counties of Kentucky in Existence in 1800; Genealogical Publishing Co., Baltimore, MD, 1966, p. 322.

Name	County	Tax List Date
Wilson, Ephraim	Bourbon	7/23/1800

1820 U. S. Census, Ripley Co., IN, NARA Roll M33_15; EN 7 Aug 1820, p. 76, line 17.
Ephraim Wilson
Males 16-25=3, Males 26-44=1, Males 45>=1, Females <10=2, Females 26-44=1, Females 45>=1.

The Pension Roll of 1835 Volume IV, The Mid-Western States, Indexed Edition, In Four Volumes; Genealogical Publishing Co., Inc., Baltimore, MD, Reprint 1968, p. 87.
Statement, &c. of Ripley county, Indiana.

INDIANA Names	Rank	Annual allow-ance.	Sums re-ceived	Description of service
Ephraim Wilson	Private	23.33	79 99	Penn. militia

When placed on pension roll	Commencement of pension	Ages	Laws under which they were formerly placed on the pension roll; and remarks.
Oct 3, 1833	March 4, 1831	75	-

A Census of Pensioners for Revolutionary or Military Services with their Names, Ages, and Places of Residence Under the Act for Taking the Sixth Census in 1840; Genealogical Publishing Co., Inc., Baltimore, Maryland, 1965. p. 184.

Names of pensioners for revolutionary or military services.	Ages	Names of heads of families with whom pensioners resided June 1, 1840.
RIPLEY COUNTY		
JOHNSON		
Ephraim Wilson	84	Henry Wilson

Toph, Violet E.; Peoples History of Ripley County, Indiana; self-published, c. 1940, p. 124-125.
Revolutionary Soldiers Who Came to Ripley County
Ephraim Wilson enlisted from Pennsylvania in May, 1774 and was discharged in July, 1774. He was drafted in 1778 and served one month, re-enlisted of his own free will and served and as substitute for one month. He again entered the service as a substitute in March 1779 and was discharged in April 1779. He was born July 18, 1756 and died March 22, 1850. He gave a total service of five months. He is buried in the old Wilson family burial ground about three miles east of Versailles. As his monument was in a bad condition, The Ripley County Historical Society secured a Government marker and placed it July 13, 1936.

O'Byrne, Mrs. Roscoe C., comp. & ed.; Roster Soldiers and Patriots of the American Revolution Buried in Indiana; Published by Indiana Daughters of the American Revolution, 1938, Reprinted Genealogical Publishing Co., Baltimore MD, 1968, p. 385.
WILSON, EPHRAIM   Ripley County
Born – July 18, 1756, Sussex Co.
Service – Enlisted from Penn. In May, 1774. Drafted in 1778 and served 1 mo. Had been discharged in July, 1774, from first enlistment. Served as substitute for 1 mo. I 1779. Re-entered in March, 1778, as a substitute again. Discharged in April, 1779. Total service, 5 mos.
Proof – Pension claim S. 32609.
Died – March 22, 1850. Buried Wilson Cemetery, Johnson Twp. Stone. Name on bronze tablet in Versailles Court House.
Married – Catherine -----, d. July 2, 1819.
Collected by Mrs. A. B. Wycoff, Batesville, Indiana.

Gibbs, A.; Ripley County Historical Society Data on Revolutionary Soldiers, 1973 review.
Exact location of marker: juncture of Cave Hill Rd. and 300S; take continuation of 300S (no longer a road, but the evidence of old road is there); go back about 1/2 mile or so; very overgrown cemetery is to the left; not visible. Old Wilson Cemetery, Johnson Tw. Ripley Co. Ind.
Gibbs, A.; Ripley County Historical Society Data on Revolutionary Soldiers,
Type of marker: Gov't and family of Ephraim & wife

Date placed: 1936?
Placed by: Ripley County Historical Society
Additional comments: on Court House tablet
    Pa. Archives Series 3; Pennsylvanians residing in Ripley Co. pr PM 30 Oct 1833 age 75.
    1840 census Ripley Co. Ind. pension list, p. 252 Ephraim Wilson 84.
    Probate A. Ripley Co. Ind. pension appl. May 1833.
Family marker: Ephraim Wilson d. Mar. 22, 1850 93yr 8mo 4da.
    Catherine, wife of Ephraim Wilson d. Jan. 28, 1819 58-8-26.

United States Headstone Applications for U.S. Military Veterans, 1925-1949, database with images; (https://familysearch.org/ark:/61903/1:1:VHZN-F57 : 17 May 2016); Affiliate Publication Number: M1916; Affiliate Publication Title: Applications for Headstones for U.S. Military; Veterans, 1925-1941; Affiliate Film Number: 131; GS Film Number: 1878280; Digital Folder Number: 004832298; Image Number: 00739. Application for Headstone; War Department O.Q.M.G. Form No. 623
Name: Wilson, Ephraim
Event Date: May 31, 1934
Name of Cemetery: Wilson Private
Located in or near: Versailles, Ind.
Death Date: March 22, 1850
Enlistment Dates: May 1774
Discharge Dates: April 1779
Rank: Private
Company: Capt. Rich'd Johnson's Co. early in Rev. War; also Capt. ZadockWright's Co. 1778; Capt. David Ricky & Col. John Cannon's Co. 1779.
To be shipped to: Ripley Co. Historical Society, Osgood, Ind., Ripley Co.
Whose post-office address is: Versailles, Ind.
This application is for the UNMARKED grave of a veteran. It is understood the stone will be furnished and delivered at the railroad station or steamboat landing above indicated, at Government expense, freight prepaid. I hereby agree to promptly accept the headstone at destination, remove it and properly place same at decedent's grave at my expense. Ripley Co. Historical Society, Applicant.
No fee should be paid in connection with this application. Applicant: Ripley Co. Historical Society, Versailles, Ind.

Tombstone Location: Wilson Family Cemetery, Johnson Twp., Ripley Co., IN

Tombstone Inscription (old stone):
                    EPHRAIM WILSON
                            DIED
                         March 22,
                            1850
Same stone: CATHARINE
                            Wife of
                          W. WILSON

DIED
[Illegible] 1819
Tombstone Inscription (new stone): EPHRAIM
WILSON
PVT CANNON'S CO
REV WAR
MARCH 22, 1850

WILYARD (WILLYARD), HENRY

Henry Wilyard did not have ties to Ripley County. Hus wife, Agnes, resided in Ripley County after his death where she applied for pension.

Patriot: Henry Wilyard
Birth:
Married Spouse 1: 2 Oct 1790, Ligonier Valley, Westmoreland Co., PA
                            Agnes Bridges (1767 - 1859)
Service state(s): PA
Rank: Private
Proof of Service: Pension application
Pension application No.: W9892
Residences: Bedford Co., PA; Westmoreland Co., PA; Hamilton Co., OH;
           Ripley Co., IN
Died: 20 Jan 1830   Hamilton Co., OH
Buried: Hamilton Co, OH
DAR Ancestor No.: None as of 7 Jun 2017.

Pension Application Abstracted from National Archives microfilm Series M804, Roll 2603, File W9892.
Pension abstract for – Henry Wilard
Service state(s): PA
Alternate spelling(s): Willyard; Willyard; Wilyard
Date: 22 Jan 1819 & Declaration 21 Aug 1820
County of: Hamilton   State of: OH
Declaration made before a Judge or Court: Court of Common Pleas
Act of: 18 Mar 1818
Age: Not stated
Residence when he entered service: Westmoreland Co., PA
Residence(s) since the war: Not stated
Residence now: Hamilton Co., OH
Volunteer, Drafted, or Substitute: Enlisted
Rank(s): Private
Statement of service-

Period	Duration	Names of General and Field Officers
Spring 1777 - end 1780	3 yrs.	8th Regt. PA Line, Capt. Wendal Oarey [or Orrey], Col. Bayard [Broadhead]; aft. Brandywine Capt. Bell. [in 1823 claims Continental establishment]

Battles: Brandywine
Discharge received: at Pittsburgh
What became of it?: Worn out, lost, or destroyed.
Person now living who can testify to service:
       On 3 Jan 1820, John Gullion, Switzerland Co., IN, made declaration that Henry Willyard, late of PA, now of Hamilton Co., OH, served as a private soldier in 1778 or 1779; served abt. 6 mos. with this deponent.

On 3 Mar 1820, Alexander Lemmon, Hamilton Co., OH, made declaration to a JP, that he was encamped with Wilyard at West Point in the winter of 1779-1780.

&

Pension abstract for – Henry Willyard
Date: 23 Dec 1823
County of: Hamilton   State of: OH
Declaration made before a Judge or Court: Common Pleas Court
Declaration: military service; schedule of property. The cabin in which he lived, and his property in it, was consumed by fire Oct. last.
Act of: 18 Mar 1818 & 1 May 1820
Age: 77 yrs.
Residence now: Hamilton Co., OH
Volunteer, Drafted, or Substitute:
Discharge received: at Pittsburgh
What became of it?: lost it descending the Ohio 22 yrs. ago.
Wife: Not named   Wife's age: 65 yrs.
Names and ages of children: None living with him, all are grown.

&

Pension abstract for – Agnes Willyard widow of Henry Willyard
Declaration: Her said husband was a regular in the Continental Service; at time of enlistment he lived in Westmoreland Co., PA, she thinks; he continued to receive a pension until the time of his death in 1830
Date: 14 Nov 1839 & 8 Jun 1842 & 8 May 1843 & 15 Nov 1849 & 27 Dec 1850
County of: Ripley   State of: IN
Act of: 4 Jul 1836 & 3 Mar 1839 & 2 Feb 1848
Age: 72 yrs. in 1839; 74 yrs, on 7 May 1842; 75 yrs, in 1843; 82 yrs. in 1849.
Residence now: Franklin Twp., Ripley Co., IN
Persons in neighborhood who certify character: Jane Wadery gave testimony she was acquainted with Agnes Willyard for 38 yrs., and Henry Willyard until time of his death.
Death of soldier: 20 Jan 1830
Marriage date and place: 2 Nov 1790   Westmoreland Co., PA
Proof of marriage: Marriage was published, she has no Record.
   On 24 Apr 1842, John Willyard, age 72, resident of Ripley Co., IN, brother of Henry Willyard gave testimony – Henry Willyard & Agnes Bridges were married, he believes, 2 Nov 1790; resident of Westmoreland Co., PA; she remained his wife until his death some time in 1830; Henry Willyard was a pensioner on the Roll of Ohio Agency.
Names and ages of children: Not stated

&

Pension abstract for – Agnes Willyard widow of Henry Willyard
Date: 29 Mar 1855
County of: Ripley   State of: IN
Declaration made before a Judge or Court: Notary Public
Act of: 3 Mar 1855

Age: 88 yrs.
Residence now: Ripley Co., IN
Persons in neighborhood who certify character: James A. Stockwell & Joseph J. Stockwell gave testimony
Death of soldier: Jan 1830 Ripley Co., IN
Marriage date and place: she stated 2 Oct 1790 [actual date 2 Nov 1790]
   she stated Bedford Co., PA
Wife's former name: Agnes Bridges
Proof of marriage: proof of the fact will be found on file in the War Office
Names and ages of children: Not stated

Letter in the Pension application for Adam Fox
Versailles Indiana September the 19th 1839
   Dear Sir Thomas Johnson who was a soldier of the Revolutionary war and who resided at the time of his death in the County of Dearborn and State of Indiana and who drew a pension for many years before his death also Ning Bell and William Lippard and <u>Henry Wilyard</u> all of whom was soldiers of the Revolutionary War and <u>resided in the county of Ripley</u> and State of Indiana and was in the receipt of pensions at the time of their death. They have all left surviving widows to wit Sarah Johnson, <u>Agnes Willyard</u>, Christina Beall, and Mary Lippard all of whom wish to apply for pensions under and by Authority of the Act of Congress of the 4th of July 1836, and the 3rd of March 1837. The said Thomas Johnson, Ning Beall, William Lipperd and <u>Henry Wilyard</u> at the time of their deaths left a draw of pensions due and in order to obtain the same, sayeth widows, was requested to surrender the pension Certificates of their deceased husbands which said Certificated I suppose has been returned to the proper office. In order to enable the widows of deceased pensioner to identify themselves as the widows of the deceased it is necessary for them to set out the original pension certificate of their deceased husbands and as they must be on file in the office over which you preside please transfer to me at Versailles Indiana the original certificated of the said Johnson, Beall, Lipperd, and <u>Wilyard</u> if it is in accordance with the custom of your office. If not, please send me a Certified Copy of the same
I herewith send the papers of Mr. Adam Fox who claims a pension. If the papers are different please point out the deficiency to me.
Let me hear from you as soon as convenient.
          Yours respectfully
          Joseph Robinson

Abstract of Final Payment Voucher; General Services Administration, Washington, DC
 NAME   Willyard, Henry
 AGENCY OF PAYMENT   INDIANA
 DATE OF ACT   1818
 DATE OF PAYMENT   1st qr 1830
 DATE OF DEATH   Jan. 20, 1830
   FINALPAYMENT VOUCHER RECEIVED FROM

THE GENERAL ACCOUNTING OFFICE   From
General Services Administration   GSA DC 70-7035   GSA DEC 69 7068

1820 U. S. Census, Hamilton Co., OH, NARA Roll M33_87; EN 7 Aug 1820, p. 374, line 15.
Henry Willyard
Males <10=1, Males 45>=1, Females 16-25=1, Females 45>=1.

Craig, Robert D.; Revolutionary Soldiers in Hamilton County, Ohio; Self-published, Salt Lake City, UT, 1965. p. 39.
HENRY WILLYARD - Born in Westmoreland Co, Penn, in 1749, joined the 8th Penn Regiment in the spring of 1777 and was in the battle of Brandywine, Delaware, 11 Sept 1777. He was discharged at Pittsurg at the end of three years service. He came down the Ohio River in 1801 to Cincinnati and lived here until his death on 20 Jan 1830. His widow was living in Ripley county, Ind., in 1843.

Dailey, Jane Dowd, State Chairman, Daughters of American Revolution of Ohio; The Official Roster of the Soldiers of the American Revolution Buried in Ohio; Daughters of the American Revolution; THE F. J. Heer Printing Co., Columbus, OH, 1929; p. 402.
WILLYARD, HENRY, (Hamilton Co.)
Br 1749, Pennsylvania. D 1830. Ref: S.A.R. Fur infor Cincinnati Chap.

Historic Sites Committee, Cincinnati Chapter Daughters of the American Revolution; Revolutionary Soldiers Buried in Hamilton County, Ohio; Little Miami Publishing Co., Milford, OH, 2010; p. 112.
TOWNSHIP UNKNOWN
WILLYARD, HENRY 1749-1830
He was born in Pennsylvania in 1849. He enlisted in Westmoreland County, Pennsylvania, in 1777, served in the 8th Pennsylvania Regiment under Colonel Brodhead and was in the battle at Brandywine. He was discharged at the end of three years in Pittsburgh, Pennsylvania, and came to Hamilton County aged seventy; however, on December 23, 1823, he gave his age at seventy-seven. His cabin and other property were lost in a fire in October 1823. He died in Hamilton County on January 20, 1830.

Margaret R. Waters; Revolutionary Soldiers Buried in Indiana (1949) With Supplement (1954) Two Volumes in One; Genealogical Publishing Company, Baltimore, MD, 1970, p. 111.
WILLYARD, HENRY   Ripley
b. ca. 1750; d. 1-20-1830; m. 11-2-1790, Ligonier Valley, Westmoreland Co., Pa. (later, wid. says Bedford Co., Pa.), Agnes Bridges, b. (see varying ages); alive 3-29-1855, ae. 88, Ripley Co. Ind. Pens appl., Cincinnati, Hamilton Co., O.; wife 65; chn. Grown up. Affid. 1-3-1820, Switzerland Co., Ind., of John Gullion ("Roster" p. 167); that he serv. With Willyard; same of Alexander Lemmon of Hamilton Co., O. Affid. 8-21-1820, Hamilton Co., O., of John Willyard, bro. of Henry, who was under age at enlistment & whose father went to camp to try to

get Henry released. Wid's appl. 7-7-1838 & 1842, ae. 74 on May 7, 1842, Ripley Co., Ind.; 82; 3-29-1855 ae., ae. 88; all Ripley Co., Ind. Affid. 11-14-1839, 40-41 yr. Affid. 6-24-1842, Ripley Co., Ind., of John Williard, ae. 72, bro. of Henry. Service: enl. Spr. 1777, 8th Regt., Pa. W.9892 Pa.; BLW 26151-160-1855.
[Note: He died and was buried in Hamilton Co., OH.]

Ohio Society of the Sons of the Revolution; <u>Year Book of The Ohio Society of the Sons of the Revolution 1895</u>; printed by Ohio Society of the Sons of the Revolution, 1895; p. 64.
Roll of Honor
Henry Willyard, born in Westmoreland county, Pa., in 1749, joined the Eighth Pennsylvania Regiment in the spring of 1777, and was in the battle of Brandywine, Delaware, September 11, 1777, when the captain of his company was killed. He was discharged at Pittsburg at the end of three years service. He came down the Ohio river in 1801 to Cincinnati. He lived and died here January 20, 1830. His widow was living in Ripley county, Indiana, in 1843. See Records of War Department.

WHITTAKER (WHITACRE), JOHN

There is another patriot by the name of John Whitacar (Whitacer) who applied for pension in Switzerland County. His pension application number is S36845. See my book Revolutionary Soldiers and the Wives of Soldiers with Ties to Switzerland County Indiana.

Patriot: John Whitteker
Birth: 1754/1757 VA
Married Spouse 1: Jane X (abt 1760 -)
Service state(s): VA Continental Line
Rank: Private
Proof of Service: Pension application
Pension application No.: S36844
Residences: VA; Ripley Co., IN
Died: 1833 Ripley Co., IN
Buried: Benham Cemetery, Benham, Ripley Co., IN
DAR Ancestor No.:None as of 7 Jun 2017.

Pension Application Abstracted from National Archives microfilm Series M804, Roll 2549, File S36844.
Pension abstract for – John Whitacar
Service state(s): VA
Alternate spellings: Whitacre, Whittacar
Date: 21 Jul 1818
County of: Ripley State of: IN
Declaration made before a Judge or Court: Circuit Court
Act of: 18 Mar 1818
Age: 64 yrs.
Residence now: Ripley Co., IN
Volunteer, Drafted, or Substitute: Enlisted
Rank(s): Private
Statement of service-

Period	Duration	Names of General and Field Officers
1777 - 1781		8th Regiment, VA Line Continental Army, Capt. Thomas Boyears [Boyer]

Battles: siege of Yorktown, was taken prisoner, remained a prisoner fourteen months until exchanged.
Discharge received: in Williamsburg, VA
&
Pension abstract for – John Whitacar
Date: 6 Feb 1822
County of: Ripley State of: IN
Declaration made before a Judge or Court: Circuit Court
Declaration: Provided certified schedule of assets; original certificate dated 7 Dec 1818, numbered 4786; a farmer, due to one of his shoulders put out of place he is unable to work.

Act of: 1 May 1820
Age: 65 yrs.
Residence now: Ripley Co., IN
Volunteer, Drafted, or Substitute: Enlisted
Statement of service-

Period	Duration	Names of General and Field Officers
1777 - 1781		Regt. of Infantry, VA Line commanded by Col. Guess, Thomas Bowyer's comp.

Battles: Taken prisoner at the Siege of Charleston, detained 14 mos., then exchanged.
Discharge received: in 1781
Wife: Not named				Wife's age: 60 yrs.
Names and ages of children: One son, age 18; one daughter, age 12.
&
Additional notes in Pension File:
Death of soldier: 1833		Ripley Co., IN

Abstract of Final Payment Voucher; General Services Administration, Washington, DC
  LAST	FINAL PAYMENT VOUCHER RECEIVED FROM
      THE GENERAL ACCOUNTING OFFICE
                              WHITTICER
NAME				~~WILLEKER~~, JOHN
AGENCY OF PAYMENT		INDIANA
DATE OF ACT			1818
DATE OF PAYMENT		March 1, 1833 (dead)
DATE OF DEATH
GENERAL SERVICES ADMINISTRATION
National Archives and Records Service	NA-286
GSA-WASH DC 54-4891			November 1953

Revolutionary War Service Records; *National Archives Publication number M881, Compiled service records of soldiers who served in the American Army during the Revolutionary War, 1775-1783.*
https://www.fold3.com/image/23098531?terms=Whitacre,%20John%20va
8 Virginia Regiment, Capt. Thomas Bowyer's Company of Foot, commanded by Col. James Wood.
Whitacre, John – Private – Muster Roll for Apr, May, Jun, Jul, Aug, Sep, Oct 1779.

Gwathmey, John H.; Historical Register of Virginians in the Revolution, Soldiers, Sailors, Marines, 1775-1783; The Dietz Press, Richmond, VA, 1938, p. 820, 823, 824.
p. 820.
Whitaker, John (Whitacre) 9 CL, 13 CL, 15 CL.
p. 823.

Whitecar, John, Inf., nbll. [Name appeared on Army Register but had not received bounty land. An extensive compilation in the War Department.] *p. 824.*
Whiteker, John (Whitaker)   15 CL.
Whiticar, John, Pvt. WD. [War Department, emphasizing that the record is there.]

Senate Documents, Vol.9, No. 988, 63rd Congress, 3d Session, Washington, 1915; "*Register of Certificates Issued by John Pierce, Esquire, Paymaster General and Commissioner of Army Accounts for the United States, to Officers and Soldiers of the Continental Army Under Act of July 4, 1783"; <u>Seventeenth report of the National Society of the Daughters of the American Revolution</u>; Genealogical Publishing Co., Inc., Baltimore, MD, 1984. p. 541.*
Men listed in this volume with the same name.
p. 541

No. of Certificate	To whom issued	Amount
22888	Whitacre, John	33.30

p. 546.

No. of Certificate	To whom issued	Amount
23139	Whitteker, John	59.10

Clark, Murtie June; <u>The Pension List of 1820 [U.S. War Department]</u>*Reprinted with an Index; Genealogical Publishing Co., Inc., Baltimore, 1991. Originally published 1820 as Letter from the Secretary of War, p. 659.*
INDIANA
Names of the Revolutionary Pensioners which have been placed on the Roll of Indiana, under the Law of the 18th of March, 1818, from the passage thereof, to this day, inclusive, with the Rank they held, and the Lines in which they served, viz.

Names	Rank	Line
John Whitacar	private	Virginia

<u>U.S. Department of Interior, Bureau of Land Management, General Land Office Records; Land Patent Search</u> – *accessed 27 June 2012.*
WHITAKER, JOHN
Accession Nr. IN0210_.305; Document Type – State Volume Patent; State - Indiana; Issue Date – 10/4/1824; Cancelled – No
Land Office – Jeffersonville; Authority – April 24, 1820 Sale-Cash Entry (3 Stat. 566); Document Nr. -825; BLM Serial Nr. – IN NO S/N; Total Acres – 80.00
Land Description: State - IN; Meridian – 2nd PM; Aliquots – 006N-012E; Section - 19; County – Ripley.

Ripley County Indiana, Recorder's Office, Tract Book 1, p. 34.
Whitaker, John   16 Oct 1822   R12, T6, S19

Ripley County, Indiana Deed Records Vol. A, 11 Aug 1818-29 Jan 1827
Page(s): 318-319.
Abstract of Deed/Patent for: John Whitaker and Jane (dower) his wife

of Ripley Co., State of Indiana.
Purchaser (Grantee) or Seller (Grantor)?: Seller
Sold to: Edward McGuffy
State & county where recorded: Ripley Co., Indiana
Date entered: 19 Nov 1825
Recorded: 2 Oct 1826
Description: Parcel of land being in Ripley Co., Brown Township, being the southwest end of the west half of the southeast quarter of Section 19, Township 6, North of Range 12 East in the district of lands for sale at Jeffersonville, containing twenty-six acres of land.
Amount paid: Thirty three and 1/3 dollars ($33.33).
Name(s) of Witnesses: Henry Hamilton & Samuel Loveless

Ripley County, Indiana Deed Records Vol. A, 11 Aug 1818-29 Jan 1827
Page(s): 320-321.
Abstract of Deed/Patent for: James Whitaker and Jane (dower) his wife of the county of Ripley, State of Indiana.
Purchaser (Grantee) or Seller (Grantor)?: Seller
Sold to: Samuel Loveless of Pendleton Co., KY
State & county where recorded: Ripley Co., Indiana
Date entered: 19 Nov 1825
Recorded: 2 Oct 1826
Description: Parcel of land being in Ripley Co., Brown Township, being the Northwest end of the west half of the southeast quarter of Section 19, in Township 6, North of Range 12 East in the district of lands for sale at Jeffersonville, containing twenty-six acres of land.
Amount paid: Thirty-three dollars ($33.00).
Name(s) of Witnesses: Henry Hamilton & Edward McGuffy.

The Pension Roll of 1835 Volume IV, The Mid-Western States, Indexed Edition, In Four Volumes; Genealogical Publishing Co., Inc., Baltimore, MD, Reprint 1968, p. 51.
Statement, &c. of Ripley county, Indiana.

INDIANA Names	Rank	Annual allowance.	Sums received	Description of service
John Whitacer	Private	96.00	1,403 86	Virginia line

When placed on pension roll	Commencement of pension	Ages	Laws under which they were formerly placed on the pension roll; and remarks.
Dec 7, 1818	July 21, 1818	65	Died in 1833.

Toph, Violet E.; Peoples History of Ripley County, Indiana; self-published, c. 1940, p. 128.
Revolutionary Soldiers Who Came to Ripley County

John Whittaker enlisted from Virginia Dec. 17, 1776 and served three years but received no discharge to the neglect of his captain. He quit the service in 1779. He was born about 1760 and was pensioned from Switzerland County.

O'Byrne, Mrs. Roscoe C., comp. & ed.; Roster Soldiers and Patriots of the American Revolution Buried in Indiana; Published by Indiana Daughters of the American Revolution, 1938, Reprinted Genealogical Publishing Co., Baltimore MD, 1968, p. 381.
WHITTAKER (WHITACRE), JOHN   Ripley County
Born – 1760.
Service – Enlisted in Vir., Dec. 1776, as pri. in Capt. George McCormick's CO., Col. Joh Gibson's Vir. Regt., 3 yrs.
Proof – Pension claim S. 36845.
Died – Sept. 12, 1825. Buried Benham, Ind. Bronze tablet in Versailles Court House.
Married – Martha -----.
Collected by Mrs. A. B. Wycoff, Batesville, Indiana.

O'Byrne, Mrs. Roscoe C., comp.; Roster of Soldiers and Patriots of the American Revolution Buried in Indiana, Vol. II; Indiana Daughters of the American Revolution, 1980, p. 108.
WHITACAR (WHITACER), JOHN   Ripley County
Born – 1754/57.
Service – First pens. appl., 1818, age 64, Ripley Co., Ind., states he enl. 1778, 8th Regt. Va. Line; Capt. Thomas Boyears. Second pens. appl., 1822, age 65, Ripley Co., Ind., states he enl. ca. 1777, Inf. Regt., Col. Guess, Capt. Thomas Boyer.
Proof – Pens. S. 36844, Va. I.A.R. No. 4786.
Died – 1833.
Married – In 1822 pens. appl. states wife age 60, one son, age 18, and one dau., age 12. No names given.
From Waters' Sup., p. 109.

Revolutionary Soldiers Buried in Indiana (1949) With Supplement (1954) Two Volumes in One; Margaret R. Waters; Genealogical Publishing Company, Baltimore, MD, 1970. p. 109.
WHITACAR, JOHN   Ripley
(Note: not to be confused with John Whittaker or Whitsore in "Roster", p. 381, given as of Ripley Co., Ind., and who, I think, should be of Switzerland Co., Ind. He is given in the 1835 Pens. List, v.3, p.33, as of Switzerland Co., Ind; was placed on pens. roll 7-22-1819, I.A.R. certif. #12,571, Pens. S.36845 Va.).
The correct Ripley Co., Ind., man is John Whitacar or Whitacer, b. 1754-1757; d. 1833; mar. (wife ae. 60 in 1822); chn.: at least son (18 in 1822); 1 dau. (12 in 1822). Pens. appl.7-21-1818, ae. 64, Ripley Co., Ind.; again 2-6-1822, ae. 65, Ripley Co., Ind. Service (1st appl.): enl. ca. 1777, Inf. Regt.; Col. Guess (Gist?), Capt. Thomas Boyer. Placed on pens. roll 12-7-1818; I.A.R. certify. #4,786.
REF: Pens. S.36844 Va.; 1835 Pens. List, Ripley Co., Ind., v.3, p. 29.

Gibbs, A.; Ripley County Historical Society Data on Revolutionary Soldiers, 1973 review.
Exact location of marker: no further information on grave site
Comments: on Court House tablet
    Probate A. Ripley Co. Ind. p. 40, 42. Dec'd by 3 Nov 1825 Court, John Whitaker Jr. adm.

Hatcher, Patricia Law, Comp.; Abstract of Graves of Revolutionary Patriots (4 volumes); Pioneer Heritage Press, Dallas, TX, 1987, Vol. 4, p. 189.
This is an abstract and an index to information reported to the Daughters of the American Revolution and published in their annual reports to the Smithsonian Institution, printed as Senate Documents (1900-1974) and published annually in the DAR magazine (1978-1987).
Published 1972 (Senate Doc. 54)
Whittaker   John   Benham Cem, Benham, Ripley Co IN 72

WYCOFF, ISAAC

There was never a patriot by the name of Isaac Wycoff. The following clarifies the name was listed in error on the 1835 Pension List.

Pension Application Abstracted from National Archives microfilm Series M804, Roll 2654, File S32619.
Pension abstract for – Jacob Wykoff
Correspondence in file:
LETTER TO COMMISSIONER OF PENSIONS -

Batesville, Indiana
March 14, 1922

Commissioner of Pensions
Washington, D.C.
Dear Sir: As a member of the Ripley County branch of the Indiana Historical Society I have been asked by a representative of the Sons of the American Revolution to locate the grave of a Revolutionary soldier named Isaac Wycoff who is supposed to be buried in our county somewhere. The list of Revolutionary soldiers drawing pension in 1835 as obtained from your office contains the name of Isaac Wycoff as a resident of Ripley County, Indiana. As a family we know absolutely nothing of Isaac Wycof except that he was born March 8, 1852 in New Jersey or Maryland and later moved to Loudoun Co., Virginia where he was living in 1796.

    Can you give me all the data to be found in the pension records in regard to this man? The family need this information to complete his record in the family history and trace his descendants if there were any.

    The Sons of the American Revolution are interested in completing their records and marking the graves of all Revolutionary soldiers.

    If any fee is required for this information, please enclose bill with letter or notify me in advance as required.

    Thanking you for this information

Most sincerely,
Minnie E. Wycoff
219 Maplewood Ave.
Batesville, Ind.

RESPONSE -

Rev. War Section
Department of the Interior
Bureau of Pensions
Washington

April 13, 1922

Minnie E. Wycoff
219 Maplewood Avenue
Batesville, Indiana
Madame:
    In response to your letter dated March 14, 1922, you are advised that a careful search of the records of this Bureau fails to show a claim for Rev War

pension or bounty land on file for any soldier named Isaac Wycoff, under any spelling of that surname.

The pensioner of Ripley County, Indiana, was Jacob Wykoff. His name was erroneously printed on the list of 1835 as Isaac.

[Letter continues with description of Jacob Wykoff's service.]

Very respectfully,

Commissioner

The Pension Roll of 1835 Volume IV, The Mid-Western States, Indexed Edition, In Four Volumes; Genealogical Publishing Co., Inc., Baltimore, MD, Reprint 1968, p. 87.

Statement, &c. of Ripley county, Indiana.

INDIANA Names	Rank	Annual allowance.	Sums received	Description of service
Isaac Wycoff	Private	80.00	240 00	N.J. State troops

When placed on pension roll	Commencement of pension	Ages	Laws under which they were formerly placed on the pension roll; and remarks.
Feb 4, 1834	March 4, 1831	76	-

Revolutionary Soldiers Buried in Indiana (1949) With Supplement (1954) Two Volumes in One; Margaret R. Waters; Genealogical Publishing Company, Baltimore, MD, 1970. p. 113.

WYCOFF, ISAAC   Ripley
Rev. sold. who died there. In 1835 Pens. List, ae. 76; pvt. In N.J. State Troops. REF: Mr. Schrum; 1835 Pens. List. V. 3, p. 65; Stryker—"Official Reg. of N.J. in Rev, War", p. 830.

WYCOFF, JACOB

Patriot: Jacob Wycoff
Birth: 3 Nov 1754   Monmouth Co., NJ
Married Spouse 1:   Susannah Allen (1762 -)
Service state(s):   NJ
Rank: Private
Proof of Service: Pension application
Pension application No.: S32619
Residences: Monmouth Co., NJ; Hunterdon Co., NJ; Dearborn Co., IN; Ripley Co., IN
Died: 8 Feb 1835   Ripley Co., IN
Buried: Private Cemetery on farm of Robert Ralston, south of Versailles, Ind.
DAR Ancestor No.:A126114

Pension Application Abstracted from National Archives microfilm Series M804, Roll 2654, File S32619.
Pension abstract for – Jacob Wykoff
Service state(s): NJ
Date: 29 Dec 1833
County of: Ripley   State of: IN
Declaration made before a Judge or Court: Judge of the Circuit Court
Act of: 7 Jun 1832
Age: 78 yrs.   Record of age:
Where and year born: Monmouth Co., NJ   3 Nov 1754
Residence when he entered service: Hunterdon Co., NJ
Residence(s) since the war: Hunterdon Co., NJ; Dearborn Co., IN in abt. 1806 for 1 yr.; Ripley Co., IN.
Residence now: Ripley Co., IN
Volunteer, Drafted, or Substitute: Volunteered
Rank(s): Private
Statement of service-

Period	Duration	Names of General and Field Officers
1 Jul 1775 - Jul 1778	3 yrs.	Thomas Patterson's company, Cols. Barber, Spencer, Chambers, Bishop.
Aug 1778	1 yr.	Capt. Potter, Col. Scudder
Aug 1779	1 yr.	Capt. Carey, Eads, Col. Chambers

Battles: Trenton, Princeton, "the Kegs" near Philadelphia, Brandywine, Germantown, Monmouth.
Discharge received: at Easton, NJ
Signed by: Col. Spencer, he thinks
What became of it?: Destroyed
Statement is supported by –
Clergyman: Mishack Hyatt
Persons in neighborhood who certify character: Elijah Boswell
Death of soldier: 8 Feb 1835

Abstract of Final Payment Voucher; General Services Administration, Washington, DC

    FINAL PAYMENT VOUCHER RECEIVED FROM
    THE GENERAL ACCOUNTING OFFICE
NAME   WYKOFF, JACOB
AGENCY OF PAYMENT INDIANA
DATE OF ACT   1832
DATE OF PAYMENT   3d Qr. 1835
DATE OF DEATH   Feb. 8, 1835
GENERAL SERVICES ADMINISTRATION
National Archives and Records Service NA-286
GSA-WASH DC 54-4891   November 1953

William S. Stryker, Adjutant General, Compiled Under Orders of His Excellency Theodore F. Randolph, Governor; Official Register of the Officers and Men of New Jersey in the Revolutionary War; by Printed by the Authority of the Legislature; Wm. T. Nicholson & Co., Printers, Trenton, NJ, 1872, Facsimile Reprint by Heritage Books, Inc., Bowie, MD, 1993; p. 819.
WICKOFF, JACOB. Captain Hankinson's company, First Regiment, Monmouth.

Toph, Violet E.; Peoples History of Ripley County, Indiana; self-published, c. 1940, p. 129.
Revolutionary Soldiers Who Came to Ripley County
Jacob Wycoff entered the service from Monmouth County, New Jersey in July, 1775 and served two years. He was born Nov. 3, 1754 and died Feb. 8, 1835. He served under Major E. Anderson and Captain Thomas Patterson and was pensioned from Ripley County. The Ripley County Historical Society secured a Government marker and it was placed at his grave on the Ralstin Farm three miles southwest of Versailles by the wife of one of his descendants, Mrs. Minnie E. Wycoff, in the Fall of 1935.

Mrs. Roscoe C. O'Byrne, comp. & ed.; Roster Soldiers and Patriots of the American Revolution Buried in Indiana; Published by Indiana Daughters of the American Revolution, 1938, Reprinted Genealogical Publishing Co., Baltimore MD, 1968, p. 392. WYCOFF, JACOB   Ripley County
Born – Nov. 3, 1754, N. J.
Service – Entered service from Monmouth Co., N. J., in July, 1775. Served 2 yrs.
Proof –Pension claim S. 32619.
Died – Feb. 18, 1835. Buried Versailles, Ind. Government marker. Name on bronze tablet in Versailles Court House.
Married – Susannah Allen, b. 1762. Ch. John, b. 1785; Daniel, b. 1787; Robert, b. 1791, m. Hannah Allen; Allen, b. 1802, m. Eleanor Simpson.
Collected by Mrs. A. B. Wycoff, Batesville, Indiana.

United States Headstone Applications for U.S. Military Veterans, 1925-1949, database with images; (https://familysearch.org/ark:/61903/1:1:VHZN-GSC : 17 May 2016); Affiliate Publication Number: M1916; Affiliate Publication Title:

Applications for Headstones for U.S. Military; Veterans, 1925-1941; Affiliate Film Number: 133; GS Film Number: 1878282; Digital Folder Number: 04832300; Image Number: 01934. Application for Headstone; War Department O.Q.M.G. Form No. 623
Name: Wycoff, Jacob
Event Date: May 31, 1934
Name of Cemetery: Private cemetery
Located in or near: Versailles, Ind.
Death Date: Feb. 8, 1835
Enlistment Dates: July, 1775
Discharge Dates: 1777
Rank: Private
Company: Capt. Thos. Patterson's Co. under Col. Barber, Spencer, Chambers & Bishop.
To be shipped to: Ripley Co. Historical Society, Osgood, Ind., Ripley Co.
Whose post-office address is: Versailles, Ind.
This application is for the UNMARKED grave of a veteran. It is understood the stone will be furnished and delivered at the railroad station or steamboat landing above indicated, at Government expense, freight prepaid. I hereby agree to promptly accept the headstone at destination, remove it and properly place same at decedent's grave at my expense. Ripley Co. Historical Society, Applicant. No fee should be paid in connection with this application.
Applicant: Mrs. A. B. Wycoff, Batesville, Ind.

Minutes of Ripley County Historical Society Board of Director Meeting, 26 Sep 1934.
President Wycoff reported she received $5.00 from Miss Edith C. Miller, Vreedersburg, Ind, for purpose of setting monument for grave of Revolutionary soldier Jacob Wycoff, situated on farm of Robert Ralston, south of Versailles.

Minutes of Ripley County Historical Society Board of Director Meeting, 19 Nov 1934.
Jacob Marker placed on 17 Oct 1934, on the southwest corner of Robert Ralston's farm adjacent to the county road, running to State Rd. 29. An added inscription by Francis Edens at the top of the marker locates the actual grave site as 60 rds NW.

Gibbs, A.; Ripley County Historical Society Data on Revolutionary Soldiers, 1973 review.
Exact location of marker: off 421, take 300S (west) about 1/3 mile; marker on north side of road at fence line. Cemetery "60 yds. Nw" stated on marker. Southwest of Versailles, Johnson Tw. Ripley Co. Ind.
Type of marker: Gov't
Date placed: Oct. 17, 1934 (R.C.H.S. Minutes)
Placed by: Ripley County Historical Society
Additional comments: on Court House tablet
Wording on marker:

Jacob Wycoff
Pvt. N.J. Troops
Rev. War
Feb. 8, 1835

YOUNGER, KANARD

Patriot: Kanard (Kennard) Younger
Birth: 1760 Frederick Co., MD
Married Spouse 1: Bond – 16 Feb 1792; Marr - 22 Feb 1792, Nelson Co., KY
    Elizabeth Cambron (1770-1820)
Married Spouse 2: bef. 1830 Mary "Polly" X (c1779 – aft 1851)
    prev. married to XX
Service state(s): MD
Rank: Private
Proof of Service: Pension application
Pension application No.: S32620
Residences: Frederick Co., MD; Fort Pitt, PA; Nelson Vo., KY, Jefferson Co., KY; Bullitt Co., KY; Henry Co., KY; Trimble Co., KY; Ripley Co., IN
Died: 2 Aug 1851 Ripley Co., IN Last Pension Payment 3rd qtr. 1848
Buried: Unknown
DAR Ancestor No.: A206165

Pension Application Abstracted from National Archives microfilm Series M804, Roll 2667, File S32620.
Pension abstract for – Kanard Younger
Service state(s): MD
Date: 21 Sep 1833
County of: Henry   State of: KY
Declaration made before a Judge or Court: Justice of the Peace
Act of: 7 Jun 1832
Age: 73 yrs.
Record of age: I have a record at home
Where and year born: Frederick Co., MD   1760
Residence when he entered service: Frederick Co., MD
Residence(s) since the war: Frederick Co., MD; Feb 1783 to Fort Pitt, now Pittsburgh; Louisville, [Jefferson Co.] KY; Bullitt Co., KY; Henry Co., KY where I now live.
Residence now: Henry Co., KY
Volunteer, Drafted, or Substitute: 1st tour - Drafted; 2nd tour – Drafted; Fort Pitt tours – Volunteered
Rank(s): Private
Statement of service-

Period	Duration	Names of General and Field Officers
Feb 1778	3 mos.	Capt. Price, Col. Bird's Regt., command of Gen. Morgan.
Jul 1781	3 mos.	Capt. Maready, Col. Respass as well as he recollects.
Mar 1783	1 mo.	Garrison under Capt. Ritchie
Apr 1783	3 mos.	Capt. Simms, down the Ohio River

against the Indians, built fort across from where Cincinnati now stands.
Battles: Siege of York – Cornwallis' defeat.
Discharge received: Received several
What became of it?: Lost them
Statement is supported by –
Documentary proof: Has none
Person now living who can testify to service: Knows no one
Clergyman: James Kidwell
Persons in neighborhood who certify character: James Kidwell, Roger Owens
&
Pension abstract for – Kanard Younger
Date: 30 May 1850
County of: Ripley   State of: IN
Declaration made before a Judge or Court: Justice of the Peace
Declaration: Requests transfer from rolls of State of Kentucky to State of Indiana where he now resides and intends to remain.
Reason for Transfer: Some years since he made arrangements to live in the family of Joshua King, a step-son-in-law during his natural life; said King having removed to Indiana he was of necessity compelled to accompany him.
&
Additional notations in file -
Death of soldier: 2 Aug 1851

Abstract of Final Payment Voucher; General Services Administration, Washington, DC

NAME	YOUNGER, Kanard
AGENCY OF PAYMENT	Ky.
DATE OF ACT	1832
DATE OF PAYMENT	3rd. qtr. 1848
DATE OF DEATH	-

Last   FINAL PAYMENT VOUCHER RECEIVED FROM
          THE GENERAL ACCOUNTING OFFICE   From
General Services Administration   GSA DC 70-7035   GSA DEC 69 7068

Newman, Harry Wright; Maryland Revolutionary Records; Tuttle Publishing, Rutland, VT, 1928. p. 56, 155.

p. 56

Maryland Revolutionary Pensioners

Name of Veteran	Birth	Rank	Establishment	Misc. facts and other State services
Younger, Kanard	1760	Pvt.	Militia	Pa. & Va. Service

p. 155.
Miscellaneous Lists Other States

Younger, Kanard	Virginia

Kentucky, County Marriages, 1797-1954; Nelson, Kentucky, United States, Madison County Courthouse, Richmond; accessed 11 April 2016 from https://familysearch.org/ark:/61903/1:1:V65Q-1RF
Name: Kennard Younger
Event Type: Marriage
Event Date: 16 Feb 1792 [Bond]
Event Place: Nelson, Kentucky, United States
Spouse's Name: Elizth Cambron
Spouse's Father's Name: James Cambron
GS Film number: 000481488;
Digital Folder Number: 004705582;
Image; Number: 00112; FHL microfilm 481,488.

Clift, G. Glens, Assistant Secretary, Kentucky Historical Society, Comp.; "Second Census" of Kentucky – 1800, A Privately Compiled and Published Enumeration of Tax Payers Appearing in the 79 Manuscript Volumes Extant of Tax Lists of the 42 Counties of Kentucky in Existence in 1800; Genealogical Publishing Co., Baltimore, MD, 1966, p. 332.

Name	County	Tax List Date
Younger, Kennard	Bullitt	8/30/1800

Quisenberry, Anderson Chenault; Revolutionary Soldiers in Kentucky, containing a roll of the officers of Virginia line who received land bounties, a roll of the Revolutionary pensioners in Kentucky, a list of the Illinois regiment who served under George Rogers Clark in the Northwest campaign, also a roster of the Virginia Navy; Reproduction of the original which appeared in Sons of the American Revolution Kentucky Society Year Book, Louisville, 1896, Southern Book Co., Baltimore, MD, 1959. p.168.
Henry County
Pensioners under the Act of June 7, 1832. Began March 4, 1831
Younger, Kanard, Private   Virginia dragoons
       December 22, 1829; $100.

The Pension Roll of 1835 Volume III, The Southeastern States, Indexed Edition, In Four Volumes; Genealogical Publishing Co., Inc., Baltimore, MD, Reprint 1968, p. 291.
Statement, &c. of Henry county, Kentucky.

KENTUCKY Names	Rank	Annual allow- ance.	Sums re- ceived	Description of service
Kanard Younger	Private	20.00	60 00	Virginia militia

When placed on pension roll	Commencement of pension	Ages	Laws under which they were formerly placed on the pension roll; and remarks.
Nov 25, 1833	Mar 4, 1831	74	-

A Census of Pensioners for Revolutionary or Military Services with their Names, Ages, and Places of Residence Under the Act for Taking the Sixth Census in 1840; Genealogical Publishing Co., Inc., Baltimore, Maryland, 1965, p. 167.

Names of pensioners for revolutionary or military services.	Ages	Names of heads of families with whom pensioners re-sided June 1, 1840.
KENTUCKY, TREMBLE COUNTY		
Kennard Younger	85	Kennard Younger

1850 U.S. Census, Johnson Twp., Ripley Co., IN; p. 239, dwelling 319, family 322, lines 4-5; National Archives Microfilm Roll M-432, Enumerated 30 Oct 1850. [Indexed as Tounger by LDS]

Name		age	b. yr.	b.p.
Kennard	Younger	100	c1750	Maryland
Polly	Younger	71	c1779	Virginia

[Step-son-in-law, Joshua King, & wife Catherine (dau.of Polly) are listed in the previous household, dwell. 318, fam. 321).

Margaret R. Waters; Revolutionary Soldiers Buried in Indiana (1949) With Supplement (1954) Two Volumes in One; Genealogical Publishing Company, Baltimore, MD, 1970, p. 114.

YOUNGER, KANARD   Ripley
b. 1760, Frederick Co., Md.; d. 8-2-1851; mar. Pens. appl. 9-1-1833, ae. 73, Henry Co., Ky. After Md. Service, ca. Feb 1783 mov. To Ft. Pitt & serv there; later mov. to Falls of Ohio at Louisville, Ky. In 1835 Pens. List, Henry Co., Ky.; pvt. In Va, Mil.; in 1840 Pens. List, Trimble Co., Ky. On 5-30-1850, Ripley Co., Ind., asks for tr. to live with step-son-in-law who has recently mov. to Ripley Co., Ind.; Pens. tr. 6-22-1851. Service: Pens. List, v.3, p. 105; 1840 Pens. List, p. 167.

O'Byrne, Mrs. Roscoe C., comp.; Roster of Soldiers and Patriots of the American Revolution Buried in Indiana, Vol. II; Indiana Daughters of the American Revolution, 1980, p. 111.

YOUNGER, KANARD   Ripley County
Born – 1760, Frederick Co., Md.
Service – Enl. Feb., 1778, Frederick Co., Md.
Proof – Pens. 32620, Md. Pens. appl. 1833, Henry Co., Ky., and on May 30, 1850, Ripley Co., Ind. asks for transfer of pension, to live with step-son-in-law. Transfer made June 22, 1851.
From Waters' Sup., p. 114.

O'Byrne, comp. Mrs. Roscoe C., comp.; Roster of Soldiers and Patriots of the American Revolution Buried in Indiana, Vol. III; Indiana Daughters of the American Revolution, 1966, p. 80.
Additional data and/or corrections received since 1966 to the records of the soldiers and patriots listed in Rosters I and II.

YOUNGER, KANARD   Roster II, p. 111   Ripley County

Died – Probate Order Book E, p. 322, Ripley Co., Ind. states the soldier d. Aug. 2, 1851. Widow Mary Younger.
Children – John; Ellen; Anna Easton, late Anna Younger; Elizabeth Ceadton, late Elizabeth Younger.

Gibbs, A.; Ripley County Historical Society Data on Revolutionary Soldiers, 1973 review.
Exact location of marker: no known marker

APPENDIX A

Soldier	State of Service
Chapman, Lemuel	CT, NY
Gookins, Samuel	CT
Mathews, Amos V.	CT
Robbins, Ephraim	CT
Welch, Daniel	CT
Cavendar, John	DE, MD, NC
Boldrey, John	MA
Fisk, Robert	MA
Maxwell, David	MA
Pratt, Jonathan	MA
Babbs, John	MD
Beall, Ninion	MD
Davis, Philmore	MD
Fox, Adam	MD, VA
Marquest, Samuel	MD
McMillin, Daniel	MD
Rutledge, Peter	MD
Whitstone, David	MD, NC
Younger, Kanard	MD
Baumgardner, Daniel	NC
Burchfield, John	NC
Burchfield, Robert	NC
Gibson, Wilbourne	NC
McCullough, John	NC
Micheller, Jacob	NC
Prothero, Thomas	NC
Tucker, John	NC
Ward, John	NC
Rollf, James	NH
Crane, Edmund	NJ
Delapp, James	NJ
Burroughs, James	NJ
Parr, John	NJ
Wycoff, Jacob	NJ
Hennegin, Joseph	NY
Benefiel, George	PA
Buchanan, George	PA
Buskirk, John	PA, VA
Collins, William	PA, VA
Dowers, Conrad	PA
Dowers, Jacob	PA
Hamilton, Benjamin	PA
House, Levi	PA, VA
Johnson, Thomas	PA
McDonald, Joseph	PA
Myers, Henry	PA
Newcomer, Peter	PA
Overturf, Martin	PA
Pendergast, Edward	PA
Stephens, Samuel	PA
Thomas, Henry	PA
Wilson, Ephraim	PA
Wilyard, Henry	PA
Hall, Benjamin	RI
Hodges, Richard	SC
Lipperd, William	SC
Arnold, James	VA
Bassett, William	VA
Christy, James	VA
Cruzan, Benjamin	VA
Grimes, James	VA
Hite, Jacob	VA
Johnson, James	VA
Johnson, Phillip	VA
Johnson, Roswell	VA
Lambert, James	VA
Levi, Isaac	VA
Livingston, George	VA
Lloyd, Indian Robin	VA
Mavity, William	VA
O'Neal, John	VA
Pennetent, John	VA
Rasor, Peter	VA
Ryan, George	VA
Stewart, Charles	VA
VanBibber, Peter	VA
Way, Isaac	VA
Wittaker, John	VA
Howlett, William	VT

APPENDIX B

Revolutionary War Patriots listed on the new Revolutionary War Patriot Memorial at the Ripley County Courthouse

The Ross' Run Chapter Daughters of the American Revolution Dedicated this new Memorial in 2018, as part of the Ripley County Bicentennial Celebration

James Arnold
John Babbs
William Bassett
Ninion Beall
John Boldrey
George Buchanan
Daniel Baumgardner
John Burchfield
Robert Burchfield
John Buskirk
Lemuel Chapman
William Collins
Edmund Crane
Benjamin Cruzan
Philmore Davis
James Delapp
Conrad Dowers
Jacob Dowers
Adam Fox
Wilbourne Gibson
Samuel Gookins
James Grimes
Benjamin Hall
Benjamin Hamilton
Joseph Hennegin
Richard Hodges
Levi House
William Howlett
James Johnson
Philip Johnson
Thomas Johnston
James Lambert
Isaac Levi
William Lipperd

George Livingston
Indian Robin Lloyd
Samuel Marquest
Amos V. Mathews
William Mavity
John McCullough
Joseph McDonald
Daniel McMillin
Jacob Micheller
Henry Myers
Peter Newcomer
John O'Neal
Martin Overturf
John Parr
Edward Pendergast
John Pennetent
Jonathan Pratt
Ephraim Robbins
James Rolff
Peter Rutledge
George Ryan
Samuel Stephens
Charles Stewart
Henry Thomas
John Tucker
Peter VanBibber
John Ward
Isaac Way
Daniel Welsh
Daniel Whitstone
Ephraim Wilson
John Wittaker
Jacob Wycoff
Kanard Younger

APPENDIX C

Interesting observations discovered during compilation of this work

Richard Burchfield witnessed deed for Richard Hodges, Ripley Co., 10 Jan 1822.

John O'Neal and William Bassett, deacons of Middle Fork (Baptist) Church purchased land for the church in May 1826.

Henry Myers married Hannah Deitch; Martin Overturf married Catherine Deitch. Were Hannah and Catherine sisters? Both men served in PA, lived in Montgomery Co., KY where they probably met and married these women.

James Grimes' son testified for Indian Robin Lloyd.

Ephraim Wilson testified for Samuel Stephens.

Ninian Beall testified for Adam Fox.

John McCullough & John Ward served in the 4th Regt. NC Continental Line.

John Boldery & Samuel Gookins came to Ripley from Ontario Co., NY – ref 1835 pension.

www.ingramcontent.com/pod-product-compliance
Lightning Source LLC
Chambersburg PA
CBHW050834230426